Terrifying Texts

ALSO EDITED BY CYNTHIA J. MILLER *and*
A. BOWDOIN VAN RIPER

---

*Divine Horror: Essays on the Cinematic Battle
Between the Sacred and the Diabolical* (2017)

Terrifying Texts

*Essays on Books of Good
and Evil in Horror Cinema*

Edited by CYNTHIA J. MILLER *and*
A. BOWDOIN VAN RIPER

McFarland & Company, Inc., Publishers
Jefferson, North Carolina

ISBN (print) 978-1-4766-7130-7 ∞
ISBN (ebook) 978-1-4766-3374-9

LIBRARY OF CONGRESS CATALOGUING DATA ARE AVAILABLE

BRITISH LIBRARY CATALOGUING DATA ARE AVAILABLE

© 2018 Cynthia J. Miller and A. Bowdoin Van Riper.
All rights reserved

No part of this book may be reproduced or transmitted in any form or by any means, electronic or mechanical, including photocopying or recording, or by any information storage and retrieval system, without permission in writing from the publisher.

Front cover image © 2018 iStock

Printed in the United States of America

*McFarland & Company, Inc., Publishers
Box 611, Jefferson, North Carolina 28640
www.mcfarlandpub.com*

For everyone who has learned that it's wise
to judge some books by their covers.

Acknowledgments

This collection owes its existence to the efforts and good will of many individuals, from colleagues whose work provided inspiration and encouragement to loved ones who graciously accepted less than our full attention and offered words of support during long days spent battling the horrors of the book. To all of them, we give our thanks. Additionally, thanks to our 19 fine contributors, for their energy, scholarship, and creativity.

Table of Contents

Acknowledgments ... vi

Introduction
    Cynthia J. Miller and A. Bowdoin Van Riper ... 1

Lovecraft and His Legacy

Monstrous Writing, Writing Monsters: Authoring Manuscripts, Ontological Horror and Human Agency
    Michael Fuchs ... 11

That Monstrous Book: The *Necronomicon* and Its Cinematic Contents
    Michael E. Heyes ... 23

Paperback *Necronomicon*: Occult Authorship in John Carpenter's *In the Mouth of Madness*
    Murray Leeder ... 33

The Book with a Thousand Faces: The Evolution of the *Necronomicon* in the *Evil Dead* Universe
    Martin J. Auernheimer ... 44

Books of Hope and Despair

The Magic Book and the Magic of Books in Murnau's *Faust* (1926)
    Thomas Prasch ... 59

Apocryphal Horror: Understanding Evil Through Lost Books of the Bible
    Jeffrey M. Tripp ... 73

Losing Your Faith for Seeing Too Much: The Anti-Bible as Indictment of American Heroism in Gregory Widen's *The Prophecy*
    Mark Henderson ... 83

I(dio)t Follows: The Seashell E-Book in *It Follows*
    Learned Foote ... 94

Perspectives on *The Babadook*

"The more you deny me, the stronger I get": "Mister Babadook" and the Monstrous Empowerment of Children's Culture
    Jessica Balanzategui ... 107

Mediating Trauma in Jennifer Kent's *The Babadook*
    MICHAEL C. REIFF   120

Bad Books and Fairy Tales: Stigmatized Guardians in *The Turn of the Screw* and *The Babadook*
    AUSTIN RIEDE   132

Diaries and Scrapbooks

Dreadful Girl Diaries and the Promise of Transparent Girlhood
    KAREN J. RENNER   145

"Do not read the Latin": The Summoning Diary in Horror Film
    LISA CUNNINGHAM   154

"That book lies!" Lost Texts and Hidden Horrors in *The Whisperer in Darkness*
    A. BOWDOIN VAN RIPER   162

Witches, Demons and Curses

Spellbound: The Significance of Spellbooks in the Depiction of Witchcraft on Screen
    EMILY BRICK   175

Horror Comedy by the Book: *Grimoire*, Carnival and *Heteroglossia* in Kenny Ortega's *Hocus Pocus* (1993)
    SUE MATHESON   186

Unraveling Julian Karswell's Runic Curse in Jacques Tourneur's *Night of the Demon*
    MICHAEL FURLONG   198

International Takes

Logical Horror: Axiomatic Magic and Strategic Murder in *Death Note*
    RICHARD J. LESKOSKY   211

Grotesque Adaptations: Bodies of Knowledge in *Maléfique* (2002)
    CYNTHIA J. MILLER   224

The Appeared (2007) by Paco Cabezas: Redefining the Book of Hidden Memories and Cyclical Time
    GRACIELA TISSERA   235

"No one who sees it lives to describe it": *The Book of Eibon* and the Power of the Unseeable in Lucio Fulci's *The Beyond*
    PHILIP L. SIMPSON   245

About the Contributors   255

Index   257

Introduction

CYNTHIA J. MILLER *and*
A. BOWDOIN VAN RIPER

"That book lies!!"[1]
Truth ... lies ... fact ... fantasy ... our complex, and often contested, relationship with books shapes our reality. Books are revered—and feared—for their ability to affect the minds and hearts of humankind. We collect them, pore over them, commit their passages to memory, censor them, and even attempt to banish them from our midst, lest they lead us to ruin.

Indeed, for better or worse, we are all "people of the book." Perhaps not in the sacred sense, as possessors of divine texts revealing knowledge imparted by God,[2] but rather in the cultural sense; we continue to prove ourselves true believers in books as repositories of knowledge, vessels of power, and keepers of ancient secrets. Through both physical form and content, books have defined and altered histories, signified and eradicated privilege, and given voice and substance to both dreams and illusions. They form a semiotic system of materiality and meaning that has been of "fundamental importance," as John Feather observes, "to understanding the essentially book-based culture of the West."[3]

Our engrained (though limited) perception of the book and its uses has a long history. For generations, we have relied on texts to serve as faithful means of making, maintaining, and communicating knowledge—as predictable, immutable, "immortal" containers of information about our own nature and that of the world. Adrian Johns argues that "[e]ven the brisk skepticism we may express about certain printed materials ... rests on it, inasmuch as we feel confident that we can readily and consistently identify what it is that we are scorning."[4] Authorship and the means of production both strive to erase their own presence in order to craft an air of authority. Thus, the printed word—a product of complex social processes—becomes disengaged from its origins and reified, and with it, our understandings and portrayals of knowledge and knowing.

Still, books are social tools—curated artifacts of society's accumulated knowledge—made all the more potent by this reification. John Feather grounds his discussions of the book in society in the web of values and relationships, material and abstract, shaped by books as both artifacts and symbols, noting that the significance that is attached to books extends "far beyond their functional role as containers of texts."[5] Robert Darnton illustrates several of these interrelationships in his seminal discussion of the history of the book, citing the intellectual, economic, social, and political complexities linked to the printed word, suggesting that it is, in fact, virtually impossible to separate the history of the book from that of society at large.⁶ First literacy, and then specialist language, deepened class divisions and social hierarchies, as books became the vessels for the codification of religious doctrine, secular laws, and normative rules, and as they imposed and affirmed order, books naturally became signifiers of high culture and social advancement. Moral character, both positive and negative, became conflated with the ability to access and use written information, as well as the means by which that was achieved. Knowledge led to power, and power was maintained through order. As Van Rensselaer Potter points out, however, "progress," "civilization," and "advancement" all rest on the uneasy tension between order and disorder.⁷ We instinctively resist disorder and the uncertainty it introduces in our social and intellectual lives, and yet, only through the confrontation of difference do we move forward. Those who possessed and controlled formal, written knowledge met challenges on several fronts: from mass culture that mimicked, yet threatened to cheapen, the power and status of the book on one side; from folkways and oral traditions—Old World knowledge based in tradition and the supernatural—on another; and from new knowledge and ideas on still another. "Dangerous knowledge" threatened to introduce chaos into order, through controversial texts—pamphlets, pages, letters, diaries, and book-length works—that questioned and confronted established, codified understandings of the social and natural worlds. Each of these eroded the cultural and intellectual establishment, introducing the unknown and challenging belief in the comprehensibility of all knowledge.

Individuals and societies thus employed the book to map their social and cultural identities, as well as their mental universes; yet, at the same time, they were constrained by it. Access, in terms of both economics and the socio-political control of materials, determined what written texts were read, by whom, and within what circumstances, while intellectual and creative conventions—as well as the construction and shifting tides of taste—set the stage for how material was received, interpreted, and discussed. This tension inherent in the experience of using books is perhaps one of the defining elements of Western society. Those who challenge the privileged status of books—questioning their truth and denying their authority—shine a powerful light on their ability to shape our collective notions of how the world works. Lies are exposed, agendas are revealed, and histories are revised, and yet, even these do not wholly erase the influence of the book's original form. While written into being by ordinary men and women, the ideas that animate volumes, diaries, scrolls, and other texts develop lives and destinies of their own; and reality, once conjured, is difficult to vanquish.

Books and Horror

Depictions of books in tales of the fantastic draw on these centuries of experience, presenting exaggerated versions of what books can be and do, while simultaneously subverting our expectations of how to interact with them. Magical books that depart from the day-to-day realities of the printed and bound page cluster in the comic-fantasy genre when the effects of the departure are benign—when a hack adventure-story writer's friend is sucked into the world of his latest poorly conceived epic, for example, or a frustrated novelist's main character comes to flesh-and-blood life—and in the realm of horror when the effects are malignant.⁸ Horror stories destabilize our perceptions of books in diverse ways, plunging us into a world where they can no longer be casually relied upon and rendering the seemingly familiar suddenly unfamiliar.

Books are, in the everyday world, essentially passive devices: tools for preserving and organizing knowledge so that readers can access it at will. Absorbing knowledge from the book (by reading) and applying it to the world (by taking action on it) are fundamentally separate processes. The spell books, grimoires, and similar magical tomes that fill horror films narrow this separation, however, merging reading and action into a single, seamless process. Reading aloud from the pages of a magical book can—without any further action on the part of the reader—summon beings of unimaginable power, open gateways between worlds or dimensions, and orchestrate magical forces capable of reshaping the world at the reader's whim. Sutter Cane, the horror writer at the heart of *In the Mouth of Madness* (1994) seemingly disappears from our world, only to be found in a town that appears on no map—one drawn from, and shaped by, the words in his best-selling novels—where he can reshape reality at will. Words read from a page are, in extreme cases, capable of completely unweaving the fabric of reality. The plot of *Warlock* (1989), for example, revolves around the struggle to control the Grand Grimoire: a book revealing the true name of God that, if called out, will unmake Creation itself, rendering the world (as it was in the beginning) "without form, and void."[9]

The ease with which books offer up their contents to reader—basic literacy opening up worlds of knowledge nearly without end—is transformed, in horror films, from a powerful benefit to a terrifying liability. Magical tomes that can be activated merely by the act of reading become, in the hands of unwitting users, weapons of immense power with no safety mechanisms or fail-safe circuits. Reading the text of a spell—regardless of whether the reader understands the forces it invokes, the effect it is meant to achieve, or even the language in which it is written—is sufficient to set it in motion. Idle curiosity is, in the hands of the impetuous or the unwary, sufficient to bring about disaster. The horrors of the *Evil Dead* films (1981, 1987, 1992) are set in motion by characters who unwittingly unleash hordes of the undead when they stumble across, and read from, the *Necronomicon*. The demon-summoning inscriptions in *Deliver Us from Evil* (2014) are even more potent. Scrawled on New York City walls as graffiti, they can be activated even when read silently by individuals who cannot (presumably) understand the languages—Latin and ancient Persian—they are written in. The trope is so well established that when a quartet of vacationing college students encounters a fearsome-looking antique book in *The Cabin in the Woods* (2012)—a horror film about the conventions of horror films—the most self-aware member of the group cautions: "Don't read the Latin!"

Those of us who use books in the everyday world are accustomed to seeing ourselves as masters of the text, but horror films introduce the possibility that the text will master us. Magical books that fall into the hands of the malevolent or the unwary can bring about destruction on an epic scale, but cursed books and manuscripts inflict terror only on the individuals unlucky enough to possess them, tearing apart the fabric of their lives rather than of reality itself. The threats they pose may be external—summoning demons and monsters, or causing otherwise harmless mishaps to spiral into fatal accidents—or disturbingly intimate. The uncanny children's book in *The Babadook* (2014), for example, materializes in the home of a grieving single mother struggling to raise a young son, whose father died on the day he was born. Seemingly innocent, if odd, at first, the book and its title character gradually insinuate themselves into her fragile psyche, fraying her grasp of reality and urging her toward murder and suicide.

The books that populate horror films need not, however, exercise magical powers in order to destabilize their characters' worlds. Even when performing their most basic function—recording and preserving information—they can reveal the dark and terrifying forces that lie beneath the surface, or lurk just beyond the margins of day-to-day reality. Secret family histories shared with the members of each new generation as they come of age shatter their dreams of a normal life. "Hidden" books of the Bible, suppressed millennia ago by the Church for fear of undermining its authority, outline the details of the impending Apocalypse, or reveal secret wars between Good and Evil in which humans are mere pawns. The hapless English professor hero of *The Whisperer in Darkness* (2011) seeks the solution of a cosmic mystery in a century-old collection of folklore—clinging to it even as the world he thought he knew turns dark and terrifying around him—only to find that it was part of an elaborate deception perpetrated by malevolent aliens bent on the conquest of the Earth. Reading a newly discovered book in a horror film may not, as in the works of H.P. Lovecraft and his literary followers, drive the reader literally insane, but to open one is to risk stepping across a threshold that cannot be re-crossed, and learning things that, once known, can never expunged from the mind.

Horror stories are, at their most basic level, tales in which characters' lives and their illusions of control over the world around them are placed in jeopardy. The books that populate onscreen horror stories attack both at once—causing their readers' worlds *and* worldviews to crumble and reform around them—and are all the more insidious because they so often seem, at first glance, to be so ordinary and benign.

Horror by the Book

Over his brief but incandescent writing career H.P. Lovecraft invented, or refined, many of the horror genre's most enduring book-related tropes. The 21 essays that comprise this collection are, therefore, led off by a set of four that consider "Lovecraft and His Legacy." It begins with Michael Fuchs' "Monstrous Writing, Writing Monsters: Authoring Manuscripts, Ontological Horror and Human Agency," which examines a familiar Lovecraftian theme—monsters from other worlds invading our own—as it plays out in films (and the video game *Alan Wake*) where "haunted manuscripts" act as a portal. The ability of such monsters to transgress the "sacred" boundary between fiction and reality and the epistemological conundrums it poses sheds critical light, Fuchs argues, on issues of agency and individual freedom in modern (or, rather, post-modern) horror. The next essay, "That Monstrous Book: The *Necronomicon* and Its Cinematic Contents," features Michael E. Heyes' exploration of the complex ways in which Lovecraft's fictional *Necronomicon* has intertwined, onscreen and off, with the real-world literature of the occult. Considering films such as *The Haunted Palace* (1963), *The Dunwich Horror* (1970), and *The Evil Dead* (1981), Heyes draws in figures ranging from Aleister Crowley to "reformed" Lovecraftian cultist William Schoeben. The essay that follows, Murray Leeder's "Paperback *Necronomicon*: Occult Authorship in John Carpenter's *In the Mouth of Madness*," explores the ways in which the director plays with the borderland between fantasy and reality inside a multilayered fictional universe. The story of a best-selling horror novelist who, by channeling the power of his readers' belief in his words, can write an entire New Hampshire town into physical existence, the film—and the essay—examine familiar Lovecraftian elements (alien god-monsters, rural New England settings, and a hero who finds the truth and wishes he hadn't) through the lens of the titular book.

The final essay in the section, Martin J. Auernheimer's "The Book with a Thousand

Faces: The Evolution of the *Necronomicon* in the *Evil Dead* Universe," focuses on the book's role in the film and television productions that have introduced it to a new generation of horror fans. The *Necronomicon* of the *Evil Dead* tales has, Auernheimer shows, evolved along a trajectory independent from Lovecraft's original—departing from, and ultimately eclipsing, the tome described by Lovecraft in 1921.

The second section, "Books of Hope and Despair," considers how books—even when operating in their traditional role as repositories of information—have the capacity to act not only as agents of courage and faith, but also as instruments of disruption, chaos, and terror. As Thomas Prasch notes in "The Magic Book and the Magic of Books in Murnau's *Faust* (1926)," F. W. Murnau's silent film adaptation of the legend shows him casting his Bible (and other, secular books) into the fire of his study before stepping onto the Devil's cloak for a flying tour of the world. Yet, Faust's conjuring of the Devil depends on a handwritten magical tome. Murnau, as Prasch shows in his close reading of the film, fills the screen with visual allusions to the early decades of print culture in Europe, from which the Faust legend sprang. The complex attitude toward books exhibited by both the film and its hero/victim reflect, Prasch argues, the fraught nature of books in the era of the Reformation. The next pair of essays in the section considers films in which the Bible, seen by many as a source of unwavering certainty in an ever-changing world, is revealed to be anything but that. "Apocryphal Horror: Understanding Evil Through Lost Books of the Bible," by Jeffrey M. Tripp, takes a broad view of "hidden" and "secret" Biblical texts in horror films: books and verses that are "not only non-canonical, but non-existent." Tripp explores how the films' use of these texts—simultaneously defining the problems that the heroes face, and providing them with the basis for a solution—presuppose that Bible verses have only one, plainly apparent meaning. They thus implicitly endorse a view of scripture associated with the small, but disproportionately loud-voiced forces of right-wing Christian fundamentalism. Mark Henderson's "Losing Your Faith for Seeing Too Much: The Anti-Bible as Indictment of American Heroism in Gregory Widen's *The Prophecy*" begins with the hero of the cult-classic film retrieving an ancient handwritten Bible from the corpse of a fallen angel. This Bible, never meant for human eyes, reveals the existence of a brutal, centuries-old struggle for control of Heaven, which has begun to engulf the Earth and draw in unwitting humans whose actions, as Henderson shows, become the film's proxies for the bloody history of U.S. expansion across North America.

The final essay of the section, "I(dio)t Follows: The Seashell E-Book in *It Follows*," by Learned Foote, follows the subtle-yet-pervasive ways in which the act of reading is woven into the fabric of a film that is, on the surface, about a tightly knit group of friends threatened by a monster. Dostoyevsky's classic, and the curious device on which the heroine Yara reads it, neither explain the monster nor mitigate its threat, but they become a vehicle for commenting on the film's central theme: coming to terms with the imminence of death.

Jennifer Kent's *The Babadook*, the story of a malevolent children's book that insinuates itself into the home and life of psychologically fragile single mother, has been widely hailed as a classic of 21st-century horror. It lends itself to widely divergent interpretations, which the three essays comprising the third section, "Perspectives on *The Babadook*," provide. Jessica Balanzategui leads off the section with "'The more you deny me, the stronger I get': 'Mister Babadook' and the Monstrous Empowerment of Children's Culture," which places the analytical focus on children, and on the ways in which children's culture—crafted *for* children by adults guided by their understanding of what it meant to be a child—reflects adult-child relations in the larger society. The book at the center of *The Babadook*, appearing and reappearing from nowhere in defiance of the central adult character's increasingly desperate wishes, breaks this pattern and thus forces both characters and viewers to reconsider the sharp, binary division of child and adult worlds.

Michael C. Reiff's "Mediating Trauma in Jennifer Kent's *The Babadook*," the next essay in the section, focuses on the decidedly adult problems faced by the film's heroine Amelia. Losing her husband has, when the film opens, left her for years in a state of emotional "living death," unable to move forward and barely able to care for herself and her son Samuel. The malevolent book's exploitation of her weakness is the source of the film's horror, Reiff argues, but it is the act of crafting and telling stories that ultimately gives Amelia the power to control the monster and leads her out of the darkness and into a better life. The section concludes with "Bad Books and Fairy Tales: Stigmatized Guardians in *The Turn of the Screw* and *The Babadook*," in which Austin Riede argues that the film and the Henry James literary classic are manifestations of "domestic horror." Riede sees both as tales in which children are terrorized by monsters, and the failure of their guardians—unaware of, or even complicit in, the terror—adds a deeper, more disturbing layer of horror.

The next section is "Diaries and Scrapbooks." These are among the most intimate forms of books: spaces within which experiences can be recorded, and inner thoughts revealed, that are never intended for the eyes of others. The next group of essays explores the ways in which these informal books are intertwined with the supernatural. Society sees young girls as emblems of uncorrupted innocence, but in "Dreadful Girl Diaries and the Promise of Transparent Girlhood," Karen J. Renner considers films that use the disturbing contents of girls' diaries to reveal the darkness behind their sweet-natured facades. The dark diaries in films such as *Fun* (1994), *Heavenly Creatures* (1994), and *The Loved Ones* might seem to subvert the innocent ideals of girlhood, Renner argues, but they still uphold the comforting presumption that the true nature of girls can always be accessed and known. Behind the obsession with the dark diary is a fantasy of feminine transparency—that girls cannot help but reveal their hearts once they pick up a pen.

Lisa Cunningham's essay, "'Do not read the Latin': The Summoning Diary in Horror Film," continues this look at evidence of evil hidden between the covers of diaries, but focuses on intrusions of the public into the private sphere. When diaries, intended by nature to be private, are violated—read by others—in films such as *Cabin in the Woods* (2012) and *Evilspeak* (1981), they summon their authors from beyond the grave, and returning to the world the evil that should have died with them.

The journal in *The Whisperer in Darkness*, kept by folklorist Eli Davenport and recovered a century later by Albert Wilmarth, records a different kind of inner thoughts: Davenport's musings on folktales of strange creatures that live in the hills of Vermont. In "'That book lies!' Lost Texts and Hidden Horrors in *The Whisperer in Darkness*," A. Bowdoin Van Riper shows how Wilmarth's deep emotional investment in the journal blinds him to the fact that that not all texts are what they seem, and that faith in the printed word is often misplaced, with disastrous results.

Deeply personal books continue to figure prominently in the section that follows, which deals with "Witches, Demons and Curses." In the opening essay, "Spellbound: The Significance of Spellbooks in the Depiction of Witchcraft on Screen," Emily Brick offers an overview of the magical books used by witches and warlocks in film and television, illustrating the ways in which secret spellbooks illuminate the characters that use them. More than just spell-casting tools, the books act as sources of exposition, objects of desire, and markers of the characters' standing within the magical community, as well as shedding light on how their magical power is produced and made manifest. Focusing on the *grimoire*, or magical encyclopedia, Sue Matheson's essay, "Horror Comedy by the Book: *Grimoire*, Carnival and *Heteroglossia* in Kenny Ortega's *Hocus Pocus* (1993)," looks at the comic portrayals of three witches and a willful spellbook, bound in human skin. Following Bakhtin, Matheson argues that the supernatural characters use the language of their magic to create both humor and horror, through the inversion of social norms. Taking a much darker turn, the last essay in this section discusses the horror classic *Night of the Demon*, in which a scholar-turned-cult-leader overthrows social norms entirely, using a cursed bit of parchment to summon a fire demon that eliminates his enemies. In "Unraveling Julian Karswell's Runic Curse in Jacques Tourneur's *Night of the Demon*," Michael Furlong traces the film's series of encounters between Karswell and American psychiatrist John Holden, a man of science who must learn to accept the existence—and power—of the supernatural if he is to survive.

The volume's final section, "International Takes," features a selection of international films that feature horrific books. It begins in Japan, with "Logical Horror: Axiomatic Magic and Strategic Murder in *Death Note*," Richard J. Leskosky's analysis of the international multimedia franchise centered on the titular Death Note: a notebook that exists for the sole purpose of taking human lives. As Leskosky illustrates, the franchise uses the notebook to call into question the morality of causing death, even for the common good, and illustrates how quickly personal interest can override higher order goals. Cynthia J. Miller's essay, "Grotesque Adaptations: Bodies of Knowledge in *Maléfique* (2002)," shifts the focus from the atmospheric horror of 1950s England to a 21st-century product of the New French Extremity: a film about a book so malevolent that it exacts a gruesome price from each of the four prison cellmates who seek to use its power to escape. Miller explores the film's layered commentary on the imprisonment of bodies and minds, and on the illusion of freedom.

Dark diaries return to the fore in Graciela Tissera's "*The Appeared* (2007) by Paco Cabezas: Redefining the Book of Hidden Memories and Cyclical Time," as a pair of Argentinian siblings discover the horrific secrets of their father's involvement in the country's Dirty War. The diary causes past and present to collapse around them, trapping them in a time of chaos and murder, as phantasmagorical figures reenact their own deaths and plead for remembrance and justice. Tissera's analysis highlights the film's use of one family's descent into supernatural horror to symbolize and comment on the larger, real-world horrors of Argentina's national past. Philip L. Simpson rounds out the volume with his essay "'No one who sees it lives to describe it': *The Book of Eibon* and the Power of the Unseeable in Lucio Fulci's *The Beyond*." Fulci's classic film is set in a forbidding Louisiana landscape that opens into a dimensional gateway revealing the fathomless realm of Hell itself. The film presents a dire warning against careless or ignorant use of magic, codified in the *Book of Eibon*. As Simpson demonstrates, the physical power of the written word—and the knowledge codified in that word—is never to be treated lightly.

NOTES

1. *The Whisperer in Darkness*, 2011
2. Such as the *Ahl al-Kitāb* described in the *Kurān*.

3. John Feather, "The Book in History and the History of the Book," *The Journal of Library History* Vol. 21, No. 1 (Winter 1986): 12.
4. Adrian Johns, *The Nature of the Book: Print and Knowledge in the Making* (Chicago: University of Chicago Press, 2009), 5.
5. Feather, "The Book in History," 12.
6. Robert Darnton, "What Is the History of Books?" *Daedalus* Vol. 111, No. 3 (Summer 1982): 70.
7. Van Rensselaer Potter, "Society and Science," *Science* Vol. 146, No. 3647 (1964): 1018.
8. The benign examples are, respectively, L. Ron Hubbard's 1940 science fiction novel *Typewriter in the Sky* and the 2012 fantasy film *Ruby Sparks*.
9. Genesis 1:2.

Lovecraft and His Legacy

Monstrous Writing, Writing Monsters
Authoring Manuscripts, Ontological Horror and Human Agency

MICHAEL FUCHS

Horace Walpole's iconic Gothic tale *The Castle of Otranto* (1764) claimed to be a manuscript "translated by William Marshall ... [f]rom the original Italian of Onuphrio Muralto," as the first edition's subtitle suggested.[1] The book thus produced its authenticity by referring to a non-existing document purportedly readily available in the "real" world, anchoring the fantastic events depicted in the story in material reality. At the same time, the subtitle highlighted the hauntedness of the original Italian manuscript (which, of course, never existed), as it brought forth the spectral hauntings displayed in the text. *The Castle of Otranto* thus not only firmly established the "haunted manuscript" trope but also tapped into the epistemological ambiguities guiding many tales of horror.

This essay will explore a particular type of "haunted manuscript" horror in which the epistemological questions Walpole's narrative raises take decidedly ontological twists: postmodernist horror tales in which monsters are quite literally written into worldly existence, exemplified by the movies *In the Mouth of Madness* (1994) and *Wes Craven's New Nightmare* (1994) and the video game *Alan Wake* (2010). Several scholars have employed the designation "postmodern horror" overzealously and indiscriminately, leading Andrew Tudor to diagnose the "proliferation in [the] use of the expression 'postmodern horror' as an apparently unproblematic descriptive term ... with little or no discussion of what that involves or implies."[2] In order to avoid making the same mistake, I should clarify that I understand "postmodernist horror" as a horror tale characterized by a high degree of self-awareness. One must keep in mind, though, that horror, as Carol J. Clover has pointed out, might well be "the most self-reflexive of cinematic genres."[3] As a result, self-awareness alone does not suffice to define postmodernist horror. However, we may (quite literally) take a page from Brian McHale's seminal book *Postmodernist Fiction* (1987), in which he introduces a useful means of defining postmodernism: Whereas the "dominant mode of modernist fiction is *epistemological*," the "dominant [mode] of postmodernist fiction is *ontological*."[4] In other words, while modernist cultural practice focuses on questions of how much and what we can know of the world we inhabit, postmodernism explores the very nature of this world, thereby raising fundamental philosophical questions about the world we live in.

From this perspective, the *Scream* movie series (1996–2011), although frequently celebrated as an exemplary case of postmodernist horror, only becomes postmodernist in very specific moments. Without doubt, the movies reference other horror films and genre conventions to such an extent that their intertextual subtext becomes "the actual *text* of the films," which allows the series to explore the influence of popular culture on our conception of the world.[5] However, the *Scream* films make sure that they do not "question the 'reality' of the film world" and thus largely sidestep the ontological questions characteristic of postmodernism.[6] Still, the movies feature a handful of truly postmodernist moments.

For example, in the third film, when the series' protagonist, Sidney Prescott (Neve Campbell), enters the set of *Stab 3*, she steps into a replica of Woodsboro, the setting of the first *Scream* (and first *Stab*) movie. Sidney goes into "her" house and up to "her" room, which cues lines of dialogue from the first film. These lines of dialogue are meant to be memories, but Sidney begins to interact with them, as present-day Sidney responds in the same way past-Sidney did in the first movie (or, more to the point, present-day Sidney knows past-Neve's lines). Suddenly, Ghostface attacks. After a wild chase through the "house" (which is as close to a shot-by-shot replication of a similar scene in *Scream* as it gets), Sidney falls off the roof to be "saved" by inept policeman Dewey (David Arquette). When she describes the attack to Detective Kincaid (Patrick Dempsey), she stresses, "I know he was there.... He was there in Woodsboro."[7] However, neither Sidney nor Ghostface was in Woodsboro, as the attack took place in a representation of Woodsboro, a model of small-town America, which begins to segue into Sidney's reality, as she can no longer confidently differentiate between fact and fiction. Indeed, one might take this idea even a step further: Since Woodsboro is a fictional place, created as a setting for the original *Scream* movie, the Woodsboro set is nothing but a copy of a copy of a copy. The resultant deferral of meaning blurs the distinctions between original and copy to the point that "the original" ceases to exist independent of its copies.

Apart from tapping into the hyperreal character of the postmodern condition, the short scene in the studio highlights the proliferation of various realities when Sidney hears voices from the past. Suddenly, multiple realities are not only beginning to co-exist simultaneously, but the alternative realities are "capable of collapsing, compromising, and even displacing the real world."[8] In the horror texts I will discuss in this essay, these multiple realities manifest in various forms, from memories invading the present moment to embedded manuscripts. In particular, I will focus on hypodiegetic stories featuring monsters trying to invade diegetic reality, transgressing the "sacred" boundaries separating fictional from real worlds.[9] While I will discuss the texts' explorations of monstrosity, which draw on fears characteristic of the postmodern age, I will argue that the three horror stories are centrally concerned with questions of agency and individual freedom—what is agency? And can we control our destinies?

Schizophrenic Narrative Structures

Horror stories, Judith Halberstam suggests in *Skin Shows* (1995), "thematize the monstrous aspects of both production and consumption—*Frankenstein* is, after all, an allegory about a production that refuses to submit to its author."[10] Halberstam decidedly uses the word "author" to emphasize the metatextual reading she proposes. This understanding of *Frankenstein* as a piece of metafiction is firmly rooted in the novel, as the text is an epistolary novel whose overall structure is akin to Chinese boxes. The resultant multiplication of stories(-within-stories) "calls attention to [the] text's constructedness," as the proliferation of narrators narrating "real" events they never witnessed reminds us of a game of Chinese whisper, in which each new version of the tale moves farther away from the original, thereby creating new versions of reality.[11] In addition to highlighting the artificial nature of the diegetic events, *Frankenstein*'s multilevel structure suggests that what is truly important lies at the heart of the narrative; that layer upon layer "must be peeled back to reveal the secret or repressed center," as Halberstam has explained.[12]

In the texts discussed in this chapter, the proliferation of narrative layers may have diverse effects on different types of recipients. Two effects are most prominent among them: Peeling off one narrative layer after another causes confusion among viewers and players who try to dissect the stories from a rational distance. In contrast, viewers and players who immerse themselves in the storyworlds experience numerous uncanny moments, generated by the texts' self-aware peeling-off-in-progress. Indeed, while Halberstam's aforementioned approach is evidently rooted in Freudian ideas surrounding repressed mental material—fears, anxieties, fantasies, and wishes which are transferred to the unconscious—*New Nightmare*, *In the Mouth of Madness*, and *Alan Wake* primarily evoke the uncanny through other means. Sigmund Freud explained that "an uncanny effect is often and easily produced when the distinction between imagination and reality is effaced, as when something that we have hitherto regarded as imaginary appears before us in reality."[13] Indeed, *Alan Wake* practically quotes Freud when an FBI detective realizes that "he had seen this moment before, read it in the page. He was transfixed by the déjà vu and the horror that he was a character in a story someone had written."[14] The incessant crossing of diegetic layers exemplified by this utterance creates textual labyrinths in which the limits between reality and fiction are not only put into question, but, in fact, disappear altogether, allowing the texts to tap into the "lingering emotion of terror as it relates to [the] loss of reality" Maria Beville considers emblematic of Gothic postmodernism.[15]

In the Mouth of Madness opens with a scene showing a couple of orderlies taking John Trent (Sam Neill) to a mental institution. This opening scene serves as a framing tale, as John begins to tell a psychiatrist how he ended up in this situation, explaining, "This all started with a disappearance. The Sutter Cane disappearance."[16] This statement cues an extended flashback, which virtually transports viewers back a few weeks (at least[17]). *Mouth of Madness* thus underlines that the events viewers will see in the following roughly 70 minutes are narrated by a man who has been declared insane—a highly unreliable narrator. Indeed, the story John relates seems crazy: A horror author named Sutter Cane (Jürgen Prochnow) went missing. While his publisher Arcane originally meant the writer's disappearance to be a publicity stunt to promote his latest book, no one knows Cane's whereabouts.

John, who investigates the insurance claim filed by Arcane, discovers that the covers of Cane's past books combine to make up a map of New England. This map reveals that Hobb's End—the preferred small-town setting of Cane's tales—is located somewhere in New Hampshire. After deciphering this hidden message, John believes that Cane must be hiding in Hobb's End. Trent's idea catches Cane's editor, Linda Styles (Julie Carmen), off-guard, as she wonders, "So, you're saying the man went someplace fictional?" However, John insists that "[i]t's a real place in a real state." But as both the two characters and the viewers will learn soon enough, the separation between reality and fiction is not as clear-cut as John suggests.

Indeed, as the story unfolds, reality, as experienced by John, and fiction, exemplified by Cane's novels, increasingly intersect, since Trent begins to live Cane's latest novel, *In the Mouth of Madness*, eventually leading John to murder a *Mouth of Madness* reader in broad daylight. Tellingly, prior to killing his victim, Trent remarks that for someone knowing the book, his gruesome attack "shouldn't come as a surprise." This murder returns the setting to the insane asylum, where the psychiatrist concludes that Trent "thinks he's fiction." The next morning, John finds not only the asylum, but the entire city abandoned. As he has nothing better to do, he goes to see *In the Mouth of Madness* in a theater. Significantly, the moving pictures Trent sees on the screen repeat images viewers had seen some time earlier, not only suggesting that Cane's novel is simultaneously inside and outside the actual movie (allowing the novel to effectively create the movie in both the diegetic world and in our world), but also holding up a mirror to the extra-filmic audience, who are meant to see themselves reflected in the filmic image. In this way, *Mouth of Madness* demonstrates that, as Linda explains at one point, "reality is just what we tell each other it is."[18] How is this situation different from fiction?

New Nightmare follows a comparable narrative pattern, as the film makes explicit its Möbius strip-like structure toward the end when Heather Langenkamp (Heather Langenkamp) finds a movie script in her son's room. On the title page, Heather notices a personal dedication from Wes Craven (Wes Craven): "Heather—thanks for having the guts to play Nancy one last time. At last Freddy's back where he belongs." Attentive viewers will notice that the intradiegetic script shares the title with the movie they are watching. As Heather begins reading the story to her son, Dylan (Miko Hughes), the script returns viewers to the beginning of the film they have been watching for the past one hundred minutes: "WE OPEN ON AN OLD WOOD BENCH. There's FIRE AND TOOLS, and a man's GRIMY HANDS building what soon is revealed as A GLEAMING SET OF CLAWS. And the claws are moving now, as if awakening from a long and unwanted sleep."[19]

By effectively returning viewers to its beginning, *New Nightmare* suggests that horror tales repeat the same pattern time and again. Indeed, similar to how Nancy (Langenkamp's role in the first and third films in the series) and other Freddy-victims-to-be tried to make sure that Freddy could not transgress the borderlines between dreams and (diegetic) reality in previous *Elm Street* movies, Heather wants to stop Krueger from crossing over

John Trent (Sam Neill) searches for Sutter Cane in *In the Mouth of Madness* (1995).

from the world of fiction to reality. *New Nightmare* mines this self-awareness to reflect on the history of horror by tracing the genre to fairy tales.[20] In addition, the movie comments on the evolution of the *Elm Street* franchise. Tellingly, at one point, Wes remarks that he is developing a script for a new movie because Freddy's story has been "water[ed] … down to make it an easier sell," implying that the franchise entries which he was not involved in did not measure up to the standards set by the original film.[21]

Yet beyond these somewhat solipsistic reflections on *New Nightmare* as well as the franchise and the genre the film participates in, confronting Heather with the story that is her life suggests that the audience is watching the narrative unfold while Wes Craven is creating it—from the death of her (fictional) husband to Freddy trying to invade reality, it's all "real": constructed in a script within the diegetic reality. The reality of the script, filmic reality, and our reality (since Heather Langenkamp stars as Heather Langenkamp, Robert Englund as Robert Englund, and so on) accordingly segue into one another, making the attempt to differentiate between these layers of reality a moot point, because the film is as "real" as extra-filmic reality, while material reality features as many artificial elements as a fiction film.

Alan Wake's narrative, finally, focuses on its titular character, a popular crime fiction, thriller, and horror author suffering from writer's block. Alan soon discovers that the events taking place in the small-town of Bright Falls in the Pacific Northwest echo his novel-in-progress *Departure*. At first, Alan is convinced that he barely started working on his new novel, but both he and players soon realize that the book is nearly finished. However, Alan has no recollection of composing it, as he suffers from a week-long memory gap, which is connected to the abduction of his wife, Alice. At first, the kidnapper appears to be a local man, possibly a crazy fan, but the mastermind behind Alice's abduction is, in fact, a dark force that needs a writer in order to exist.

In the course of the game, Alan and the player learn that the events unfolding in front of their eyes (and on their screens, respectively) do not simply mirror the events depicted in the novel; they are, in fact, created by Alan's writing. However, this is not the end of the proliferation of narrative layers, as Alan-the-writer is possibly a character in a story authored by Thomas Zane, who had purportedly died 30 years before Alan set foot in Bright Falls and who appears as a quite literal "Author-God" in the gameworld.[22] As Alan tries to save his wife, he faces the challenges of confronting not only an unknown foe, but also generic conventions. Indeed, about half-way through the game, he comes to understand that while he had conceived of *Departure* as a crime thriller, "the genre of the story shifted," as "it's becoming a horror story."[23] He knows that this generic shift does not bode well for his wife and becomes convinced that in order to save Alice, he must change *Departure*'s ending.

Writing Monsters

At the heart of these confusing narratives are manuscripts in progress: Sutter Cane is working on his latest novel, called *In the Mouth of Madness*, Wes Craven is developing the script for his latest movie, *New Nightmare*, and Alan Wake is writing his latest novel, *Departure*. Since "the monster exists only to be read," as Jeffrey Jerome Cohen has suggested, the emphasis on the writing process reveals insights into the monsters the characters (and their creators) employ in their stories.[24]

Mouth of Madness does not waste any time in establishing its focus on the production of books, as the opening credits are displayed over images of a printing press, as thousands of copies of Sutter Cane's novel *The Hobb's End Horror* (whose back announces the upcoming release of *In the Mouth of Madness*) are rolling off the line. While *Mouth of Madness* begins to inquire into the nature of reality early on, the interconnections between diegetic reality and the reality of *Hobb's End Horror* become central to the narrative once John and Linda arrive in Hobb's End. There, they begin to unravel the intricate connections between Cane's books and the small-town they are in. As they are walking through the town, John is reading *Hobb's End Horror* and comments that the novel is "like … a guidebook" to the town.[25]

The story's level of weirdness increases exponentially when Linda finds Cane in an old, dark, and eerie church. As he is typing his manuscript, he comments, "For years, I thought I was making all this up, but they were telling me what to write." The camera focuses on a door, locked with iron chains, which appears to be alive and seems to restrain something that should not be released. Cane continues that they were "giving [him] the power to make it all real." When Trent meets Cane soon thereafter (after repeatedly failing to leave Hobb's End, as he returns to its main street despite driving away from the town time and again), the writer explains, "When people lose their ability to know the difference between fantasy and reality, the Old Ones can begin their journey back."[26] As Cane opens the gateway for the Lovecraftian creatures, the pounding door transforms into a piece of paper which has been torn apart.

This self-aware moment draws on the notion that books allow readers to enter different worlds: "avowedly fictional spaces that provide an escape from a disenchanted modernity into self-subsistent realms of wonder."[27] In addition, the scene reflects on how horror seeks to address that which eludes verbalization and/or visualization—"The things Cane writes are indescribable; beyond description," remarks Linda at one point.[28] Tellingly, Tzvetan Todorov noted that the "supernatural is born out of language," as supernatural creatures "exist only in words."[29] Of course, Todorov wrote about fiction, but what is true of literature is—in this case—also true of multimodal texts such as films. Without Cane's writing, without *In the Mouth of Madness* (the movie), the monsters might lurk in the darkness, but they are only set free by the creative process and, more importantly, produced in discourse.

While in *Mouth of Madness*, Sutter Cane's writing opens a gateway to a different dimension, *New Nightmare* suggests that it exists to contain Evil. In a lengthy, highly self-aware exchange between Wes and Heather, Craven explains that Evil "can be captured … by storytellers, of all things. I mean, every so often, they imagine a story good enough to sort of catch its essence, and then, for a while, it's held prisoner in the story…. But the problem comes when the story dies" because "when the story dies, the evil is set free." Significantly, earlier in their conversation, Wes refers to "the evil" as "this entity—whatever you want to call it," while Heather, for a lack of a more appropriate descriptor, simply calls it "this thing."[30] In this way, the dialogue acknowledges what Halberstam has referred to as the monster's "vertiginous excess of meaning."[31] Since the "monstrous body is pure culture," it may symbolize whatever one wants it to represent.[32] However, this semantic openness in fact annuls the monster's meaning, as its meaning relies on discourse; in fact, the monster only exists in discourse. In addition, the entire scene self-reflexively "invokes psychoanalytic considerations," as Andrew Tudor put it, by suggesting that horror stories help us understand and/or come to terms with suppressed and repressed material.[33]

Alan Wake highlights the centrality of writing in its opening cinematic by tipping its proverbial hat to Stephen King (who is referenced repeatedly in the course of the game) and by emphasizing Alan's status as a writer.[34] Indeed, in *Alan Wake*, players may find dozens of pages of the manuscript Alan is working on. According to Thomas Vogler, these representations of a book may be referred to as "book objects," since they are "not books, even though their whole being exists in relation to the book."[35] Johanna Drucker has taken up Vogler's ideas on "book objects" and explained that one of the most prolific tropes in this context is the "book-as-repository-of-secret-knowledge."[36] The secret knowledge the manuscript pages in *Alan Wake* hold is knowledge about the future. For example, Alan discovers the following manuscript page at one point.

Only seconds later, Alan can hear the sounds of a chainsaw announcing a slew of opponents approaching. The exposure to the manuscript prophesying the future produces two kinds of uncanny effects here: On the one hand, the past narration, present player performance, and future-as-foretold-in-the-past-narration become one, as temporal demarcations disintegrate. On the other hand, the embedded narrative of the manuscript does not simply predict the future-to-come, but, in fact, *creates* the diegetic future. Thus, the manuscript is not only embedded in the gameworld, but simultaneously frames it.

The concurrent proliferation and conflation of various worlds, produced through the multi-level structure, draws on Jean Baudrillard's idea that the postmodern age is not

> The night had been one desperate situation after another. I was exhausted and my body felt as though it had been chewed up and spat out.
>
> The flashlight was heavy in my hand, and each pull of the trigger sent a painful shock up my arm. But I was finally out of the woods and things were looking up.
>
> That's when I heard the chainsaw.

Departure (written in the past) foretells the future, which becomes the present (Xbox 360 edition of *Alan Wake* © Microsoft Game Studios, 2010).

defined by the mere excess of signs, but rather characterized by a process through which "the signs of the real" first precede and eventually replace "the real."[37] This increasing entanglement of (what we believe to be) fiction with (what we believe to be) reality has led Slavoj Žižek to diagnose that a "paranoiac fantasy" has been haunting postmodern America, namely "that of an individual living in a small idyllic Californian city ... who suddenly starts to suspect that the world he is living in is ... a spectacle staged to convince him that he is living in the real world."[38]

Tellingly, Alan believes he can see through the spectacle and the layers and layers of illusions creating realities. Indeed, he becomes convinced that if he were to stop writing, the world (that he is actually part of) would cease to exist. Since Alice's life thus depends on his skills as an author, he becomes intent on finishing his novel and coming up with a conclusion that sees him save Alice. However, Alan is very much aware of the spectral presence of Thomas Zane, who possibly created Alan. Accordingly, *Alan Wake* raises the question of how much agency Alan actually has in the world he inhabits.

Agency in a Predetermined World

To be sure, *Alan Wake* is not the only one of the texts discussed here to explore human agency. Toward the end of *New Nightmare*, Heather begins to understand that her recent encounters with other people mirrored similar moments in *A Nightmare on Elm Street* (1984), making her wonder how "real" these encounters may have been. When coming across the *New Nightmare* script for the first time, she reads, "The more she read[,] the more she realized what she had in her hands was nothing more or less than her life itself. That everything she had experienced and thought was bound within these

```
She searches the vast room, then stops, hearing something
fluttering - like the wings of a wounded bird or... She
turns.

IN HER POV - ACROSS THE CHAMBER - past falling water and
ruined pillars there is visible - A SCRIPT.  Its pages
flapping in the hissing wind.

HEATHER CROSSES.  Cautiously kneels and picks it up.
Checking over her shoulder once, she opens to a page at
random.

CLOSE ON THE SCRIPT.  HEATHER'S VOICE can be heard READING
OS:
                    HEATHER (OS)
                (reading)
          The more she read the more she
          realized what she had in her hands
          was nothing more or less than her
          life itself.  That everything she
```

Nancy reads the movie script that is her life in *New Nightmare* (2011).

pages. There was no movie. There was only ... her ... life...."³⁹ The script page thus highlights that Heather's life (Heather's, not just Nancy's) is prescribed by the manuscript. Indeed, when looking at the pieces of the script one can actually see, the manuscript details the very steps she took to get to the document.

In *Mouth of Madness*, Trent asserts early on that "I'm my own man. Nobody pulls my strings." This moment echoes in the scene in which Cane opens the gate to the other dimension, as John maintains, "I know what's real. I know who I am, and nobody pulls my strings." However, Cane claims, "You are what I write. Like this town. It wasn't here before I wrote it. And neither were you," before turning René Descartes's famous dictum *cogito ergo sum* on its head by asserting, "I think therefore you are."⁴⁰ And, indeed, since John's life unfolds in ways eerily reminiscent of the intradiegetic manuscript (and its film adaptation), Cane appears to have created the world Trent inhabits. However, the question of agency is more of a secondary subtext in *Mouth of Madness* and *New Nightmare*.

Alan Wake, in contrast, zeroes in on the topic of self- vs. pre-determination, which takes a decidedly meta-ludic dimension in the video game. This aspect is introduced as early as the opening cinematic, which re-creates one of Alan's nightmares. In the nightmare, he runs over a hitchhiker. When Alan steps out of the car to check up on the hitchhiker, the body has disappeared. In this moment, the uncontrollable world of cinematics smoothly transitions to interactive gameplay. Alan occupies a dual position in this moment: On the one hand, Alan is the avatar, the player's embodiment in the digital world⁴¹; on the other, Alan acts as a voiceover narrator who relates the actions performed by the player in the past tense. In combination with the interactive gameplay, the voiceover narration in the past tense generates a friction, since playing "has a basic sense of happening ... *now*."⁴² Here, *Alan Wake* teases the metaludic games players will be confronted with throughout the game by highlighting that players participate in events which have already taken shape. Put differently, players may simply act out *Departure*.

This interrelation between the gameworld and the manuscript becomes most explicit in the concluding hours of the game, since objects are depicted as words hovering around in the gameworld. When Alan points his flashlight at one of these words, the signifier magically turns into the signified, as the word transforms into the object, to the sound of a typewriter. These surreal

In a meta-linguistic play, signifiers turn into signifieds to the sound of a typewriter in *Alan Wake* (Xbox 360 edition of *Alan Wake* © Microsoft Game Studios, 2010).

moments are crucial for *Alan Wake*'s metatextual and metaludic games, since up until this point, players are made to believe that *Departure* has been finished and Alan re-enacting it. Suddenly, Alan and the player are quite literally writing the story while they are experiencing it.

At least, that is the surface meaning *Alan Wake* communicates. On second thought, though, one may wonder: Who put the words into the gameworld, to begin with? Alan? Thomas Zane? Leaving the narrative behind, the only correct answer seems to be the developers, but even they are distanced from the words on the screen by the code they use to program the game. Irrespective of who (or what) may, in fact, be the origin of the letters, *Alan Wake* highlights that neither Alan nor the players are free in their choices. While they may opt for different routes to approach certain tasks in the gameworld, these choices are pre-fabricated, underlining that, at the end of the day, "all playing is a being-played."[43]

If, as Jerrold E. Hogle has argued, horror "helps us address and disguise some of the most important desires, quandaries, and sources of anxiety, from the most internal and mental to the widely social and cultural," *In Mouth of Madness*, *Wes Craven's New Nightmare*, and *Alan Wake* suggest that the "elision between reality and fiction" is, indeed, one of the main anxieties plaguing contemporary subjects.[44] Yet beyond this characteristic of the postmodern condition, all three texts tap into the growing awareness, possibly even fear, that neo-liberalism breeds self-determining and free subjects. Of course, "self-determining and free" might have a positive ring to it, but, what Nikolas Rose referred to as the "aspiration to self-control" has been replaced by the "burdens of freedom."[45] The most central "burden of freedom" is making life meaningful through narratives of free choice. These decisions, however, are generally offered by the market, rendering these choices anything but autonomous. By toying with the interplay between pre-determined and self-determined lives, *In the Mouth of Madness*, *Wes Craven's New Nightmare*, and *Alan Wake* thus suggest that one of the most constricting fears in our contemporary world is that we have little to no control over the lives we live.

NOTES

1. Walpole, *Castle of Otranto*, 1.
2. Tudor, "From Paranoia to Postmodernism," 105.
3. Clover, *Men, Women, and Chain Saws*, 168.
4. McHale, *Postmodernist Fiction*, 9–10; italics in original.
5. Wee, "The *Scream* Trilogy," 44; italics in original.
6. Tudor, "From Paranoia to Postmodernism," 110.
7. *Scream 3*.
8. Sconce, *Haunted Media*, 18.
9. Genette, *Narrative Discourse*, 236.
10. Halberstam, *Skin Shows*, 12.
11. Benford, "'Listen to my tale,'" 325.
12. Halberstam, *Skin Shows*, 21.
13. Freud, "Uncanny," 244.
14. *Alan Wake*.
15. Beville, *Gothic-Postmodernism*, 10.
16. *Mouth of Madness*.
17. In typical postmodernist manner, the chronology of events is not clear—and, indeed, shouldn't be. In addition, after having visited the town of Hobb's End, John can no longer remember certain events, such as delivering Cane's manuscript "months ago."
18. *Mouth of Madness*.
19. *New Nightmare*; capitalization in original.
20. On the interrelation between fairy tales, folklore, and horror, see Mikel J. Koven's *Film, Folklore, and Urban Legends* (2008).

21. *New Nightmare.*
22. Barthes, "Death of the Author," 146.
23. *Alan Wake.*
24. Cohen, "Monster Culture," 4.
25. *Mouth of Madness.*
26. *Ibid.*
27. Saler, *As If*, 7.
28. *Mouth of Madness.*
29. Todorov, *The Fantastic*, 82.
30. *New Nightmare.*
31. Halberstam, *Skin Shows*, 2.
32. Cohen, "Monster Culture," 4.
33. Tudor, "Why Horror," 446.
34. For more on the role of writing in *Alan Wake*, see Fuchs (44–46).
35. Vogler, "When a Book," 459.
36. Drucker, "Digital Codex," 220.
37. Baudrillard, "Precession of Simulacra," 2.
38. Žižek, *Welcome*, 12.
39. *New Nightmare.*
40. *Mouth of Madness.*
41. There is yet another set of dualisms at work here, as Alan is both avatar and character; as avatar, Alan is both part of the real world occupied by the player and part of the gameworld. However, developing these points would take this piece into a different direction than intended.
42. Juul, "Introduction," 134.
43. Gadamer, *Truth and Method*, 104.
44. Hogle, "Introduction," 3; Vidler, *Architectural Uncanny*, 9.
45. Rose, *Powers of Freedom*, 45, 107.

BIBLIOGRAPHY

Alan Wake. Developed by Remedy Entertainment. Microsoft Game Studios, 2010. Xbox 360.
Barthes, Roland. "The Death of the Author," translated by Stephen Heath. In *Image—Music—Text*, edited by Stephen Heath, 142–48. New York: Hill & Wang, 1978.
Baudrillard, Jean. "The Precession of Simulacra," translated by Sheila Faria Glaser. In *Simulacra and Simulation*, 1–42. Ann Arbor: University of Michigan Press, 1994.
Benford, Criscilla. "'Listen to my tale': Multilevel Structure, Narrative Sense Making, and the Inassimilable in Mary Shelley's *Frankenstein*." *Narrative* 18, no. 3 (2010): 324–46.
Beville, Maria. *Gothic-Postmodernism: Voicing the Terrors of Postmodernity*. Amsterdam: Rodopi, 2009.
Clover, Carol J. *Men, Women, and Chain Saws: Gender in the Modern Horror Film*. Princeton: Princeton University Press, 1992.
Cohen, Jeffrey Jerome. "Monster Culture (Seven Theses)." In *Monster Theory: Reading Culture*, edited by Jeffrey Jerome Cohen, 3–24. Minneapolis: University of Minnesota Press, 1996.
Drucker, Johanna. "The Digital Codex from Page Space to E-Space." In *A Companion to Digital Literary Studies*, edited by Ray Siemens and Susan Schreibman, 216–32. Malden, MA: Wiley-Blackwell, 2008.
Freud, Sigmund. "The 'Uncanny,'" translated by James Strachey, Anna Freud, Alix Strachey, and Alan Tyson. In *The Standard Edition of the Complete Psychological Works of Sigmund Freud, Vol. 17*: An Infantile Neurosis *and Other Works*, edited by James Strachey, 217–56. London: Vintage, 2001.
Fuchs, Michael. "A Different Kind of Monster: Uncanny Media and *Alan Wake*'s Textual Monstrosity." In *Contemporary Research on Intertextuality in Video Games*, edited by Christophe Duret and Christian-Marie Pons, 39–53. Hershey: IGI Global, 2016.
Gadamer, Hans-Georg. *Truth and Method*, translated by Joel C. Weinsheimer and Donald G. Marshall. London: Continuum, 2004.
Genette, Gérard. *Narrative Discourse: An Essay in Method*, translated by Jane E. Lewin. Ithaca: Cornell University Press, 1980.
Halberstam, Judith. *Skin Shows: Gothic Horror and the Monstrosity of Monsters*. Durham: Duke University Press, 1995.
Hogle, Jerrold E. "Introduction: The Gothic in Western Culture." In *The Cambridge Companion to Gothic Fiction*, edited by Jerrold E. Hogle, 3–20. Cambridge: Cambridge University Press, 2002.
In the Mouth of Madness. Directed by John Carpenter. 1994. Warner Home Video, 2013. Blu-Ray.
Juul, Jesper. "Introduction to Game Time." In *First Person: New Media as Story, Performance, and Game*, edited by Pat Harrigan and Noah Wardrip-Fruin, 131–42. Cambridge: MIT Press, 2004.
Koven, Mikel J. *Film, Folklore, and Urban Legends*. Lanham, MD: Scarecrow Press, 2008.
McHale, Brian. *Postmodernist Fiction*. London: Routledge, 1987.
New Nightmare. Directed by Wes Craven. 1994. New Line Cinema, 2011. Blu-Ray.

Rose, Nikolas. *Powers of Freedom: Reframing Political Thought*. Cambridge: Cambridge University Press, 1999.
Saler, Michael. *As If: Modern Enchantment and the Literary Prehistory of Virtual Reality*. Oxford: Oxford University Press, 2012.
Sconce, Jeff. *Haunted Media: Electronic Presence from Telegraphy to Television*. Durham: Duke University Press, 2000.
Scream 3. Directed by Wes Craven. 2000. Studiocanal, 2011. Blu-Ray.
Todorov, Tzvetan. *The Fantastic: A Structural Approach to a Literary Genre*, translated by Richard Howard. Ithaca: Cornell University Press, 1975.
Tudor, Andrew. "From Paranoia to Postmodernism? The Horror Movie in Late Modern Society." In *Genre and Contemporary Hollywood*, edited by Steve Neal, 105–16. London: BFI Publishing, 2002.
———. "Why Horror? The Peculiar Pleasures of a Popular Genre." *Cultural Studies* 11, no. 3 (1997): 443–63.
Vidler, Anthony. *The Architectural Uncanny: Essays in the Modern Unhomely*. Cambridge: MIT Press, 1992.
Vogler, Thomas A. "When a Book Is Not a Book." In *A Book of the Book: Some Works and Projections about the Book and Writing*, edited by Jerome Rothenberg and Steven Clay, 448–66. New York: Granary Books, 2000.
Walpole, Horace. *The Castle of Otranto*, edited by Michael Gamer. London: Penguin, 2001.
Wee, Valerie. "The *Scream* Trilogy, 'Hyperpostmodernism,' and the Late-Nineties Teen Slasher Film." *Journal of Film and Video* 57, no. 3 (2005): 44–61.
Žižek, Slavoj. *Welcome to the Desert of the Real!* New York: Verso, 2002.

That Monstrous Book

The Necronomicon *and Its Cinematic Contents*

MICHAEL E. HEYES

In 1924, H.P. Lovecraft published "The Hound" in *Weird Tales* and first introduced the reading public to the *Necronomicon*: "Immediately upon beholding this amulet we knew that we must possess it.... Alien it indeed was to all art and literature which sane and balanced readers know, but we recognized it as the thing hinted of in the forbidden *Necronomicon* of the mad Arab Abdul Alhazred."[1]

This passage is indicative of the way in which Lovecraft wrote about the *Necronomicon*, in language full of "things hinted," but short on detail. This creates a curious disjunction in Lovecraft's writing, with the *Necronomicon* being present for the characters, who handle and read it, but absent for the reader. Despite its narrative presence, there are no descriptions of its appearance; despite the book being read, there is little-to-no information given about the contents of the book, and quotations are rare.

This strategy of concealment works in literature, but visual media such as film and television cannot render the disjunction: When a character reads from a book, they must read *something*; when a character performs rites, they must take actions that look like a ritual to the audience. In a literary context, the *Necronomicon* functions as a hypertext[2]—an amorphous, shadowy work that could theoretically take an infinite number of forms—but when translated to film, one of these forms must be actualized: the book must be filled with something.

There is, I will argue, a pattern to this "filling." Rather than invent content for the *Necronomicon* wholesale, directors instead appropriate works, practices and rituals associated with actual religious or magical practices to fill the dread book's pages. In the films under consideration in this chapter, this material is drawn from Spiritualism, Aleister Crowley and his tradition of Thelema, and the Simon *Necronomicon*. The term Spiritualism is used here to apply to a wide variety of traditions indebted to Emmanuel Swedenborg and Franz Mesmer that believed humans were spirits enshrined in bodies, that after death this corporeal form was shed, and that man could participate in this spiritual nature in the present life in a variety of ways. After his tenure as part of the occult organization the Golden Dawn, Aleister Crowley, the British ceremonial magician and artist once dubbed "the wickedest man in the world" by the *Sunday Express*, developed a tradition of ritual magic governed by the creed "Do what thou wilt shall be the whole of the Law." Finally, the Simon *Necronomicon* is one of several works that claim to be the "actual" *Necronomicon* of which Lovecraft wrote, and was published by the pseudonymous "Simon" in 1977 as a book of ritual magic, a book that the author claimed in 2006 had sold 800,000 copies.[3] However, this process of importation does not transmit an accurate and complex picture of the tradition from which it borrows. Rather, filmmakers bring a Christian frame of understanding—just as absent from Lovecraft's work as the practices themselves—to the rituals, effectively demonizing the tradition for their target American audience.

The Haunted Palace *(1963)*

In many ways, Roger Corman's work is a natural place to start when querying the *Necronomicon*. As Migliore and Strysik point out "*The Haunted Palace* is a seminal film for Lovecraft lovers. It's the first motion picture to introduce HPL's creations to a general audience, including the ever-popular *Necronomicon*."[4]

Based loosely on *The Case of Charles Dexter Ward*, the film features Vincent Price in two different roles: Joseph Curwen, a devotee of the "dark gods" and owner of a copy of the *Necronomicon*, and Charles Dexter Ward, an heir to Curwen's home who bears a mysterious resemblance to his forebear. The opening of the film establishes the threat that Curwen poses to the small town of Arkham: by night, he hypnotically draws women out of their homes to participate in sexual experiments, experiments aimed at crossbreeding humans with a monstrous creature that dwells below Curwen's castle. Burnt for his crimes, Curwen receives another chance at life when Ward enters the castle to claim his inheritance. Slowly, Curwen exerts a disembodied hold over Ward until he possesses him completely, terrorizing the town by immolating the descendants of his murderers.

Wilbur Whateley (Dean Stockwell), a character inspired by Aleister Crowley, carries out dark rituals in *The Dunwich Horror* (1970).

Though Ward's wife, Ann (Debra Paget), attempts to stop the transformation with the help of Dr. Willett (Frank Maxwell), a sympathetic Arkhamite, the castle is eventually destroyed by the townspeople and Curwen escapes in Ward's body.

While the *Necronomicon* does not make many appearances throughout the film, it nevertheless features as a narrative hinge around which the plot swings. A dialogue between Willet and Ward reveals a major element of this importance:

> WARD: I'm sure that every warlock or witch who died in America left a curse. Why should Curwen's be taken so seriously?
>
> WILLET: It was thought that he had gained possession of a book called the *Necronomicon* ... they claimed it held enough secrets to give a man absolute power. Of course, every mythology has such a book, but the *Necronomicon* supposedly contained formulas through which one could communicate with or even summon the elder gods: the dark ones from beyond who had once ruled the world and now are merely waiting for an opportunity to regain that control.

The importance of the *Necronomicon* is further underscored when Curwen gains control of Ward for the first time. As he becomes aware of his surroundings, he sees one of his servants holding a voluminous tome: "The book. The book!" Curwen cries while grasping at it desperately. The audience is shown the cover which contains the title *Necronomicon* in block letters. "Good ... good" Curwen declares, clearly relieved at the book's survival.

As Ward points out, warlock curses are a dime-a-dozen and not to be taken seriously. The only reason the townsfolk place any stock in Curwen's curse is that he possessed the *Necronomicon*, a book that gives to its holder "absolute power." While the totality of the book's contents is not divulged, this dialogue suggests that Curwen acquires his mysterious powers from the book, as well as his hybrid breeding program. This obfuscation of the book's contents extends even to its owner: Before his castle's destruction, Curwen tells Willett about the breeding program, claiming it is "the most important [project] ever attempted of humans, more important than you can ever imagine and therefore, I fear, beyond your understanding.... As a matter of fact, we don't fully understand ourselves. We obey. That is all. We obey."

The majority of Curwen's unusual abilities appear to involve a kind of hypnosis. Even before the *Necronomicon* appears on screen, the viewer sees evidence of the strange hypnotic powers Curwen is capable of exerting over his victims. As the men of the town drink at a local tavern, they see a glassy-eyed woman plodding towards the castle, the most recent victim of Curwen's reproductive program. Her trance-like motion is matched by behaviors an audience would associate with hypnosis: the woman accepts commands from Curwen and responds to pressures placed on her body but otherwise does not speak or act on her own. When the townsfolk approach the castle with torches and pitchforks, Curwen produces the woman and tells the mob that "she visits us frequently. Don't you, Miss Fitch? *Don't you*?" The woman responds with a hollow "Yes." Yet, when questioned by the townsfolk she stares blankly, prompting the leader of the mob to declare, "You see? He's taken her mind, her soul ... the good Lord knows what else."

This hypnotic power appears related to Curwen's possession of, and resurrection within, the body of Charles Dexter Ward. When Ward first arrives in the castle, he sees a painting of Curwen. Throughout the film, when Ward approaches the painting, the interactions are shot to call attention to the painting's eyes, which are piercing and intense, and Ward's, which are confused and clouded. Alternating shots of the painting and Ward create the impression that the two are staring into each other's eyes, not unlike the popular image of a hypnotist and his hypnotized patient/victim.[5] This hypnotic exchange results in Curwen possessing the body of Ward little by little until Curwen eventually declares: "I have him now.... Charles Dexter Ward is dead."

The supernatural abilities that Curwen gains from his study of the *Necronomicon* reveal some of the film's occult influences: the matrix of ideas drawn from Mesmerism and the credo "man is a spirit here and now." While this matrix influenced several different traditions (e.g., New Thought, Theosophy, etc.), Spiritualism is likely the most well-known to American viewers due to its immense popularity in the 19th and early 20th centuries. Arthur Conan Doyle, for example, describes the same combination of hypnosis and the freeing of the personality from the body when he recounts the life of early American spiritualist Andrew Jackson Davis:

> In his later boyhood, Davis's latent psychic powers began to develop.... His full capacity was tapped, however, by the chance that a travelling showman who exhibited the wonders of mesmerism came to the village and experimented upon Davis.... It was soon found that Davis had very remarkable clairvoyant powers.... Davis's ministrations were not confined to those who were in his presence, but his soul or etheric body could be liberated by the magnetic manipulation of his employer, and could be sent forth like a carrier pigeon with the certainty that it would come home again bearing any desired information. Apart from the humanitarian mission on which it was usually engaged it would sometimes roam at will...[6]

The passage also highlights the difference between Mesmerism and hypnosis: before the latter was relegated to its current, narrow therapeutic and stage use, the former allowed for the manifestation and development of a variety of seemingly supernatural abilities such as those that Davis displayed (and which Curwen does as well).[7]

Curwen also, curiously, displays the ability to return the dead to life—a power associated with neither Mesmerism nor Spiritualism. The audience sees this conjuration in action when Curwen and his aides exhume the body of his dead lover in preparation for her resurrection. Looming over the casket, Curwen reverently recites in Latin: "All you powers of darkness, give to this woman eternal life. Let her live, let her live, let her live...."[8] This ritual does not appear to emerge out of any particular religious or spiritual tradition, but seems to be an inversion of traditional Christian notions of eternal life. Curwen's words echo the claims made by Jesus in John 10:27–28 (KJV): "My sheep hear my voice.... I give unto them eternal life; and they shall never perish." However, it is not through a miracle that Curwen accomplishes this, but by explicitly calling upon "all you powers of darkness."

Through this inversion, the director introduces a Christian mythic structure and moral framework into the narrative, an addition that is all the more striking due to the absence of such a framework from the source material created by Lovecraft—an avowed atheist and materialist. This framework appears again and again throughout the film as characters refer to Curwen as "Satan himself" and "the Devil himself."

This mythic structure also underscores the generic nature of the *Necronomicon*'s filling in the film. Curwen's character codes as somewhat "demonic" in his supernatural abilities: were it not for the hypnotic component, one could interpret Curwen's possession of Ward as demonic possession, and his invocation of "all you powers of darkness" fits the "generic" trope of the necromancer or witch who work their dark powers under the aegis of demons. The Spiritualist practices only underscore this element in a horror film where such practices often summon demons or other malevolent spirits.[9] The result is a compilation of anti–Christian elements that ultimately depend upon Spiritualism for their substance, but represent a general reflection of it rather than a conscious modeling of it.

The Dunwich Horror (1970)

Daniel Haller's *The Dunwich Horror*—based on the Lovecraft short story of the same name—is more deliberate in its filling of the *Necronomicon*. The narrative revolves around Wilbur Whateley (Dean Stockwell) and his attempt to bring the "Old Ones" back to Earth. He requires the *Necronomicon* to accomplish this task, and travels to Miskatonic University in Arkham to acquire it. Though he is allowed to peruse the book by Nancy Wagner (Sandra Dee), his studies are cut short by the arrival of Dr. Henry Armitage (Ed Begley) who is aware of the Wilbur family's questionable past, a portion of which is revealed in the beginning of the film when Whateley's mother, Lavinia (Joanne Moore Jordan), gives birth to him. Despite Armitage's warnings, Wagner finds Whateley entrancing, eventually driving him back to his family home. There, Whateley covertly sabotages her car and drugs her, and Wagner agrees to stay the weekend at his home. Over the course of the next two days, Wagner experiences disturbing dreams, is a participant/sacrifice in fertility rituals in "The Devil's Hopyard," and mutely watches Whateley bury his grandfather. Concurrently, Armitage begins to uncover the sinister story of the Whateley family and their participation in a similar set of fertility rituals that led to the birth of twins: Wilbur Whateley and his otherworldly brother. The film ends as Whateley's brother runs amok through the town and Whateley takes Wagner to the Devil's Hopyard to conclude the rituals and bring the Old Ones back to this world, a disastrous course ultimately stymied by the appearance of Armitage. Whateley and his monstrous brother die in flames, and Dr. Wagner claims "the last of the Whateleys is dead," just before the camera fixes on Wagner's belly to reveal a shadowy infant and quiet heartbeat.

Haller fills his *Necronomicon* by collapsing the fictional character Wilbur Whateley with the historical figure Aleister Crowley. The first evidence of such a collapse is in the rituals Whateley enacts. While Whateley reads the *Necronomicon*, scenes of figures in dark robes and crashing waves alternate, superimposed over the image of Whateley in the library of Mistakonic University. These same elements—dark robed figures and crashing waves—are a feature of the fertility rituals carried out by Whateley and his family, both those that surround Whateley's own birth and those he practices with Wagner. Thus, the *Necronomicon* appears as both the source for these rituals, and—later in the film—a necessary prop for their completion.

The rituals from the *Necronomicon* are shockingly close to Crowley's Thelemic rituals, as John Wisdom Gonce III has noted:

> The entire ritual seems reminiscent of a working designed to produce a *homunculus* (a human baby with the spirit of a demon)

Aleister Crowley, "the wickedest man in the world."

described by Aleister Crowley in both his novel *Moonchild* (1917) and in a ninth-degree OTO document entitled "De Homunculo Epistola" (1914). When he evokes Yog-Sothoth, Wilbur makes the "Vir" sign of the horned beast used by Aleister Crowley, with fists held beside his head, palms facing the ears, thumbs sticking out like little horns [pictured]. This gesture is used in two Thelemic Rituals of the Pentagram: "The Star Ruby" and "Liber V vel Reguli," also called "The Ritual of the Mark of the Beast."[10]

To take the comparison one step further, "The Star Ruby" ritual also includes the instruction "Drawing the hands to the eyes, fling it forth, making the sign of Horus and roar ΘHPION [THĒRION] (translation: "wild beast")."[11] To perform the "sign of Horus," the magician is instructed to "advance the left foot..., throw forward the body, and let the hands (drawn back to the side of the eyes) shoot out,"[12] a gesture and pose similar to the one struck by Whateley in a magical duel with Dr. Armitage (who, it is revealed, is also a student of the *Necronomicon*) at the close of the film. Similarly, Whateley displays for the audience many different ways of saying "Yog-Sothoth," some versions are spoken quietly, some shouted, some with alternating pitch. Corresponding notes in "The Star Ruby" instruct the practitioner in the way to repeat particular names: e.g., "whisper BABALON," "bellow HADIT, "cry IAΩ [IAŌ]."[13]

Indeed, Whateley seems something of a picture of Crowley himself. While the antagonist of Lovecraft's short story "The Dunwich Horror" is a "goatish" and "teratologically fabulous"[14] creature, the Whateley of the film is strikingly good-looking and charming, as Crowley himself was as a young man. He easily seduces Wagner with his magnetic stare and soft-spoken eroticism, speaking intensely and sensuously about sexual matters.

In this attention to sex, another widely known element of Crowley's Thelemic practice emerges. While Lovecraft treats the subject of sex only obliquely in his narrative, *The Dunwich Horror's* Whateley is a source of eroticism and a practitioner of sexualized rituals, like Crowley himself. In 1899, Crowley "learned something of the esoteric techniques of Indian Tantra, and soon began to engage in sexual magic with his partner, Rose Kelly."[15] His later creation of Thelema was supposed to be "a utopian community in which every desire could be gratified and every impulse expressed through free experimentation in drugs, sex, and physical excess."[16] Moreover, this sexual magic is similar to Whateley's in that it seeks to create a new world out of the old. For Crowley, "this secret of sexual magic was really the key to his entire vision of a new Aeon based on the full affirmation of the Will and the complete liberation from the repressive, oppressive religions of the past."[17]

However, while Crowley's new Aeon is a liberated utopia, Haller's Whateley struggles for an anti–Christian apocalypse. In a discussion between Armitage and Dr. Cory (Lloyd Bochner), the physician who claimed to have delivered Whateley, the nature of this end-of-the-world scenario is revealed:

> Armitage: The legend of the *Necronomicon* has it that long ago the earth was inhabited by a species from another dimension. With certain chants from the book, coupled with ancient rites and sacrifices, this race, the Old Ones, can be brought back.
> Cory: And mankind?
> Armitage: Destroyed.

After Whateley sabotages her car and drugs her, Wagner has a brief vision of such "ancient rites," involving painted individuals and a goat near the seashore. While this vision is brief, it becomes more developed when Wagner dreams in the Whateley house: half-naked, laughing men and women surround her bed (now inexplicably positioned at the seashore) and attempt to draw her into an orgy of writhing bodies. Although the ecstatic participants appear to be hippies, the introduction of a goat into the mix recodes the erotic dream as a Witches' Sabbath: the ceremony that witches supposedly attended that included the devil appearing as a goat, wild dancing, and sexual exploits.[18]

These evocations of witchcraft and forbidden sex are reinforced by the ritual altar used throughout the film. When Whateley first takes Wagner to "the Devil's Hopyard," a set of four pillars surrounding a stone altar clearly designed to accommodate a human body, he indicates that the site was once used for "fertility rites." The scene quickly shifts from a casual conversation to Wagner writhing and moaning sensuously upon the altar while black clad celebrants—faces obscured but cleavage exposed—offer liquids and oils before her. At the apex of this gyration, Whateley positions himself between Wagner's open legs and removes his shirt, exposing a mass of tattoos. He then proceeds to fondle Wagner while the theremin plays an encore until the end of the fertility rite. This depiction of nudity and bondage, combined with elements of horror such as human sacrifice and masked figures, place *The Dunwich Horror* in the familiar territory of sexploitation, a fact underscored by the use of such imagery on the film's poster.

The film's fertility imagery connects with Christian apocalyptic imagery through the scenes depicting Whateley's birth. At the beginning of the film, the elder Whateley (Sam Jaffe) looks on as Lavinia Whateley is in the throes of labor, overseen by two women dressed in a fashion similar to the celebrants in Wagner's fertility rite. As Lavinia's pain crescendos, Whateley picks up his staff and begins to lead her out the door. The film then shifts to a blue and black image of a pregnant woman and a man with a staff, characters meant to represent the elder Whateley and Lavinia but equally reminiscent of Joseph and Mary. Slowly, it becomes apparent that they are walking upon a face, a face that belongs to a stylized Devil who then tosses Lavinia into his mouth. The Devil's hand then becomes a snake that stares at the viewer before exposing its tongue to reveal the two figures again. The landscape gradually transmutes into figures of the black-clad celebrants, Lavinia lying on an altar (presumably, the Devil's Hopyard), the umbilical cord of her child being cut, and then her holding the child upside down by the feet. It is difficult to read these images as anything other than the prospective birth of the anti–Christ, especially since the film was released only two years after Roman Polanski's *Rosemary's Baby* (1968). The baleful nature of pregnancies in the film is later confirmed at the end when Dr. Armitage claims that Whateley's father was "not of this world." As Armitage leads Wagner away, the ominous heartbeat and the shadowy image of a fetus superimposed over her belly herald the birth of another hybrid (presumably) with apocalyptic desires.

The Evil Dead *(1981)*

Perhaps the most enduringly popular of the three films under consideration, Sam Raimi's *The Evil Dead* follows five students who vacation in a remote cabin for spring break. Unfortunately, this cabin holds the research of an ill-fated professor, research that leads to the students conjuring a "Kandarian demon" that proceeds to possess and kill them one by one.

By the time of the movie's creation, several authors had published their own versions of the *Necronomicon*, with little commercial success. This changed in 1977 when the pseudonymous "Simon" combined the narrative elements of Lovecraft with primary source material from Babylon[19] to produce the Simon *Necronomicon*.

Although neither the *Necronomicon* nor its contents receive much screen time in Sam Raimi's *The Evil Dead*, the Simon *Necronomicon* likely served as Raimi's inspiration. As the recorded voice of the professor comes on over the speaker, the audience hears:

> I believe I have made a significant find in the Kandarian ruins, a volume of ancient Sumerian burial practices and funerary incantations. It is entitled "*Naturam Demonto*," roughly translated: "Book of the Dead."[20] The book is bound in human flesh and inked in human blood. It deals with demons and demon resurrection and those forces which roam the forest and dark bowers of man's domain. The first few pages warn that these enduring creatures may lie dormant but are never truly dead. They may be recalled to active life through the incantations presented in this book. It is through the recitation of these passages that the demons are given license to possess the living.

The film reflects a particularly Simonian understanding of the relationship between Lovecraft and Crowley, in which both men—though they never met in person—"stretched their legs across the world, and in the Seven League Boots of the mind they *did* meet, and on common soil.... Sumeria."[21] Simon makes this claim, but it appears to be a creation of his own design: Crowley has no particular interest in Sumer in his writings and Lovecraft was explicit about the *Necronomicon*'s origins in "History of the Necronomicon," a history that includes no reference to Sumer.[22] That the film adopts Simon's conceit is strong evidence for its influence. Similarly, "The Testimony of the Mad Arab" which starts the text of the *Necronomicon* identifies the text as "the Book of the Dead, the Book of the Black Earth, that I have writ down at the peril of my life."[23]

The professor's narration in *The Evil Dead* also echoes some of the warnings in Simon's *Necronomicon*. Namely, the Simon *Necronomicon* warns of demonic possession and cautions the reader that "*there are no effective banishings for the forces invoked in the NECRONOMICON itself!*"[24] Thus, demonic possession is the horror *du jour* of *The Evil Dead*, with the voice on the recorder cautioning the listener, "the only way to stop those possessed by the spirits of the book is through the act of bodily dismemberment."

While the Simon *Necronomicon* attempts to create an alien religious "ecosystem" by weaving Babylonian material into Lovecraft's narrative framework, *The Evil Dead* contains no such framework. Rather, the focus on demonic possession "defaults" the film once again to interpretation within a Christian frame of reference, a frame that already contains an etiology of possession and a well-developed notion of demons.

Quite unplanned, it also brings us full circle back to *The Haunted Palace* and the trappings of Spiritualism. While the Simon *Necronomicon* provides the frame for summoning the Kandarian demon, it manifests itself before possession through the trappings of Spiritualism. When they arrive at the cabin, Cheryl (Ellen Sandweiss) offers a display of automatic writing (a common Spiritualist technique) when her hand—seemingly of its own volition—draws a picture of the Book of the Dead. Likewise, Cheryl's possession reveals itself through her success at a version of the "card guessing trick" developed by Zener and Rhine in the wake of Spiritualism and resultant field of parapsychology. As previously noted, Spiritualism and its trappings are typically coded in horror films as a method to contact or raise demonic entities, once more aligning the production of the film with a Christian worldview.

Conclusion

In his chapter opening to "Many a Quaint and Curious Volume," Daniel Harms notes that "a literary work is not an extension of the author, but rather exists apart from their intentions and can sometimes travel in surprising directions."[25] He goes on to describe the various forgeries of the *Necronomicon* (20 entries in all), a literary construct that has clearly slipped from the grasp of the author and transformed into something Lovecraft could never have anticipated.

One of these slippages is from the page onto film. For example, just as Harms refers to the Simon *Necronomicon*, a text created by Simon and filled with material from Babylon, one could just as easily refer to Haller's *Necronomicon* in *The Dunwich Horror*. In fact, John Todd, a Christian public speaker in the 1970s, claimed to have been involved in a vast occult conspiracy in which the *Necronomicon* featured prominently. He likely acquired this idea from *The Dunwich Horror*, which Todd claimed was "one of the strongest movies, truthful, about witchcraft and their beliefs that existed."[26] Todd also echoes Whateley's claim about the *Necronomicon*—"I'm a student of the occult and that book is like a Bible"—when he remarked to one of his audiences that the *Necronomicon* was "the original occult bible."[27]

This challenges the dichotomous relationship between fact and fiction, and it is not an isolated incident: The religious milieu in the United States is increasingly influenced—and even created—by film, television, and fiction.[28] In the past five decades, Lovecraft's work has been a source for several religious traditions, including LaVeyan Satanism, the Order of the Trapezoid, and the Cult of Cthulhu. With Lovecraftian religious groups operating in the United States—groups that rely on media to form their rituals and doctrines—there is an increasing possibility of a blurring of reality that might bring conservative Christian denominations and these invented traditions into conflict. Much as the *Necronomicon* has metamorphosed from literary device to literary work, the film versions of that monstrous book have transformed into potential reflections of reality.

NOTES

1. Lovecraft, *Complete Fiction*, 234.
2. Braune, "How to Analyze Texts."
3. Harms, "Reviving Dead Names," 172.
4. Migliore and Strysik, "The Haunted Palace."
5. Examples of many of these popular tropes, including disembodied motion of hypnotists, can be found in the 1931 film *Svengali*.
6. Doyle, *History of Spiritualism*, 37–39.
7. This transition is marked by Crabtree, "Mesmerism and the Psychological Dimension of Mediumship."
8. Translation mine. While most of the film's audience might not understand the language, Corman's choice to use understandable Latin rather than gibberish suggests his investment in the notion that Curwen is diabolical.
9. Most famously, the use of the Ouija Board that invites the demonic entity "Captain Howdy" into Regan in *The Exorcist* (1973), but connections between the Ouija Board and malevolent spirits are also made much earlier in Raupert, *The New Black Magic* (published in 1919), and films such as *The Uninvited* (1944) and *Thirteen Ghosts* (1960).
10. Harms and Gonce, *Necronomicon Files*, 237.
11. Duquette, *The Magick of Thelema*, 89.
12. *Ibid.*, 61–66.
13. *Ibid.*, 89.
14. Lovecraft, *The Complete Fiction*, 691.
15. Urban, "Beast with Two Backs," 9.
16. *Ibid.*, 10

17. Urban, "Unleashing the Beast," 150.
18. See for instance Goode and Ben-Yehuda, *Moral Panics*. 2nd ed. esp. chapter 10, "The Renaissance Witch Craze."
19. See Harm and Gonce, *The Necronomicon Files*, 46–48, for a more detailed exploration of the sources used in Simon's filling of his *Necronomicon*.
20. It may be that a purist of the film would object to me placing *The Evil Dead* into a discussion of the *Necronomicon* as it is only in the remake (*Evil Dead II* [1987]) that the book is actually referred to as the *Necronomicon*. However, the translation of the nonsensical Latin into "Book of the Dead," its similarity to Simon's *Necronomicon*, and the warning that "enduring creatures may lie dormant but are never truly dead" (compare: "That is not dead which can eternal lie" from Lovecraft's "The Nameless City" and "The Call of Cthulhu") suggests an obvious debt to Lovecraft and his later interpreters.
21. Simon, *The Necronomicon*, xvii.
22. Lovecraft, *The Complete Fiction*, 672–73
23. Simon, *Necronomicon*, 5.
24. *Ibid.*, liii.
25. Harms and Gonce, *The Necronomicon Files*, 29.
26. Walker, *The United States of Paranoia*, 192.
27. Walker, *The United States of Paranoia*, 190.
28. See for instance Nelson, *Gothicka*.

Bibliography

Braune, Sean. "How to Analyze Texts That Were Burned, Lost, Fragmented, or Never Written." *Symploke* 21, no. 1 (December 22, 2013): 239–55.
Crabtree, Adam. "Mesmerism and the Psychological Dimension of Mediumship." In *Handbook of Spiritualism and Channeling*, 9–31. Leiden: Brill, 2015.
Conan Doyle, Arthur. *The History of Spiritualism, Vol. 1*. 2 vols. London: Cassell, 1926.
Duquette, Lon Milo. *The Magick of Thelema: A Handbook of the Rituals of Aleister Crowley*. Boston: Weiser Books, 1993.
Goode, Erich, and Nachman Ben-Yehuda. *Moral Panics: The Social Construction of Deviance*, 2nd ed. Malden, MA: Wiley-Blackwell, 2009.
Harms, Dan. "Reviving Dead Names: Strategies of Legitimization in the Necronomicon of Simon and the Dark Aesthetic." In *Magic in the Modern World: Strategies of Repression and Legitimization*, edited by Edward Bever and Randall Styers, 171–96. University Park: Pennsylvania State University Press, 2017.
Harms, Daniel, and John Wisdom Gonce III. *The Necronomicon Files: The Truth Behind The Legend*. York Beach, ME: Red Wheel/Weiser, 2003.
Lovecraft, H.P. *The Complete Fiction of H.P. Lovecraft*. New York: Chartwell Books, 2016.
Migliore, Andrew, and John Strysik. "The Haunted Palace." *The Lurker in the Lobby: A Guide to the Cinema of H.P. Lovecraft*. Accessed July 17, 2017. http://www.thelurker.com/features/hauntedpalace.htm.
Nelson, Victoria. *Gothicka: Vampire Heroes, Human Gods, and the New Supernatural*. Cambridge: Harvard University Press, 2013.
Raupert, John Godfrey. *The New Black Magic and the Truth About the Ouija-Board*. New York: The Devin-Adair Company, 1919.
Simon. *The Necronomicon*, 1st ed. New York: Avon, 1980.
Urban, Hugh B. "The Beast with Two Backs: Aleister Crowley, Sex Magic and the Exhaustion of Modernity." *Nova Religio: The Journal of Alternative and Emergent Religions* 7, no. 3 (2004): 7–25.
———. "Unleashing the Beast: Aleister Crowley, Tantra and Sex Magic in Late Victorian England." *Esoterica: The Journal of Esoteric Studies* 5 (2003): 138–92.
Walker, Jesse. *The United States of Paranoia: A Conspiracy Theory*. New York: Harper, 2013.

Paperback *Necronomicon*
Occult Authorship in John Carpenter's In the Mouth of Madness

MURRAY LEEDER

> The thing I can't remember is what came first: us, or the book.
> —Simon (Wilhelm von Homburg), *In the Mouth of Madness* (1994)

In late 1990s, early in the digital era and the commercialization of the Internet, my teenage web-surfing took me to cthulhu.org,[1] an irreverent site related to the writings of H.P. Lovecraft. One limerick, credited to Dennis Maggard, has stuck in my mind for close to two decades:

> The Necronomicon?? *You* can't be shown one!
> While the libraries *never* will loan one!
> But if it's so rare
> And guarded with care
> Why does every nut case seem to own one?[2]

The *Necronomicon* referenced here is, of course, the famous fictional grimoire created by H.P. Lovecraft as part of the body of linked stories would retrospectively be labeled "the Cthulhu Mythos." A rare and powerful occult manuscript that provides access to forbidden secrets and worlds, prone to driving its readers insane, *Necronomicon* or *Al Azif* and its author, the "Mad Arab" Abdul Alhazred, are key elements of the Mythos,[3] with certain stories (like "The Nameless City" [1921]) affiliated with the Mythos solely for referencing them. In the enormous body of Lovecraft pastiches and fiction that otherwise references Lovecraft, references to the *Necronomicon* are extremely commonplace, popping up everywhere from the writings of authors like Ramsey Campbell, Brian Lumley and Alan Moore to *The Evil Dead* (1981) and television's *The Real Ghostbusters* (1986-1991). In DC Comics, the *Necronomicon* has been in the possession of Swamp Thing's nemesis Anton Arcane; it was also detailed in the 1980 *Dungeons and Dragons* supplement *Deities & Demigods*,[4] and *The Simpsons* (1989-) had Bob Dole reading from it at a meeting of the Springfield Republican Party.[5] In fact, Guillermo del Toro nixed a reference to the *Necronomicon* in *Hellboy* (2004) because of its overexposure.[6] The *Necronomicon* seems to embody the modern paradox of the occult (etymologically related to "hidden," "secret") becoming popular, nigh ubiquitous.

Sticking strictly to Lovecraft's own stories, Maggard's limerick is not quite accurate; though frequently quoted, the *Necronomicon* only plays an active role in a handful of stories and is generally found in libraries. It is in the extended multi-author Mythos (and Lovecraft-influenced works more broadly) that the *Necronomicon* seems to be omnipresent despite its rarity. Yet read differently, the nutcase in Maggard's poem could have been me: a paperback copy of the *Necronomicon* sat on my bookshelf, right next to Lovecraft reprint collections from Arkham House. In this case, it was the so-called "Simon *Necronomicon*," first published in 1977.[7] The saga of this and other commercial *Necronomicon*s has been covered by a number of authors,[8] but I will quote from Philip A. Sheffler, also in 1977:

> Apparently, Lovecraft had done such a convincing of making his grimoire sound authentic ... that some of HPL's readers started out in search of the book. For a time, librarians and bookstore owners were annoyed by people trying to buy or borrow the *Necronomicon*.... Yet it is a fact that a New York bookseller listed a copy of the *Necronomicon* in his catalog for $375 ... And it is also a fact that the John Hay Library at Providence, Rhode Island's Brown University does indeed hold a copy of [the *Necronomicon*], written in Duraic and published by the Owl's Wick Press of Philadelphia in 1973. It seems that where Lovecraft is concerned, truth and fiction are merely relative.[9]

Or, as a character in John Carpenter's *In the Mouth of Madness* puts it, "Reality isn't what it used to be."

"Do you read Sutter Cane?"

In the Mouth of Madness is regarded as the third film in Carpenter's informal "Apocalypse Trilogy," after *The Thing* (1982) and *Prince of Darkness* (1987). It concerns bestselling horror novelist Sutter Cane (Jürgen Prochnow), who has recently disappeared without a trace and without completing his next novel, also entitled *In the Mouth of Madness*. His publisher, Jackson Harglow (Charlton Heston), recruits insurance investigator John Trent (Sam Neill) to find him. Trent cynically suspects the disappearance might be a publicity stunt but he and editor Linda Styles (Julie Carmen) trace the missing author to Hobb's End, New Hampshire ... a town that seems to exist only in Cane's fiction. Hobb's End is just as Cane described it, however, dominated by an imposing church within which Cane is found composing a novel that seems to become horrific reality even as he writes it. Cane claims that extra-dimensional god-monsters are using him as a vehicle to enter our world, essentially rewriting reality through the power of his readers' belief; Cane has also, apparently, been transformed into a liminal being, as omnipresent as his writings. Trent encounters increasingly disturbing phenomena and begins to believe that he is the protagonist in Cane's book. He tries vainly to prevent its publication but is locked away in an insane asylum. An attack by unseen monsters frees Trent, who wanders through an apocalyptic landscape until he finds an abandoned movie theatre showing the film adaptation of *In the Mouth of Madness* starring ... himself. As he watches the film, his sanity comes unglued entirely.

Though Cane's subject matter is unmistakably Lovecraftian (as explicated below), his level of success is exponentially greater than the modest recognition Lovecraft received during his lifetime. Cane is described as "this century's most widely read author," yet he is a pastiche, not of Agatha Christie or Danielle Steel, but of Stephen King.[10] *In the Mouth of Madness* acts as a commentary on, to borrow a book title, "the Stephen King phenomenon"[11]: King's astonishing productivity, popularity and cultural presence. King was the face of the revival in popular horror fiction in the 1970s and 1980s, other key members of which included John Farris, John Saul, Dean Koontz, Clive Barker, Whitley Strieber, Peter Straub and Anne Rice.[12] The popularity of this group secured an increasing presence of horror in popular culture and media, a trend that attracted moral consternation from some quarters,[13] and also inspired scholarly criticism. S.T. Joshi, a vocal King naysayer, holds that King's "weird conceptions are unoriginal and poorly conceived, his morality conventional and unadventurous, and his characterizations hackneyed and sentimental."[14] Joshi argues that King's academic admirers are either sycophants, ignorant of the broader tradition King works within, or are "so dazzled by King's fame and reputation that they fancy there must be something to the fellow (the hoary and fallacious argument, 'Millions of readers can't be wrong')."[15] Yet *In the Mouth of Madness* plays this claim straight: millions of readers of Sutter Cane can't be wrong, or perhaps more accurately, the books themselves can't be wrong if millions read and, in some strange way, *believe* them.

Interviewed in 1998 for the American newsmagazine program *60 Minutes* (1968–), King described himself as "the literary equivalent of a Big Mac and fries,"[16] cheerfully embracing his low and "pop" authorial star persona, the same status that ultimately allows Cane his vast and terrifying reach. To borrow Walter Benjamin's terminology,[17] grimoires like the *Necronomicon* are "auratic"—their value, occult or monetary, is related to scarcity and obscurity. In "The Dunwich Horror" (1929), Wilbur Whateley tries to steal a copy of the *Necronomicon* from Miskatonic University because his family's version lacks page 751, vital to a ritual he is attempting. It would be a very different story if Wilbur could simply saunter to the local bookstore and buy a copy. Cane's writings are non-auratic products of the age of technological reproducibility, a fact reinforced by the opening montage of printing presses churning out copies of *The Hobb's End Horror*. *In the Mouth of Madness*, then, constitutes a kind of horror story for the age of mechanical reproducibility, where it is not the aura but its decline that threatens the world. The cult of the celebrity author (underlined by the repeated line "Do you read Sutter Cane?") reflects Benjamin's affiliation of movie star cults with "that magic of the personality has long been no more than the putrid magic of its own commodity character,"[18] in turn linked to the fascist cult of the dictator.

With only fleeting exceptions, *In the Mouth of Madness* visualizes Cane's books in paperback, the format associated with the explosion of the mass reading public in the 19th and 20th centuries. The bookstore display that Trent visits early in the film conspicuously lacks any hardcover editions, and even the displays in the publisher's offices are dominated by paperbacks.[19] This decision works to associate Cane's writings both with low culture, easily dismissed and ignored ("that horror crap"), and the cultural omnipresence and apparent disposability of the paperback novel; these themes are visually reinforced when Trent discovers his fingers are smeared with cheap paperback ink.

The fictional Cane novel titles largely pay homage to Lovecraft: *The Whisperer of the Dark* to "The Whisperer in Darkness" (1931), *The Thing in the Basement* to "The Thing on the Doorstep" (1937), *Haunter Out of Time* to "The Haunter of the Dark" (1936) and "The Shadow Out of Time" (1936), *In the Mouth of Madness* to *At the Mountains of Madness* (1936). The title *The Feeding* references King instead, specifically *The Shining* (1977), as well the vogue of similarly titled works that followed (*The Burning* (1981), *The Nesting* (1981), etc.; *The Breathing Tunnel* might reference the King novella *The Breathing*

Method (1982) or simply King and Lovecraft's shared fondness for subterranean passages. A more complex intertextual web is at work with *The Hobb's End Horror*, which simultaneously references Lovecraft's "The Dunwich Horror" (1929), the fictional London Underground station "Hobbs End" in *Quatermass and the Pit* (1967, also *Five Million Years to Earth*), written by Carpenter favorite Nigel Kneale,[20] and the King story "Crouch End" (1980). The latter takes place in the eponymous London neighborhood and is one of King's few overt Lovecraft pastiches, originally published in the collection *New Tales of the Cthulhu Mythos* (1980).[21] Another Lovecraft story referenced in *In the Mouth of Madness* is "Pickman's Model" (1927), where an investigation into the missing artist Richard Upton Pickman ultimately reveals that the warped figures in his paintings were faithful representations of real monsters.[22] Sutter Cane is a Pickman figure, a degenerate artist in whose works the lines between imagination and reality blur.

Another key link between Lovecraft, King and Cane involves place: the New England roots of each author, and in particular the creation of a fictionalized New England setting where many related stories unfold. Lovecraft's fictional cosmology is centered on Massachusetts, with Arkham, loosely approximating Salem, coexisting with real and fictional places. King's works set in his native Maine include recurring fictional locales like Little Tall Island, 'Salem's Lot, Derry and most famously Castle Rock; the latter, as evidenced by lending its name to the recent King-derived drama on Hulu, has become the exemplary King locale. Certain King novels have provided maps to help orient their readers and to fill out the world, and King's website supplies a map of Maine with locations for settings of various stories. Cane's state is New Hampshire, and his version contains the town of Hobb's End, found on no map save for the one concealed within the covers of Sutter Cane paperbacks.[23]

Lovecraft, King and Cane are unified by the practice of world-building, and not just of a geographical sort. Lovecraft's gallery of extra-dimensional monsters (Yog-Sothoth, Azathoth, Nyarlathotep, Great Cthulhu, et al.) were echoed in recurring King figures like the Crimson King and Randall Flagg; indeed, the mythology of King's *The Dark Tower* series (1982–2004) eventually swells out to encompass huge swaths of King's writings. Certain fictional worlds, like those of Arthur Conan Doyle, J.R.R. Tolkien, J.K. Rowling or George R.R. Martin, are compellingly detailed and coherent, achieving a kind of convincing reality in themselves. The writings of Sutter Cane, "a deadly mad prophet of the printed page," achieve something more than convincingness.

The field of subcreation studies distinguishes between "Secondary Worlds" and the "Primary World" occupied by its creator and consumers.[24] This language allows differentiation from the real (Primary) Maine that lacks a Castle Rock and the fictional (Secondary) Maine that has one. And yet for many readers, Castle Rock or other Secondary locales may *feel* just as real as Primary locations. Michael Saler uses the term "double consciousness" to describe the capability of modern subjects of "living simultaneously in multiple worlds without experiencing cognitive dissonance."[25] Lovecraft provides one of Saler's test studies, for the sprawling and continually expanding modern mythology spawned by his works: "Like the imaginary worlds of Conan Doyle and Tolkien, Lovecraft's Cthulhu Mythos has become a virtual reality shared by successive generations. The Mythos has an extended literary genealogy—a 1999 concordance lists 2631 works— and has also inspired films, comics, games, pseudo-histories, and even a colourful line of plush toys."[26] Interestingly, a real occult organization named "The Esoteric Order of Dagon" or EOD (named for the church featured in Lovecraft's "The Shadow Over Innsmouth" [1936]) holds that Lovecraft was himself a Pickman-like visionary artist: "For the EOD, Lovecraft's 'visions' are very real, or at least contain aspects of the real. This perspective has led to the EOD embracing a philosophical and magical discipline that seeks to invoke and gain access to the power of the Lovecraftian pantheon, or whatever entities Lovecraft as channeling from beyond the void."[27] The EOD's reformulation of Lovecraft as a "conveyor" rather than a creator resembles the Baker Street Irregulars' "diminishment" of Arthur Conan Doyle to the status of Sherlock Holmes's "literary agent," which led to the opposition of Doyle's estate.[28]

For the EOD, the distinction between Primary and Secondary world has vanished altogether, and the same process unfolds in *In the Mouth of Madness*. There may be no Hobb's End, but when Trent uncovers its location and drives there, the town is precisely as Cane described it. Cane asserts, "This town ... wasn't here before I wrote it"; his Secondary World is starting to overwrite and remake the Primary one. In fact, Cane has been a mouthpiece for a group of Lovecraftian monsters using his novels as a conduit for their return to the world. Though Cane was apparently not always a conscious participant ("For years, I thought I was making all this up. But they were telling me what to write, giving me the power to make it real"), he has by now wholeheartedly embraced his role as their prophet. Operating from the distorted church, Cane offers his works as a new Bible, asserting that religion "doesn't understand the true nature of creation. No one's ever believed it enough to make it real. The same cannot be said of my work" and that more people believe in his works than in the Bible. He asserts that the naysayer Trent is in fact his own fictional character, and warps Descartes's dictum "Cogito, ergo sum" into "I think, therefore you are." Simon (an homage to the "Simon *Necronomicon*"?), one of the warped Hobb's End locals, expresses doubts that they existed before Cane's book. By the end, Trent has to accept this nightmarish new reality, and his sanity finally comes uncoupled in a movie theatre, watching a film called *In the Mouth of Madness*.

The Film of the Book

In the Mouth of Madness is a peculiar text relative to adaptation and authorship. While it putatively comes from an original screenplay by Michael De Luca,[29] it also clearly and unapologetically "adapts" extensively from Lovecraft and King (to say nothing of Nigel Kneale). Thomas Leitch notes that where adaptations of novelists like Henry James or Charles Dickens are concerned, the criterion of "fidelity" is measured less against the individual work being adapted than the broader cultural constellation of the "Jamesian" or "Dickensian," "measured not only against the novels they explicitly adapt but against the distinctive world or style or tone associated with the author in general."[30] Likewise, *In the Mouth of Madness* adapts the "Lovecraftian" and the "Kingian" in recognizable ways without adapting specific stories in the formal, legal sense (comparable to the "Kingian"—and "Spielbergian"—affinities of *Stranger Things* (2016–), or even how *The Dark Tower* (2017) adapts "Stephen King" itself more than any specific tale). The film adaptation of the diegetic *In the Mouth of Madness* alludes to the considerable adaptability that King's works has proved to have. As Bill Warren wrote in 1982, "It was only natural that the movies and Stephen King would get together. His books are not only laden with references to movies, his writing is intensely cinematic.... The thickest of King's books often seem like richly detailed novelizations of films."[31] Indeed, it was largely Brian De

Palma's adaptation of *Carrie* (1976) that put King on the cultural map.[32] King has been adapted dozens of times since, including by significant directors George A. Romero, Tobe Hooper, Stanley Kubrick, Kimberly Peirce, Frank Darabont, Bryan Singer and indeed John Carpenter (*Christine* [1983]). Adaptation (and not only in cinema) has created a Stephen King brand that swells far beyond his writings, expanding and securing his cultural status.

Carol J. Clover writes that horror may be, "intentionally or unintentionally, the most self-reflexive of cinematic genres."[33] Something similar, however, can be said of literary horror in its preponderance of stories about writers and writing. King is prolific in this "metahorror" subgenre: novels like *Salem's Lot, The Shining, Misery* (1987), *The Dead Zone* (1989), and *Bag of Bones* (1998) and short stories like "Word Processor of the Gods" (1985), "Secret Window, Secret Garden" (1990) and "1408" (2002) are just the most obvious examples. Indeed, King himself appears as a character within his own fiction late in the *Dark Tower* series. Lovecraft, too, had many writer protagonists, including his signature character Randolph Carter and Robert Blake (an homage to Robert Bloch) in "The Haunter of the Dark" (1936). *In the Mouth of Madness* is a reflexive horror film through and through, all about the experience of horror, the writing of horror, the marketing of horror and even the distribution of horror. If metafiction is "a discrete discursive phenomenon [where a text] thematizes its fictitiousness,"[34] *In the Mouth of Madness* proves exemplary.

As a reflexive film about literature, *In the Mouth of Madness* faces a challenge similar to *Atonement* (2007), Joe Wright's adaptation of the 2001 Ian McEwan novel. The final reveal is that much of what we have been seeing and hearing does not have the internal ontological status of "truth" or "reality," but rather is a fiction constructed by the aged Briony Tallis (Vanessa Redgrave). While based on her own life, Briony has rewritten events to provide a happy ending denied by harsh reality. But the adaptation for the screen creates an inevitable mediumistic rupture: If these events happen only in Briony's prose, how is it that we perceive them audiovisually as a film? *In the Mouth of Madness* embraces this literary-film disjuncture by drawing adaptation itself into its intertextual web. It works to collapse the distinction between cinema and literature in a couple of different ways, even as it ironically reinforces their different cultural registers.

Early on, editor Styles mentions that the film rights to Cane's next book have already sold as evidence of Cane's success and value to her company; later, when Trent fruitlessly tries to persuade publisher Harglow to pull the book *In the Mouth of Madness* by saying, "This book will drive people crazy," Harglow answers, "Well, let's hope so. The movie comes out next month." We are thus repeatedly reminded that Sutter Cane is a multimedia property ("a billion-dollar franchise," Styles calls him at one point), fixed neither in literature nor cinema but resident in both, plus merchandise: the billboards, posters, shirts, hats and mugs we see. And in this exchange, *In the Mouth of Madness* acknowledges film's apparently greater cultural reach:

> TRENT: It's Cane's story, and it'll spread with each new reader. That's how it gets its power.
> Dr. Wrenn (David Warner): What about the people who don't read?
> TRENT: There's a movie.

The theme of collapsing media distinctions is reinforced formally. When Styles discovers Cane in the church, he entrances her and thrusts her face into his looseleaf manuscript, which glows with white light (like a projector?). This action seems to trigger a

A breach between worlds and between media in *In the Mouth of Madness* (1995).

fast-cut montage of horrific images, some of them from different parts of the film, blurring the acts of reading and viewing; it is implied that the audience is perceiving what Styles experiences. The act of manipulating cinematic images through editing comes to represent Cane's disorienting reworking of the narrative world. Styles returns to Trent raving, "I saw the book," as if the acts of seeing and reading are indistinguishable. Cane is again associated with unearthly white light when he confronts Trent in the church's confessional; here again Cane triggers a montage and a scene change seemingly at will. He later adds cinematography to his arsenal by casually turning the world blue (his favorite color) as Trent rides a cross-country bus. His own spectacularly cinematic transformation into the printed word speaks to film's own collapse of cinema and literature—complete with torn pages crisscrossing the screen—distinctions between media becoming meaningless as the diegetic world and the world created by Cane's authorial will collapse into one.

Kevin Heffernan notes that "In many horror films, the narrative's storytelling process is often enacted in a magician or trickster figure who accompanies his acts of sorcery with elaborate gestures to the audience that have their origins in the deliberately distracting sleight-of-hand of the stage magician."[35] Heffernan sees this *monstrateur* figure as a successor to the showman-magicians of early cinema like Georges Méliès, whose presence in, and magical mastery over, cinematic form speaks to the initial non-closure of the diegetic world. Horror films in general and reflexive ones like *In the Mouth of Madness* in particular represent a continuation of that tradition, and Cane serves as a sort of *monstrateur* writ large, an internal figure of authorship at both the level of narrative (even able to write a character out of existence, as he does with Styles) and cinematic form.

The film's climax provides the final expression of reflexivity, when Trent comes upon a movie theatre showing the film he is in. The marquee calls it

IN THE MOUTH
OF MADNESS
WITH JOHN TRENT

and its poster lists all of the real film's personnel, except for its cast. It says, "STARRING JOHN TRENT LINDA STYLES JACKSON HARGLOW," in place of the names Sam Neill, Julie Carmen and Charlton Heston.

Trent sits in the first row of the empty theatre, his overflowing tub of popcorn signifying his ironic transformation into the kind of mindless consumer he has decried throughout the film. What follows is a sort of "recap montage" of the film, intercut with Trent's face rippling with the light from the screen. The images of the film-within-a-film are framed by the theatre's curtains. From Trent's point of view, we initially see three successive segments from earlier in the film. Without any cuts back to Trent's face, the three shots play continuously, implying that the version of *In the Mouth of Madness* that Trent is watching is not exactly the one we have seen but rather a non-narrative selection of key moments. The film cuts back to Trent beginning to laugh in the theatre, and to Trent on screen, now framed to exclude the curtains, illustrating the dissolving lines between mediums, as well as between fiction and reality.

Appropriately, the screen-Trent yells, "This is not a Sutter Cane story! This is reality!" This footage does not actually appear elsewhere in the film, though the line is close to Trent's statement to Simon, "We are not living in a Sutter Cane story! This is reality!" and shares the bar setting and the framing—evidently a literal "alternate take." To further emphasize Cane's role as editor, jump cuts twice provide slightly different takes of the line "Not reality!" the audio of which continues even after we cut back to Trent, his laughter growing more and more unhinged.

Among the images in the final montage-recap that frames Trent's final disintegration into madness are one last look at Cane's face and six of his paperbacks (seemingly an alternate take from the scene where Trent identifies the map hidden in their covers). Raiford Guins and Omayra Zaragoza Cruz read *In the Mouth of Madness* as a commentary on capitalism and mass culture, noting that its apocalypse shows "the entire world descending into … [a] special kind of madness: a schizophrenia of consumption."[36] To further develop this argument, the identification of Cane as a "franchise" and a "tent pole" speaks to the untethering of authorship from a specific individual and its redistribution through a corporate, transmedia web, as epitomized by the final adaptation. The apotheosis of Sutter Cane the brand/cult figure/god is accompanied by the extinction of his personal, physical presence, his transformation into text.

The Peril of Fiction

In "What is an Author?" (1969), Michel Foucault spoke of "the great peril, the great danger with which fiction threatens our world"[37] through the proliferation of signification; the attribution of authorship to a single individual (the "author function"), Foucault argues, works to stem that peril. One could say that *In the Mouth of Madness* has it both ways: Cane's name is spoken some 50 times and his presence looms over the film to a degree vastly incommensurate with his brief screen time, and yet ultimately, he too, by his own admission, is just a functionary in the process of meaning-making, and of meaning-destroying. Conspicuously, on the movie poster Trent examines, *In the Mouth of Madness* is identified both as "A JOHN CARPENTER FILM" and from "DIRECTOR JOHN CARPENTER."[38] De Luca is identified as its writer and the name "Sutter Cane" does not appear on the poster, possibly because the name itself is now redundant in an entire world authored by Cane. His name's absence from the movie poster near the film's end may disclose the true mastermind behind *In the Mouth of Madness*'s twisting of narrative and film form ("Carpenter, the filmmaker, is also the magician who is capable of making it all seem 'real'"[39]). But it might simultaneously do the opposite, suggesting the equivalent arbitrariness of the author name "John Carpenter"[40]—just another empty, corporatized signifier at the fall of meaning.

In the Mouth of Madness replaces the rarity of Lovecraft's maddening *Necronomicon* with the ubiquity of a mass market paperback. Furthermore, it narrativizes this transition, as the internal *In the Mouth of Madness* moves from a manuscript that seemingly only exists in one place, to a widely distributed novel, to a movie—and Trent is almost comically unable to prevent its increasing spread. *In the Mouth of Madness* imagines Foucault's "great peril" as a virus transmitted through fiction, transforming its readers into monstrous things. Certainly, the film thumbs its nose at the moral guardians by playing their claims to straight and thus revealing them to be "outrageously hilarious,"[41] but it also provides a something rarer: a provocative examination of the horror genre itself and its own mass popularity.

Notes

1. The earliest record of the site on web.archive.org is from March 1997. As of this writing, it still exists.
2. "Slimy Songs and Tentacled Tales—Limericks," *Cthulhu.org*, http://www.cthulhu.org/cthulhu/other.html.
3. S.T. Joshi lists "an ever-growing library of occult books, both ancient and modern" as a characteristic of the Mythos ("Cthulhu Mythos," 99).
4. Ward and Kuntz, *Deities & Demigods*. The debut of Chaosium's Lovecraft-themed role playing game *Call of Cthulhu* in 1981 necessitated the removal of Lovecraftian elements from *D&D*. They have occasionally crept back in, including a reference to the *Necronomicon* in Collins and Cordell's *Libris Mortis*, 4.
5. "Brawl in the Family," season 13, episode 7; January 6, 2002.
6. Commentary Track, *Hellboy*, ctd. in Harms, "Reviving Dead Names," 192.
7. Simon, *Necronomicon*.
8. For example, see Colavito, *Cult of Alien Gods*, esp. 171–74; Harms and Gonce, *Necronomicon Files*; Davies, *Grimoires*, esp. 262–77; Laycock, *Dangerous Games*, 270–71; Poole, *In the Mountains of Madness*, esp. 210–15, 289–92; Harms, "Reviving Dead Names."
9. Shreffler, *Lovecraft Companion*, 172–73. Shreffler is here referencing the hoax book "*Al Azif*," written by George Scithers in a fictional language and bearing an introduction by Lovecraft biographer L. Sprague de Camp.
10. The film twice references Stephen King as a writer whom Cane outsells.
11. Collings, *Stephen King Phenomenon*.
12. See Murphy, "Rise of Popular Horror."
13. Poole, *Satan in America*, esp. 155–84.
14. Joshi, *Modern Weird Tale*, 95.
15. *Ibid.*, 94.
16. *60 Minutes*, season 29, episode 22; February 16, 1997.
17. Benjamin, "Work of Art."
18. *Ibid.*, 33.
19. For a panoramic treatment of the paperbacks of the horror boom and their covers, see Hendrix, *Paperbacks from Hell*.
20. Kneale's Quatermass cycle in general and *Quatermass and the Pit* in particular have been described as having Lovecraftian qualities (see Mitchell, *Complete H.P. Lovecraft Filmography*, 16).
21. Another Lovecraftian King story, "Jerusalem's Lot" (1978), concerns a church built over a pagan site that is consumed by the force it was meant to contain, just like *In the Mouth of Madness* (and Lovecraft's "The Haunter in the Dark"). The *Necronomicon* itself briefly appears in King's story "I Know What You Need" (1976).
22. The character Mrs. Pickman (Frances Bey) in *In the Mouth of Madness*, also associated with an unearthly painting, is a clear homage to "Pickman's Model."
23. For the importance of maps in world-building, see Wolf, *Building Imaginary Worlds*, esp. 77–78; think, too, of the opening sequence of *Game of Thrones* (2011–), which visualizes the process of world-building on a vast virtual map.
24. Wolf, *Building Imaginary Worlds*.
25. Saler, *As If*, 13.
26. *Ibid.*, 133.
27. Engle, "Cults of Lovecraft," 92. Engle describes EOD as only the most extreme example of Lovecraft-inspired occult practice.

28. Saler, *As If,* 109. Other works have fiction have also treated Lovecraft as a participant in his own fictional world, including the Canadian TV movie *Out of Mind: The Stories of H.P. Lovecraft* (1998), the film *Necronomicon: Book of the Dead* (1993) and the manga *Nyaruka: Crawling with Love* (2009–2014).

29. As a student, De Luca wrote a 12-minute adaptation of King's story "The Lawnmower Man" (1977), one of the so-called "Dollar Babies," instances where King licensed adaptations of his short fiction for a single dollar. De Luca later wrote the notorious *Star Trek: Voyager* episode "Threshold" (1996), often considered the worst episode of all of *Trek,* before settling into the role of movie producer, earning Oscar nominations for *Moneyball* (2011) and *Captain Phillips* (2013).

30. Leitch, "Twelve Fallacies," 164.

31. Warren, "The Movies and Mr. King," 105.

32. Adaptations of Lovecraft have a very different arc, not appearing until decades after his death (*The Haunted Palace* [1963], *Die, Monster, Die!* [1965] and *The Dunwich Horror* [1970]) and becoming more numerous from the 1980s on but never especially commonplace; the broadly "Lovecraftian" cinema is much more successful, including items like *Quatermass and the Pit, Alien* (1979) and other Carpenter films including *The Fog* (1980), *The Thing* and *Prince of Darkness.* There is a persistent sense that his mode of "cosmic dread" makes his work "just impossible to visualize" (Carpenter in Mitchell 7), in contrast to King's ready adaptability. See also Dixon, *Second Century of Cinema,* 60–75; Smith, *H.P. Lovecraft in Popular Culture*; Petley, "The Unfilmable?"; Sharrett, "The Haunter of the Dark," 22–26; Leeder, "Poe/Lovecraft/Corman."

33. Clover, *Men, Women and Chain Saws,* 168.

34. Quendler, *From Romantic Irony to Postmodern Metafiction,* 25. Much like Wes Craven's *New Nightmare* (1994), which similarly unperformed, *In the Mouth of Madness* represents a thoughtful and serious expression of "meta-horror" before the more irreverent *Scream* franchise (1996–). For more on *In the Mouth of Madness* as a piece of postmodern, meta-horror, see Fuchs, "Horrific Welcome to the Desert of the Real," 84–86.

35. Heffernan, *Ghouls, Gimmicks, and Gold,* 26.

36. Guins and Cruz, "Revisionings," 160.

37. Foucault, "What Is an Author?" 118.

38. However, it does not refer to the film as "John Carpenter's *In the Mouth of Madness,*" as the film's actual advertisements did.

39. Mulvey-Roberts, "A Spook Ride on Film,'" 86.

40. This is not the first time Carpenter was "name-checked" in his own films; in *They Live* (1988), parodies of Gene Siskel and Roger Ebert, actually aliens, criticize the sex and violence in films: "I'm fed up with it. Filmmakers like George Romero and John Carpenter have to show some restraint."

41. Carpenter, interviewed by Gilles Boulenger (*John Carpenter,* 229).

Bibliography

Benjamin, Walter. "The Work of Art in the Age of Its Technological Reproducibility." In *The Work of Art in the Age of Its Technological Reproducibility and Other Writings on Media,* edited by Michael W. Jennings, Brigid Doherty and Thomas Y. Levin, 19–55. Cambridge: Belknap Press of Harvard University Press, 2008.

Boulenger, Gilles. *John Carpenter: The Prince of Darkness.* Los Angeles: Silman-James Press, 2003.

Clover, Carol J. *Men, Women and Chain Saws: Gender in the Modern Horror Film.* Princeton: Princeton University Press, 1992.

Colavito, Jason. *The Cult of Alien Gods: H.P. Lovecraft and Extraterrestrial Pop Culture.* Amherst, NY: Prometheus, 2005.

Collings, Michael R. *The Stephen King Phenomenon.* Mercer Island, WA: Starmount House, 1987.

Collins, Andy, and Bruce R. Cordell. *Libris Mortis: The Book of Undead.* Renton, WA: Wizards of the Coast, 2004.

Davies, Owen. *Grimoires: A History of Magic Books.* Oxford: Oxford University Press, 2010.

Dixon, Wheeler Winston. *The Second Century of Cinema: The Past and Future of the Moving Image.* Albany: State University of New York Press, 2000.

Engle, John. "Cults of Lovecraft: The Impact of H.P. Lovecraft's Fiction on Contemporary Occult Practices." *Mythlore* 33, no. 1 (Fall/Winter 2014): 85–98.

Foucault, Michel. "What Is an Author?" In *The Foucault Reader,* edited by Paul Rabinow, 101–20. New York: Pantheon, 1984.

Fuchs, Michael. "A Horrific Welcome to the Desert of the Real: Simulacra, Simulations, and Postmodern Horror." In *Landscapes of Postmodernity: Concepts and Paradigms of Critical Theory,* edited by Petra Eckhard, Michael Fuchs and Walter W. Hölbling, 71–91. Vienna: LIT Verlag, 2010.

Guins, Raiford, and Omayra Zaragoza Cruz. "Revisionings: Repetition as Creative Nostalgia in the Films of John Carpenter." In *The Cinema of John Carpenter: The Technique of Terror,* edited by Ian Conrich and David Woods, 155–66. London: Wallflower, 2004.

Harms, Dan. "Reviving Dead Names: Strategies of Legitimization in the *Necronomicon* of Simon and the Dark Aesthetic." In *Magic in the Modern World: Strategies of Repression and Legitimization,* edited by Edward Bever and Randall Styers, 171–96. University Park: Pennsylvania State University Press, 2017.

Harms, Daniel, and John Wisdom Gonce III, eds. *Necronomicon Files: The Truth Behind Lovecraft's Legend.* Newburyport, MA: Red Wheel/Weiser, 2003.
Heffernan, Kevin. *Ghouls, Gimmicks, and Gold: Horror Films and the American Movie Business, 1953–1968.* Durham: Duke University Press, 2004.
Hendrix, Grady. *Paperbacks from Hell: The Twisted History of '70s and '80s Horror Fiction.* Philadelphia: Quirk Books, 2017.
Joshi, S. T. "The Cthulhu Mythos." In *Icons of Horror and the Supernatural: An Encyclopedia of Our Worst Nightmares*, vol. 1, edited by S. T. Joshi, 97–128. Westport, CT: Greenwood Press, 2007.
_____. *The Modern Weird Tale.* Jefferson, NC: McFarland, 2001.
Laycock, Joe. *Dangerous Games: What the Moral Panic over Role-Playing Games Says about Play, Religion, and Imagined Worlds.* Oakland: University of California Press, 2015.
Leeder, Murray. "Poe/Lovecraft/Corman: The Case of *The Haunted Palace* (1963)." In *The Lovecraftian Poe: Essays on Influence, Reception, Interpretation, and Transformation*, edited by Sean Moreland, 163–77. Bethlehem, PA: Lehigh University Press, 2017.
Leitch, Thomas, "Twelve Fallacies in Contemporary Adaptation Theory." *Criticism* 45, no. 2 (Spring 2003): 149–71.
Mitchell, Charles P. *The Complete H.P. Lovecraft Filmography.* Westport, CT: Greenwood Press, 2001.
Mulvey-Roberts, Marie. "'A Spook Ride on Film': Carpenter and the Gothic." In *The Cinema of John Carpenter: The Technique of Terror*, edited by Ian Conrich and David Woods, 78–90. London: Wallflower, 2004.
Murphy, Bernice M. "The Rise of Popular Horror, 1971–2000." In *Horror: A Literary History*, edited by Xavier Aldana Reyes, 159–87. London: British Library, 2016.
Petley, Julian. "The Unfilmable? H.P. Lovecraft and the Cinema," in *Monstrous Adaptations: Generic and Thematic Mutations in Horror Films*, edited by Richard J. Hand and Jay McRoy, 35–47. Manchester: Manchester University Press, 2007.
Poole, W. Scott. *In the Mountains of Madness: The Life and Extraordinary Afterlife of H.P. Lovecraft.* Berkeley: Soft Skull Press, 2016.
Quendler, Christian. *From Romantic Irony to Postmodern Metafiction.* Frankfurt: Peter Lang, 2005.
Poole, W. Scott. *Satan in America: The Devil We Know.* Lanham, MD: Rowman & Littlefield, 2009.
Saler, Michael. *As If: The Literary Prehistory of Virtual Reality.* Oxford: Oxford University Press, 2012.
Sharrett, Christopher. "The Haunter of the Dark: H.P. Lovecraft and Modern Horror Cinema." *Cineaste* 22 (Winter 2015): 22–26.
Shreffler, Philip A. *The Lovecraft Companion.* Westport, CT: Greenwood Press, 1977.
Simon. *The Necronomicon.* New York: Avon, 1977.
Smith, Don G. *H.P. Lovecraft in Popular Culture: The Works and Their Adaptations in Film, Television, Comics, Music and Games.* Jefferson, NC: McFarland, 2006.
Ward, James M., and Robert J. Kuntz. *Deities & Demigods: Cyclopedia of Gods and Heroes from Myth and Legend.* Lake Geneva, WI: TSR, 1980.
Warren, Bill. "The Movies and Mr. King." In *Fear Itself: The Horror Fiction of Stephen King*, edited by Tim Underwood and Chuck Miller, 125–48. San Francisco: Underwood-Miller, 1982.
Wolf, Mark J. P. *Building Imaginary Worlds: The Theory and History of Subcreation.* London: Routledge, 2012.

The Book with a Thousand Faces

The Evolution of the Necronomicon *in the* Evil Dead *Universe*

MARTIN J. AUERNHEIMER

The *Necronomicon* is probably the best-known occult "evil book" in the world. The book itself does not exist, although some conspiracy theorists might claim otherwise; it is rather a creation of the well-known horror author H.P Lovecraft. The *Necronomicon* has been evolving and mutating in popular culture since Lovecraft created it—it was borrowed by members of his literary circle, incorporated into pastiches and homages, and turned into a "real" thing at least a couple of times. But the most powerful force in this process has been the *Evil Dead* films, which have created a version of the *Necronomicon* that has now eclipsed the original in the minds of most horror fans. The evolution of the *Necronomicon*—its sources, inspirations and depiction in the *Evil Dead* universe—are the subject of this essay, which will first give an overview of Lovecraft's *Necronomicon*, followed by a discussion of the book in the *Evil Dead* universe, that considers its visual and diegetic aspects, as well as the forces associated with it.

The Basis: Lovecraft's Necronomicon

Lovecraft used the *Necronomicon* as a recurring prop and plot device in his works of fiction. It is described as containing forbidden and dark knowledge about the cosmology of the "Great Old Ones," evil deities central to his tales. The book links seemingly unrelated stories and contributes to the creation of a universe similar to the real world. It is first mentioned in Lovecraft's short story "The Nameless City" (1921) before appearing in famous tales such as "The Call of Cthulhu" (1928), "The Dunwich Horror" (1929), and *At The Mountains of Madness* (1936). Because it became such an important reference in Lovecraft's tales—and also to keep from contradicting himself—he wrote a fictitious history of the book: In 700 AD, Abdul Alhazred, the "mad poet" of Sanaa, wrote the *Al Azif*, which was translated into Greek and named *Necronomicon* in 950 AD. Lovecraft describes many episodes in the book's history featuring real historical persons such as Pope Gregory IX or John Dee. Copies of the book are described as very rare and only to be found in a few libraries worldwide.[1]

By invoking real historical people and places, the chronology of the *Necronomicon* blurs the boundaries between fact and fiction. This pseudo-reality is intensified by the fact that the book appears not only in Lovecraft's tales, but also in stories by other authors of his literary circle. These writers, in turn, created their own fictional grimoires, such as Robert E. Howard's *Unaussprechlichen Kulten,* which enjoyed the same treatment as the *Necronomicon*. The books are mentioned in seemingly unrelated stories by different authors and are even listed (in "The Festival," for example) next to real occult works, thereby creating a "synthetic folklore,"[2] which the reader cannot easily identify as fiction. This strategy was a great success: Lovecraft mentioned in letters to other authors that many readers asked him about the existence of the *Necronomicon* and other occult books.[3]

Because the *Necronomicon* continued to appear in the works of authors such as Clark Ashton Smith and Brian Lumley even after Lovecraft's death in 1937, it became increasingly independent from its creator. The line between fact and fiction was blurred further, although mostly in form of parody or practical jokes; there exists pseudo-scientific research about the *Necronomicon*[4] and there were even faked records for the book in the library card catalogs of well known universities such as Berkeley and Yale.[5] The apparent reality of the tome was so convincing that many antiquarians and book-sellers received requests for the book. In the late 1970s the gap in the market was filled when several different versions of the *Necronomicon* were released, the best known being the *Necronomicon* by an author merely known as Simon (1977), also known as *Simonomicon*.[6]

Lovecraft maintained that the name *Necronomicon* came to him in a dream.[7] He translated it as "an image of the law of the dead."[8] The name *Necronomicon* also bears similarities to the *Poeticon Astronomica* by Hyginus or the *Astronomica* by Marcus Manilius (both 1st century BC), both of which describe stellar constellations—a topic also prominent in Lovecraft's stories. The material quoted from the *Necronomicon* in Lovecraft's tales describes the cosmology of the "Great Old Ones," as well as spells and rituals linked to them. It is thus the most important tool used by cultists of these dark gods to reach their goals.

The Metamorphosis: The Necronomicon *of* The Evil Dead

Depictions of the *Necronomicon* in film were initially closely linked to Lovecraft's works. It first appears on screen in Roger Corman's *The Haunted Palace* (1963), an adaptation of Lovecraft's *The Case of Charles Dexter Ward* (1941), and also plays an important role in the film adaptation of *The Dunwich Horror* (1970). Just like the literary adaptations, the *Necronomicon* in film became increasingly independent from Lovecraft's original description over time. Through its fame it has evolved into a symbol of the occult.[9]

The *Evil Dead* movies, however, made the *Necronomicon* the most famous "evil book" in film history. *The Evil Dead* (1981), *Evil Dead II* (1987) and *Army of Darkness* (1992) have become horror-cult phenomena and are well known for their mix of slapstick and gore, which greatly influenced the horror-comedy genre. The satirical, over-the-top depiction of violence shows influences of classic comedy such as the Three Stooges shorts: camera angles, edits, and sounds mix slapstick with horror.[10] The success of these three movies spawned a remake of the first film in 2013, as well as the television series *Ash vs. Evil Dead* (2015–2018) and many unofficial fan projects. The references in popular culture to the *Evil Dead* films are numerous and other spin-offs were planned.

The Evil Dead shows a classical horror topos: five college students want to spend a fun weekend in a cabin in the woods; in the cellar, they find a mysterious book called *Naturom Demonto*, as well as a dagger and a tape recorder. On the tape Professor Knowby, to whom the cabin belongs, documents his discovery of the book and recites passages from it, awakening the evil in the forest. One by one, the college students are possessed, and only bodily dismemberment can exorcise the demons. In the end, Ash (Bruce Campbell), the sole survivor, throws the book into the fire, thereby destroying it and the demons. In *Evil Dead II*, the *Naturom Demonto* is called *Necronomicon Ex Mortis*. The second film reprises the plot of the first, but reduces the five students to just Ash and his girlfriend Linda. Ash kills the possessed Linda and cuts off his own possessed hand with a chainsaw while defending himself against the demons in the cabin. Knowby's daughter and three others bring missing pages of the *Necronomicon* to the cabin and are possessed one by one. Ash, using a spell found in the missing pages, banishes the evil spirits through a portal, but is ultimately sucked into the portal himself.

In *Army of Darkness* Ash finds himself in the year 1300 AD, where he must locate the *Necronomicon* in order to return to his own time. On his journey, he battles demonic powers as well as his own evil twin. He finds the book, but fails to use the right magic formula while picking it up, thereby awakening the Army of Darkness, led by his evil twin, who sets out to find the *Necronomicon* and destroy humankind. Ash leads the medieval villagers around him to victory against the Army and then returns to his own time using a spell from the *Necronomicon*.

The plot of the television series *Ash vs. Evil Dead* begins 30 years after *Army of Darkness*. Ash reads from the *Necronomicon* while under the influence of drugs, inad-

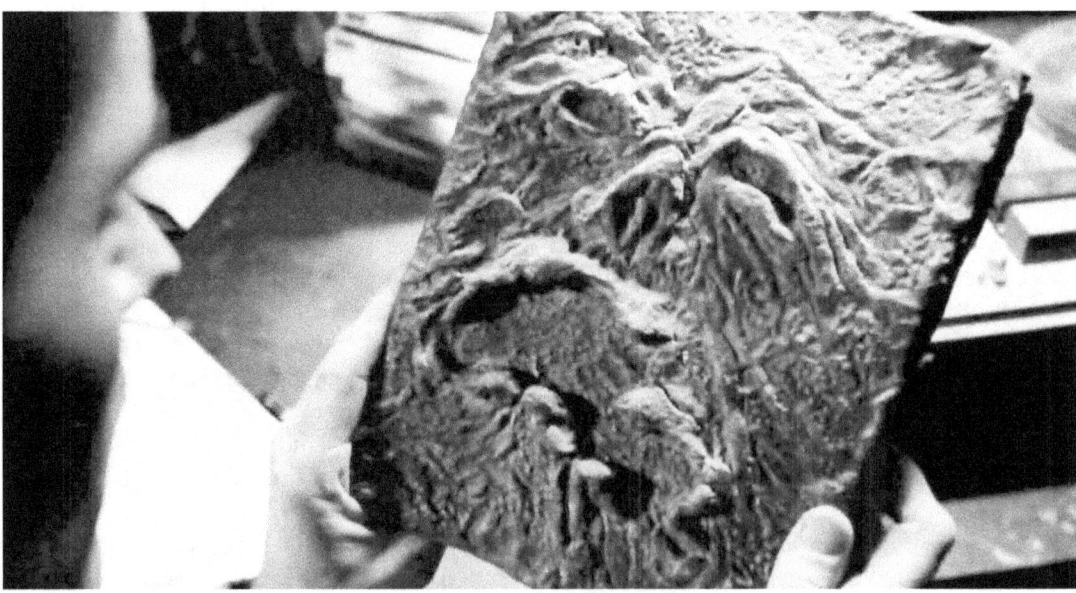

The Necronomicon in *Evil Dead II* (1987).

vertently summoning the evil forces once again. With his colleagues Kelly and Pablo, he tries to banish the demons and restore normality. After two seasons, they apparently succeed in vanquishing evil and banishing the *Necronomicon* to the underworld. The remake from 2013 shares the title *Evil Dead* with the other films, but shows a slightly different diegetic universe, because it is a "serious" horror film that updates the shocking effects of the 1981 original for modern audiences. The plot is largely the same, although the reason for the trip to the cabin is the main character Mia's fight against drug addiction.

The Incarnation: Visual Depictions of the Necronomicon in the Evil Dead Universe

Because each installment of the *Evil Dead* universe was produced by a different studio, none of which would relinquish the rights to the design, the visual depiction of the *Necronomicon* evolves significantly across the series of films.[11] The different manifestations nonetheless share two key features: they are bound in human skin and inked in human blood. In *The Evil Dead*, the book is small, and a leathery human face is visible on its cover. *Evil Dead II*'s *Necronomicon* is "cleaner" and the face becomes more prominent, even showing subtle motions. In *Army of Darkness* the face is more subtle, although still well visible. *Ash vs. Evil Dead*'s *Necronomicon* echoes the depiction in *Evil Dead II*, with a strongly defined face and fiery eyes and mouth, when the book "speaks" with Ash. The interior of the book evolves as well: the pages, which are inked in human blood, are described in *Ash vs. Evil Dead* as being cut from the bodies of the damned. Since its first appearance, the tome features anatomical drawings of humans and otherworldly creatures as well as maps and symbols imitating ancient Mesopotamian cuneiform writing. The installments that follow contain even more detailed and distinct depictions. Since *Evil Dead II* the book shows a drawing of the "chosen one" (Ash), who is prophesied to defeat evil. In *Ash vs. Evil Dead* the book also features translations and commentaries on its pages, which have been added to the book.

The depiction of the *Necronomicon* in *Evil Dead* (2013) doesn't feature a face on the cover at all, although it is still bound in human flesh. Because of the comedic elements in the earlier films, a new design is used, so as not to dilute the horror of the new movie through associations with slapstick from the other *Evil Dead* installments. The book's design is, instead, meant to be menacing. Its content is, similarly, designed to distinguish it from the volumes in the other *Evil Dead* films. It drops the oriental aspects in favor of a Christian-inflected occult evil to which the audience can better relate or by which it can be more easily scared. There are no anatomical drawings, but a mix of satanic, occult, and alchemical symbols; the cuneiform is exchanged for writings in Latin and woodcut-style drawings or prints, which remind of classic tarot card artwork and foreshadow plot developments. The book is written with ink, but there are also some smeared notes in blood—apparently for lack of proper ink. This depiction may be inspired by the grimoire in the film *Equinox* (1970), which features similar design elements.

The use of human skin to bind books is historical fact and was mostly used for works with an obvious link to death: anatomical books, such as *De Humanis Corpore Fabrica* by Andreas Vesalius (1543, bound in human skin in 1867), or books telling of the exploits and punishment of famous criminals, such as William Burke, who was hanged in 1829,[12] were sometimes bound this way. In the latter case, the binding served as a deterrence and warning, because it was bound in the skin of the criminal it described. The principal inspiration for the human face on the cover of the *Necronomicon* in the *Evil Dead* films seems to be a book about Father Henry Garnet, who was executed in 1606 for his apparent involvement in the Gunpowder Plot—a failed attempt to blow up Britain's Houses of Parliament. The book is bound in Garnet's skin and one can make out a ghostly face on its cover.[13]

Other books bound in human skin include a collection of Hans Holbein the Younger's *Danse Macabre*, which may have inspired the fictitious anatomical drawings in the *Necronomicon*, and the woodcut-style artwork in the 2013 version. Two copies of it are now located in the John Hay Library of Brown University in Providence, Rhode Island—H.P. Lovecraft's place of birth. Although he never described his *Necronomicon* physically to further the eeriness of his creation,[14] Lovecraft mentions human skin as a cover for morbid artworks in his tale "The Hound."[15] In the 20th century there were also other items crafted from human skin, which may have served as inspiration. The notorious serial killer Ed Gein crafted masks from faces of the dead (amongst other things) and was an inspiration for the character "Leatherface" from *Texas Chainsaw Massacre* (1974), who wears a mask made from a human face while swinging a chainsaw. Bruce Campbell has stated that this movie was an influence on the *Evil Dead* movies.[16]

The inspiration for the use of blood in place of ink in the *Necronomicon* refers to the well-known theme of pacts with dark forces (such as that in *Faust*[17]), which are often sealed this way, and associate the book with evil forces or magic. There is, however, no historical evidence for an entire real book written in blood.

The interior of the *Necronomicon* in *Evil Dead II* featuring pseudo-cuneiform writing and anatomical drawings.

The Coming to Life: The Evil Dead Necronomicon's Influences on the Plot

The development of the *Necronomicon* in the *Evil Dead* universe is not, however, limited to its physical depiction. The book evolves from a passive prop to an active element influencing the plot. In *The Evil Dead,* the book is merely a book. As a MacGuffin, it has little screen time, merely providing the impulse for the story's development. At the end of the movie, it becomes clear that the summoned demons are strongly connected to the book: while burning, the face on the cover of the book squirms in a stop-motion animation and mirrors the other demons' demise. The *Naturom Demonto* is no lifeless object, in other words, but a living entity as well as a portal for evil forces.

Evil Dead II only hints at the tome's active influence. During the introduction, the book moves its face slightly, but remains still for the rest of the film. The most active role is taken here by the missing pages, which are used to open the portal. The book's influence on the plot is indirect at best, present mostly in the fact that the demons are introduced as "spirits of the book,"[18] although one could argue that the demons act as 'extensions' of the *Necronomicon*. *Army of Darkness* also only features a rather passive *Necronomicon*, even though imitations of the book attack Ash by flying around him and biting him. The "real" *Necronomicon*, which shapes the goals of all characters in the film, remains a motionless MacGuffin.

Ash vs. Evil Dead features a significant evolution of the *Necronomicon*: The book is, at first, a MacGuffin that amplifies the intentions of its readers but cannot act independently, making it "harmless, unless wielded by someone very evil or very stupid."[19] Later in the series, however, it starts communicating with Pablo by causing him to hear voices and even flies at him from out of a box.[20] At the end of the first season, the *Necronomicon* becomes an active character in the series: after contact with Ash's blood it starts breathing and speaking to him, trying to exploit his inner conflict in order to trick him into using its dark magic.[21] The book's attempted seduction of Ash recalls similar elements in works such as *Star Wars*, *The Lord of the Rings*, and *Conan the Barbarian*.[22] The book now has a "mind of its own,"[23] executive producer Craig DiGregorio noted, emphasizing its similarities to Tolkien's One Ring. The book, once it exhibits agency, becomes one with the demons and attempts to directly influence other characters to summon evil forces. It also begins to show human-like emotions such as pain.[24] Like other demons, it has the ability to possess humans: the face on its cover attaches itself to Pablo's head and makes him vomit (or "give birth to") summoned demons through their common mouth. Later, the book becomes a parasite in Pablo's body, turning him slowly into the new *Necronomicon*: cuneiform symbols appear on his skin, making him a human incarnation of the book. When the *Necronomicon* is finally banished from Pablo's body, it returns to its original status of a mere plot device.

The Background: Forces Associated with the Necronomicon *in the* Evil Dead *Universe*

The *Necronomicon* in the *Evil Dead* universe is an ancient text that describes Sumerian rites. This connection to Sumerian culture ties it not to Lovecraft's *Necronomicon* (written by an Arab in 700 AD) but to the aforementioned *Simonomicon*, the best-known "real-world" version of the *Necronomicon*. The *Simonomicon* was created by a group of enthusiasts around an occult bookstore in New York for their own use, and intended as a mere practical joke. The authors were shocked when they found out that their book had been released, calling it an "occult minefield," that shouldn't be bought or used by anyone, because of its dangerous incantations.[25] Similarities between the *Necronomicon* of the *Evil Dead* and the *Necronomicon Tapes* (1981),[26] which features explanations about the *Simonomicon* by its apparent author, are also significant. Just as in the movie, the author records the correct pronunciation of the incantations on tape and even mentions the words "*klaatu verrata nicto*,"[27] which are inspired by the almost identical words "*klaatu barada nikto*," voiced in *The Day the Earth Stood Still* (1951) as a quasi-incantation used to control a powerful robot, and are also uttered in *Army of Darkness* as a magic spell. The *Evil Dead* films illustrate the consequences of using the book and, like the authors of the *Simonomicon*, Ash warns that it "was never meant for the world of the living"[28]—that is, for the eyes of the average individual.

The apparent Oriental origins of both Lovecraft's and *Evil Dead*'s *Necronomicon*, which is found in the ruins of Kandar,[29] and also the *Simonomicon*, are obvious. Middle Eastern cultures have been associated with magic and necromancy by Western observers since antiquity.[30] The *Simonomicon* combines Sumerian with later Assyrian and Babylonian myths, thus the Assyrian-Babylonian spirit "Pazuzu" is presented as Sumerian.[31] It thus appropriates the spirit that, in *The Exorcist* (1973), possesses a young girl who is then saved by Catholic priests. *The Exorcist* also influenced the depiction of demons in the *Evil Dead* universe: their unnatural eyes, strength, resistance to injuries, and ability to float in the air; the Christian connotation of an ancient Oriental evil personified by the character Baal in *Ash vs. Evil Dead* also refers to the horror classic.[32] In the television series, the ancient Mesopotamian background is pushed aside in favor of a more Christianized evil, as was already the case in 2013's *Evil Dead*. Thus, portals in the remake and the series do not lead to the "evil worlds beyond"[33] but to "Hell" and "the underworld."[34]

The forces associated with the *Necronomicon* in the *Evil Dead* universe also evoke many other well-known horror motifs, such as necromancy and undeath. Emphasized through the codicil "ex mortis," it reflects the many film representations of zombies, demons, and vampires, as well as literary adaptations of works from Lovecraft's circle. Part of the summoning formula in *Evil Dead II* is the word "Nosferatos," referring to vampires. Evil is connected to nighttime and is partially driven back by the sunrise. The demons themselves, also called "deadites," are reminiscent of other undead monsters such as zombies, whose conditions are transferred to humans through bites and infection of the blood. The themes of infection and corruption thus established in other horror films are intensified in the *Evil Dead* movies through allusions to venereal disease, rape and defilement, which are meant to shock and disgust the audience. The evil forces assault the moral and bodily integrity of their victims, although the staging remains satirical due to its over-the-top depictions: in *Evil Dead II*, evil possesses Ash's hand, which then acts autonomously like "Thing," the disembodied hand from *The Addams Family*. In *Army of Darkness*, an evil twin spawns from Ash's body in a clear allusion to Dr. Jekyll and Mr. Hyde, and in *Ash vs. Evil Dead* the possessed hand spawns another twin of Ash.

Some aspects of the *Evil Dead* universe's *Necronomicon* can originally be found in the work of Lovecraft and other authors. "Bodily dismemberment" and the reanimation of single pieces of the body through the *Necronomicon* are featured in stories by Lovecraft's friend and colleague Clark Ashton Smith,[35] and Brian Lumley mentions the "Dark Ones," who are said to have written the book in the *Evil Dead* films.[36] Much like Lovecraft's creations, death is of no consequence to the demons of the *Evil Dead*. Knowby explains that "these creatures may lie dormant but are never truly dead. They may be recalled to active life through the incantations in this book. It is through recitation of these passages that the Demons are given license to possess the living."[37] This refers to an iconic quote from Lovecraft's *Necronomicon*: "That is not dead which can eternal lie and with strange aeons even death may die."[38] Lovecraft evokes a distant and gruesome sacral-spiritual past, which emphasizes the eternal life of the demons in contrast to humanity's volatility. The description of the *Necronomicon* in *Evil Dead II*'s introductions also refers to this by mentioning that the book was "written long ago, when the seas ran red with blood"[39] which evokes biblical plagues[40] as well as Cthulhu, the best-known of Lovecraft's Great Old Ones, who is associated with the ocean.[41]

The impossibility of physically describing otherworldly horrors, a recurring theme in Lovecraft's stories, manifests in the movies through "force shots": surging point-of-view shots of a not clearly defined entity or force, which is witnessed in horror by the characters.[42] Similar shots are used in the 1970s film adaptation of *The Dunwich Horror*, in which the monster is invisible.

The potential to open portals and gateways for evil entities or forces is another central aspect of both Lovecraft's[43] and *Evil Dead*'s versions of the *Necronomicon*. In *The Evil Dead*, the gateway remains symbolic, represented through the destruction of the cabin's windows by marauding plants and the sexual assault on Sheila by animate trees in the forest. *Evil Dead II*, in which portals are portrayed as the main reason for the book's existence,[44] shows many similarities to Lovecraft's story "The Dunwich Horror": in both, missing pages are used to create the portal and the evil spirit must be made visible through the use of a spell in order to be banished. In *Ash vs. Evil Dead*, Ruby guards the *Necronomicon* and is therefore called "Gatekeeper," just like Yog-Sothoth in Lovecraft's tale.

Dark forests have long been associated with dark forces and monstrous creatures. The representation of nature, particularly forests, as hostile contrast to rational civilization in Lovecraft's "The Dunwich Horror,"[45] is also evident in the *Evil Dead* universe. The force shots and other evidence of demonic presences in the *Evil Dead* films all start in the forest: the ground moves and characters are assaulted by plants, which later attack inhabited areas, forcing their way into buildings by (in force shots) breaking windows in order to fall upon the human inhabitants. Because the evil force draws its power from the forest, the possessed Linda returns to haunt Ash from her grave in front of the cabin. By contrast, many aspects of human civilization, such as books, lamps, cars, and even the entire cabin, become possessed in the *Evil Dead* universe. Ash vanquishes the hostile forces of nature, replacing his possessed hand with the chainsaw he used to amputate it, and in *Army of Darkness* the evil hordes are defeated through the use of modern technology, with Ash declaring, "Say hello to the 21st century!" The films show a struggle between the rational, familiar, and controllable reality of the characters' civilized world, and the dangerous, unknown, and terrifying reality of nature, which engulfs them. The incarnation of the evil spirit in *Evil Dead II* as a twisted tree and the book's pseudo-Latin name *Naturom Demonto* emphasize this.[46]

The forces associated with the *Necronomicon* in 2013's *Evil Dead* differ, once again, from those referenced in the other installments, even though they influenced the representation of the book in *Ash vs. Evil Dead*. The remake drops the humorous aspects of the earlier films and the theme of possession is combined with psychological problems, drug use and detoxification. Therefore, the boundaries between hallucination and the supernatural blur. Mia must overcome the influence of both drugs *and* the *Necronomicon* in order to leave the cabin. Evil manifests itself as a girl, in the style of *The Ring* (2002) and other Asian horror films, and is named "Evil Entity" and "Taker of Souls," which refers to the Christian devil, who prepares to rise from "Hell." The "purification by fire" of possessed humans points simultaneously toward the 1981 original and historical witch burnings. Contrary to the original movie, the *Necronomicon* of the remake cannot be harmed by fire, which heightens its otherworldly quality. Other Christian references include Mia's resurrection from the grave to confront the evil entity—which evokes the Last Judgment and the war between Christ and Antichrist, as foretold in Revelations— and the "crucifixion" of a long-haired and bearded man through the use of a nail gun.

Conclusion

Because of its distinctive design, the *Necronomicon* of the *Evil Dead* universe is as closely linked to the franchise as Ash and his chainsaw-hand. The book has evolved into an unmistakable element of popular culture. Depictions of the *Necronomicon* bound in human skin derive almost exclusively from the *Evil Dead* films and its fan fiction or homages. *Evil Dead*'s depiction of the *Necronomicon* has also influenced the popular understanding of Lovecraft's *Necronomicon*: In *The Dunwich Horror* (2009) it is linked to ancient Mesopotamia, not to its origin in the 8th century, as described by Lovecraft.

To this day, the *Necronomicon*'s appearance in all horror-associated sections of popular culture, such as literature, music, film and video games (and where its development continues), is largely due to the fame it gained through the *Evil Dead* films.[47] On one hand, the book has become a symbol for a film and literary genre, on the other hand it is a autonomous phenomenon, which is taken seriously by some occultists, who ignore its fictitious origin.[48]

Satirical depictions of the *Necronomicon*, and of evil books in general, are particularly influenced by the grotesque humor of the *Evil Dead* movies. In *Evil Toons* (1992) a nameless book shares many characteristics with *Evil Dead*'s *Necronomicon*. The German comedy *Erkan und Stefan gegen die Mächte der Finsternis* (2002) links the book to the devil and portrays it as an extension of the antagonistic warlock, who seeks world domination through it. Even the creators of the *Evil Dead* universe—Raimi, Tapert and Campbell— do not limit themselves to "their" *Necronomicon*: the television series *Hercules: The Legendary Journeys* (1995–1999), in which all three participated, features another *Necronomicon*, although without references to the *Evil Dead* version. The possibility for further manifestations of the book are, therefore, endless!

николаевич Notes

1. Lovecraft, "History of the Necronomicon," 240–41.
2. Lovecraft, letter to William Frederick Anger.
3. Lovecraft, "Quotes regarding the Necronomicon from Lovecraft's Letters."
4. A collection of 'scientific material' concerning the Necronomicon (see Price, *Necronomicon*, 240–41).
5. Reichart, "Necronomicon," 76.
6. For a large summary see Harms, "'Many a Quaint and Curious Volume…'"
7. Lovecraft, letter to Harry O. Fisher.
8. Price proposes other translations in "Critical Commentary on the *Necronomicon*."

9. For example, *Necronomicon—geträumte Sünden* (1973) and *Giger's Necronomicon* (1975). For a general overview see Gonce, "Unspeakable Cuts."
10. For a thorough analysis of visual comedy in *Evil Dead* see Hoxter, "The Evil Dead."
11. The same is the case for the different Lindas in the *Evil Dead* Films, which are all played by different actors.
12. "Surgeon's Hall Museums. Pocketbook Made from Burke's Skin."
13. "Spooky 'Face' of Gunpowder Plot" and "Never Yet Melted."
14. Lovecraft, letter to Jim Blish and William Miller, Jr.
15. Lovecraft, "The Hound," 84.
16. Leighton, "Ash vs. Evil Dead Star Bruce Campbell."
17. Johann Wolfgang von Goethe, "Faust, Der Tragödie erster Teil," 67.
18. *Evil Dead II.*
19. "Books from Beyond," *Ash vs. Evil Dead.* Season 1, Episode 3.
20. "The Killer of Killers," *Ash vs. Evil Dead.* Season 1, Episode 6.
21. "Bound in Flesh," *Ash vs. Evil Dead.* Season 1, Episode 9.
22. *Star Wars* features many attempts to seduce characters to the "dark side of the force," the One Ring in *The Lord of the Rings* wants its bearer to wear it, so that the agents of evil can find him. In *Conan the Barbarian* the antagonistic Thulsa Doom tries to convice Conan, that he is his spiritual father and that he has made him what he is now through the slaughter of his people.
23. "Bound in Flesh," *Ash vs. Evil Dead.* Season 1, Episode 9. Behind the scenes.
24. "Bound in Flesh," *Ash vs. Evil Dead.* Season 1, Episode 9.
25. Since the *Necronomicon Tapes* were released in the same year with *The Evil Dead*, they may be to young to have had an influence on the film. The similarities are obvious though. The summonings in the *Simonomicon* do not feature protective barriers and the use of certain paraphernalia is designed to summoned spirits. Also, the book doesn't feature spells to banish summoned entities, which are even found in the *Evil Dead* Necronomicon. See Gonce, "A Plague of *Necronomicons*" and "Simon, Slater and the Gang."
26. *Army of Darkness.*
27. Gonce, "Simon, Slater and the Gang."
28. *Army of Darkness.*
29. There are many settlements in Tunisia, Pakistan and Iraq with the name Kandar. In *The Dunwich Horror*, a phonetically similar place called Kadath is mentioned, which may have been the inspiration for Kandar: "Kadath in the cold waste hath known Them, and what man knows Kadath?" (Lovecraft, "Dunwich Horror," 275–76).
30. Strabo, *Geography*, XVI, 2. Section 39.
31. Gonce, "A Plague of *Necronomicons*," 146–56.
32. Baal is based upon a Semitic deity that was demonized in early Christianity and became an aspect of the devil (Beelzebub). In ancient Mesopotamia, Ba'al was a name used for many deities, meaning "Lord" or "Master."
33. *Evil Dead II.*
34. "Books from Beyond," *Ash vs. Evil Dead.* Season 1, Episode 3.
35. "Most readily can the corpse be animated if all its members have remained intact; and yet there are cases in which the excelling will of the wizard hath reared up from death the sundered pieces of a body hewn in many fragments and hath caused them to serves his end, either separately or in a temporary reunion" (Smith, "Eldritch Dark: The Return of the Sorcerer"); "I fear that the only way to stop those possessed by the spirits of the book is through the act of bodily dismemberment" (*The Evil Dead*).
36. "Legend has it that it was written by the dark one: Necronomicon ex Mortis" (*Evil Dead II*); "All claimed to work their Wonders through Intercourse with dead & departed Spirits, but I fear that often such Spirits were evil Angels, the Messengers of the Dark One & yet more ancient evils" (Brian Lumley, "Aunt Hester" [1977], quoted in Price, "Critical Commentary," 310).
37. *The Evil Dead.*
38. Lovecraft, "Nameless City," 24.
39. *Evil Dead II.*
40. Exodus 7:20–22.
41. Lovecraft, "Call of Cthulhu."
42. In *Ash vs. Evil Dead* the nature of the "force-shots" is revealed as fog, therefore the eerie unknown is put into perspective. "Brujo," *Ash vs. Evil Dead.* Season 1, Episode 4.
43. Lovecraft, "Dunwich Horror."
44. "Passageway to the evil worlds beyond" (*Evil Dead II*).
45. "They walk unseen and foul in lonely places where the Words have been spoken and the Rites howled through at their Seasons. The wind gibbers with Their voices and the earth mutters with Their Conciousness. They bend the forest and crush the city, yet may not forest or city behold the hand that smites" (Lovecraft, "Dunwich Horror," 275–76). "It deals with demons, demon resurrection and those forces which roam the forests and dark bowers of man's domain" (*The Evil Dead*).

46. "*Naturom Demonto*" may actually mean "*naturam demonstro*," which means "I show nature" and demonstrates the true quality of the world, including invisible entities from different dimensions. Presumably, the words "nature" and "demon" were pseudo-Latinized, even though the translation "book of the dead" given in the film is far-fetched.

47. Reichart, "Necronomicon"; Gonce, "Unspeakable Cuts"; Gonce, "Call of the Cathode Ray Tube"; Mitchel, *Complete H.P. Lovecraft Filmography*; Smith, *H.P. Lovecraft in Popular Culture*.

48. Reichart, "Necronomicon," 86–87.

BIBLIOGRAPHY

Army of Darkness. Directed by Sam Raimi. 1992. Los Angeles: Universal Home Entertainment, 2013. DVD.
Ash vs. Evil Dead. 2015. Renaissance Pictures/Starz! Seattle: Amazon Prime, 2017. Streaming.
The Evil Dead. Directed by Sam Raimi. 1981. Beverley Hills: Starz/Anchor Bay Entertainment, 2002. DVD.
Evil Dead. Directed by Fede Alvarez. 2013. Culver City, CA: Sony Pictures Home Entertainment, 2013. DVD.
Evil Dead II. Directed by Sam Raimi. 1987. Seattle: Amazon Prime, 2017. Streaming.
Goethe, Johann Wolfgang von. "Faust, Der Tragödie erster Teil." In *Werke: Sechster Band: Faust I, Faust II*. Frankfurt am Main: Insel Verlag, 1981.
Gonce, John Wisdom III. "Call of the Cathode Ray Tube: The *Necronomicon* on Television." In *Necronomicon Files*, ed. Harms and Gonce, 281–95.
_____. "A Plague of *Necronomicons*." In *Necronomicon Files*, ed. Harms and Gonce, 127–71.
_____. "Simon, Slater and the Gang: True Origins of the *Necronomicon*." In *Necronomicon Files*, ed. Harms and Gonce, 173–96.
_____. "Unspeakable Cuts: The *Necronomicon* on Film." In *Necronomicon Files*, ed. Harms and Gonce, 225–82.
Harms, Daniel. "'Many a Quaint and Curious Volume…': The *Necronomicon* Made Flesh." In *Necronomicon Files*, ed. Harms and Gonce, 29–59.
Harms, Daniel, and John Wisdom Gonce III, eds. *The Necronomicon Files. The Truth Behind Lovecraft's Legend. Revised ad Expanded Edition*. Boston: Weiser Books, 2003.
Hoxter, Julian. "The Evil Dead. Die and Chase: From Slapstick to Splatstick." In *Necronomicon. The Journal of Horror and Erotic Cinema, Book One*, edited by Andy Black, 71–83. London: Creation Books, 1996.
Leighton, Susan. "Ash vs. Evil Dead Star Bruce Campbell: 'Put Ash on my Tombstone!'" *Fansided*. November 7, 2017. https://1428elm.com/2017/11/09/ash-vs-evil-dead-bruce-campbell-put-ash-on-my-tombstone/.
Lovecraft, H.P. "History of the Necronomicon (An Outline)." In *The Necronomicon: Selected Stories and Essays Concerning the Blasphemous Tome of the Mad Arab*, edited by Robert M. Price, 240–241. Oakland: Chaosium, 1996.
_____. Letter to William Frederick Anger. August 14, 1934. http://www.hplovecraft.com/creation/necron/letters.aspx.
_____. "Quotes regarding the Necronomicon from Lovecraft's Letters." http://www.hplovecraft.com/creation/necron/letters.aspx.
_____. "The Call of Cthulhu." *Necronomicon. The Best Weird Tales of H.P. Lovecraft. Commemorative Edition*. Edited with an Afterword by Stephen Jones, 201–25. London: Gollancz, 2008.
_____. "The Dunwich Horror." In *Necronomicon: The Best Weird Tales of H.P. Lovecraft*, commemorative ed., edited and with an afterword by Stephen Jones, 264–97. London: Gollancz, 2008.
_____. "The Festival." http://www.hplovecraft.com/writings/texts/fiction/f.aspx.
_____. "The Hound." In *Necronomicon: The Best Weird Tales of H.P. Lovecraft, Commemorative Edition*, commemorative ed., edited and with an afterword by Stephen Jones. London: Gollancz, 2008.
_____. Letter to Harry O. Fischer, February 1937. http://www.hplovecraft.com/creation/necron/letters.aspx
_____. Letter to Jim Blish and William Miller, Jr. In *The Rise, Fall and Rise of the Cthulhu Mythos*, edited by S.T. Joshi. Poplar Bluff, MO: Mythos Books, 2008.
_____. "The Nameless City." In *Necronomicon. The Best Weird Tales of H.P. Lovecraft*, commemorative ed., edited and with an afterword by Stephen Jones, 24–33. London: Gollancz, 2008. 24.
Mitchel, Charles P. *The Complete H.P. Lovecraft filmography*. Westport, CT: Greenwood Press, 2001.
"Never Yet Melted. Anthropodermic Book Associated with Gunpowder Plot to Be Auctioned Tomorrow." http://neveryetmelted.com/tags/henry-garnet/.
Price, Robert M. "A Critical Commentary on the *Necronomicon*." In *The Necronomicon: Selected Stories and Essays Concerning the Blasphemous Tome of the Mad Arab*, edited by Robert M. Price, 256–334. Oakland: Chaosium, 1996.
_____, ed. *The Necronomicon. Selected Stories and Essays Concerning the Blasphemous Tome of the Mad Arab*. Oakland: Chaosium, 1996.
Reichart, André. "Necronomicon: Das Buch das nicht sein durfte." In *Wissenschaft meets Pop. Eine interdisziplinäre Annäherung an die Populärkultur*, edited by Wiebke Ohlendorf, André Reichart, and Gunnar Schmidtchen, 61–90. Bielefeld: Transcript Verlag, 2015.
Smith, Clark Ashton. "Eldritch Dark: The Return of the Sorcerer." http://www.eldritchdark.com /writings/short-stories/183/the-return-of-the-sorcerer.

Smith, Don G. *H.P. Lovecraft in Popular Culture. The Works and Their Adaptations on Film, Television, Comics, Music and Games.* Jefferson, NC: McFarland, 2005.
"The spooky 'face' of Gunpowder Plot priest revealed on skin-bound book." Daily Mail Online. http://www.dailymail.co.uk/news/article-496936/The-spooky-face-Gunpowder-Plot-priest-revealed-skin-bound-book.html.
Strabo. *Geography*, XVI, 2. Section 39. http://www.perseus.tufts.edu/hopper/text?doc=Perseus%3Atext%3A1999.01.0239%3Abook%3D16%3Achapter%3D2%3Asection%3D39.
"Surgeon's Hall Museums. Pocketbook made from Burke's Skin." https://museum.rcsed.ac.uk /the-collection/key-collections/key-object-page/pocketbook-made-from-burkes-skin.

Books of Hope and Despair

The Magic Book and the Magic of Books in Murnau's *Faust* (1926)

THOMAS PRASCH

In a dazzling display of cinematic magic in F. W. Murnau's *Faust: Eine deutsche Volkssage* (*Faust: A German Folktale*, 1926), Mephisto invites the freshly rejuvenated scholar (magically restored to his youth): "Step onto my cloak ... and the spinning world will spread before you!" Faust steps on, the windows burst open, and they fly away. Hans Kyser's scenario describes the journey: over "hills, valleys, and forests"; past "cliffs" (*Felsenwände*), "mountain lakes, plunging waterfalls" and "Gothic church towers"; on to "Alpine vistas" (the film adds active volcanoes erupting, unmentioned in the scenario); then over the "endless sea," where the "surf foams against the reefs" and "ships battle storms"; onward above "Southern lands," with "wide arcades" lined with "palms"; back into the sky to fly surrounded by dragons ("fantastic great birds," Kyser calls them, but they look very dragonish); past the "silhouettes of cities and dark cypress gardens"; up into a night sky marked by the "shimmering moonlight" to see the "fireworks of the stars"; and finally down toward Parma, where "dancing maidens" on the "Italianate terrace" mark the wedding Mephisto and Faust arrive in time to disrupt.[1]

Suzanne Cowan calls the flight "one of the most sensational episodes of the picture. The architecutral [sic] sets, built in the expressionist style ... emphasized the tension and drama of the story."[2] Lotte Eisner similarly writes: "The journey through the skies on the cloak of Mephisto whirls through gliding landscapes, the mists making the models seem entirely authentic.... This plastic quality, this *volume* gives the film its power."[3] Roger Ebert notes the sequence's seductive power: "when Mephisto takes Faust on a flight through the sky, we really do seem to see the earth unreeling beneath us."[4] For Philip Kemp, "Faust's aerial journey ... over intricately modelled rooftops, rivers, mountains, and plains" typifies "Murnau's pictorial genius at its height."[5] David Sterritt highlights the scene in asserting that Murnau's film "set mid–Twenties records for cinematic derring-do."[6] French filmmaker Eric Rohmer rhapsodizes about how "Murnau was able to mobilize all the means at his disposal to ensure a total mastery of [cinematic] space."[7] Rohmer's description of the film as "a kind of visual opera" corresponds to Murnau's own account of his method: "the fluid architecture ... the interplay of lines rising, falling, disappearing; the encounter of surfaces, stimulation and its opposite, calm; construction and collapse; the formation and destruction of a hitherto almost unsuspected life; all this adds up to a symphony made up of the harmony of bodies and the rhythm of space; the *play of pure movement*, vigorous and abundant."[8] Even Siegfried Kracauer admits, "Their flight was a celestial sensation," and he did not even like the film.[9]

But note one key detail: as the window bursts open and the pair take flight, there, in the lower right corner of the frame, lies an open book, its pages flapping in the wind Mephisto's cloak generates. It is literally the last thing we see of Faust's study. The image pulls us back to the bookish heart of the story: to the one magic book that enabled Faust to conjure up Mephisto; and to the world of books that Faust, to that point, had been committed. Indeed, Mephisto had mocked him for his bookishness to lure him into their pact, offering his own alternative: "Your life was only the dust and mold of books! Pleasure is all!" Faust's study features piles and piles of heavy tomes, Murnau's knowing nod to the sources of his tale, and to the magic not just of a conjuring book but of books themselves at the dawn of the print age.

John Flood records the awed perspective of a range of Reformation thinkers to the printing press: "Printing was 'God's highest and extremist Grace,' said Luther … echoed by the English martyrologist John Foxe in 1572–1573 when he offered thanks,to the high providence of almighty God for the excellent art of printing.' Similarly [Philip] Melanchthon [a close ally of Luther's] said 'printing is truly an art communicated by God to mankind.' Even 80 years after the invention of printing it must have seemed a miracle, a divine gift, to the contemporaries."[10]

As Faust's conjuring book shows, however, the miracle of printing could also attach itself to unholy ends, and early Reformers, Jean-François Gilmont argues, came rapidly to recognize the downside of the print revolution: "Luther and many of his contemporaries had several reservations regarding the rapid multiplication of printed books…. In his eyes, there was an abundance of useless and even harmful books."[11] In terms of this balance between usefulness and harm, the Faust story holds an interestingly equivocal place: his own books include both the Bible and the tome with the spell for conjuring a demon; books about Faust both provided moral lessons and undermined them with tales of his magic.

Writing about how to interpret the *Faustbuch* (1587), a key source for Murnau (as for Marlowe and Goethe before him), Reformation scholar Gerald Strauss writes: "How we see a subject depends first and foremost on how we have framed it."[12] But for the Faust story, both at its origin point and in its transmutation across media and over time, those frames are multiple. Faust's origins, Strauss notes, occur at the crux of both the spread of Renaissance humanism to the north and the working out of the Reformation project by Luther and his followers in Germany.[13] It simultaneously, first as text and then in other media (stage drama, puppet play, and eventually film), must be framed in terms of popular culture, the dynamics of which print fundamentally transformed.

Faust among his books in *Faust: A German Folktale* (1926).

To frame the story fully, we must first trace its roots, to the historical Faust and his legendary, then literary, and finally cinematic afterlife. We can then note the interplay between magical books, and the magic of books, and those three broad cultural movements of Renaissance, Reformation, and a popular-cultural sphere reshaped by print, connecting these strands back to the Faust story. Finally, we can return to Murnau's film, to examine the role books (and one magic book in particular) play in this filmic incarnation of the tale.

Sources: From Faust *to* Faustbuch *to* Faust

The historical Faust (Georg or Johann; Faust or Faustus; the precise name varies[14]), variably labelled sorcerer, astrologer, necromancer, sodomite,[15] and magician, figures in some 20 texts of the 15th century, ten of them during his lifetime (c. 1466–c. 1539).[16] He was a somewhat older contemporary of Luther's (entering university the year Luther was born; dying—or spirited off to Hell—half a dozen years before Luther's demise), and indeed Luther mentions Faust by name twice in *Table Talk*. Faust first appears in recorded talk from 1533 to 1535: "When one evening at the table a sorcerer named Faustus was mentioned, Doctor Martin said in a serious tone: 'The devil does not make use of the services of sorcerers against me.'" In 1537, he comes up again: "Much was said about Fausto, who called the devil his brother-in-law, and the remark was made: 'If I, Martin Luther, had given him even my hand, he would have destroyed me; but I would not have been afraid of him,—with God as my protector, I would have given him my hand in the name of the Lord.'"[17] Luther takes Faust's satanic pact seriously. In other contemporaneous accounts, Faust is refused entry to several cities, provides astrologic or prophetic services in others, brags about his powers, and is dismissed as a charlatan.

The tone begins to change after 1540. As Karl Wentersdorf notes: "It was not until after Faust's death, which took place about 1539–1540, that bizarre stories about his feats began to appear in print."[18] The legendary Faust takes shape, then, in the unreconstructable space between oral lore and print culture. Several of these new tales involve posthumously published recollections of Phillip Melanchthon. In lectures delivered between 1549 and 1560, Melanchthon tells one story of Faust in Venice trying to fly like the earlier Simon Magus had (and like his predecessor failing), and, more strangely, this tale: "The devil is a marvellous craftsman, for he is able by some device to accomplish things which are natural but which we do not understand.... Faust, the magician, devoured at Vienna another magician who was discovered a few days later in a certain cave."[19] Johannes Manlius's collection of conversations and lecture notes goes further, quoting Melanchthon as saying, "I knew a certain man by the name of Faust," calling him "a vile beast and a sink of many devils," and providing an account of his magical schooling in Cracow, his death, several escapes from authorities, and Faust's claim that his dog was the devil.[20] Assorted chronicles, sermons, and pamphlets of the era expand and elaborate such claims.

The Faust legend becomes codified—although not in any sense finalized—in the *Faustbuch* published (and perhaps written) by Johann Spies in 1587.[21] The relationship between the text and the historic figure is complex. As Karl Wentersdorf notes of the "wild anecdotes incorporated into the Faust-book, some may have had a small basis in fact, some date from before Faust's time; with most, their fictional nature is obvious."[22]

Lyndal Roper demonstrates the *Faustbuch*'s debt to the popular *Teufelsbuch* (literally, devil's book) genre of the era, and in particular shows that a "fantastic version of the flying carpet story" from the tract compilation, *Theatre of Witches* (1586) "was lifted almost verbatim the next year by the author of the Faust book, where it forms part of the fabulous anti–Catholic tour the Devil gives Faust."[23] Roper also points out that several tall tales about devils and magical tricksters from Luther's *Table Talk* are repeated in the *Faustbuch,* ascribed (as they were not by Luther) to Faust.[24] Ioan Couliano notes the *Faustbuch*'s heavy borrowings from earlier accounts of Simon Magus (including, most notably, the materialization of Helen of Troy), as well as from far earlier stories of magicians Cyprian of Antioch and Theophilus of Adana.[25]

The Spies *Faustbuch* opens with a brief biographical account of Faust's life (much augmenting the sources from his own time, and relocating Faust's university and home to Wittenberg, Luther's base of operations), leading to his turn to necromancy. Much of the text recounts discourses between Faust and Mephistopheles about core religious and cosmological questions. These are followed by assorted magic tricks and adventures (including trips to Heaven and Hell, around the world, and to the courts of Constantinople, Rome, and the imperial city of Anhalt). In the final chapters, Faust, nearing the end date for his pact, rues and regrets and warns his students against magic before his death and damnation. The story's close is moralistic (we "should learn to fear God, [and] to flee sorcery, conjuration of spirits, and other works of the devil"[26]), but the excitement of the adventures undercut the moral ending.

The *Faustbuch* was hugely popular; it went through multiple editions in the first year of its publication, with many more versions, variants, and translations in the years following. Eric Bockstael counts 22 reissues of the volume to 1599, as well as English (1592), Dutch (1592), and French (1598) translations, plus a range of sequels (starting with an account of his servant and heir Wagner in 1593).[27] And, as H. G. Haile observes, a "characteristic of the history of the Faust Book since its first printing in 1587 is constant expansion of previous versions through interpolation of factual historical material, Faust legend, older folk tales transferred to the Faust figure, and general enrichment with pansophic material of all sorts."[28] Of particular note, Kuno Fischer observes, is a 1590 expanded version, adding Erfurt stories and a range of new locations for Faust's travels.[29] As the book expanded, it was above all else tales of Faust's tricks and travels, rather than the moral lesson of the conclusion, that tended to accumulate.

The English "translation" of 1592, ascribed to "P. F., *Gent.*," preserves the broad structure of the German original, but adds to it significantly and magnifies the comic content.[30] R. W. Maslan summarizes the changes: "P. F. adds many new details about, among other things, the city of Kraków and the tomb of Virgilius near Naples. Details like these make the central section of his translation read like a supernatural Rough Guide ... and it is in these central sections that the master magician is permitted most unequivocally to assume the status of jestbook hero, punching the pope and stealing his food without a peep of authorial indignation."[31] This spirit, and many of the details, carries over into the first major literary adaptation of the story, Christopher Marlowe's *Doctor Faustus*.[32] Again, the new version entails shifts: new travel locations and different magical stunts, but, more importantly, a more detailed account of the actual conjuration. Indeed, Marlowe's version resulted both in stories of actual demon manifestations on stage when the play was performed and accusations that Marlowe might know more than was proper about magic.[33]

In an interesting twist of the direction of influence, English traveling players brought back to the Continent staged versions of the Faust drama (Marlowe's or any of a number of contemporaneous variations).[34] The touring plays informed the development (although again with variations) of puppet-theater versions popular in Germany through the 18th century.[35] Such puppet plays provided the form of the Faust story Goethe and Lessing encountered.[36]

Lessing never finished his Faust project (a fragment was published in 1759).[37] But Goethe's Romantic *Faust* (part I published in 1808; part II posthumously printed in 1832) fundamentally remade the story. Most significantly, he recast the tone (shifting away from the comic business that dominated from Marlowe, or "P. F.," through the puppet plays); dispensed with much of the Reformation-era religious disputation of the original *Faustbuch*; added a prologue in Heaven that sets up the struggle for Faust's soul as a bet between the Lord and Mephistopheles (with clear parallels to Job); introduced a tragic romance plot (Faust falls in love with Gretchen, kills her brother, and impregnates then abandons her; a maddened Gretchen kills her child and is convicted to die for her crime, but a divine voice announces her forgiveness); and, in Part II (after a series of further adventures), insisted upon Faust's own salvation.[38]

In the 20th century, the Faust tale proved deeply attractive to practitioners of the new popular form of film. Helmut Schanze counts some 50 film versions of the tale, including works by two of the medium's pioneers, Louis Lumiere and Georges Méliès.[39] Tales of magical derring-do had a particular enchantment to the magic makers of the new medium, who could better the effects of staged/puppet versions with stop-action vanishings and materializations, image colorizing, and the play of light and shadow. But the philosophical depth and religious significance of the earlier Fausts tended to get lost in the effects.

The Cultural Context of the Book: Renaissance, Reformation, and Popular Culture

Sarah Wall-Randell writes that John Foxe, giving an account of the printing press, that "'divine and miraculous' gift of God to the Protestant cause," credited it in his first edition (1563) to "Jhon Guttenbergh in Strawsborow," but in his revision of 1570 changed the story: "he reassigns the credit for inventing the printing press to 'a Germaine ... named Joan. Faustus, a goldesmith." She goes on to aver: "the connection between Faustus the inventor and associate of Gutenberg and Faustus the spectacularly damned sorcerer appears persistently throughout the early history of the technology of printing. The inseparable entwining of the two legends necessarily highlights ... a diabolical dimension to the experience of reading and the form of the book."[40] Book historian Elizabeth Eisenstein labels "unfounded" this "legend that linked the figure of John Fust and Dr. Faustus," but concedes at the same time: "The now discredited, long-lived legend linking Gutenberg's partner Johann Fust with the historical prototype for Dr. Faustus ... suggests the new status-role achieved by the Renaissance magus. Printing itself was originally regarded as a 'magical' invention."[41] Foxe and his contemporaries, however, would not have the benefit of Eisenstein's scholarship; for them, there was something inextricably magic, and implicitly dark, in the new invention of print. In that early-modern era, the press provided an impetus for fundamental transformation—for the spread of Renaissance humanism northward; for the progress of the Reformation movement; for a new vital form of popular culture (especially in the illustrated *Flugblätter*, or broadsheets,[42] that proliferated in the period)—but at the same time it opened up more arcane and heterodox possibilities, which lead repeatedly back to the figure of Faust.

The Renaissance picture is complex, given the dependence of early humanist thought on scribal copying and an attendant resistance to print (especially in the Renaissance's home territory of Italy). As Elizabeth Eisenstein observes: "Some puzzling featured associated with this revival [of classical learning] can be explained by recognizing that it was initiated in the age of scribes and perpetuated in the age of printers.... It encompasses two distinctly different cultures which were shaped by two distinctly different communications systems."[43] Murnau's *Faust* actually includes a nod to this complexity: many of the scholar's tomes are clearly print products (including, it would appear, his Bible), although at least one, the magic book, is a scribal text. But, in the long run, print's supplanting of the scribal text secures the advance and spread of Renaissance humanism, if also transforming its character in the process. As Eisenstein observes: "these limits [of scribal-text humanism] were transcended in a manner that reoriented the Italian movement and ... reflected the impact of print.... Humanism not only crossed the Alps but it also expanded to encompass the very occupational groups who had been the special enemies of early humanism," especially in northern universities.[44] The character of print also contributed to what Eisenstein calls the "permanent renaissance,"[45] predicated on the continuous availability of published classical texts.

But the proliferation of print also secured new territory for that more heterodox figure, the Renaissance magus: that learned humanist who, exploring the less familiar terrains of ancient lore, encountered their magic and arcane lore. This is the territory of Renaissance figures like Marcilio Ficino, Giovanni Pico della Mirandola, and Giordano Bruno (and Bruno's fate, executed for heresy, suggests the dangers of the terrain).[46] Print culture contributed to the spread of this range of knowledge as well. Eisenstein observes, "The sort of book learning that was cultivated by Doctor Faustus was correctly perceived as endangering orthodoxy."[47] Frank Baron points out that the University of Heidelberg, at the time the historical Faust was studying there, was a hotbed of activity around Renaissance arcana: "the entire humanistic school was very much under the influence of the neoplatonic and hermetic writings of Ficino and Pico in Florence. The revival of Hermes Trismegistus made magic respectable in the scholarly world."[48] The *Faustbuch* directly links Faust's magic to his more arcane classical studies: he "dealt in Chaldean, Persian, Arabic and Greek words, *figurae, characteres, coniurationes,* [and] *incantationes*."[49] Faust's position as Renaissance magus is instrumental in his devilish pact.

The place of print in the development of the Reformation is far clearer, although it also entails a significant problem when it comes to control of the new medium. As François Gilmont observes: "Already in the sixteenth century, certain participants in the Reformation movement were keenly aware of the fundamental role of printing in the spread of Reformation ideas. Following in their footsteps, historians have repeated from generation to generation that the Reformation was Gutenberg's child."[50] Critical to the role of the press is the differential spread of print technology. As Andrew Pettegree and Matthew Hall demonstrate, Reformation Germany had a far more fully installed but also more widely distributed print culture (with print centers even in smaller towns in the German states). The key features Pettegree and Hall argue had been achieved by the 1520s in Germany include "evangelical dominance of print"; "rapid spread of print to multiple printing centres; popular texts spread by local reprints"; "difficulty of control assisting spread of dissident ideas"; "victory of vernacular over Latin"; and the "importance of illustration in spreading message to the non-literate."[51] Crucially, this cuts two ways: both in favor of Reformation ideas, and in the direction of difficult-to-control dissidence even in the wake of the Reformation.

On the one hand, the Reformation's dependence on print for its success is clear. In Andrew Pettegree's recent study, the alliance between Luther and artist/printer Lucas Cranach, together creating a distinctive new print form, consolidates a "Brand Luther" that secures the dominance of his work in the print field. The key innovation was Cranach's "radically new solution" to the problem of creating an attractive title page: "a title-page frame, not made up of separate panels but a single woodcut.... It was a masterpiece of design innovation" and "a major and decisive breakthrough in the history of the book."[52] The new book form consolidated the popularity of Luther's text and Wittenberg's centrality to the German states' burgeoning print culture.

But, on the other hand, the new print media was deeply resistant to control, even by Lutheran reformers. Gerald Strauss, in *Luther's House of Learning*, maps out in detail the Lutheran campaign to regiment early-modern German society through pages and pages of print. As the reformers saw it, Strauss writes: "Religious and moral instruction was a necessary stage in the sanctification of the Christian individual and a precondition of reform in society. The religious and social agitation of the 1520s [especially the "Peasant" Rebellion of 1525] made it a matter of urgency to begin such a program of instruction as soon as possible."[53] Thus Lutheran print centers produced primers for schools, catechisms

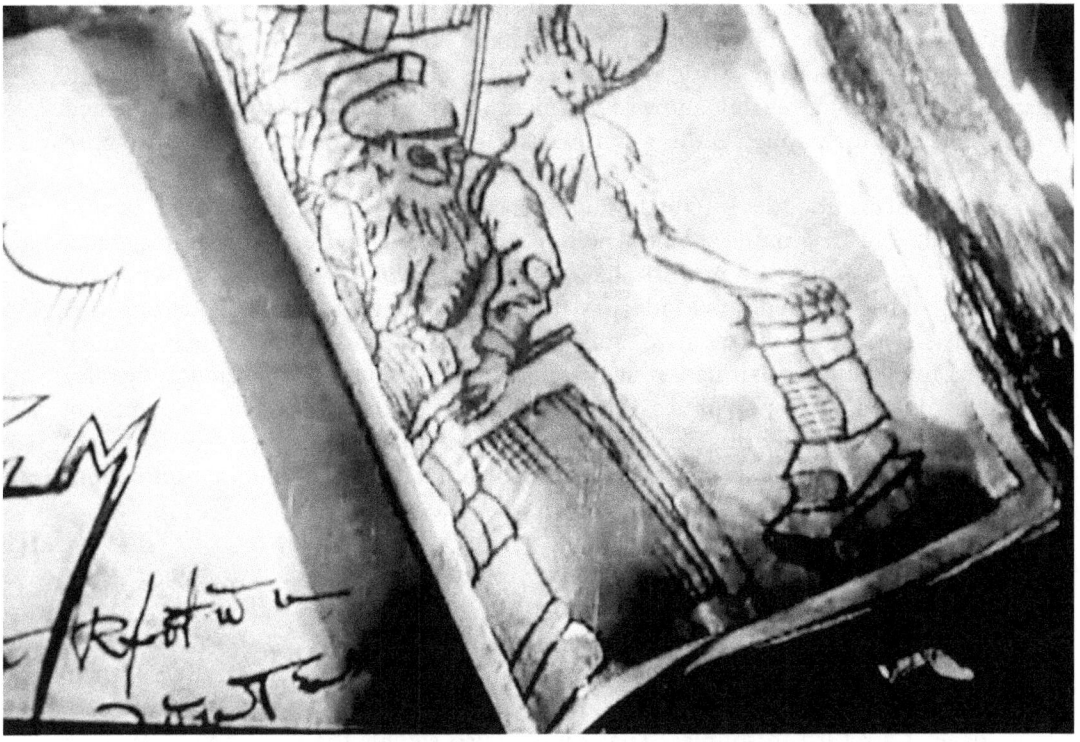

An image of piled books in *Faust: A German Folktale* (1926).

for churches, *Hausvater* literature to guide household management, and massive quantities of sermons and tracts to outline points of doctrine. When, late in the 16th century, visitations to parishes were conducted to assess the results, the outcome was dismal. Lutheran churchmen "fulminated against … 'unchristian, pagan, idolatrous, frivolous, fictitious and unfounded, lying, deceiving, seductive, ungodly, devilish' cult…. They also instructed visitors to probe in every parish for soothsayers, cunning women, crystal gazers, casters of spells, witches, and other practitioners of forbidden arts. Yearly interrogations turned up massive evidence of a proliferating undergrowth of magic practices flourishing amid the doctrines and ceremonies of official Christianity."[54] For those conducting visitations, as for Strauss, the magic was evidence of the failure to suppress pre-existing popular belief systems. But print plays a role here, too: if, as Roper notes, Faust's books are a temptation toward unorthodoxy, then it also true that the *Faustbuch*, especially as it expands to incorporate new tales of magic tricks, can be such a temptation as well.

So, on the one hand, the orthodox intention of the *Faustbuch* is abundantly evident, its Protestant credentials clear. Strauss notes of its publisher: "In the early 1580s Spies belonged to the orthodox wing of German Lutheranism…. Spies supported the conservative position by publishing … works by leading theologians and controversialists, also sermons, jurisprudence, and official documents."[55] Spies followed this with the *Faustbuch,* which argued (especially in the disputations) clearly orthodox Lutheran positions, while also insistently damning Faust for his magical practices.[56] The relocation of Faust's home to Wittenberg placed him at the Reformation's center, while his travels (to Rome and Anhalt) allow critique and comedy at the expense of the Reformation's Catholic foes. But Strauss also concedes, of the book's "censorious titillation," that "the book probably worked against itself. Emphatic as it is in its declarations of disapproval, these condemnations are embroidered with such rich anecdotal detail that what remains in the memory is an entertaining story, not a grave and salutary caution."[57] As the book expanded to include more tales, and was reprinted with variations, and was transformed for the stage and for puppetry, the way it works against itself doubtless became more pronounced.

In that process, too, the interaction between the Faust legend and popular culture becomes clear. The original *Faustbuch* interlarded historical sources with oral legends, local gossip, and tales from other works like whatever *Teufelbuch* was handy. This process was ongoing: subsequent editions and translations add more tales, stage adaptations shift the emphasis away from the didactic and toward the spectacular, puppet plays reduce the lessons to a minimal damnation at the close. In this sense, the *Faustbuch* typifies print's dynamic place in a refigured popular culture more broadly. *Flugblätter*, regularly adapting (albeit in cruder forms) the woodcut-text combinations pioneered by Cranach, focus on the excessive and strange: monstrosities and atrocities dominate production. And within that range, witchcraft pamphlets have pride of place.

The Vanishing Book

From this body of Faust materials, Murnau and Kyser sample eclectically.[58] If their main title seemed to promise an adaptation of Goethe, the subtitle—"A German Folktale"—suggests a return to sources. That subtitle also signals the film's temporal shift: relocating the material to the medieval era (even if, in the matter of books, that introduces an anachronism). Klaus Kleimeier argues that the medievalism is consistent with a broader, studio-wide Ufa dynamic, also evident, for example, in Fritz Lang's *Niebelungen*, which he sees as an escapist reaction to Weimar's insecure modernity.[59] The medieval setting also provides firm ground for the plague motif; in Murnau's version, Mephisto's first action after making his bargain is to bring pestilence to the city, and it is Faust's disenchantment with his inability to use his knowledge to provide cures for the dying that leads him first to reject his books and then to use the spell to materialize his demon.[60]

Faust tutoring his students in *Faust: A German Folktale* (1926).

From Goethe, Murnau lifts both the prologue that sets forth the bargain (in Murnau's version, between Mephisto and an Archangel) and the Gretchen subplot, although with differences in treatment; indeed, Murnau shifts attention away from Faust entirely in his film's second half to focus on Gretchen's plight, alone in the winter night with her newborn bastard child (with heavy no-room-at-the-inn nativity echoes absent in Goethe's version).[61] From Goethe, too, Murnau takes (although again with variation) Faust's salvation. In the film, the magician, old again, dies with Gretchen at the stake, and is declared saved in an epilogue that echoes the opening archangelic encounter; love is his salvation, a far simpler resolution than Goethe offered. Faust's ride on Mephisto's cloak is straight from the *Faustbuch,* although Murnau jettisons the text's specific destinations. The Parma locale where Murnau ends that journey comes from the puppet plays.[62]

Murnau emphatically, in the early part of the film, underlines Faust's association with books. In the first view we have of him, he holds an open volume as he lectures to his students. His study is crammed with books: on every surface, against every wall, piles and piles of massive tomes. But he also turns away from them: when he cannot cure the plague for all his book-learning, he casts armfuls of books into his hearthfire. He hesitates over the Bible, but then tosses it into the flames.[63] As the fire consumes most of the books, one resists the flames: the magic book Murnau hauls to the crossroads for his act of conjuration.

Beyond books, however, Murnau makes a broad range of allusions to the other visual arts, and especially the rich print culture that was also part of the Gutenberg revolution. The film's opening image—of skeletal horsemen riding through the night—recalls both Albrecht Dürer's apocalyptic horsemen and the medievally rooted Dance of Death motif (later reworked as a popular print series by Hans Holbein). Eric Rohmer identifies a range of echoes of artworks, including Rembrandt's *Faust* drawing,[64] Dürer's *St. Jerome*, and Vermeer's *Women with a Pearl Necklace.*[65] Robert Herlth says of the landscapes he helped design for the cape-riding flight that they derived from Albrecht Altdorfer.[66] Faust brooding in the mountains alludes to Caspar David Friedrich's Romantic landscapes.[67] Gretchen, in her wintery plight, suggests quattrocento Madonnas (a fitting allusion, given the Nativity echoes of the sequence).[68] Schanze notes a range of visual references: "Murnau uses the Faust iconography as created by Delacroix, Kaulbach, Cornelius, Retzsch, and von Kreling in the nineteenth century. And he uses Cranach, Altdorfer, and Baldung to establish a sixteenth-century environment."[69] The visual cues thus point to both the era of Faust's inception and the Romantic period in which Goethe reimagined the tale.

Meanwhile, Murnau also provides a knowing nod to the other forms of popular culture in which Faust's image was developed. On the stage that stands in the town square, costumed actors entertain the crowds. Shadow-puppet plays are cast on hanging sheets. Books and print culture, however, are far more emphasized.

But recall that book, its pages flapping as Faust's flight takes off. It is the last book we see in the film. Once Faust has made his pact with Mephisto, books are banished from the film's frame. We never return to Faust's study (even though he does return to the town). There is no book in his hands as he broods on the mountaintop.

The absence of books makes sense, in terms of the film's basic plot: books had failed Faust, so he turned to magic (even if it took one last book to pull that off); Mephisto had mocked his wasted, bookish life, promising pure pleasure as an alternative. But Murnau also alludes here to the fundamental shift that his own medium presents. For Rohmer, although Murnau's film is rife with allusions to that past print culture, it is "in the representation of motion, rather than immobility that he is able to achieve pictorial beauty."[70] From the magic of the flight through space and time to the miracles of instant materialization and dematerialization that provide Mephisto with the tricks of his trade, film magic in Murnau supplants stage effects or print's promise.

Walter Benjamin, in his influential essay "The Work of Art in the Age of Technological Reproducibility," argues the "aura" associated with the individual work of art had become irrelevant in the modern age as art becomes increasingly reproducible. He tracks the development forward from the innovation of print: "Graphic art was first made technologically reproducible by the woodcut." This was followed by "The enormous changes brought about in literature by movable type, the technological reproducibility of writing." This in turn "was supplemented by engraving and etching, and at the beginning of the nineteenth century by lithography." And after that, "but only a few decades after the invention of lithography, graphic art was surpassed by photography." Photography led to film. He concludes: "Around 1900, technological reproduction not only had reached a standard to permit to reproduce all known works of art … but it also had captured a place of its own among the artistic processes."[71] For Benjamin, the destruction of the aura had revolutionary potential: "the greatly increased mass of participants has produced a different kind of participation."[72] The destruction of the aura unleashed a democratization of the arts. And for him, the new mass art of film perfectly realized this potential. Murnau reenacts in *Faust* precisely this process: enshrining in his range of references the previous cultural modes of print culture, while giving it all a new form, that "cinematic space" Rohmer credits to Murnau. When Mephisto can magically materialize the emperor's crown in his hand, whatever aura that original object had has been lost, but the spectacle of cinematic magic does much the same work that aura once did.

Faustian Bargains

Faust was Murnau's last German film. He left for Hollywood the same year, where he would make his last four movies. In 1931, just a week before his final film, *Tabu*, premiered, he would die in a car crash on the Pacific Coast Highway, under mysterious circumstances.[73]

Two years later, the German people would make their own Faustian bargain. Books would burn. Evil would take control of the German soul.

Notes

1. Hans Kyser's scenario for the scene is quoted in full in Matt Erlin, "Tradition as Intellectual Montage: F. W. Murnau's *Faust* (1926)," 226; my translation. The sequence required innovative filming techniques, described in detail by set designer Robert Herlth: "We designed a trolley with a very low platform and heavy solid wheels" for the camera. "And so we were able to shoot the flight through the air. We did so in a shed 35 metres long and 20 wide…. The landscape—plains, rivers, waterfalls, forests, mountains, and cities—was a relief model, with working miniatures of birds and animals of all kinds." Lotte H. Eisner, *Murnau*, 68.

2. Suzanne Cowan, "Faust in Film: A Modern Medium for a Traditional Legend," 486.

3. Eisner, *Murnau*, 165. See also Lotte Eisner, *The Haunted Screen: Expressionism in the German Cinema and the Influence of Max Reinhardt*, 291.

4. Roger Ebert, "*Faust*" (2005).

5. Philip Kemp, "New Releases: *Faust*" (2012), 112.

6. David Sterritt, "*Faust*: A German Folktale," 62.

7. Eric Rohmer, "L'organisation de l'espace dans le Faust de Murnau" (1972), quoted in Erlin, "Tradition as Intellectual Montage," 155; Erlin's translation.

8. Rohmer quoted in Helmut Schanze, "On Murnau's *Faust*: A Generic Gesamtwerk?" 230. Murnau quoted in Eisner, *Murnau*, 84.

9. Siegfried Kracauer, *From Caligari to Hitler: A Psychological Study of the German Film*, 148. Kracauer goes on to grumble: "But neither the roller coaster nor Gerhart Hauptmann could compensate for the futility of a film which misrepresented, if not ignored, all the significant motifs inherent in the subject matter" (*ibid.*). Hauptmann, however, although initially drafted to do titles for the movie, did not contribute to the final product; the film's titles are Kyser's. On the failed collaboration with Hauptmann, see Klaus Kreimeier, *The Ufa Story: A History of Germany's Greatest Film Company 1918-1945*, 137. Given the Reformation ground of *Faust*, it is interesting to note that Kyser later directed his own biopic of the Reformation leader, *Luther* (1927). See Eisner, *Haunted Screen*, 327.

10. John Flood, "The Book in Reformation Germany," 25.

11. Jean-François Gilmont, "Introduction," 2.

12. Gerald Strauss, "How to Read a *Volksbuch*: The *Faust Book* of 1587," 27.

13. *Ibid.*, 27–29, reading these as an "effort on the part of Europe's ruling groups to undermine, and ultimately to replace, the expressions of popular culture" (29).

14. On the variable names, see Frank Baron, *Doctor Faustus from History to Legend* 11–16; Karl P. Wentersdort, "Some Observations on the Historical Faust," 203–04.

15. This might seem a version of "one of these words is not like the others," but Ioan P. Couliano insists on the consistency of the labels within the early modern framework; "Dr. Faust, Great Sodomite and Necromancer," esp. 272–74.

16. The clearest chronology of Faust's life is provided by E. A. Bucchianeri, *Faust: My Soul Be Damned for the World*, I: 100–103; Baron settles on a similar date for Faust's death in *Doctor Faustus*, 67–69. Bucchianeri provides 28 texts, the last from 1617, in his Appendix I (although some are summarized rather than fully translated). Twenty documents are translated by Eric Bockstael (in a selection described as a "free translation and adaptation of A. Dabexies, *Le Myth de Faust* [1972]"), *Lives of Doctor Faust*, ch. 2; twenty as well by Paul A. Bates, *Faust: Sources, Works, Criticism*, ch. 1.

17. Martin Luther, *Table Talk*, quoted in Bucchianeri, *Faust*, 399.

18. Wentersdorf, "Some Observations," 203.

19. Christopher Pezelius, comp., *Explicationes Melanthoniae* (1594), in Bockstael, *Lives*, 43.

20. Johannes Malius, *Locorum Communium Collectanea* (1563), in Bockstael, *Lives*, 45.

21. The work's full title is *Historia and Tale of Doctor Johannes Faustus the Sorcerer: wherein is described specifically and veraciously: His entire life and death, how he did oblige himself for a certain time unto the Devil, and what happened to him, and how he at last got his well-deserved reward*, so we will continue to call it *Faustbuch*. Debate has long raged over the possible existence of an earlier (c. 1580) Latin compilation of Faust tales. H. G. Haile, for example, seeks to reconstruct a Latin original working backward from the disputations in various, and varied, editions in "Reconstruction of the Faust Book: The Disputations."

22. Wentersdorf, "Some Observations," 206.

23. Lyndal Roper, "Witchcraft and the Western Imagination," 130.

24. Lyndal Roper, "Martin Luther's Body: The 'Stout Doctor' and His Biographers," 369–70.

25. Couliano, "Dr. Faust, Great Sodomite and Necromancer," 274–76.

26. *Faustbuch*, ch. 44.

27. Bockstael, *Lives of Faust*, 236.

28. Haile, "Reconstruction of the Faust Book," 176–77.

29. Kuno Fischer, *Goethe's Faust*, 98, 126–27.

70   Books of Hope and Despair

30. The English *Historie of the damnable life, and deserved death of Doctor John Faustus* (1592) is reprinted in full in Bockstael, *Lives of Faust*, ch. 3, and in Bates, *Faust*, 9–44 (there somewhat misleadingly titled "Johann Spies, *Faustbuch*").

31. R. W. Maslen, "Magical Journeys in Sixteenth-Century Prose Fiction," 44.

32. There are some dating problems here. The scholarly consensus argues for the play's composition around 1588–1589, before the English *Faustbook* was in print (although earlier, non-extant versions might have circulated in manuscript; the German version was out already, but there is no evidence Marlowe could have read it, although he could managed a Latin urtext, if it actually existed). Some of the details in the English version, however, seem clear sources for Marlowe (like the manifestation of Helen and the clowning at the papal court). The play was likely first staged around 1592. The issue of Marlowe's play is further complicated by two very different printed texts (1604 and 1616, the latter significantly longer). For a discussion of the issues, see Charles Nicholl, "'Faustus' and the Politics of Magic" and Richard Hillman, "Marlowe's *Doctor Faustus* and the French Translation of the *Faustbuch*" (Hillman proposes, as his title suggests, an entirely different core source for Marlowe).

33. Nichols, "'Faustus' and the Politics of Magic," 18; David Hawkes, *The Faust Myth: Religion and the Rise of Representation*, 54–57.

34. Bockstael, *Lives of Doctor Faust*, 236–37; Fischer, *Goethe's "Faust,"* 172, 177.

35. Fischer, *Goethe's "Faust,"* 183–99; Bockstael, *Lives of Doctor Faust*, ch. 6 (including a full text of an 1850 version of the puppet play).

36. On the influence of the puppet plays on Goethe, see Fischer, *Goethe's "Faust,"* 185; Jane K. Brown, *Goethe's Faust: The German Tragedy*, 71; Eudo Colecestra Mason, *Goethe's Faust: Its Genesis and Purport*, 4.

37. For details on Lessing's project and his relationship with Goethe, see Fischer, *Goethe's Faust*, ch. 10.

38. Johann Wolfgang von Goethe, *Faust*.

39. Schanze, "On Murnau's *Faust*," 224. The repository for all cultural knowledge, YouTube, includes both Lumiere's *L'Apparation de Méphistophélès* (1897) and Méliès *La Damnation de Faust* (1898). Inez Hedges claims that Méliès worked on several versions of the Faust story between 1897 and 1904 (*Framing Faust: Twentieth-Century Cultural Struggles*, 16–18), although his films were also sometimes simply retitled for international distribution.

40. Sarah Wall-Randall, "*Doctor Faustus* and the Printer's Devil," 259, 260.

41. Elizabeth L. Eisenstein, *The Printing Press as Agent of Change: Communications and Cultural Transformations in Early-Modern Europe*, I: 50, 277 n.340.

42. We lose something of the contempt for the form by not translating literally: "fly paper." See F. J. Stopp, "The Early German Broadsheet and Related Ephemera: A Bibliographical Survey."

43. Elizabeth L. Eisenstein, "The Advent of Printing and the Problem of the Renaissance," 76.

44. Eisenstein, *Printing Press*, 176.

45. *Ibid.*, 181.

46. See Frank L. Borchardt, "The Magus as Renaissance Man." Borchardt notes that Renaissance magi regularly expressed disenchantment with the limited fruits of their arcane labors, a trope that resonates strongly with Faustian themes.

47. Eisenstein, *Printing Press*, 438. The same print circulation that spread the lore of the magus also spread fear of it, above all else in witchcraft tracts: "The spread of print ... accounts for ... 'the new epidemic of witchcraft and the authority ... given ... to suppress it.'" *Ibid.*, 436; final two ellipses Eisenstein's. Both witches and their persecutors thus depended on print.

48. Baron, *Doctor Faustus*, 20.

49. *Faustbuch*, ch. 1; the shift to Latin suggests the danger in even the words. Similar language recurs in the English version; see Bockstael, *Lives of Doctor Faust*, 64. Marlowe, Sarah Wall-Randell argues, takes this further: "Faustus moves rapidly through a series of books, mentioning authors and specific titles, and quoting freely from each" in what amounts to "a plausible inventory of what have been on a university scholar's desk in 1592." "'Doctor Faustus' and the Printer's Devil," 265.

50. Gilmont, "Introduction," 1. The clearly implied "however" to this is the recognition of the dangers of print by those same 16th-century printers. See, for an interesting account of the deep penetration of print culture even into artisan homes (and note the regular presence in such homes not just of Bibles and sermons, but of a *Teufelsbuch* or two), Michael Hackenberg, "Books in Artisan Homes of Sixteenth-Century Germany."

51. Andrew Pettegree and Matthew Hall, "The Reformation and the Book: A Reconsideration," 789.

52. Andrew Pettegree, *Brand Luther: 1517, Printing, and the Making of the Reformation*, 158, and, generally, ch. 6.

53. Strauss, *Luther's House of Learning*, 135.

54. *Ibid.*, 303, and for details of the visitations and their results, chs. 12–13.

55. Strauss, "How to Read a *Volksbuch*," 32.

56. *Ibid.*, 33–36. See also Clifford Davidson, "Doctor Faustus of Wittenberg."

57. Strauss, "How to Read a *Volksbuch*," 36.

58. Eisner notes Murnau's heavy revisions of Kyser's treatment. With a few exceptions, however (like the elimination of a *Walpurgisnacht* scene), Murnau does not change basic content. See Eisner, *Murnau*, 53–58.

59. Kreimeier, *The Ufa Story*, 108–09.
60. The plague motif does have a slight sourcing in Goethe. In the early episode "Outside the Gate," Faust laments that neither he nor his also-necromancing father could develop a cure for the plague: "Patients died.... I myself gave the poison to thousands/who withered away." Goethe, *Faust*, 42. Faust's disenchantment with the arts of the magus, as noted, reflects a typical Renaissance theme.
61. Much of the critical response to the film decried this shift in focus to Gretchen, and critiqued the film's second half as melodramatic. See Hedges, *Framing Faust*, 34–35; Kracauer, *From Caligari to Hitler*, 148–49; Erlin, "Tradition as Intellectual Montage," 156.
62. On the puppet plays as source for the Parma locale, see Fischer, *Goethe's Faust*, 195–196; Mason, *Goethe's Faust*, 4. Schanze also notes the influence on Kyser and Murnau of Ludwig Berger's *Das verlorene Paradies* (*Paradise Lost*), presumably an earlier film treatment; see "On Murnau's *Faust*," 224.
63. Modern viewers will leap from this scene to Nazi book burnings, but those were still several years in the future when Murnau's film was released, commencing in 1933.
64. Whether that unlabeled drawing is really Faust at all is another question; for extended discussion, see H. Van De Waal and J. Seeger, "Rembrandt's Faust Etching, a Socinian document, and the Iconography of the Inspired Scholar."
65. All listed in Inez Hedges, *Framing Faust: Twentieth-Century Struggles*, 34.
66. Eisner, *Murnau*, 69.
67. Hedges thinks so too: *Framing Faust*, 27.
68. *Ibid.*, 38. The Madonna image also refers back to the statue of the Virgin—presumably polychrome wood, that typically German form—enshrined in a niche in Gretchen's home.
69. Schanze, "On Murnau's *Faust*," 228.
70. Quoted in *Ibid.*, 35.
71. Walter Benjamin, "The Work of Art in the Age of Technological Reproducibility (Third Version)," 253. Italics of the original removed.
72. *Ibid.*, 267. Italics of the original removed.
73. On the murky details of Murnau's death, see Eisner, *Murnau*, 221–24.

Bibliography

Allen, Marguerite de Huszar. "The Reception of the *Historia von D. Johann Fausten*." *German Quarterly* 59, no. 4 (Autumn 1986): 582–94.
Baron, Frank. *Doctor Faustus from History to Legend*. Munich: Humanistische Bibliothek, 1978.
Bates, Paul A., ed. *Faust: Sources, Works, Criticism*. New York: Harcourt, Brace & World, 1969.
Benjamin, Walter. "The Work of Art in the Age of Technological Reproducibility (Third Version)" (1939). In *Selected Writings, Volume 4 1938–1940*, edited by Howard Eiland and Michael W. Jennings, translated by Edmund Jephcott et al., 251–83. Cambridge: Harvard University Press, 2003.
Bockstael, Eric, ed. *The Lives of Doctor Faust*. Detroit: University Studies and Weekend College of Lifelong Learning, Wayne State College, 1976.
Borchartdt, Frank L. "The Magus as Renaissance Man." *Sixteenth Century Journal* 21, no. 1 (Spring 1990): 57–76.
Brown, Jane K. *Goethe's Faust: The German Tragedy*. Ithaca: Cornell University Press, 1987.
Buccianeri, E. A. *Faust: My Soul Be Damned for the World*. 2 vols. Lavergne, TN: Batalha Publishers, 2010.
Couliano, Ioan P. "Dr. Faust, Great Sodomite and Necromancer." *Revue de l'histoire des religions* 207, no. 3 (July–September 1990): 261–88.
Cowan, Suzanne. "Faust in Film: A Modern Medium for a Traditional Legend." In *The Lives of Doctor Faust*, edited by Eric Bockstael, 467–77. Detroit: University Studies and Weekend College of Lifelong Learning, Wayne State College, 1976 Lives of Doctor Faust.
Davidson, Clifford. "Doctor Faustus of Wittenberg." *Studies of Philology* 59, no. 3 (July 1962): 514–23.
Ebert, Roger. "Faust." *Chicago Sun-Times*, 8 May 2005, at http://www.rogerebert.com /reviews/great-movie-faust-1926.
Eisenstein, Elizabeth L. "The Advent of Printing and the Problem of the Renaissance." *Past & Present* 45 (November 1969): 19–89.
_____. *The Printing Press as an Agent of Change: Communications and Cultural Transformations in Early-Modern Europe*. 2 vols. Cambridge: Cambridge University Press, 2009.
Eisner, Lotte. *The Haunted Screen: Expressionism in the German Cinema and the Influence of Max Reinhardt*. Berkeley: University of California Press, 1969.
_____. *Murnau*. Berkeley: University of California Press, 1973.
Erlin, Matt. "Tradition as Intellectual Montage: F. W. Murnau's *Faust* (1926)." In Noah William Isenberg, ed., *Weimar Cinema: An Essential Guide to Films of the Era*, 155–72. New York: Columbia University Pres, 2009.
Faust. Directed by F. W. Murnau. 1926. Restored version, Kino Lorber, 2009. DVD
Fischer, Kuno. *Goethe's "Faust."* 2 vols., 3d ed. Manchester, IA: H. R. Wolcott, 1895.
Flood, John. "The Book in Reformation Germany." In *The Reformation and the Book*, edited by Jean-François Gilmont, 21–104. 1990. New York: Routledge, 2016.

72 Books of Hope and Despair

Gilmont, Jean-François. "Introduction." In *The Reformation and the Book*, edited by Jean-François Gilmon, 1–9. 1990. New York: Routledge, 2016.

Goethe, Johann Wolfgang von. *Faust: Part One and Part Two*. Edited and translated by Carl R. Mueller. Hanover, NH: Smith and Kraus, 2004.

Hackenberg, Michael. "Books in Artisan Homes in Sixteenth-Century Germany." *Journal of Library History* 21, no. 1 (Winter 1986): 72–91.

Haile, H. G. "Reconstruction of the Faust Book: The Disputations." *PMLA* 78, no. 3 (June 1963): 175–89.

Hawkes, David. *The Faust Myth: Religion and the Rise of Representation*. Basingstoke: Palgrave Macmillan, 2007.

Hedges, Inez. *Framing Faust: Twentieth-Century Cultural Struggles*. Carbondale: Southern Illinois University Press, 2009.

Hillman, Richard. "Marlowe's *Doctor Faustus* and the French Translation of the *Faustbuch*." *Modern Language Review* 112, no. 1 (January 2017): 20–34.

Historia and Tale of Doctor Johannes Faustus the Sorcerer: wherein is described specifically and veraciously: His entire life and death, how he did oblige himself for a certain time unto the Devil, and what happened to him, and how he at last got his well-deserved reward. 1587. In both modern English and German translation by J. W. Worthy at http://lettersfromthedustbowl.com/faustus.html.

Kemp, Philip. "New Releases: FAUST." *Sight & Sound* 24, no. 9 (September 2014): 112.

Kracauer, Siegfried. *From Caligari to Hitler: A Psychological Study of the German Film*. 1947. New York: Noonday Press, 1959.

Kreimeier, Klaus. *The Ufa Story: A History of Germany's Greatest Film Company 1918–1945*. New York: Hill and Wang, 1886.

Maslen, R. W. "Magical Journeys in Sixteenth-Century Prose Fiction." *Yearbook of English Studies* 41, no. 1 (2011): 35–50.

Marlowe, Christopher. *The Tragical History of Doctor Faustus*. Edited by Frederick S. Boas. London: Gordian Press, 1966.

Mason, Eudo Colecestra. *Goethe's Faust: Its Genesis and Purport*. Berkeley: University of California Press, 1967.

Nicholl, Charles. "'Faustus' and the Politics of Magic." *London Review of Books* 12, no. 5 (8 March 1990): 18–19.

Pettegree, Andrew. *Brand Luther: 1517, Printing, and the Making of the Reformation*. New York: Penguin, 2016.

Pettegree, Andrew, and Matthew Hall. "The Reformation and the Book: A Reconsideration." *Historical Journal* 47, no. 4 (December 2004): 785–808.

Roper, Lyndal. "Martin Luther's Body: The 'Stout Doctor' and His biographers." *American Historical Review* 115 no. 2 (April 2010): 351–384.

Roper, Lyndal. "Witchcraft and the Western Imagination." *Transactions of the Royal Historical Society*, 6th Series 16 (2006): 117–141.

Schanze, Helmut. "On Murnau's *Faust*: A Generic Gesamtwerk?" In *Expressionist Film: New Perspective*, edited by Dietrich Scheunemann, 223–236. Rochester: Camden House, 2003.

Sterritt, David. "*Faust: A German Folktale*." *Cineaste* 41, no. 2 (Spring 2016): 62–64.

Stopp, F. J. "The Early German Broadsheet and Related Ephemera: A Bibliographical Survey." *Transactions of the Cambridge Bibliographical Society* 5, no. 2 (1970): 81–89.

Strauss, Gerald. "How to Read a *Volksbuch*: The *Faust Book* of 1587," chapter 13 (original pagination of the reprinted article maintained in the book 27–39). In *Enacting the Reformation in Germany: Essays on Institution and Reception*. Brookfield, VT: Ashgate Press, 1993.

———. *Luther's House of Learning: Indoctrination of the Young in the German Reformation*. Baltimore: John Hopkins University Press, 1978.

Van De Waal, H. and J. Seeger. "Rembrandt's Faust Etching, a Socinian Document, and the Iconography of the Inspired Scholar." *Oud Holland* 79, no. 1 (1964), 6–35, 37–48.

Wall-Randell, Sarah. "*Doctor Faustus* and the Printer's Devil." *Studies in English Literature, 1500–1900* 48, no. 2 (Spring 2008): 259–81.

Wentersdorf, Karl P. "Some Observations on the Historical Faust." *Folklore* 89, no. 2 (1978): 201–23.

Apocryphal Horror

Understanding Evil Through Lost Books of the Bible

JEFFREY M. TRIPP

About a decade and a half ago, Mary Ann Beavis called attention to the use of the Bible in horror movies. Toward the end of her article, she notes the invention of "pseudapocrypha": "scriptures that are not only non-canonical but non-existent."[1] Beavis briefly examines the *Book of the Sins of Women* in *Carrie* (1976) and a Book of Hebron in *Omen III: The Final Conflict* (1981)—neither of which exists outside of these films—along with an additional chapter of Revelation in *The Prophecy* (1995) and a non-existent passage from Deuteronomy 17 in *Lost Souls* (2000). Beavis criticizes the lack of biblical literacy assumed (or demonstrated) by the makers of *Lost Souls*, who do not anticipate that anyone will spot a fake passage from Deuteronomy. Yet she observes that "even in a film that shows no real knowledge of the content of the Bible and expects its viewers to be equally uninformed, there is still an appeal to a 'scriptural' basis."[2]

Beavis draws needed attention the use of pseudo-biblical texts in horror cinema, but her treatment is brief and in some cases, lacks nuance. While the films show no knowledge of the content of the Bible, it does not necessarily follow that the filmmakers are similarly ignorant. Instead, the audience's ignorance of the biblical texts—real and imagined—aligns with that of the characters, providing a constructive reason to create fictional apocryphal passages in the Bible. Unlike more obviously fictional texts, like the *Necronomicon*, the Bible has strong cultural, intellectual, and emotional resonances for Western audiences. Its use on screen grounds the narrative in (our) reality and heightens the gravity of the threat. None of these cinematic works may adapt themselves neatly into the apocalyptic scheme of canonical scripture, but they present the characters and circumstances rhetorically within a biblical framework. In addition to their importance as specifically *biblical* artifacts, the content of each alternative Bible plays an important role in driving the plot. This essay, then, will broaden and deepen Beavis' original analysis in order to examine why apocryphal biblical texts have become a recent cinematic trope, beginning with three of the films she examines—*Omen III*, *The Prophecy*, and *Lost Souls*—before adding more recent examples.

Apocryphal Texts in Horror Cinema

The earliest film that Beavis mentions, *Omen III*, follows Damien Thorn, the Antichrist—a child in the first two *Omen* films, now grown to adulthood—as he attempts to bring on the Apocalypse, from which he assumes he will emerge victorious. He cites a passage from the fictitious Book of Hebron predicting that the Lamb of God will appear in "the Angel Isle," leading him to conclude that the Messiah will be born in England. Damien acquires the ambassadorship to Great Britain as part of a plan to prevent the Messiah's birth. The film locates Hebron in "the Septuagint Bible," an actual ancient Greek translation of the Hebrew Scriptures that does contain additional Greek texts—although not Hebron, which Damien cites in Latin.[3] Fortunately for Damien, England (Anglia) was named after the Angles rather than the Saxons or some other group, or else the punning on "angels" would not work.[4]

The Prophecy, by contrast, follows a detective and former seminarian, Thomas Dagget, who discovers an angel is killed in New York. The angel carries a 2nd-century Latin Bible with the augmented version of Revelation. Angels have been fighting a second war in Heaven since Christ's resurrection,[5] and the rebel angels, led by Gabriel, seek an evil human soul to lead them into battle. The predicted soul is hidden by a loyalist angel in the body of a little girl, and the monstrous Gabriel terrorizes her trying to recover it.

The alternate version of Revelation is not the only fictional biblical passage in *The Prophecy*. Earlier, Thomas narrates: "of all the gospels I learned in seminary school, a verse from Saint Paul stands out. It is perhaps the strangest passage in all the Bible, which says, 'Even now in Heaven there were angels carrying savage weapons.'"[6] Of course Paul did not write gospels, and the line does not exist in his letters. Either the canonical Bible of *The Prophecy* differs from ours, or, since Thomas received visions of angels while in seminary, he "learned" the passage not through study but through divine revelation.

Finally, Beavis mentions *Lost Souls*, in which a team of Catholic investigators tracks down the Antichrist, a disinterested atheist whose body is intended to incarnate Satan in imitation of Christ. The fictional passage from Deuteronomy 17 provides one of the criteria by which they identify the Antichrist.

The trend of using pseudo-biblical passages continues in later action-oriented, apocalyptic horror movies and TV shows. The eponymous hero of *Constantine* (2005) is a freelance exorcist trying to earn his way back into Heaven after a failed suicide attempt.[7] In this world, full angels and demons do not have access to Earth, but lower-ranking "half-breeds" do. Mammon, the son of the Devil and a full demon, attempts to gain entry to our realm with the help of Gabriel (once again a rebel angel) using the spear that pierced Jesus on the cross (see John 19:34). When Mammon possesses Angela, a police detective and client of Constantine's, the exorcist must fight through demons to save her and stop Mammon. While he investigates what Mammon is up to, his attention is drawn to an uncharacteristically apocalyptic 17th chapter of (First?) Corinthians; the canonical text has only 16 chapters, but "the Bible in Hell" is longer.[8]

Finally, the horror TV show, *Supernatural* (2005–2017), which features two brothers who hunt monsters and demons, builds to the biblical Apocalypse over the first few seasons. Sensing they are in over their heads, Sam and Dean Winchester consult an augmented version of Revelation, longer than the "widely distributed version just for tourists."[9]

Literalist Readings of the Bible

There is a likely link between the specifically apocalyptic nature of the horrors in these works, and patterns in their use of apocryphal but authoritative biblical texts. The films feature visions, angels and demons operating in Heaven or Hell (actual places, to which characters journey), and an imminent, eschatological catastrophe—frequent features of ancient apocalypses (as a literary genre).[10] Appropriately then, the only literary apocalypse of the Hebrew Bible, Daniel, presents itself as a previously hidden text only discovered in time for the sages to understand the evil currently facing them.[11]

In order to understand the use of hidden, pseudo-biblical texts, it is important to note how they are read and how they function within each story-world. Characters read (pseudo-) Bibles through a notably literalist, even fundamentalist hermeneutic. The Bible in horror cinema, as in literalist Christian circles, is framed as readable, relevant, and above all, right. It is through the Bible that characters come to understand the present evil facing them. Reading the Bible is unambiguously and invariably helpful; failing to read it leads to catastrophe.

Since, from a literalist viewpoint, the Bible was written through direct, divine inspiration, it does not contain mistakes. It is not only infallible (i.e., reliable and true), but factually inerrant. Many literalists stop short of claiming it to be the direct dictation of God's word, and absolute inerrancy may be credited only to the original manuscripts.[12] Practically speaking, though, there is no difference between what God wanted the authors to write, what they wrote, and what has survived in the manuscripts. So, if the Bible contains information about a threat, the information is accurate. If it makes a prediction, that prediction will always come true—eventually.

Literalists appeal to the "plain sense" of the Bible, rejecting the need for critical scholarship or even a critical reading.[13] Making sense to an average modern reader becomes the primary standard of interpretation: The Bible says what it means, and means what it says (to us). Of course, someone has to translate the Bible (from Hebrew, Aramaic, and Greek into English), but this is, in the literalist worldview, a simple matter for linguists who can produce a reliable one-to-one mapping of meaning from one language to another. Literalists do not recognize the ambiguities of translation, much less how translation inherently distorts meaning. Instead, they contend that idioms, euphemisms, or turns of phrase in ancient languages can be easily understood outside of their cultural contexts, even when taken literally.

Devotional readings are self-centered, almost by nature: I want to know what meaning the Bible has for *me*, in *my* life. Critical readings, focused as they are on the meanings the text has for other people in diverse cultural, historical, or religious contexts, are viewed as basically useless in a literalist devotional context. Within literalist circles, the assumption of relevance dominates the interpretation of prophecies unfulfilled already in Christ. Prophetic material, and so also apocalyptic material (the critical distinction between the two genres is ignored), is always predictive regarding *us*.

Christians have, of course, read Daniel and Revelation as predictions of future events for centuries, trying to decipher when they will take place. The End is always near: William Miller convinced thousands in the 1830s to expect Christ's earthly arrival in 1843, while fundamentalist interpreter Hal Lindsey, in *The Late Great Planet Earth* (first published in 1970), gave the world only until 1988.[14] Countless examples of failed Second Comings could be added, but far from cautioning against interpreting biblical apocalypses

76   Books of Hope and Despair

as datable predictions of an impending End, earlier interpretations of this sort are instead easily dismissed. The reasons are simple: they were wrong (and only one interpretation can be right), and they were so because they did not predict the End *now*, at the time of the present reader. A detailed and accurate prediction of the fall of the Ottoman Empire, for example, might be mildly interesting, but its irrelevance to the present concerns of believers makes it unworthy of the full weight of the Bible.

The Literalist "Bible" in Apocalyptic Horror Cinema

All of the pseudo-biblical texts under examination are positioned specifically as ancient predictions of an evil, apocalyptic threat actually facing the world *now*. Thomas, the hero of *The Prophecy*, translates the following from Revelation 23: "And there shall be a dark soul, and this soul will eat other dark souls, and so become their inheritor. This

Above and opposite: Biblical prophesies becoming reality in *Constantine* (2005), featuring Tilda Swinton as the angel Gabriel stabbing Rachel Weisz as Angela.

soul will not rest in an angel but in a man, and he shall be a warrior."[15] That soul belongs to a deranged army colonel who has recently died, and Gabriel, along with his angels is currently searching for it. *Lost Souls*, likewise, opens with a quote from "Deuteronomy, Book [not chapter] 17":

> A man born of incest
> Will become Satan
> And the world as we know it
> Will be no more.[16]

Although the phrasing ("the world as we know it") is decidedly modern, within the film the Antichrist has in fact already been born as the result of incest.

Constantine also opens with a quotation, but without a cited source. Although it sounds vaguely oracular in a B-movie sort of way ("He who possesses the Spear of Destiny holds the fate of the world in his hands"), the source of the statement is actually not as important as the implication that such an apt quote exists, and is available for citation. Later, however, a friend of the exorcist translates a passage from Corinthians, "Act" (not chapter) 17: "The sins of the father will only be exceeded by the sins of the son." The passage goes on to name the demon Mammon as the Devil's son, and woodcarvings show first a cruciform symbol, then an angel stabbing a person with a spear as a hand claws its way out of her, then another of Mammon emerging from the body. Again, this exact set of circumstances is currently taking place in Constantine's neighborhood, and his friend Angela is the intended victim of the sacrificial ritual that will give Mammon access to Earth. The early seasons of *Supernatural* similarly feature demons attempting to gain greater access to the human world. The show is generally episodic, with a "monster of the week" structure, but an ongoing storyline sees the demon, Azazel,[17] attempting to initiate the biblical (?) Apocalypse. The first time the Winchester brothers learn there is an alternative Bible, a friend informs them it contains a prophecy that 66 seals must be broken before Lucifer can be let loose upon the Earth.[18] Later a demon cites a passage from the augmented Revelation: "The first seal shall be broken when the righteous man sheds blood in Hell. As he breaks, so shall it break."[19] Dean Winchester, who spent time in between seasons torturing souls in Hell, is that righteous man. His brother Sam will inadvertently break the 66th seal.

In every case the passages are predictions stated in the future tense. This is not, however, the way that biblical prophecies typically appear in canonical texts, even if we may choose to read them as predictions. When Revelation, for example, describes the seven seals being broken and releasing the Four Horsemen, it is as a past-tense description of what happened in John's vision: "And I *watched* when the Lamb *opened* the first of the seven seals, and I *heard* one of the four living creatures saying with a voice like thunder, 'Come!'"[20] The future tense is used in fictional passages to highlight that they are predictive, and the occasional use of "shall" gives them a more biblical sound. In fact, the future orientation of the text is necessary so that it can unambiguously point to the heroes' current predicament and drive the plot forward. In every case, the characters attempt either to fulfill the prediction or to thwart it.

The texts, then, are not only always relevant, but accessible and readable when the heroes need them. Most of the apocryphal texts are in Latin. It is possible that the filmmakers perceive Latin as ancient and esoteric (compare the Latinisms in the *Harry Potter* series), but Latin is nevertheless a language that the audience is probably aware of. Apocryphal texts often survive only in languages that would be unfamiliar to the average moviegoer: Syriac, Coptic, Slavonic, etc. The ability to translate these languages is quite rare and requires special training—expertise the heroes simply would not have. Thomas, now a police detective, competently translates an ancient manuscript with only a former seminarian's education, one unlikely to include Syriac. Constantine does consult an expert, but one who works out of the back of a bowling alley rather than a near Eastern languages department at a university. The Winchesters' resident expert, Bobby, ran a junkyard with a high school education before he hunted monsters. These average Joes do not have time to learn languages the audience never heard of. The heroes possess ancient, rare knowledge within their special Bibles, but knowledge presented in a form they might plausibly access. As with literalist confidence in the ease of translating biblical texts, the language of pseudo-biblical texts never creates an overwhelming obstacle to reading them.

From a literalist perspective, the Bible is inerrant because it was in some way written with the participation of the Holy Spirit—that is, of God. *Supernatural* suggests an even more direct form of divine authorship. The Winchesters discover a series of pulp novels in which they are the heroes, and which contain remarkably accurate descriptions of their adventures. The author, Chuck Shurley (the pun on "surely" is made explicit in the 11th-season episode, "Don't Call Me Shurley"), is introduced as a prophet of the Lord: He appears to know as much as he does about the Winchesters through divine inspiration. The ostensibly fictional books he is writing will one day be known as the Winchester Gospel, a new scripture. The Winchesters later discover that Chuck is not in fact an ordinary man chosen to be a prophet, as he first seems, but God posing as a prophet writing a new holy text. This opens the possibility that the current Bible (the obscure, expanded one at least) was written directly by God, without human mediation.

If these hidden Bibles are right, then, what are they right about? Put another way, for what purpose does horror cinema introduce pseudo-biblical texts? In every case, the Bible helps the heroes to understand evil, and not evil generally but the specific embodiment of evil they face *now*. If Thomas had not read Revelation 23, he would have absolutely no reason to suspect that a dead army colonel's soul was hidden in a little girl's body, that the homicidal sociopath pursuing her is actually the angel Gabriel, or that the stakes were so incredibly high should Gabriel succeed. After all, in a world at least somewhat like ours, who *would*? Constantine's version of Corinthians details the name of the demon pursuing Angela, what it intends to do with the spear, and even that an angel will assist in the ritual. The Winchesters' Bible lays out the precise means by which Lucifer will be released (against God's will, in contrast to our Bible).[21] They are all horribly informative and clear about the threats faced by the protagonists.

The demons only get close to victory in these films because God is seemingly indifferent, because the angels are incompetent or in rebellion, and most importantly, because humans are ignorant. Only in *The Prophecy* have people been unable to read the (true) Bible prior to the crisis. Thomas would be completely justified in shaking his head at the odd coroner's report on the dead angel, or at most making a phone call to Arizona (where the girl lives) to let a sheriff know the colonel's obituary turned up at the scene of a murder, the suspect in which is still at large. Instead the world is saved because Thomas inexplicably takes his newfound Bible seriously and literally, and travels from New York to Arizona.

Constantine and *Supernatural*, meanwhile, argue that the world is only in peril because the heroes didn't know their Bible already. As soon as the spear appeared in his city at a time of increased demonic activity, Constantine should have been on the lookout for Mammon. After all, his name is right there in the text, and an exorcist who has spent time in Hell has no reason to doubt Mammon is real. When Dean Winchester is captured and brought to Hell, he is offered the chance to relieve his suffering by torturing wicked souls. He knows he does not belong there, but after months of torture he gives in. Yet soon after, he is rescued by angels. Had he known the prophecy that the first seal would be broken by a just man, a man like him, shedding blood in Hell, he might have held out long enough to prevent the Apocalypse.

Omen III makes a similar point, but with a twist. Here it is the evil character, the Antichrist, who cites a highly informative passage from Hebron, which he describes as "one of the more obscure backwaters of the Septuagint Bible." Whether it is obscure or not, it is evidently available to read in translations of the Apocrypha, as are Judith, Tobit, and other apocryphal books from the Septuagint. Damien the Antichrist believes he has an advantage over the forces of good, perhaps even over the Messiah, since he reads his Bible. He is thwarted, however, because he does not read the Bible thoroughly enough. As Beavis points out,[22] Damien assumes Christ will be born as a child like he was the first time (and as Damien was in the first *Omen*), but another citation highlights that he should have known better:

> Behold the Lion of Judah
> The Messiah, who came first as a child
> But returns not as a child
> But now as the King of Kings
> To rule in power and glory forever![23]

As in each of the works surveyed here, Damien learns about evil from the Bible, but he fails to learn about the (righteous) enemy who threatens him—not because the Bible fails to inform him, but because he fails to read it.

Conclusion

Horror cinema presents the Bible as a repository of information about evil: how it is embodied, what it is planning, and how to defeat it. Yet the Bible is useful only if read through a literalist hermeneutic that is often, and most devoutly, employed by conservative evangelicals and Christian fundamentalists. The literalism corresponds with other fundamentalist perspectives. For example, the ethics of each film reflects a rigid, black-and-white dualism, where both good and evil are clearly defined and unambiguously separable. Such a perspective is appropriate given the prevalent apocalyptic themes, since ethical dualism is a common feature of apocalypses.[24] It is also, however, an ethical perspective embraced by fundamentalists.[25]

There is some tension between the superficial Catholic trappings of many of the films, and their literalist approach to scripture. The Roman Catholic Church embraces historical and literary methods of interpretation, and Catholic hermeneutics can be quite diverse, embracing allegorical and figurative interpretations.[26] They are often influenced by the non-literal interpretations of the ancient Church Fathers. Indeed, Catholic interpretations generally take a literal reading as only a first step toward a fuller, more spiritual interpretation.[27] The Bible is thus a sufficient but unnecessary part of Catholic tradition, in contrast to its centrality in *sola scriptura* ("scripture alone") forms of Protestantism, particularly fundamentalist ones. In the horror films discussed here, the Bible is indispensable to understanding evil, and none of the films suggest that spiritual readings would be anything but a distraction from the *information* spelled out literally in the text (truth in terms of mere facticity). While Catholicism shapes their visual aesthetics, likely influenced by the success of *The Exorcist* (1973), it is literalism applied with the stringency (and simplicity) of Protestant fundamentalist interpretation that dictates how the Bible is read by the characters.[28]

The voices of literalists are disproportionately loud in American culture.[29] Public biblical arguments regarding creationism or sexuality appear in the media almost invariably voiced in terms of a clearly defined good versus a clearly defined *and present* evil, which one can discern with a "plain sense" reading of the Bible. Counter-arguments to literalist positions, meanwhile, are rarely crafted from a biblical perspective—even when they are made by Jews and Christians who may employ alternative reading strategies. Someone with little personal experience of the diverse styles of interpreting the Bible might conclude from these debates that it is a text that informs the reader about good and evil in a relevant, easily discernible way, but only if it is read literally. This is just how a Bible works.

That is not to say that the religious or political viewpoint of these films aligns with literalist interpretations of Christianity. The God in each work is distant and indifferent, while God's angels are uninformed, incompetent, or defiant. The interpretive method is similar, but the theology and texts differ. In these cinematic fantasy worlds, when the heroes are faced with cataclysmic evil, they require what literalists believe they already have in the Bible in order to defeat it. Yet the filmmakers are consistently reluctant to build their narratives on the Bible they know. It may only be reassuring for a popular audience to imagine black-and-white explanations for evil—and to imagine an informative, effective tool like the Bible for combatting it.

There are also important distinctions in how the films present their protagonists as readers of the Bible. The heroes are not devout, chaste, or even penitent churchgoers. They are rarely believers, and if circumstances force them to be, they do not spend their time bringing people to the Church. Fundamentalists emphasize a personal relationship with God. In fact, it is often embracing a personal relationship with God, and so accepting the influence of his Spirit, that allows someone to read the Bible through a proper, literal lens.[30] Yet in these films, and in their apocryphal texts, the author of scripture is too distant to engage in such a relationship.

Since there is (according to these films) only one way to read scripture, a different God seems to require new texts. The apocalyptic pseudo-biblical texts are everything literalists wish the Bible was: blatantly predictive about the evils they themselves face, and more importantly, loaded with plentiful, specific, and unambiguous details. The End, in these story-worlds, is in fact nigh. From a literalist perspective, the plots play out just as they should in real life: God gave very specific instructions about the evils facing the world, but only a privileged minority knows to read the Bible literally in order to defeat them.

Notes

1. Beavis, "Savage Weapons," 17.
2. *Ibid.*
3. Damien incorrectly (or fictionally?) refers to "the original Latin." The Septuagint was translated into Latin almost half a millennium later.
4. Bede makes a similar pun on angels/Angles in the Latin *Ecclesiastical History of the English People* (8th century CE). While the pun is ancient, it does not work in Greek.
5. The first war is the primordial, Miltonian war resulting from Lucifer's rebellion.
6. This line inspires the title of Beavis' essay ("Savage Weapons"). For a full transcript of the final script, see http://www.script-o-rama.com/movie_scripts/p/prophecy-script-transcript-christopher-walken.html (accessed November 15, 2017).
7. The later NBC show, *Constantine* (2014–2015), shares source material in the DC comic book series, *Hellblazer*, but is not based on the movie.
8. For the problems with the presentation of this text, see Tripp, "Gabriel," 68 n.32. When the Latin text is shown on screen, the end of chapter 16 does not match the canonical 1 Corinthians 16. Second Corinthians has only 13 chapters.
9. "Are You There, God? It's Me, Dean Winchester," *Supernatural*, season 4, episode 2.
10. Consider an oft-cited definition of "apocalypse": "revelatory literature within a narrative framework, in which a revelation is mediated by an otherworldly being to a human recipient, disclosing a transcendent reality which is both temporal, insofar as it envisages eschatological salvation, and spatial insofar as it involves another supernatural world" (cited in Collins, "What Is Apocalyptic Literature?" 2), later emended to include that an apocalypse is "intended to interpret present, earthly circumstances in light of the supernatural world of the future" (*ibid.*, 5).
11. Daniel 8:26; 12:4, 9.
12. Boone, *The Bible Tells Them So*, 23–37. That is, literalists theoretically acknowledge that corruptions may have entered into the text over time, but they view them as minimal and easily detectable.
13. *Ibid.*, 13, 39–41; also Crapanzano, *Serving the Word*, 2–3.
14. Lindsey and Carlson, *Late Great Planet Earth*, esp. 42–58. On Miller, see Rowe, *God's Strange Work*.
15. See above, n.6.
16. Although Deuteronomy does predict the arrival of a prophet like Moses (Deuteronomy 18:15–19), a prediction applied to Jesus in the New Testament (Meeks, *The Prophet-King*), there is little eschatological material in Deuteronomy, and nothing about Satan or demons. Such ideas post-date Deuteronomy by a number of centuries.
17. cf. Leviticus 16; 1 Enoch 8.
18. The relationship to the familiar Revelation, with its seven seals, is not clear. The Four Horsemen, who appear as the first four seals are broken (Revelation 6:1–8), are characters on the show (sent by the Devil

rather than God). The 66 seals are an obvious echo of the number of the Beast, 666 (Revelation 13:18), one amplified when the brothers learn there are "around 600 seals. Only 66 need to be broken" (season 4, episode 9). In contrast to Revelation, where they are wax seals on a scroll, so that access to the *text* is what is important, those in *Supernatural* are seals on a cage holding Lucifer, probably written spells.
   19. *Supernatural*, season 4, episode 16.
   20. Revelation 6:1.
   21. cf. Revelation 20:3.
   22. Beavis, "Savage Weapons," 18–19.
   23. cf. Genesis 49:9; Revelation 5:5.
   24. Frey, "Apocalyptic Dualism."
   25. Collins, "What Is Apocalyptic Literature?" 10–11.
   26. See, for example, the encyclical *Dei Verbum* (1965).
   27. Viviano, "The Senses of Scripture," 1–2.
   28. *Supernatural* has the fewest Catholic trappings, although priests play a larger role in the first season. The show's aesthetics quickly veered away from Catholicism and mainly toward esoteric Judaism, with "Enochian script" (an echo of the Enochic literature, *1–3 Enoch*), no mention of Christ (even in the storyline based on Revelation), and its depiction of a decidedly non–Trinitarian God in later seasons.
   29. According to a Pew Research poll of 35,000 Americans (http://www.pewforum.org/religious-landscape-study/#religions), only 31 percent of respondents claimed "holy scripture is the Word of God" and "should be taken literally" (Gallup puts it lower at only 24 percent, see Saad, "Record Few Americans Believe Bible Is Literal Word of God"). Despite this decline, literalists have influenced even 10 percent of Religiously Unaffiliated respondents to agree that religious people should read scripture as the literal word of God.
   30. Crapanzano, *Serving the Word*, 84–91.

Bibliography

Beavis, Mary Ann. "'Angels Carrying Savage Weapons': Uses of the Bible in Contemporary Horror Films." *Journal of Religion and Film* 7, no. 2 (2003): 1–23.

Boone, Kathleen C. *The Bible Tells Them So: The Discourse of Protestant Fundamentalism*. Albany: State University of New York Press, 1989.

Collins, John J. "What Is Apocalyptic Literature?" In *The Oxford Handbook of Apocalyptic Literature*, edited by John J. Collins, 1–16. New York: Oxford University Press, 2014.

Crapanzano, Vincent. *Serving the Word: Literalism in America from the Pulpit to the Bench*. New York: The New Press, 2000.

Frey, Jörg. "Apocalyptic Dualism." In *The Oxford Handbook of Apocalyptic Literature*, edited by John J. Collins, 271–94. New York: Oxford University Press, 2014.

Lindsey, Hal, and Carole C. Carlson. *The Late Great Planet Earth*. Grand Rapids: Zondervan, 1970.

Meeks, Wayne A. *The Prophet-King: Moses Traditions and the Johannine Christology*. Novum Testamentum Supplement 14. Boston: Brill, 1967.

Rowe, David L. *God's Strange Work: William Miller and the End of the World*. Grand Rapids: Eerdmans, 2008.

Saad, Lydia. "Record Few Americans Believe Bible Is Literal Word of God." 2017. http://news.gallup.com/poll/210704/record-few-americans-believe-bible-literal-word-god.aspx.

Tripp, Jeffrey M. "Gabriel, Abortion, and Anti-Annunciation in *The Prophecy, Constantine*, and *Legion*." *Journal of Religion and Popular Culture* 27, no. 1 (2015): 57–70.

Viviano, Pauline. "The Senses of Scripture." In *The Word of God in the Life and Mission of the Church: Celebrating the Catechetical Year 2009–2009 with Resources for Catechetical Sunday 2008*, 1–4. Washington, D.C.: United States Conference of Catholic Bishops, 2008.

Losing Your Faith for Seeing Too Much
The Anti-Bible as Indictment of American Heroism in Gregory Widen's The Prophecy

MARK HENDERSON

Gregory Widen's 1995 fantasy-horror film *The Prophecy*, despite its lack of critical acclaim,[1] is a cult classic. Central to contextualizing its remarkable plot is a handwritten 2nd-century Bible found on the corpse of a fallen angel named Uziel (Jeff Cadiente). The text contains an extra chapter in the Book of Revelations that reveals the existence of a *second* war in Heaven—one that occurs *after* the defeat of Lucifer and his followers,[2] with the rebel faction this time being led by the angel Gabriel (Christopher Walken)—and prophesies the existence of a dark earthly soul to be used as a decisive weapon within this war.

This stark reorientation of a character such as Gabriel, who is depicted so favorably in the Bible—interpreting the apocalyptic visions of the prophet Daniel and revealing the miraculous pregnancies of both Elizabeth and Mary—obviously upsets fundamental theological notions.[3] Knowledge of the *completeness* of the handwritten Bible is what makes it an *anti*-Bible and thus defines Thomas Dagget's (Elias Koteas) loss of faith as well as the general loss of faith experienced by characters in the film. What is most significant is that this loss, as Thomas notes, comes not "because Heaven shows [...] too little, but [...] because Heaven shows [...] too much," ultimately making one question whether or not faith (one's "voice," as Thomas calls it) is something better not to have to begin with. This anti–Bible provides an unwelcome revelation that brings a painful end to the innocence created by an incomplete and more naïve body of religious knowledge, and sheds further light upon the darker implications of known biblical texts.

The characters' loss of faith is also shaped by the film's setting: the western state of Arizona. Such a location calls for a specifically American critique, engaging the myths and ideologies that have come to define American heroism. The object of the rebel angels' earthly pursuit is, after all, the evil soul of the recently deceased Korean War veteran Colonel Arnold Hawthorne who, as is later discovered, was guilty of horrible war crimes against his Chinese adversaries during the war. At the time of his death, however, he was given a hero's funeral in his hometown of Chimney Rock, by friends and neighbors obviously unaware of the darker aspects of his military service. What makes Hawthorne's soul so valuable is its embodiment of an evil of which apparently even rebel angels are not capable, which gives it the potential to turn the tide of battle in the great heavenly war. The value of this particular soul further reinforces the need for a close and sober look at the dark and only begrudgingly acknowledged underbelly of American "heroism." As the film unfolds, it becomes increasingly apparent that the actions of the angels, even the "good" ones who fight in defense of God, are meant to parallel this aspect of American history: an uncomfortable and accusatory metaphorical mirror held up, by the filmmakers, to the self-assured and naïve American psyche.

That the film is meant as a specifically American critique is further underscored by the prominence of Native American characters. The ultimate vessel for Hawthorne's dark soul, and thus the ultimate spiritual battleground, is a young Native American girl, Mary (Moriah Shining Dove Snyder), and the successful exorcism of Hawthorne's soul from her body is apparently accomplished not by Christian rituals but by traditional Native American ones. The film is thus positioned to indict the darker side of American military exploits in both the Korean War *and* the various Indian wars. One can neither ignore nor deny that notions of Anglocentric Christian exceptionalism are imbedded in the myths defining American heroism—and how such notions were given voice during the country's earliest colonial days by both the Pilgrims and the Puritans. A consequence of this self-privileging and self-validation is the demonizing of the immediately present Other: the Native Americans of the surrounding wilderness.

The film addresses this prejudicial demonization through one of its most startling ironies: The *deus ex machina* who resolves the plot is none other than Lucifer (Viggo Mortensen) himself, who opposes Gabriel's efforts to create a second Hell in Heaven. The traditional, clear-cut God-good/Devil-bad dichotomy, thus reversed, is further complicated by the refusal of both white and Native American mortals to place themselves in league with Lucifer. This suggests the film's complicated and ambiguous acknowledgment of the *current* American identity and state of American heroism. *The Prophecy*, with its central narrative device of the anti–Bible, is thus both an acknowledgment of America's problematic past *and* an optimistic yet sober coming to terms with the country's present. This essay will explore and analyze the film's progression from using upsetting theology to indict notions of American heroism to reconciling some of the harder and darker facts of American history.

Bad Angels...

The Prophecy presents the loss and recovery of Thomas' religious faith through his visions of and encounters with angels, which reveal an angelic nature far darker and more malevolent than Thomas had initially imagined. His crisis begins when, just as he is about to be ordained into the priesthood as a Catholic seminary student, a sudden vision of war among angels (complete with bloody wings and screaming, grimacing faces) leaves him screaming and hysterical. This traumatic event is clearly what drives Thomas from the priesthood to his work as a Los Angeles Police Department detective. He finds the aforementioned Bible on Uziel, who was killed during an altercation with another angel, Simon (Eric Stoltz), who had visited Thomas in his apartment, told him that he was in the church while Thomas was having his vision, and warned him of upcoming events. Simon, already wounded by Uziel, is ultimately tortured and killed by Gabriel—

for whom Uziel was working—for his refusal to tell Gabriel the whereabouts of Colonel Hawthorne's soul. Simon had, in fact, already sucked out the soul from Hawthorne's corpse and breathed it into the body of little Mary, rendering her ill and possessed. With the help of Lucifer, who tears out Gabriel's heart and drags him to Hell, Gabriel is thwarted and the soul is exorcised from Mary. Thomas, along with virtually everyone present, demonstrates his recovered faith by refusing Lucifer's invitation to join him.

As a plot device, the Bible found on Uziel presents a *counter*-narrative to long-held but erroneous beliefs formed from too little information. This anti–Bible thus effectively sets the mood for world-shattering disillusionment. Accordingly, and from its beginning, *The Prophecy* pulls no punches in undermining any simplistically romantic or sentimental investment in angels as benevolent and ethereal beings. Gone are any childhood bedtime stories about gentle and protective "guardian" angels. Whether "good" or "evil" (the quotation marks here indicating the film's consistent moral ambiguity), the angels are remarkably *earthy* and animal-like: they perch—be it on a rooftop or on the back of a chair—like birds, and they can pick up on one another's scents with a conspicuous sniff. They are beasts, brutes—corporeally limited in the mortal realm and hypocritically dependent on the very human beings who both Gabriel and Lucifer arrogantly deride as "talking monkeys." Gabriel—even more than Lucifer, the film's apotheosis of the "bad" angel—demonstrates this dependence in its coldest extreme. He forcibly recruits mortals on the brink of death to assist him with the practical functions of transportation and negotiating other unfamiliar technologies. He accomplishes this by cheating these desperate souls of the immediate boon of death and placing them in a state of limbo. Jerry (Adam Goldberg), a suicide, pleadingly complains to Gabriel of his world-weary fatigue, and the terminally ill and recently flat-lined Rachael (Amanda Plummer), bitterly weeps upon being resuscitated and seeing Gabriel.

The second angelic war in Heaven, as described in the extra chapter of Uziel's Bible, goes so far against traditional Christian doctrine that *The Prophecy*'s (1995) *deus ex machina* turns out to be the Devil himself (Viggo Mortensen).

The earthiness and brutishness of the angels is matched by their potential for violent conflict—evident not only in the war waged by Lucifer, but in the current war begun by Gabriel. As the film opens, a somber Simon, standing over what are apparently the skeletal remains of a fallen angel, laments how "a third of Heaven's legion [has been] banished ... and now my brothers are no longer brothers." Furthermore, and appropriately, Thomas is disturbed by something he had read in "St. Paul's gospel" concerning "angels carrying savage weapons." This reference, though entirely fictitious, draws attention to a crucial irony surrounding the film's anti–Bible: its revelations are, in fact, but an extension of disturbing insinuations existing within the Bible proper. Take, for instance, this passage from Revelation concerning the fall of Lucifer: "And I heard a loud voice in heaven, saying, 'Now the salvation and the power and the kingdom of our God and the authority of his Christ have come, for the accuser of our brethren has been thrown down, who accuses them day and night before our God.'"[4] Can this not be read as a hint or a warning of possible *other* sources of insurrectionist sentiment besides Lucifer and his followers? Finally—as Thomas bitterly points out to Mary's teacher, Katherine (Virginia Madsen)—when God needed a killing in the Bible, he sent an angel. Thomas chillingly considers what such a creature must be like: "A whole existence spent praising your God ... with one wing dipped in blood.... Would you ever really want to *see* an angel?"

As the quintessentially "bad" angel, Gabriel confirms Thomas' dark assessment of angels. In answer to Katherine's horrified plea of "Why?" Gabriel replies: "I'm an angel. I kill firstborns while their mamas watch. I turn cities into salt.[5] I even, when I feel like it, rip the souls from little girls. And from now until kingdom come, the only thing you can count on in your existence is never understanding why." He thus reaffirms Thomas' conclusions by calling attention to the apparent, confounding incongruity (if not incompatibility) between the angelic moral compass and the human one. In spite of such acts as torturing Simon all night with fire before ultimately ripping his heart out in the morning, it is clear that Gabriel considers himself to be in the right. Though Lucifer–like in his actions toward God, Gabriel does not want, as he explains to Simon, to *be* or *surmount* God; he just wants things to be as they were before the creation of humankind. This is perhaps most curiously reflected by Gabriel's persistent irritability at hearing the Lord's name taken in vain—at such profanities as "goddamn" and "Jesus Christ"—as well as his blessing of Uziel's corpse with holy water before setting it on fire in the morgue. Yet, this righteous sense of angelic rectitude is put forth in the film as *worse* than Lucifer's less ambiguously adversarial hatred and break with Heaven!

...And Bad Patriots

In spite of Gabriel's hatred for human beings, it appears to be lost on him how much he actually identifies with them and, in the case of such evil individuals as Colonel Hawthorne, even respects them. Upon seeing Hawthorne's casket after Jerry has exhumed it, Gabriel describes the colonel as "the cleverest, meanest, sickest-talking monkey—I love him!" Lucifer, by comparison, has no such moral blind spots; he is far more honest with both himself and Katherine in his admiration of human iniquity, to the point of understanding Gabriel perhaps better than Gabriel understands himself: "Humans—and how I love you talking monkeys for this—know more about war and treachery of the spirit than any angel. Gabriel is well aware of this and has found a way to steal the blackest soul on Earth to fight for him." A direct metaphorical parallel is thus established between the bad angel Gabriel and the bad patriot Colonel Hawthorne—and, further, between a sober and less-illusioned view of the nature of angels and a sober and less-illusioned view of the nature of American heroism (Manifest Destiny and expansionism). By further extension, the anti–Bible's counter-narrative (represented by Gabriel) parallels the white-washed historical narrative of American rectitude (represented by Hawthorne).

The most climactic example of these parallels is the uncanny similarity between the crayon drawings that Mary (now possessed by Hawthorne's evil spirit) makes of impaled soldiers and the terrible vision of a multitude of impaled angels shared by Thomas and Katherine in the abandoned mine inhabited by Gabriel, The truth behind Mary's drawings is confirmed by Thomas' finding evidence of war crimes in Hawthorne's home: articles hinting at "human sacrifices," film reels showing mutilations and dismemberments on the battlefield, court martial footage, and actual facial skins taken from enemy combatants. Such evidence belies the traditional, mythical notions of exceptionalism and moral superiority foundational to the idea of American heroism while elucidating the messy, complicated facts behind many of America's "heroic" historical exploits. Widen (who also wrote the film) situates Hawthorne's war crimes within Battle of Chosin Reservoir, a campaign described by retired general Lemuel C. Shepherd as "heartbreaking [and] an epic of individual heroism and physical hardship" by the Marines and soldiers of the United States Army's X Corps.[6] The horror of Hawthorne's actions are rendered morally ambiguous by the desperate nature of the conflict at Chosin.

Ordered by General Douglas MacArthur to prevent retreat by the North Korean army, the U.S. Eighth Army and other UN forces pressed further into North Korea, reaching the snow-covered Chosin Reservoir Plateau, where the Yalu River forms the natural boundary between China and North Korea.[7] Approximately 30,000 of these UN troops ("The Chosin Few") were suddenly encircled and attacked by approximately 120,000 troops of the Chinese Ninth Army, who had hidden in the woods surrounding the reservoir. A brutal seventeen-day battle—much of it fought hand-to-hand, and all of it in freezing weather—followed, with the UN forces ultimately making a fighting withdrawal from the encirclement and inflicting crippling losses on the Chinese.[8] As described by Eric M. Hammel, it must have seemed to the UN forces during this so-called First Phase Offensive "that whole Chinese divisions emerged from the ether,"[9] with no warning and no time to think.

In the context of such an ordeal, extremes of violent behavior would hardly be far-fetched possibilities, and Widen finds his creative springboard in the troubling line drawn

The horrifying vision of a multitude of impaled angels in *The Prophecy* (1995), seen by Thomas and Katherine in Gabriel's cave hideout, present the casualties of the second war in Heaven as not as all dissimilar to the horrors of human war, particularly Colonel Hawthorne's crimes against humanity during the Korean War.

between the urgent necessities of a harrowing moment and war crimes. Hawthorne's soul, speaking through the possessed Mary, underscores this as it recalls the campaign in terms both chilling and revealing: "Ever cut off a Chinaman's head? They don't bleed. Not like we do. Or maybe it was just the cold. You could always tell when they were coming. Those songs. They'd charge through the snow. The guns froze. But that was okay. Because we were better. At Chosin, we were colder than anyone." Surviving such an ordeal is undeniably heroic, but the equally undeniable sentiments of tribalism, nationalism and racial prejudice behind Hawthorne's projected words darken and contaminate that heroism. Through the example of this fictional episode from the Korean War, they call into question *all* military and expansionist exploits defining American history. If the heroic narrative of this specific war has been called into question, undermined, and sullied, what of the other wars, of greater scope and seemingly greater righteousness?

Even the relatively "good" angel Simon is not free from ties to the dark underbelly of American history. He intuits enough of the uneasy connection between angelhood and being an American "hero" to know where to find the most evil human soul; Thomas' finding of Hawthorne's obituary in Simon's apartment is proof of Simon's having been aware of this connection for quite some time. This critical moral link between angel and American hero is perhaps best reinforced by the image of Simon's sucking the evil soul out of the mouth of Hawthorne's corpse, during which the camera deliberately pans out to include the American flag draped over Hawthorne's casket. One of the last statements that Simon makes to Gabriel before being killed is also chillingly reminiscent of a war criminal's retrospective defense: "I'm not sure who's right, who's wrong, but it doesn't matter. Sometimes you just have to do what you're told. That's who we are." One can very well imagine Hawthorne having made a similar statement while defending his actions at the Chosin Reservoir. Throughout military history (not just American military history), excuses about merely "doing the job" and "following orders" for the sake of personal and national survival have drawn a disturbingly blurred line between patriotism and atrocity. Even Simon's transfer of Hawthorne's soul into Mary's body—from his mouth to hers, in what is ostensibly a kiss following enticing eye contact—is not only eerily pedophilic, but calls to mind historical instances of wartime rape and sexual exploitation.

Given the obvious second-guessing and undermining of angelic moral authority that such behavior from Gabriel and Simon inspires, as well as the grudging respect that the audience is encouraged to comparatively have for Lucifer, one cannot help but to recall with irony what the country's earliest European settlers distinguished what was "good" and "evil"—what was of God and what was of the Devil. A significant early contributor to the American worldview, Cotton Mather presumptuously spoke of the early Puritan settlers of New England having "all the vultures of hell trodden under our feet" and attributed the Salem witch trials to a "terrible plague of evil angels"[10]:

> The New Englanders are a people of God settled in those, which were once the devil's territories; and it may easily be supposed that the devil was exceedingly disturbed, when he perceived such a people here accomplishing the promise of old made unto our blessed Jesus, that He should have the utmost parts of the earth for His possession.... I believe that never were more satanical devices used for the unsettling of any people under the sun, than what have been employed for the extirpation of the vine which God has here planted, casting out *the heathen* [emphasis added].[11]

Mather was an infamous figure in the Salem witchcraft panic—one of the most embarrassing chapters in early American history, out of which came the deaths of innocents—and his writings provide a uniquely startling account of how chauvinistic moral certainty can yield potentially disastrous results. According to Peter N. Carroll, Mather's self-assured ideology reflected that of the colonial Puritan collective, for whom New England paradoxically signified both "the New Canaan" and "a land of spiritual darkness" beckoning the faithful as a sort of supreme religious test.[12] It does not take a great stretch of the imagination to identify the "heathen" to which Mather refers. Carroll speaks directly to what Mather rather transparently insinuates: to the Puritan settlers in the New World, the obvious embodiment of the "savage state of the wilderness [which] signified Satanic power" was "the Indians," who, as "true instruments" of the Devil's "malice," would act fervently in opposition to the "incursion of Christianity into the wilderness."[13]

Such designations of the wilderness as Satanic—as wild, foreign, Other—also provided a convenient endorsement for the Eurocentric doctrine of Manifest Destiny, a phrase by John L. O'Sullivan in 1845 that imputed divine sanction to America's ongoing westward expansion for "the development of our yearly multiplying millions."[14] Those millions, however, clearly did not include the Native Americans and Mexicans who stood so inconveniently in the way of this "destiny," and the Judeo-Christian overtones of divine sanction implied by Manifest Destiny unburdened the expansionist conscience of any guilt or moral crisis for atrocities committed in its name. According to Richard Slotkin, these atrocities became further incorporated into a myth of "regeneration through violence" that, in turn, became "the structuring metaphor of the American experience"— both the psychological and physical inspiration for the earliest American colonizers to regenerate "their fortunes, their spirits, and the power of *the church and nation*."[15] However, as Frederick Jackson Turner tellingly pointed out, this belief in the manifest destiny of one's country can ultimately work "for good *and* for evil."[16] The early Puritan idea of the New World as the New Canaan thus fits, making even clearer the parallel between angels and patriots in *The Prophecy*. Just as the Israelites, having escaped Egypt, found divine sanction through the idea of the Promised Land for the serial genocides that they committed throughout Canaan,[17] early American colonizers found sanction through Manifest Destiny for the actions committed against Native Americans.

The Prophecy takes place in the present, in the American West, long after westward expansion has been geographically realized, and assigned a place in the ongoing American narrative that coincides with the supernatural present represented by the anti–Bible. The locus for the events of the film is Chimney Rock, Arizona—specifically the rundown charity school where Mary attends and Katherine teaches. As Katherine explains to Thomas, the economic plight of the school and the surrounding region are due to the closure of the town's copper mine. Both the school and the town, then, act as microcosmic echoes of Manifest Destiny; having been exploited to the limit of its usefulness, the land around Window Rock as been abandoned by those who can afford to leave. What remains are the vestiges not only of the economic opportunity brought by the mine but also, in the longer view, of American westward expansion. The students at the charity school appear to be an even mix of white and brown- skinned children, descendants of the out-of-work employees who could not leave and of those whose (Mexican and Native American) ancestors were victimized in the name of Manifest Destiny.

This microcosmic melting pot of children represents the newest generation and thus the most current American identity. They highlight the central problem posed by this present-day identity: what to do *now*, after westward expansion has been realized. The obvious representative for this current, multicultural identity is the afflicted Mary:

Native American, but clearly exposed to other cultures through the school's curriculum (she is shown happily singing Christian hymns in the school choir) and her friendships with non–Native students. The battle for Mary's soul is thus a battle for the soul of present-day America. When labeling a victor in the battle, however, or even defining the moral terms that would signify a victory, the expected designations of "good," "evil," "hero," or "villain" simply fail—rendered problematic by the rather discouraging revelations pertaining to angelic/patriotic behavior. How, then, can America's present be reconciled with its past?

Exorcism and Reconciliation

Thomas's temptation by two different agents—the morally self-assured Gabriel and the unabashedly evil Lucifer—highlights the failure of the simplistic God-good/Devil-bad dichotomy to usefully differentiate the opposing sides in the battle for Mary's soul and in the film's larger angelic war. Granted, Lucifer is partially redeemed by advising Thomas on how to defeat Gabriel, and by his appearance to ostensibly save the day by tearing out Gabriel's heart, but his ultimate invitation to join him in Hell reminds the audience, as well as Thomas and everyone else present at Mary's exorcism, just who they are dealing with. Even when functions as a *deus ex machina*, Lucifer's motives are undeniably and unapologetically self-centered; he jealously wants to prevent Gabriel's insurrectionist creation of another Hell for the sake of his (Lucifer's) own sovereignty and exclusivity. As he explains to Gabriel before killing him, the current angelic war (Gabriel's) is based on arrogance, which is evil, and that is *Lucifer's* territory. Lucifer, however, is the relative better in this case he does not directly harm any human during the film: He merely *threatens* to fill Katherine' mouth with her dead mother's feces if she will not talk with him. Gabriel, on the other hand, has been dismissively harming and killing humans at will, the last two being the police officers who drive away, with him in the back of the squad car, from the site of Mary's motor-home explosion.

Gabriel's temptation is also the more significant, for it reinforces the angel-patriot parallel established by the anti–Bible and coincides with the popularly accepted narrative of American history. Upon his arrival to disrupt Mary's exorcism, Gabriel's invitation to Thomas to join him smacks simultaneously of an angel's darker actions *and* of the historical atrocities committed by the likes of American "patriots" like Colonel Hawthorne: "You get to kill all day, all night, just like an angel!" For Thomas, this is the greater temptation because he and Gabriel have far more in common—namely, a loss of faith. Lucifer recognizes this and advises Thomas, having firsthand experience of what shaky faith feels like, to use Gabriel's lack of faith against him. One notices, however, how Lucifer predatorially embraces Thomas from behind, sneaking up on him and getting in his ear, while imparting this advice. Lucifer clearly wants to take Thomas with him back to Hell. He will do so with Gabriel, by force, but again, Gabriel is the more immediate and tangible threat, and more so for the odd identification between him and Thomas. Thomas' fight against Gabriel is a fight against himself as a modern American, to finally come to terms with and reconcile the national past to which he is heir.

The Native American site to which Thomas and Katherine flee with Mary and her family provides a fitting arena for Mary's exorcism, for it lies culturally outside of the exclusively Judeo-Christian purview that has thus far proven so fraught and untrustworthy.

The site, however, does not lie outside the purview of American-ness. Mary's people are, by definition, are among the *first* Americans, and the modern, post-expansion American character is multicultural—a hybrid of definitive cross-cultural encounters that, through better and worse (and *for* better *or* worse), have shaped an identity undeniably new, unique, and different from those claimed by the forefathers of each integrated part. The site, with its gathering of Native and non–Native, pagan and Christian, is the new America.

Even the evil soul of Colonel of Hawthorne, embodied by the possessed Mary, appears to be reappropriated for purposes that are actually helpful to those trying to escape Gabriel and aid in Mary's exorcism. The advice given to Thomas by Hawthorne's soul on how to defeat a terrestrial angel is oddly reminiscent of Hawthorne's earlier "Chinaman" comments: "On Earth, they're not immortal. They're not like you and me. You've got to cut their hearts out." The Other-izing language (*us* versus *them*) and casual reference to bodily mutilation recalls the horrors committed by Hawthorne at the Chosin Reservoir, yet the desperate necessity of the moment not only calls attention to the vivid threat of the present adversary but casts a more ambiguous light over the morality of Hawthorne's original actions. The next advice given to Thomas by Hawthorne's soul seems, in fact, to be purely practical in terms of military strategy; referring to the Native American site, he says: "This is a good place. Separate water source. Stocked grain. Only one possible approach. And you may could, with the proper defenses, hold off an entire battalion."

But one must remember that this voice of Hawthorne's soul is coming from Mary—from *her* vocal cords and through *her* mouth. This vocalizing during the state of possession is thus a fundamental act of reappropriation in itself. It can't *not* be. Mary is, after all, conscious, lucid, and aware of—even distressed by—what she is saying during moments when Hawthorne's soul speaks through her. The current American identity, as the latest manifestation of the ongoing American narrative, is thus defined by not only a sober awareness of the past, but by an incorporation of the practical components of even the darkest moments of that past; to resort to a cliché, one must know not to throw the proverbial baby out with the bathwater in desperate times.

Having not only a "soul," but "faith" as well, seems to be the key to Thomas' redemption—and, by extension, that of Mary and all the other human beings present at the site. Having a soul is central to his refusal of Gabriel; a soul being what distinguishes humans from angels. Yet the potential for faith, along with the possession of a soul, also allows Thomas to understand Gabriel's anger, hurt, and jealousy; Gabriel is capable of faith—having, according to Lucifer, apparently lost it. Thomas too, of course, had lost his faith, but the example of both Gabriel and Lucifer have revealed to him the possible, dire consequences of such a loss—not only to the individual but to the collective (angels, humanity, all of Creation) to which one belongs, begrudgingly or otherwise. Ultimately, in the specific geographical context of *The Prophecy*, the collective to which one belongs is, once the lines of metaphorical extension provided by the film's supernatural and philosophical elements are drawn in, America. As morning comes, after Gabriel's defeat and Mary's exorcism, Thomas comments on the nature of faith, what it means to be truly human, and how faith "can be lost—for a man, an angel, or the Devil himself": "[I]f faith means never completely understanding God's plan, then maybe understanding just a part of it, *our* part, is what it is to have a soul, and maybe in the end that's what being human is after all." And being an American—which is being *part* of an enduring experiment, an experiment in which your *part* has been provided, defined, and differentiated by other, past, and possibly horrible parts.

The conclusion of *The Prophecy*, however, offers a less satisfying closure than might, at first, seem to be the case. Indeed, barring any willful feel-good amnesia for the details of the plot and the troubling ambiguities of the characters, the film ends on a rather uncomfortable note. The similarity of Thomas' concluding talk of playing one's "part" in a grander "plan" to Simon's talk of having to sometimes do what one is told is chilling and foreboding. The troubles and the horrors hardly seem to be over. Is history doomed to repeat itself? Does Lucifer's killing of Gabriel, which directly coincides with the release of Hawthorne's soul from Mary's body, imply that, to negotiate the historical present, the best that one can do is to make the best of a Faustian pact from the distant past? Perhaps. The film did, after all, spawn four sequels, suggesting further complications in the plot. But the developments in the first two sequels are encouraging. In *The Prophecy 2*, Gabriel is kicked out of Hell and returns to Earth, where he tries to prevent the birth of a Nephilim (the offspring of a mortal and an angel), but fails and is punished by being made completely mortal. In *The Prophecy 3: Ascent*, amazingly, Gabriel is ultimately redeemed for his now-human remorse for his past actions.

If the fate of Gabriel is any reflection of the humans he was so hatefully resistant to identifying with (and specifically of these American humans) then the lesson appears to be one of resolve—of hope and endurance, and a transcendent reconciliation of the past with the imperfect but improving present. Prophecies inferred from newly discovered, apocryphal anti–Bibles, though revelatory reflections of the "book" ever-written through the living-out of American history (and of history in general), need not be irrevocable. Nor must beliefs necessarily be forsaken if earlier, more naïve understandings of them have been shown to be inaccurate if not outright false. A heavenly beam does shoot down from the sky to dissipate the Hawthorne's evil soul after it is expelled from Mary, nor does the film offer any other sign to encourage continued belief—in God, humanity, America, or anything still worthy of promise and potential, individually or collectively. The trick is not only to endure but to *change*—evolve and progress. After all, the titular prophecy provided by Uziel's anti–Bible, like the forebodings within the current state of America's historical narrative, turns out to not be set in stone. It is a warning and a call to action, not an irrevocable damnation.

Notes

1. Among other negative-to-lukewarm reviews, David Kronke of the *Los Angeles Times* described it as "simply too loopy ... to render ... in any credible fashion," and Owen Gleiberman of *Entertainment Weekly* called it an "inert ... occult freakshow."
2. This is generally agreed to be recounted in Revelation 12:3–9.
3. Daniel 8:15–27 and 9:20–27; Luke 1.
4. Revelation 12:10.
5. God's sending of an angel to kill the first-borns of Egypt in Exodus 11:1–12:36; the destruction of Sodom and Gomorrah in Genesis 18–19.
6. Shepherd, "Introduction," xi.
7. Ibid., x.
8. Appleman, *Disaster in Korea*, 24.
9. Hammel, *Chosin*, 5.
10. Mather, *Wonders of the Invisible World*, 152.
11. Ibid., 151.
12. Carroll, *Puritanism and the Wilderness*, 8.
13. Ibid., 10–11.
14. O'Sullivan, "Annexation," 5.
15. Slotkin, *Regeneration through Violence*, 5; emphasis added.

16. Turner, *Frontier in American History*, 38; emphasis added.
17. Joshua 2:12.

BIBLIOGRAPHY

Appleman, Roy E. *Disaster in Korea: The Chinese Confront MacArthur*. College Station: Texas A&M University Press, 1989.
Carroll, Peter N. *Puritanism and the Wilderness: The Intellectual Significance of the New England Frontier 1629–1700*. New York: Columbia University Press, 1969.
Gleiberman, Owen. "*The Prophecy*." *Entertainment Weekly*, September 22, 1995. http://ew.com/article/1995/09/22/prophecy-2/.
Hammel, Eric M. *Chosin: Heroic Ordeal of the Korean War*. New York: Vanguard, 1981.
Kronke, David. "*Prophecy*: Sequel to Lucifer's Fall, Only with Guns, Cars." *Los Angeles Times*, September 4, 1995. http://articles.latimes.com/1995-09-04/entertainment/ca 42096_1_angel.
Mather, Cotton. "From *The Wonders of the Invisible World*." In *The Norton Anthology of American Literature*, shorter 8th ed., edited by Nina Baym, I: 151–55. New York: Norton, 2013.
The New Oxford Annotated Bible with the Apocrypha, rev. standard ed. New York: Oxford University Press, 1977.
O'Sullivan, John L. "Annexation." *United States Democratic Review* 17 (July–August 1845): 5.
The Prophecy. Directed by Gregory Widen. First Look Pictures, 1995. DVD.
Shepherd, Lemuel C., Jr. "Introduction." In Eric M. Hammel, *Chosin: Heroic Ordeal of the Korean War*. New York: Vanguard, 1981.
Slotkin, Richard. *Regeneration through Violence: The Mythology of the American Frontier, 1600–1860*. Norman: University of Oklahoma Press, 1973.
Turner, Frederick Jackson. *The Frontier in American History*. Charleston, SC: Bibliobazaar, 2008.

I(dio)t Follows

The Seashell E-Book
in It Follows

LEARNED FOOTE

The object described in this essay is not precisely a book; nor is it not a book. It is a prop from the 2015 horror film *It Follows*: a pink hand-held compact in the shape of a seashell, which opens to reveal an illuminated screen (complete with clock and wi-fi meter). The touch-screen shows about a hundred words at once. Its owner, a young woman named Yara, applies her thumb, and the words scroll smoothly upwards into that electronic ether where all words go once they leave our viewing screens. The book Yara reads on her seashell is Dostoevsky's *The Idiot* (1868–1869). This seashell book plays a relatively minor role in *It Follows*, taking up less than five minutes of screen-time and barely affecting the plot. While the story plays out with a strong dose of sex and supernatural monsters, Yara is merely a supporting character. Sometimes we see her in the background of a scene, reading from her seashell or using it as a flashlight. So why write about this seashell book?

When we trace this unusual object through the film, *It Follows* reveals its depths. Far more than the archetypal scary movie involving teenagers having sex and then being killed by a mysterious monster, *It Follows* is a meditation on the uncertainty of life and the role that art and friendship play in our efforts to make sense of the universe: mysterious, murderous, mundane and beautiful. The object plays a key aesthetic role by locating the film in a unique setting beyond the confines of space-time. It acts as a vacuum that sucks its contemporary audience into the film's universe. Over the course of the film, the characters discuss the seashell book three times: twice in brief and casual conversations, and ultimately in the film's final lines of dialogue. The seashell is a means to creatively explore the film's central thematic concern of inevitable, impending death. Yet these explorations never feel heavy-handed. The seashell book is not a tool to convey dogma or give answers. Rather, the book is a locus of poetic meaning and creative interpretation. It helps the characters come to terms with the monster and their own existence, even if it never promises to give an explanation of either. Likewise, *It Follows* retains a richly ambiguous and uncertain atmosphere up to its final moment, one that asks its audience to interpret its meaning for themselves. The seashell book acts as an unobtrusive symbol of these powerful poetic qualities.

The seashell e-book of *It Follows* (2015).

Teenagers Having Sex

Yara and her seashell play a deceptively small part in the movie. Most of the screen time is instead devoted to Jay, a young woman living in a Detroit suburb. Her life descends into horror when she has sex with a young man she doesn't know well in an abandoned parking lot. Afterwards, he chloroforms and kidnaps her. She wakes up tied to a wheelchair in a dark factory warehouse. The man seems agitated, looking out the window and uttering cryptic words about an impending threat. He explains that something is following him, and that he "gave it" to Jay in the car. "It can look like people you know, or it can be a stranger in a crowd. Whatever helps it get close to you." Suddenly he runs to the window. "I see it."

Jay too sees the monster: a silhouette of a naked woman. As Jay begins to scream for help, the woman comes closer and closer, one step at a time, until the man finally grabs the wheelchair and pulls her out of reach. "Never go anywhere that doesn't have more than one way out," he says as he leads them away from the slowly arriving monster, "it's very slow, but it's not dumb."

After this horrific encounter, the man dumps Jay back with her friends and disappears without any trace the police can find. As Jay discovers over the coming days, though she would rather not believe it, something indeed is following her, invisible to all who have not been initiated into the hellish ritual. She can pass the curse along by sleeping with someone else, but if the monster kills that person, it will again pursue her. She can run, but it's only a matter of time before the thing again approaches. Her best bet is to sleep in a room with many windows, each hung with bottles suspended from strings, so that she has a chance of waking in time to escape should the thing arrive while she sleeps. The remainder of the film deals with how Jay and her close-knit circle of friends deal with this strange being.

Breaking the Space-Time Barrier

Given all the supernatural excitement described above, why should we turn our attention to a little seashell e-book possessed by a minor character? For one (excepting a brief prologue), Yara is the only character to possess anything like a cell phone. Thus a prosaic object becomes an unsettling hint of the film's unstable sense of space-time. In and of itself, the e-book has its foot in multiple decades: a 1960s exterior, a 21st-century wi-fi meter, and a screen that displays words from a 19th-century Russian novel in an early 20th-century English translation. Director and screenwriter David Robert Mitchell explained in an interview how the production team transformed an old compact into a book, and how the film is constructed using elements from several different decades, lending the film a displaced and dream-like feeling: "I wanted an e-reader in there and I didn't want a particular model that everyone would date by a particular year. I felt like it would feel strange within the film. It would be too grounded in the moment. There's sort of a lot of odd, anachronistic production design elements, and it's all sort of to somewhat confuse you, to be honest. It's about not allowing the audience to place it within a specific moment in time, so it's somewhat timeless and it's also something that resembles things out of a dream to some degree."[1]

For the most part, the film has a distinctly retro feel, with dated pop-culture references and fashions. Yet the seashell book seems almost futuristic, and the wi-fi meter makes it evident that we're partly in the Internet age. The film offers no logical explanation for why Yara is the only character with access to wi-fi, or why none of the other characters have cell phones. Instead, the seashell hints that the film takes place in dreamland. Yara's book is the one point of reference that connects the film to the contemporary technology its audience takes for granted. Yet the technology appears in the form of an unfamiliar device, both grounding the film's universe in our own familiar world, and yet pointing to how the film's universe is wholly beyond our world.

Subtle Introductions

In the scene where we first meet Yara and her seashell book, we have few initial clues about the book's dreamlike and uncanny qualities. Initially, the focus of the scene is Jay, whom we meet lounging alone in her pool (she casually drowns an insect, her only companion). Jay's sister Kelly tells her that their friends Paul and Yara have arrived to watch a movie. Jay declines the offer to join the group because she wants to meet a man (the one who will impart the curse). As Jay, still the center of the scene, enters the house, an establishing wide shot shows nearly all the main characters of the film. On the far left sits her mother, facing away from the camera and holding a glass of wine in her hand. Jay's sister, along with Paul and Yara, sits on the couch facing a television. Jay pauses a moment to watch the TV with her friends, a towel wrapped around her waist. Yara sits furthest to the right, barely noticeable.

We see the seashell first as a half-moon unobtrusively sticking out of Yara's palm. She is intently focused on the device, wearing a neutral expression, perhaps a slight frown. At first glance, the sight is all-too-familiar: a young person apparently lost in their smartphone. Meanwhile the other characters stare dully at the TV screen, seemingly all in private technologically-bound universes even as they share the same couch. No wonder Jay prefers to ditch her friends in favor of some old-fashioned flesh-and-blood interaction.

At that moment, however, the film goes on to take a closer look. We move into a medium shot showing Paul and Yara, and then into a close-up of the device Yara holds.

Yara's (Olivia Luccardi) e-book seems to replace human companionship as she sits beside Paul (Kier Gilchrist) to watch a movie in *It Follows* (2015).

Now we see it is not a smartphone but rather an e-book. The lines on its screen come from Eva Martin's 1915 English translation of Dostoevsky's *The Idiot*, which is available on Project Gutenberg. I like to imagine that Yara chose the version she could download for free.

Jay asks Yara what she's reading (thus implying she knows Yara to be a bookworm and therefore illustrating the hidden depths of the characters' friendship). Yara answers her: "*The Idiot*." "Is it good?" Jay asks. "I don't know yet," Yara says, then quips: "It's about Paul." She tells her friends: "Hey, I've got an idea," and when they ask what it is, she shifts in her seat and farts, saying, "It got away."

The seashell thus acts to subvert our expectations about the characters. In the first shot, the tableau depicts bored teenagers alienated from each other and engrossed in technology. Yet the technology is not what it seems; Yara's device is not a mundane object, but rather a unique and subtly disorienting example of the film's dream-like logic. To add to the unexpectedness, we find that Yara is reading Dostoevsky, not in a dreary and pretentious manner, but rather as an opportunity for gentle ribbing and fart jokes. Finally, we find that Yara is not at all alienated from her friends. Even though she seems distracted by an electronic device, the scene demonstrates how mindfully attuned she is to the interactions between them. She makes a "*tsk*" sound at Paul's attempts to flirt with Jay, and she notices when Jay leaves the group.

The moments described above occupy mere seconds of screen time. Yet the film manages to convey quite a bit in this scene. Here is a group of friends that has known each other since childhood, with a complex interweaving of relationships defined both by sympathy and gentle mocking. Jay belongs to a community shaped not so much by parental figures (the mother is a spectral presence defined by alcohol and aloofness) as by friends that care about her. It is this connection with others that gives *It Follows* so much of its heart, and its sense of hopefulness in the face of the horror that will soon descend. Our introduction to Yara and her seashell is brief. As Jay moves on to her date, the audience quickly moves on to sexy, audience-pleasing scares. However, these moments hint at the thematic ground that come to define the heart of *It Follows*.

Passing the Time: Novels, Card Games and Drinking on the Porch

The next scene featuring Yara and her book occurs immediately after Jay has first encountered the monster while strapped to a wheelchair. As Jay faces down sexuality and horror, Yara, Paul, and Kelly sit up at night playing cards on the porch. While they play, Yara multitasks, reading from her seashell. She reads a passage to her friends:

> YARA: Listen to this. "I think that if one is faced by inevitable destruction—if a house is falling upon you, for instance—one must feel a great longing to sit down, close one's eyes and wait, come what may..."
> KELLY: That's why we're drinking on the porch.

Here, the book serves as a means to tie the friends together. As before, in an age of smartphones, one could easily read Yara's engrossment in an electronic device as an example of an individual being disconnected from the game she's playing with her friends. Yet, precisely the opposite is the case. Yara is invested in the card game, and she also takes her solitary reading experience and brings it to the group. Moreover, when she does so, Kelly identifies with the passage. She takes a circumstance from a Russian novel, and creatively connects it to the group's communal experience, thereby reinterpreting their lives in light of Yara's contribution.

Kelly's brief comment reveals an underlying imaginative structure that is at play whenever we identify with someone else. In the relevant scene in the Dostoevsky novel, the idiot Prince Myshkin is telling a story of seeing a prisoner about to be executed. Identifying with the prisoner, he imagines how he would feel if he were in the prisoner's shoes. As Richard Pevear notes in his introduction to his translation of *The Idiot*, this passage is based upon Dostoevsky's own experience of nearly being executed as a young man.[2] So in Dostoevsky, a fictional character identifies with another fictional character, whose own experience is based on the artist's. And in *It Follows*, another fictional character identifies with Dostoevsky's fictional characters. We could also understand Yara as a reflection of David Robert Mitchell's own experience reading Dostoevsky and then quoting it to his "friends" (in this case being the audience of his film), an analogy which places us in the role of Kelly, assigning meanings on top of this quotation. Art spurs these sorts of identifications. Yet how valid is Kelly's identification with Dostoevsky's words of the man who will be executed?

The passage appears to relate far more closely to Jay's experience with the monster, which is ongoing even as the friends (as yet, unknowingly) relax on the porch. Thanks to the curse, Jay has just been gifted with the awareness of a constantly impending "inevitable destruction" like the one that Dostoevsky describes. She can literally see death coming for her at all times. The monster is impelled towards her as if by gravitational force: it will walk up and down stairs, crawl through spaces, break windows, or whatever else is necessary to reach Jay. Yara's Dostoevsky passage describes the human inclination to give up in the face of the knowledge of death. *It Follows* depicts an example of this inclination in its opening prologue, in which a woman flees the invisible monster, only to sit on a beach and wait for the monster to come. She calls to tell her father she loves him, having apparently given up on survival. The screenplay specifies that in the scene before Yara reads this passage on the porch, Jay's "eyes are heavy." This suggests that David Robert Mitchell understands Jay to be feeling some of that same desire to give up.

Jay wrestles with the resignation that Dostoevsky describes. But unlike the first victim in the film, she does not give up.

Her persistence in the face of the monster's threat to her stems, in part, from her friends drinking on the porch. They support her tirelessly, even when she runs away from them. They stay up at night with her to try and keep her safe, they help her in her search to find out where the monster came from, they put themselves in physical danger, and—when necessary—they run with her. Self-preservation is never their only goal. Jay is struck with a murderous curse, and as far as they're concerned, this is an issue for the group.

So even though Jay is the one with the curse of seeing "inevitable destruction" as Dostoevsky's idiot describes, it seems that Kelly is also right to identify with the idiot. Kelly never sees death coming for her in the extraordinary way that Jay does, but as she sits in the mundane circumstances drinking on the porch, she is willing to admit that this is how she feels. It is this identification that helps the friends to gather around Jay and support her. The way that Kelly reframes the Dostoevsky quote is revealing. As Yara describes, "one" faces destruction as an individual. This is the way that the man who curses Jay leaves her at the end of this scene, when he dumps her alone on the side of the road by her house. But as Kelly says, "that's why we're drinking on the porch." It's no longer "one," but "we." And though Jay is left momentarily alone, her friends rush from the porch to help her and to stand by her.

As the idiot identifies with the prisoner to be executed, and Kelly identifies with the idiot in the novel, we as the audience can identify with the characters in the film. Though we may not see death as a supernatural entity walking towards us as Jay does, it is easy to identify with Kelly and Yara drinking on the porch, passing the time with card games. Such circumstances feel familiar. Likewise we pass the time with friends, in meaningless card games, or in fictional universes like Dostoevsky's or that of *It Follows* itself. Kelly's observation is that death comes at all times, even in the boring moments when the clock ticks one slow step at a time. Boredom and death by supernatural sex monster are not so far apart.

The way Yara uses her e-reader is thus significant: The book passes the time, but it imputes meaning to time as it passes. Yara does not use it to escape from community. Rather, although it affords her moments of private reflection (the screenplay specifies in one moment cut from the film that "Yara's eyes dart excitedly over her cell phone screen. She smiles and nods to herself—enjoying some undisclosed prose"[3]), her experience with the novel is ultimately something that she brings to the group, thereby deepening the bond between them. Likewise, these fictional universes interpenetrate with our own; we imaginatively project ourselves into the characters' lives, and the fiction gives new meaning to our lives. It provides the ground for conversation, creates the opportunity for imaginative identification, and helps to foment the bonds of community.

Identifying with Scary Art

Art—even heavily stylized art like a supernatural horror film—can reflect our experiences. We see this in the way Yara and Kelly interpret Dostoevsky, and *It Follows* provides another example in a scene where Jay encounters the monster. In this scene, Jay sits in a college classroom while a professor reads from T. S. Eliot's "The Love Song of J. Alfred Prufrock." The professor reads the passage where the narrator reflects on a "head (grown slightly bald)," further linking the monster to the normal flow of life in which death follows us, bit by bit. The professor continues reading:

> I have seen the moment of my greatness flicker,
> And I have seen the eternal Footman hold my coat, and snicker,
> And in short, I was afraid…
> "I am Lazarus, come from the dead,
> Come back to tell you all, I shall tell you all."

She reads these words just as Jay catches sight of an elderly woman in a nightgown slowly making her way across the college campus towards her (one might even imagine that Jay is seeing her own future as an elderly woman approach her). The lines from the poem are carefully timed with horrific images and sounds, to suggest that the monster bears some resonance with this "eternal Footman," this "Lazarus." The poem's own literary references, in turn, evoke Lazarus of Bethany from the Gospel of John. Such resonance is not conveyed by logical argument, but instead by emotional correspondence. Jay is afraid at the moment that the poet is afraid and the audience is afraid. The emotions and images spill into each other, tightening our bond both with Jay and with T. S. Eliot. This emotional identification is one of the hallmarks of the horror genre. As Noël Carroll argues in "The Nature of Horror," the genre defines itself in terms of the emotion that it provokes in its audience: horror imparts fear. Moreover, he says, "horror appears to be one of those genres in which, ideally, the emotive responses the audience run parallel to the emotions of characters. Indeed, in works of horror the responses of characters often seem to cue the emotional responses of the audience."[4]

It Follows is a typical horror film by Carroll's definition, in that it creates fear by showing us characters who are afraid of a monster. Yet its literary references deepen and complicate our sense of fear. By associating the impending supernatural monster with passages from Dostoevsky and Eliot, the film not only associates the monster with a grotesque sex-demon, but also forges links with our awareness of the human condition of uncertain death that approaches with every moment of aging. As the audience of a scary movie, we feel visceral panic for the obvious reason that a deadly monster is on screen. Yet this panic mingles with our reception of Eliot's lines about a "head (grown

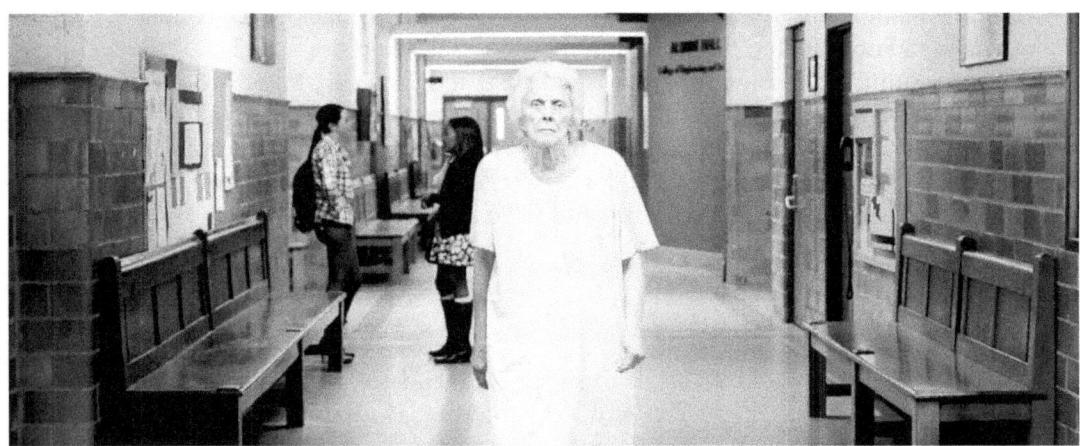

An elderly woman in a nightgown (Ingrid Mortimer) makes her way toward Jay in *It Follows* (2015)

slightly bald)." Our fear of impending death is no longer distant and easy to ignore, but instead becomes as urgent as a monster stalking us.

Stuart Hanscomb argues that art-horror acts precisely by using imaginative and fantastic contexts to force a confrontation with real existential crises: "the contingency of what exists and the nothingness of the self are ideas that are difficult to call to mind and attain heat for the individual, and thus they readily become buried under the clutter of the everyday."[5] Horror invokes emotion that shakes us out of this stupor; but, as Hanscomb goes on to say, it is "up to the individual as to whether the roots and implications of what is awakened are pursued and refined."[6] *It Follows* is remarkable for the way it artfully suggests these implications. One such implication is visible in the nature of the monster itself.

What Is the Monster?

One of Carroll's main points in defining the monster of art-horror (building on Mary Douglas's work on purity codes in the book of Leviticus) is that the monster tends to transgress boundaries of "me/not me, inside/outside, and living/dead" as do common objects of disgust, such as "feces … spittle, blood, tears, sweat, hair clippings, nail clippings, pieces of flesh, and so on."[7] He goes on to say that the "frequent references to monsters by means of pronouns like "it" and "them" suggests that these creatures are not classifiable according to our standard categories."[8] The very name *It Follows* lends support to Carroll's observation, but one remarkable aspect of the monster in the film is how *ordinary* it appears. It always takes a human guise (frequently a friend or family member), and often one that is defined by abjection in terms of social convention: the monster appears naked, or urinating on itself, or as an elderly woman wearing a nightgown in public. As Hanscomb suggests, one of the fears monsters evoke stems from "our concern for our own ambiguous ontology."[9] Part of the fear of the monster is that it represents such a broad swath of humanity, including those aspects we prefer to keep hidden (sickness, old age, death).

Carroll also observes that monsters tend to be "unnatural relative to a culture's conceptual scheme of nature…. Monsters are not only physically threatening; they are cognitively threatening."[10] As Timothy Morton pointed out to me in one of our conversations about the film, the title *It Follows* carries a connotation of logic, a sort of inevitable QED that can never be escaped. Yet everything about the formless, shape-shifting, yet human-appearing monster suggests a simultaneous irrationality that lurks beneath. As the tagline for the movie states: "It doesn't think … it follows." The monster represents, in Carroll's terms, a threat to knowledge.

This emphasis on irrationality proved troubling for many viewers of *It Follows*. In particular, the monster at times appeared to be breaking the rules that Jay learned from her kidnapper. For example, Quentin Tarantino argued that David Robert Mitchell "broke his mythology left, right, and center."[11] Examples occur when we see the monster standing perfectly still, breaking the pattern of slow advancement, one step at a time. *It Follows* is interesting, however, precisely because of this threat to knowledge. My reaction to these scenes in the initial days after seeing the film (during which I always made sure I was in a room with more than one exit) was to frantically browse the Internet, searching for fan theories and explanations, almost as if I could gain enough information to stave off some existential threat. Mitchell seems to anticipate this reaction in an interview with Yahoo:

The only rules that we hear are rules that we're told by a character within the film, who has access to limited information. If you look at the film enough, you can start to understand how he may be figuring these things out and how he has gotten the information that he has. But you also have to understand that they're not rules on a stone's [sic] tablet; they're a character's best guess about what's happening to them. So, you know, they seem mostly right. But for me, that's kind of fun, in that there might be some gaps in information, some things that he doesn't understand and neither do we.[12]

There Are No Answers to be Found in Books

As Mitchell says, part of the fun of *It Follows* comes from the way in which the monster defies rationality and breaks the "rules on a stone's tablet." Here his reference to the Ten Commandments emphasizes the insufficiency of dogma. The monster doesn't quite seem to fit the rules that the characters impart to each other.

It's understandable that the characters in the film (and the audiences) seem so intent on figuring out the mechanics or the rules for just how the monster works. Such a desire to impose order is akin to the desire to impose order (whether religious or philosophical) on the chaos of existence. As H.P. Lovecraft writes in "Supernatural Horror in Literature," the horror genre is defined in particular by the "fear of the unknown" (or a monster that refuses to follow the rules), a "psychological pattern or tradition as real and as deeply grounded in mental experience as any other pattern or tradition of mankind; coeval with the religious feeling and closely related to many aspects of it."[13] *It Follows* is powerful because it evokes strong emotions, which are tied to our deepest fears of what it means to be human, grow old, and die. Yet in the face of this dilemma, *It Follows* tends to offer questions more than answers, poetry rather than dogma. Though the film provides a series of rules for how to deal with the monster, these inevitably fall short of describing what we actually witness of the monster's behavior.

Here is where Yara and her seashell book become important. The more we learn about the monster, the more we find that it is described better by poetry than law. The rules about the monster's behavior fail to explain its ambiguous and irrational ontology. In contrast, the poetic analogies—both Yara and her seashell book, and the professor reading T. S. Eliot—seem to get to the heart of what the monster is. A skeptic might say that these poetic resonances succeed where dogma fails because they give less helpful advice (even if the clear-cut rules don't always explain the monster, at least they give some helpful tips for temporarily avoiding it). In contrast, the poetic analogies, though they describe the monster well, do not offer Jay any answers for how to deal with it. In the scene introducing the seashell, the characters are watching television. Specifically, they're watching *Killers from Space*, which also has an odd resonance with their experiences in facing the monster.[14] The characters in the black-and-white film talk about how "you can't tap enough electricity wherever you get it from," which echoes a situation faced by the characters near the film's climax. But this doesn't help them in getting rid of the monster; it only points out that their plan is doomed to fail in advance. Considered collectively, these books and movies don't seem to help the characters in any concrete way. There are no strict definitions, no how-to guides. Rather, what *It Follows* reveals in its quotations from literature is a dense web of symbols, a shock of recognition and reinterpretation, a means of describing the indescribable in a roundabout way.

The final scene with dialogue (though not the last scene of the film itself, which is beautiful and wordless) features Yara reading from her seashell book, as Jay listens: "And the most terrible agony may not be in the wounds themselves, but in knowing for certain that within an hour, then within ten minutes, then within half a minute, now at this very instant—your soul will leave your body and you will no longer be a person, and that this is certain; the worst thing is that it is certain." In one respect, these words speak clearly to the threat that the monster poses, both in terms of its literal appearance in the movie, and of its metaphoric significance to the audience. The monster comes closer and closer, with the aim of killing. The time of death is uncertain, but it inevitably draws closer.

The larger significance of the scene, however, lies not merely in these rather depressing words but in the fact that they are spoken by a friend who is sitting up in a hospital bed, injured perhaps, but for the moment avoiding death. The passage from *The Idiot* that she reads in the final scene comes *before* the section that she read out loud to her friends on the porch, suggesting she has read and re-read the book with close attention. Moreover, the scene suggests she chose lines to share with Jay, an act of generosity that mirrors Jay coming to visit her friend in the hospital. The underlying subtext of the scene, never stated through dialogue, but visible nonetheless, is that these are people who care about each other: who have come to an awareness of death, but continue to live as death comes ever closer.

Yara makes a dour pronouncement when she describes the monster, but she does it with her mouth full, chewing cheerfully. The impression is not only that these friends support each other, but that Dostoevsky supports them too, offering a glimpse of shared experience that is its own kind of comfort. The seashell book doesn't do away with the monster. But it acts as one of the supports that help them survive as a group of friends, even if only for an hour, for ten minutes, in this very instant.

Notes

1. Hayes, "'It Follows' Director David Robert Mitchell."
2. Pevear, "Introduction," xix.
3. Mitchell, *It Follows* (script).
4. Carroll, "Nature of Horror," 52.
5. Hanscomb, "Existentialism and Art-Horror," 17.
6. *Ibid.*
7. Carroll, "Nature of Horror," 55.
8. *Ibid.*
9. Hanscomb, "Existentialism and Art-Horror," 15.
10. Carroll, "Nature of Horror," 56.
11. Brown, "In Conversation: Quentin Tarantino."
12. Watkins, "Yahoo Movies Interview."
13. Lovecraft, "Supernatural Horror in Literature."
14. I came upon this comparison in one of the many Internet fan-theories when I first saw the film, but could not find an original source.

Bibliography

Brown, Lane. "In Conversation: Quentin Tarantino," *New York Magazine*, August 24, 2015. http://www.vulture.com/2015/08/quentin-tarantino-lane-brown-in-conversation.html

Carroll, Noël, "The Nature of Horror." *The Journal of Aesthetics and Art Criticism*, Vol. 46, No. 1, Autumn, 1987. http://www.jstor.org/stable/431308

Hanscomb, Stuart. "Existentialism and Art-Horror." *Sartre Studies International*, Vol. 16, No. 1, 2010. http://www.jstor.org/stable/23512850

Hayes, Britt. "'It Follows' Director David Robert Mitchell On His Distinctive and Timeless Horror Film," March 2014. http://screencrush.com/it-follows-david-robert-mitchell-interview/

It Follows. Directed by David Robert Mitchell. 2015. Beverley Hills, CA: Anchor Bay Entertainment, 2015. DVD.

Lovecraft, H.P. "Supernatural Horror in Literature." 1927. http://www.hplovecraft.com/writings/texts/essays/shil.aspx.

Mitchell, David Robert. *It Follows*. Film script. 2013. http://la-screenwriter.com/wp-content/uploads/2016/03/IT-FOLLOWS-2015-by-David-Robert-Mitchell.pdf.

Pevear, Richard. "Introduction." In *The Idiot*, by Fyodor Dostoevsky, translated by Richard Pevear and Larissa Volokhonsky. New York: Vintage Classics, 2001.

Watkins, Gwynne. "The Yahoo Movies Interview: '*It Follows*' Director David Robert Mitchell on his Surprise Horror Hit." March 21, 2015. https://www.yahoo.com/movies/the-yahoo-movies-interview-it-follows-director-114138739632.html.

Perspectives on *The Babadook*

"The more you deny me, the stronger I get"
"Mister Babadook" and the Monstrous Empowerment of Children's Culture

Jessica Balanzategui

In *The Babadook* (2014), a children's picture book called "Mister Babadook" that mysteriously appears—and relentlessly *reappears*—in the household of a single mother and her young son functions as the vessel for a monstrous bogeyman. The book echoes the familiar form and aesthetics of interactive pop-up books for young children, featuring large, evocative pop-up and lift-the-flap illustrations, and simple text which follows a nursery rhyme-esque poetic pattern incorporating onomatopoeia, rhymes, rhythmic repetition, and nonsensical textual play. Yet while the book adopts the innocent, playful form of literature for very young children, "Mister Babadook" holds monstrous power. The book becomes the crucible for the mother and son's social isolation, the disintegration of their relationship and household, and the monstrous resurfacing of their suppressed familial traumas. As a result, the text functions as a Gothic subversion of children's literature, and monstrously empowers the realm of children's culture so that it holds sway over the life and imagination of the adult as well as the child, with horrifying results.

In this essay I argue that, through its monstrous pop-up book, *The Babadook* expresses potent anxieties about the growing power of children's culture over adult realities in the early 21st century. The movement from childhood to adulthood tends to be conceived as a "growing out" of children's culture, as is represented by the diminishing power of fictional texts and images—particularly those representative of children's culture—over adult lives and psyches. As Marina Warner suggests, in childhood "the stories and other materials summoning the bogeyman in one guise or another not only give existing fears a face and form, but can also excite them and shape them in the first place."[1] As a result, a key barometer marking the shift from childhood into adulthood is that "we learn to live peaceably with this power of images to conjure realities."[2] By reinstating the threat represented by the bogeyman of children's literature, *The Babadook* depicts a monstrous retrogression from adulthood into childhood, as the bogeyman—an embodiment of childish fears—becomes a source of anxiety for the adult protagonist and viewer.

The Supernatural Irrationality of Children's Culture

In the second decade of the 21st century, one of the central recurring preoccupations of the horror genre has been the supernaturally-charged empowerment of the texts and images representative of children's culture. These films center their horrors around the (re)positioning of a child character's seemingly imaginary bogeyman as a threat to both the adult protagonist and the assumed adult audience (these films tend to be firmly adult-oriented with ratings ranging from PG–13 to R). As well as *The Babadook*, these films include *Don't Be Afraid of the Dark* (2010), *Mama* (2013), *Intruders* (2011), *Sinister* (2012), *The Conjuring 2* (2016) and *Before I Wake* (2016). Each of these films dramatizes the violent eruption of the previously subjugated realm of children's culture—as signified by images, stories, toys and lullaby-like nonsense expressions—into the adult's reality. In all of these films, a childhood bogeyman, initially dismissed as a harmless and insignificant figment of the child's imagination by the adult characters, comes to terrorize not just the children, but the adult characters and viewers as well. Thus, these films construct the adult's disregard for the power of the child's imaginary and culture as their undoing.

As Steven Bruhm suggests, the repeated emphasis on children in contemporary Gothic texts "has a particular emotive force for us because it brings into high relief exactly what the child knows…. Invariably, the Gothic child knows too much, and that knowledge makes us more than a little nervous."[3] In these supernatural bogeyman films, however, it is not the *quantity* of the child's knowledge that is unsettling, but the *quality*: it is not that the children are revealed to possess too much knowledge about the adult world, but that the modes of knowledge that we perceive as unique to childhood are suddenly empowered and defy their marginalized existence. These films thus enact a shift in the traditional power balance between children and their adult guardians, whereby "childish" fears become adult ones. This preoccupation entails a subversion of the very connotations of childishness, in turn illuminating contemporary cultural contortions surrounding the shifting power balances and conceptual relationships between childhood and adulthood in the 21st century.

The child has long been defined through a comparative lack of reason and knowledge in relation to the rational, experienced and knowledgeable adult. That the child's conceptual constitution is underpinned by this comparative *lack* of adult understanding justifies the child's subordination within a family unit and institutionalized processes of socialization. The roots of these ideologies about childhood can be seen in Enlightenment philosopher John Locke's famous contention that the child is born a "white paper"—a *tabula rasa* or blank slate—and is gradually filled with knowledge on the path towards adulthood,[4] and the ideologies of Romantic poets and philosophers such as Jean-Jacques Rousseau and William Wordsworth which idealize this "blank" child as a natural, pre-rational being. These 18th- and early 19th-century concepts continue to buttress contemporary, common-sense understandings of the child. Yet while the Romantic notion that "childhood is the sleep of reason"[5] remains a key component of 21st-century definitions of childhood, this notion also constructs the child as an empty and enigmatic figure who can motivate anxiety and ambivalence. As Spanish painter Francisco Goya suggests in the title of one of his most unsettling works, "the sleep of reason produces monsters."

As is illuminated by the recent cycle of monstrous bogeymen films, the child's symbolically-charged "sleep of reason" has become an increasingly complex and ambivalent signifier of childhood's demarcation from adulthood throughout the late 20th and 21st centuries. As Chris Jenks elucidates, the child has come to represent a "continuous paradox, albeit expressed in a variety of forms. Simply stated, the child is familiar to us and yet strange; he or she inhabits our world and yet seems to answer to another; he or she is essentially of ourselves and yet appears to display a systematically different order of being."[6] The psychic realm of childhood is romanticized in paradoxical ways that delineate this "systematically different order of being." The pre-rationality and pre-logicism of childhood is bound to childhood's relational definition as socially and cognitively inferior to adulthood, while at the same time being associated with a unique and precious insight that extends beyond the perceptual capabilities of adulthood. Philippe Ariès, one of the first and most influential theorists of childhood, illustrates how the development of the modern schooling system was integral to the formation of such ambivalent borders of separation between the mental life of the child and the adult. As Richard Sennett explains, Ariès found that by the mid–18th century "adults were beginning to think of themselves as fundamentally different kinds of creatures from those who were their children. The child was no longer thought of as a little adult. Childhood was conceived as a special and vulnerable stage; adulthood was defined in reversed terms."[7] As Ariès states, the development of institutions of schooling towards the end of the 17th century revolved around conceptions of "the weakness of childhood ... [but a weakness] associated with its innocence ... and which placed education in the front rank of man's obligations."[8] He points out that the Romantic idea of innocence as inherent to childhood subsequently resulted in two kinds of attitudes towards socialization and education that remain central to understandings of the child, "firstly, safeguarding it against pollution by life, and secondly strengthening it by developing character and reason."[9]

The modern education system is thus structured around "the association of childhood with primitivism and irrationalism or prelogicism"[10]: a process of institutionalized inferiority that Marina Warner suggests has paradoxically become central to childhood's symbolic power. She asserts that the unreason of children is typically realized in the popular imaginary as an "intimate connection, above all, to a wonderful, free-floating world of the imagination. Their observable, active fantasy life, and their fluid make-believe play seem to give them access to a world of wisdom."[11] Recent bogeymen films expose the Gothic underside to this myth: not yet inculcated into the world of adult reason, the children in these films are gifted with a supernatural insight that penetrates beyond accepted adult discourse. These films anxiously aestheticize the empowerment of children's pre-rational culture, as the child's rich, fantasy realm—embodied by the bogeyman—comes to overwhelm the adult's own logical, rational modes of being. Thus, the bogeyman derails the epistemological structures that undergird the primacy and dominance of adult knowledge and perception, in so doing unsettling long-entrenched adult/child power relations.

As a result, in line with Warner's suggestion, the child's quasi-sacred lack of reason comes to be characterized as a "supernatural irrationality,"[12] revealing the extent to which "childhood, placed at a tangent to adulthood, perceived as special and magical, precious and dangerous at once, has turned into some volatile stuff—hydrogen, or mercury, which has to be contained."[13] Recent bogeyman films thus interrogate the tendency Warner identifies in contemporary culture in which "the separate condition of the child has never been so bounded by thinking, so established in law as it is today," playing upon a revelation that many of our anxiously-determined contradictions surrounding the child arise from this very "concept that childhood and adult life are separate when they are inextricably intertwined."[14]

Childhood/Adulthood Bogeymen

Refracting such anxieties about the shadowy borderlands between child and adult life, the recent cycle of bogeyman horror films play out the fear that the supposedly fictional, "childish" bogeymen of children's culture are slipping into the adult real in insidious ways, and that it is their depiction in children's art and stories which functions as the channel for this slippage. Such a fixation is heralded by some of the taglines of these films, which include "Fear Is Never Just Make Believe" (*Don't Be Afraid of the Dark*), "The Nightmare Is Real" (*Intruders*), "Once you see him, nothing can save you" (*Sinister*), "Fear Your Dreams" (*Before I Wake*) and "If it's in a word, or in a book, you can't get rid of the Babadook" (*The Babadook*). As the taglines suggest, the films imply that adult culture's dismissal of the power of children's culture allows bogeymen to creep into adult realities, empowered through this very dismissal. These films tend to structure their supernatural horror plots around the monstrous eruption of the bogeyman into the adult's world after the adult protagonist sees him visually depicted in a child's drawing or storybook, a narrative mechanism that is paralleled for the viewer by the gradual infiltration of the supernatural into the seemingly realist, adult-centered diegesis initially established in each film. As a result, the viewer functions as the adult protagonist's proxy, terrorized by the replacement of the rationally-grounded diegesis with a supernatural one emergent from the "supernatural irrationality" of children's culture.

Foregrounding the bogeyman's threat to viewers in a way that parallels the diegetic threat he poses to adult characters, the marketing campaigns for these films tend to extend the supernatural power of their bogeyman images beyond the fictional realm of the film and into the viewer's reality. For instance, the poster for *Sinister* depicts a little girl creating a macabre fingerpainting of the face of the film's bogeyman figure—known to the children in the film as "Mr Boogie" and to the adult characters as "Baguul"—using what appears to be blood. This poster image references the climactic set-piece of the film, in which the central child figure, a little girl named Ashley, uses her parents' blood to draw pictures of "Mr. Boogie" on the walls of her house after murdering her family with a hatchet, an act carried out at the bogeyman's bidding. The film's aforementioned tagline, "Once You See Him, Nothing Can Save You," references the narrative conceit that Mr. Boogie draws his power from the images that depict him: once his image has been seen, he will never stop haunting or pursuing his victim. In tandem with this tagline, a viral marketing campaign was launched which revolved around the film's website, "haveyouseenhim.com," which encouraged visitors to report on apparent sightings of the bogeyman's image in their local public spaces. This tagline and marketing campaign imply that Mr. Boogie's reach extends beyond not only the child character's imagination and into the adult character's reality, but also beyond the fictional diegesis of the film and into our own reality.

Similarly, *The Babadook*'s marketing campaign extra-diegetically reinforced the uncontainable power of the bogeyman's depiction in text and images. The film's tagline is drawn from the children's storybook in which the eponymous bogeyman first appears: "If it's in a word or in a look, you can't get rid of the Babadook." The film's poster couples this nursery rhyme-esque phrase with a childlike drawing of the monster—which evokes a crude chalk drawing on a blackboard—clearly rendering this monster as emergent from children's culture, while at the same time suggesting that these very images and words are imbued with a monstrous force that cannot be dismissed or excised once these materials have been seen. Like *Sinister*, *The Babadook* was advertised in Europe via a viral marketing campaign which asked participants via Twitter whether they had seen "the Babadook," as images of the creature were circulated without context across the internet and on the pavements or walls of various cities. Furthermore, subsequent to the film's release, real-life, material versions of the pop-up storybook which conjures "Mister Babadook" in the film were created by the filmmakers in collaboration with illustrator Alex Juhasz, published in limited edition by pop-up book specialist Insight Editions. As the film's website explained in its call-out for crowd-funding to support the book's publication: "join Mister Babadook in his plans for world domination by helping him get his very own pop-up book published."

Thus, the marketing material for both *Sinister* and *The Babadook* heralds each film's preoccupation with the "power of images to conjure realities" in the child's psyche, a power that we typically learn to "live peaceably with" upon our entrance into adulthood.[15] The horrors of these films center upon the renewed power of this "magic of make-believe,"[16] as the visual materials that summon the bogeyman in the child's imagination gradually craft him into a real-life presence: as the tagline for *Don't be Afraid of the Dark* suggests, "Fear Is Never Just Make-Believe." As a result, these films pivot on the gradual revelation that the monsters that inhabit the child's "sleep of reason" are not contained within the subjugated domain of childhood, but are *shared* between child and adult, challenging the previously secure distinctions between child and adult worlds. Chris Jenks

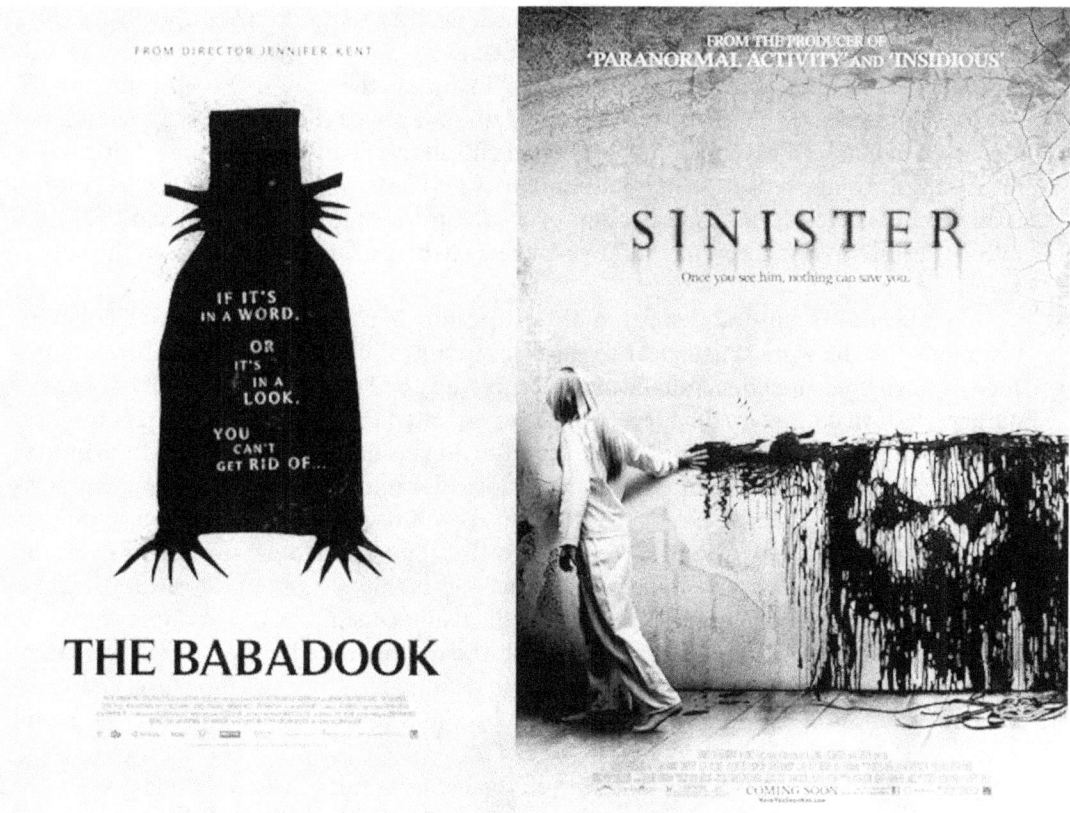

The Babadook (2014) and *Sinister* (2012) posters.

suggests that in contrast to children's culture, the adult's world tends to be characterized as "firmly established, rational.... This adult world is not only assumed to be complete, recognizable in stasis, but also, and perhaps most significantly, desirable. It is a benevolent and coherent totality."[17] *Sinister*'s Mr. Boogie and *The Babadook*'s Mister Babadook violently undermine the adult world's "coherent totality" in relation to the "supernatural irrationality"[18] of childhood—a challenge staged at the interface between individual child and adult identities, and between child and adult culture wholesale. This undermining of clear boundaries of separation between child and adult culture is made most explicit in *The Babadook* by the fact that the monster is located in, and summoned by, one of the most archetypal signifiers of children's culture: a pop-up storybook.

Fear Is Never Just Make-Believe: Horrifying Retrogressions

The child's storybook "Mister Babadook" is thus depicted as horrifying for the way in which it draws into the adult's rational present the irrational power of childish make-believe. Such cultural anxieties about the ontological status of children's culture and "make-believe" are pervasive in the contemporary cultural moment, also being embedded in the moral panic that has come to surround "The Slenderman": a bogeyman-like figure of internet folklore, who in 2014 became implicated in an attempted murder committed by two 12-year-old girls against one of their friends. As I and my co-author Naja Later suggest in a previous study, this bogeyman came "to enact in unnerving ways a simultaneous personal and cultural regression, a fusion at the core of Freud's uncanny."[19] According to Freud, the unsettling cognitive dissonance of the uncanny is the result of repressed beliefs and psychical material from childhood resurfacing in the adult psyche, provoking a strange sensation of both familiarity and unfamiliarity. On a parallel cultural level, Freud suggests that the uncanny is related to the return, or confirmation in the rational present, of surmounted cultural beliefs such as magic, animism, and the supernatural.[20]

While Freud's cultural definition of the uncanny betrays an unquestioned colonialism related to the work's historical context, it remains the case that supernatural figures such as bogeymen are conceptualized as a repressed and "surmounted" belief of contemporary Western culture on dual levels: both surmounted in the present "coherent totality" of the adult psyche, and on a cultural level following earlier historical stages of primitive belief. As Bliss Cua Lim explains, modern historical frameworks place supernatural folklore as a crude, early stage of human and cultural evolution in relation to Western modernity. Supernatural mediations of reality are thus "positioned as already known and surmounted precursors, not something disturbing that persists alongside and within the modern but as relics of superseded chronological antecedents."[21] The fictional children's bogeymen of recent horror films thus disturb the disenchanted, rational frameworks of the modernist present on a cultural level, and in simultaneity invoke a monstrous personal retrogression as the mental life of adulthood becomes invaded by the ghouls that haunt childhood.

This retrogression unseats long-entrenched child-adult power relations because, as Gareth Matthews explains, a defining feature of childhood is that the child is considered to be "'unfinished' relative to human *telos*,"[22] while the adult is, to return to Jenks' terms, "complete, recognizable in stasis."[23] As Jenks states elsewhere, the result of this ideological construction is that the child is defined as ascending on a set linear trajectory, with "adult competence being journey's end—the modernist project writ small!"[24] Thus, that the child's bogeyman is suddenly positioned in these films as a source of widespread cultural fear beyond the realm of children's culture points to the unraveling of the twinned personal and cultural "modernist project" of disenchantment conceptually embedded in child/adult relations: the child's epistemic "incompleteness" is challenged by the empowerment of bogeymen in tandem with the undermining of adulthood's "completeness." As a result, via a combined personal and cultural retrogression, these films express a complex constellation of anxieties related to the wavering of boundaries between adult and childhood cultures, refracting as a source of horror Warner's identification of the contemporary collision of child/adult worlds: "Children's culture has been gradually growing closer to the culture of adults, as children themselves—their psychology, their concerns, their dreams and desire—have become more and more central to art and culture."[25] By attaching the horrors of this collision to a child's pop-up storybook *The Babadook* explicitly works through the cultural tensions underlying shifting relationships between child and adult worlds.

Mister Babadook

The Babadook depicts the story of young single mother, Amelia, and her child, Samuel. The two live alone together as Samuel's father died on the same day that he was born. From the beginning of the film, Samuel is terrified of a seemingly imaginary monster, to the point that he creates makeshift weapons to protect himself from this bogeyman and, in a familiar childhood ritual, requests that his mother check his cupboards and under his bed every night to ensure that the monster is not there. One night following this ritual, Samuel produces a pop-up storybook of mysterious origins from his shelf for his mother to read to him—the aforementioned "Mister Babadook"—which playfully depicts the eponymous monster terrorizing a young boy. A Gothic incarnation of tactile children's literature, this hardcover book consists of black-and-white pop-up and lift-the-flap illustrations that evoke a hybrid of the unsettling Gothic drawings of American illustrator Edward Gorey—for instance, the drawing "Donald Imagined Things"[26] and those from the abecedarian book *Gashlycrumb Tinies*[27]—and the pop-up ghouls of Maurice Sendak's famous pop-up book *Mommy?*[28] These images—which include an interactive illustration of "Mister Babadook" popping out of a closet and peering at a little boy while he sleeps—are accompanied by rhythmic meters and rhyming patterns infused with onomatopoeia and made-up words reminiscent of Dr. Seuss. The book begins with a passage referencing the privileged insight of childhood: "If you're a really clever one, and know what it is to see, you could make friends with a special one, a friend of you and me." Later the book details the audible portents of Mister Babadook's presence: "A rumbling sound and three sharp knocks, ba-BA-ba DOOK! DOOK! DOOK! That's when you'll know that he's around. You'll see him if you look." As in many classic children's texts, such as "The Three Little Pigs," this playful, rhythmic phraseology associates the conditions for Mister Babadook's emergence with a repetitive, sound-based ritual. This familiar feature of children's culture is subsequently enacted in the film as a source of terror, as these noises come to herald Mister Babadook's real-life appearance. Furthermore, like the eponymous monster in children's books like *The Gruffalo*,[29] Mister Babadook's name is an onomatopoeia for the sound he creates.

In an instance of the process Warner identifies whereby "the stories and other materials summoning the bogeyman ... give existing fears a face,"[30] the storybook gives form to Samuel's pre-existing fears of the monster, and he becomes convinced that it is Mister Babadook who has been terrorizing he and his mother. Thus, from the moment Amelia reads Samuel the book, his fears and the rituals he deploys in an attempt to manage them intensify. Amelia becomes increasingly frustrated as Samuel stubbornly resists her continual dismissals of his ever-escalating fears. Because we are positioned to identify with Amelia throughout the first half of the film rather than her child—whose motivations and thought-processes are initially obscure to both the audience and his mother—the audience is invited to share in Amelia's exasperation and exhaustion as Samuel keeps her awake each night with his demands to sleep in her bed, even after she dutifully fulfills the ritual of checking the house for monsters. As a result, the audience is also invited to empathize with Amelia's attempts to quash the child's unhealthy fixation with the creature when she insists that "this monster thing has got to stop," that "if the Babadook was real we would see it, right now, wouldn't we," and that "it's just a book, it can't hurt you."

When Samuel's obsession with both the book and the bogeyman fails to subside, Amelia tears up the book in exasperation and throws it away. However, her denial of the pop-up book's power—and by extension, the agency and power of the children's culture it represents—only serves to facilitate its insidious invasion of her own reality. After Amelia—and the audience—hear a booming noise that evokes the sounds conjured by onomatopoeia in the story (ba-BA-ba-DOOK! DOOK! DOOK!), the book reappears on Amelia's doorstep, crudely glued back together and including extra pages that detail Amelia's own possession by Mister Babadook. These gruesome pop-up images—which, now that the adult is the target of the monster, frighten Amelia as much as the book first did Samuel—are accompanied by the warning: "the more you deny me, the stronger I get." Amelia subsequently burns the book in terror, at which point the film undergoes a sudden shift in which she too starts to see Mister Babadook: the events narrated in the pop-up book erupt in monstrous form into her own reality, and in parallel the bleak domestic realism that structures the first half of the film shifts into surreal, supernatural horror as the adult audience sees and hears Mister Babadook as he repeatedly emerges from Amelia's closet and towers over her bed.

Thus, while Amelia initially exercises her parental control over the storybook—taking it from Samuel, ripping it to pieces and throwing it in the rubbish bin—the events depicted in the book overpower her own agency and cleaving to rational frameworks of meaning. That these hauntings are a monstrous amplification of the repetitive, childish phrases and images from the storybook aestheticizes the growing power of the children's culture from which the story emerges. Throughout the film, the various regulatory gatekeepers of the epistemic regimes of adult culture—doctors, teachers, and police officers—are powerless to confront this supernaturally-charged expression of children's culture, for they do not believe in, let alone respect or understand, its existence. The pop-up illustrations in the book thus come to metaphorize the power of images to burst from the realm of fiction and into not only the child's but the adult's lived reality: a tactile and intrusive incarnation of "the magic of make-believe" that comes to represent, to use Warner's description of the childish power of images, "such a convincing semblance of actuality that it supplants real life."[31] This power is crystallized in the scene in which

Amelia frantically thumbs through the book after it returns, glued back together, on her doorstep: this time as she reads it, the pop-up images erupt from the pages to dominate both her own entire field of vision and the whole screen. The images are sonically accompanied by a dissonant yet rhythmic, ever-crescendoing cacophony of children's voices chanting indecipherably. Thus, just as Samuel did earlier in the film, the adult protagonist and viewer become enraptured by and enfolded in the illustrations that burst from the book's pages. From this moment in the film, the book holds sway over both the adult's own existence and the diegetic world of the film.

The bogeyman becomes symbolically implicated in both Amelia's trauma surrounding her husband's death and Samuel's fear that his mother does not love him, which only serves to reinforce the film's eerie collapsing of boundaries between the psychic realms of childhood and adulthood. The bogeyman exerts its power at the interface of both identities, functioning as a complex embodiment of both the child's and adult's fears. Yet while Samuel has been preparing to confront Mister Babadook since the beginning of the film, Amelia's denial of the monster's existence until it is too late leaves her vulnerable to the bogeyman's power. At the film's climax, Samuel is forced to perform an impromptu exorcism on his mother, which helps to free her from the monster's influence—in turn, Amelia rises to protect Samuel when the monster seeks vengeance against him. Thus, the film's bogeyman demands that the child and adult relate to each other on more equal terms, shifting the coordinates of the adult's unquestioned epistemological power over her son.

By conjuring a child's supposedly non-existent bogeyman in the diegetic real, the film's storybook thus catalyzes a crisis to the primacy of the adult's perception of reality. This collision of epistemic perspectives is sewed into the film's narrative and aesthetic structure, as the coherent, rational totality of the adult world is increasingly invaded and eventually overwhelmed by the supernatural irrationality of childhood. This shift in diegetic registers is signaled both by the Babadook's visual and audible presence, and by a tinkling, nursery rhyme-esque melody that gradually permeates the film's sparse score. Following the return of the book, this diegetic collision is overtly enacted in a scene in which Samuel's previously invisible supernatural perception of reality intrudes into his mother's own staid, domestic existence. As Amelia does the dishes at the kitchen sink, she stares absent-mindedly out of her own window and into the window of her elderly neighbor. Suddenly, she sees the Babadook lurking in the shadowy space behind her neighbor, staring back at her through the window. The shock of this vision compels Amelia to drop and smash the plate that she was washing. This moment shifts the film's narrative and aesthetic axis—from this point, Amelia and the audience repeatedly see the Babadook emerging from dark corners of the house—while simultaneously impelling a shift in power between child and adult, as Amelia becomes hopelessly dependent upon her child in a reversal of their relationship up until this point in the film. Immediately after Amelia's first vision of the bogeyman at the kitchen sink, Samuel appears in the kitchen and declares he is exhausted and ready to go to bed. However, Amelia encourages her son to stay awake with her so as to alleviate her anxiety. This moment thus overturns the child-adult relationship previously established in the film, in which Amelia was forced to undergo the tedious rituals of bed and closet monster-checks in order to make her son feel at ease. The film's structure thus dramatizes the belatedness of the adult character's perception of this otherworldly realm, an unwillingness to appreciate the power and vitality of the child's imaginary which proves to be almost deadly for Amelia.

Children's Consumer Culture

The shift in power balance that the film enacts can be related more broadly to the changing landscape of children's culture in the late 20th and early 21st century, shifts in large part incited by the increasing commodification of children's entertainment and leisure, as well as children's technology-enabled access to information previously cordoned off from children's culture. Shirley Steinberg and Joe Kincheloe argue that these shifts have led to the emergence of a new "kinderculture": a new form of children's culture that emerged in the late 20th century driven by "changing economic realities coupled with children's access to information about the adult world."[32] As they suggest, in tandem with "the corporate production of popular kinderculture"[33] from the 1980s onwards, "the information explosion so characteristic of our contemporary era has played a central role in undermining traditional notions of childhood."[34] Steinberg and Kincheloe, as well as other children's culture scholars including Stephen Kline, Dominic Lennard, and Juliet B. Schor, highlight that children's consumer culture powered by new forms of marketing aimed directly at children flourished from the 1980s onward. As Kline suggests, "during the 1980s a major transformation took place in children's [television] scheduling thanks to the interest of toy merchandisers."[35] He elucidates that "the removal of long-established restrictions on advertising realism and tie-ins during the 1980s allowed marketers to explore new ways of communicating with children."[36]

As Lennard points out, these shifts meant that "throughout the 1980s, understandings of childhood were increasingly mediated by advertising and consumer culture" as "the specific targeting of their desires positioned the child as an active force in consumption."[37] Lennard argues that these new conditions underpin the anxieties expressed in a number of late 20th-century horror films, including the monstrous living-doll film *Child's Play* (1988), which positions the child's new economic bargaining power within the fractured family unit as a terrifying threat. Using this film as a metonymic example, Lennard suggests that from the 1980s onwards, children's culture—rather than the child herself—has been increasingly positioned in the horror genre as a sinister and insidious force. Marina Warner also suggests that the commodification of children's culture has led to tense ambivalence about the child's social position: "economic individualism has brought us the ultimate nightmare—not just the child as commodity, but the child consumer.... The child, as a focus of worship, has been privatized as an economic unit, has become a link in the circulation of money and desire."[38] This social repositioning of childhood desires and interests has been intensified by the central presence of the internet in children's everyday lives and the rapid decline of broadcast television as a key source of children's entertainment, particularly as broadcast television regimented children's content and viewing practices through its regulatory scheduling, such as the 9 p.m. watershed. Children's entertainment has become diversified and segmented by these broader shifts in the media environment, providing children with more control and power over their entertainment and leisure time.

These complex anxieties about the empowered social position of children's culture can be related to the monstrous pop-up book in *The Babadook*, and are signaled in a number of ways throughout the film. When Samuel first produces the book from his shelf, Amelia is confused as she does not know where he got it from: when she asks Samuel where the book came from, he simply replies "on the shelf." That Amelia herself did not buy this book for Samuel is thus a source of tension in the film, as it suggests that the child has other means of acquiring goods outside of his mother's control. The book's origins remain ominously veiled throughout the film. Augmenting the fraught uncertainty surrounding where and how the child acquired the book, Samuel is depicted throughout the film crafting elaborate tools of violence to defend himself against the bogeyman, and despite her best efforts his mother is unable to limit this activity. It is not clear where Samuel has acquired the various objects that go into his monster-defense weapons, and his mother remains powerless to dispossess him of them: for instance, without her knowledge Samuel takes a make-shift cross-bow he has made to school, which results in her having to answer for her child's actions in the principal's office. At another point in the film he is seen dangerously throwing fire-crackers around the house. When Amelia chastises him and demands to know where he got them, he nonchalantly responds, "I got them from the internet."

Thus, the child's entertainment and leisure time takes on a threatening charge with his seemingly unmitigated access to the resources of his choosing: he does not have to negotiate his acquisitions with an adult gatekeeper. Tying these concerns to the "supernatural irrationality" of the children's culture in which Samuel is immersed are the repeated depictions of the magic DVDs he enjoys watching. When his mother becomes exasperated with the child, she demands that he goes to "put on a DVD." While Samuel obeys, yet again Amelia's power is challenged by his choice of entertainment: although she has told him "no more magic," he repeatedly chooses to play a DVD about magic tricks. As the magician-host on the DVD declares: "Life is not always as it seems. It can be a wondrous thing. But, it can also be very treacherous." Samuel memorizes this line and is seen repeating it in the film when in the basement carrying out some of his dangerous—and disallowed—magic tricks. The line captures the film's anxieties about the growing power of children's culture over adult realities: like Samuel's tricks, the magic of childhood make-believe is a source of both wonder and treachery in supernatural bogeyman films like *The Babadook*.

Conclusion

The Babadook coheres and makes explicit a dominant preoccupation of the horror genre in the 21st century: the under-appreciated power of children's culture. The film's monstrous pop-up book both thematizes and aestheticizes the "supernatural irrationality" of the child's imaginary, in turn counteracting the adult viewer's and protagonist's reliance on rationality and attendant logic-based dismissals of the child's concerns. The film ultimately suggests that a new form of receptiveness to the mental and cultural realm of childhood is required of adults if children and adults are to work together effectively to resolve personal and cultural traumas. Furthermore, "Mister Babadook" unsettles a primary condition of children's culture that sustains child-adult power relations: as Jacqueline Rose famously suggests, literature and entertainment for children cannot be considered a product *of* childhood, because it is adults that craft these works in relation to their own imagined "inner child."[39] Yet rather than being benevolently bought or created for the benefit of the child by his adult guardian, Samuel's "Mister Babadook" has no clear adult origin, simply being produced by the child one night from his bookshelf. Thus, at the crux of the film's tensions is a growing awareness that the binary separation between child and adult worlds—worlds demarcated by the child's relative lack and the adult's relative abundance of knowledge and understanding—can no longer sustain child/adult relations as it once did.

Notes

1. Marina Warner, *Monsters of Our Own Making*, 379.
2. *Ibid.*
3. Bruhm, "Nightmare on Sesame Street," 103.
4. Locke, *Essay on Human Understanding*, xix, 6–24.
5. Rousseau, *Emile*, 80.
6. Jenks, *Childhood*, 56.
7. Sennett, *Fall of Public Man*, 92.
8. Ariès. *Centuries of Childhood*, 111.
9. *Ibid.*, 116.
10. *Ibid.*
11. Warner, *Managing Monsters*, 37.
12. *Ibid.*, 42.
13. *Ibid.*, 36.
14. *Ibid.*, 48.
15. Warner, *Monsters of Our Own Making*, 379.
16. *Ibid.*, 381.
17. Jenks, *Childhood*, 9.
18. Warner, *Six Myths*, 42.
19. Balanzategui and Later, "'Dark and Wicked Things,'" 79.
20. Freud, *The Uncanny*.
21. Lim, *Translating Time*, 16.
22. Matthews, "Socrates's Children," 21.
23. Jenks, *Childhood*, 9.
24. *Ibid.*, 75.
25. Warner, *Monsters of Our Own Making*, 391.
26. Neumeyer and Gorey, *Donald and the…*.
27. Gorey, *Gashlycrumb Tinies*.
28. Sendak, Yorinks and Reinhart, *Mommy?*
29. Donaldson and Scheffler, *The Gruffalo*.
30. Warner, *Monsters of Our Own Making*, 381.
31. *Ibid.*, 381.
32. Steinberg and Kincheloe, eds., *Kinderculture*, 4.
33. *Ibid.*, 3.
34. *Ibid.*, 1.
35. Kline, *Out of the Garden*, 140.
36. *Ibid.*, 237.
37. Lennard, "All fun and games…"
38. Warner, *Six Myths*, 47.
39. Rose, *Case of Peter Pan*, 1–2.

Bibliography

Ariès, Philippe. *Centuries of Childhood: A Social History of Family Life*. Translated by Robert Baldick. New York: Alfred A. Knopf, 1962.
Balanzategui, Jessica, and Naja Later. "'Dark and Wicked Things': The Slenderman, Tween Girlhood and Deadly Liminalities." In *Misfit Children: An Inquiry into Childhood Belongings*, edited by Markus P. J. Bohlman. Lanham, MD: Lexington Books, 2016.
Bruhm, Steven. "Nightmare on Sesame Street: or, The Self-Possessed Child." *Gothic Studies* 8, no. 2 (2006): 98–210.
Donaldson, Julia, and Alex Scheffler. *The Gruffalo*. London: Macmillan, 1999.
Freud, Sigmund. *The Uncanny*. Translated by David McLintock. New York: Penguin, 2003.
Jenks, Chris. *Childhood: Second Edition*. New York: Routledge, 2005.
The Babadook. Directed by Jennifer Kent. 2015. Melbourne: Umbrella Entertainment, 2015. Blu-Ray.
Kline, Stephen. *Out of the Garden: Toys, TV, and Children's Culture in the Age of Marketing*. London: Verso, 1995.
Lennard, Dominic. "All fun and games…: children's culture in the horror film, from Deep Red (1975) to Child's Play (1988)." *Continuum: Journal of Media & Cultural Studies* 26, no. 1 (2012): 133–42.
Lim, Bliss Cua. *Translating Time: Cinema, the Fantastic, and Temporal Critique*. Durham: Duke University Press, 2009.

Locke, John. *An Essay on Human Understanding*. Edited by Kenneth P. Winkler. Indianapolis: Hackett, 1996.
Matthews, Gareth B. "Socrates's Children." In *The Philosopher's Child: Critical Essay in the Western Tradition*, edited by Susan M. Turner and Gareth B. Matthews. Rochester: University of Rochester Press, 1998.
Neumeyer, Peter F., and Edward Gorey. *Donald and the....* New York: Harry N. Abrams, 2004.
Rose, Jacqueline. *The Case of Peter Pan, or the Impossibility of Children's Fiction*, 3d ed. Philadelphia: University of Pennsylvania Press, 1999.
Rousseau, Jean-Jacques. *Emile, or On Education*. Sioux Falls: NuVision Publications, 2007.
Sendak, Maurice, Arthur Yorkins, and Matthew Reinhart. *Mommy?* New York: Scholastic, 2006.
Sennett, Richard. *The Fall of Public Man*. London: Faber & Faber, 1993.
Steinberg, Shirley R., and Joe L. Kincheloe, eds. *Kinderculture: The Corporate Construction of Childhood*. Boulder: Westview Press, 1997.
Warner, Marina. *Managing Monsters: Six Myths of Our Time*. London: Vintage, 1994.
_____. *Monsters of Our Own Making: The Peculiar Pleasures of Fear*. Lexington: University of Kentucky Press, 2007.

Mediating Trauma in Jennifer Kent's *The Babadook*

MICHAEL C. REIFF

Why do we tell stories?

In his 2015 book *Sapiens*, Yuval Harari argues that stories are what set *Homo sapiens* apart from their genetic kin. What made them different. What made them dominant.

But are stories simply for organization … for control … for power? Rebecca Solnit has a different idea. In her 2017 collection of essays *The Mother of All Questions*, she writes that "being unable to tell your story is a living death and sometimes a literal one," declaring that "silence is the ocean of the unsaid, the unspeakable, the repressed, the erased, the unheard."[1] Solnit goes on to note that the antidote to erasure, to repression, to unspeakability, is to *speak*. In the end, "stories save your life." But Solnit also notes that while stories can be liberating, they can be problematic too: "We are our stories, stories that can be both prison and the crowbar to break open the door of that prison."[2]

Stories can liberate us. Stories can imprison us.

Jennifer Kent's 2014 film *The Babadook* brings this conversation down to the human level. It uses the horror genre in general, and a haunted book in particular, to humanize the paradoxical power of the story.

The Babadook is a film about trauma, the stories we are given, and the stories we create. It is a horror film with a monster and blood, but also a film of speech and silence. It is a film about how stories can dominate us, and how we can allow them to dominate us. It is also a film about how struggling with stories—those within and without ourselves—is crucial to survival. *The Babadook* shows how breaking our own silence is crucial. It suggests that facing the toxic stories around us, and those we create, is necessary—even existential.

The Babadook is a film about a woman who needs to save her life, and the life of her son. She is experiencing Solnit's "living death." She is surrounded, consumed, and possessed by stories—sometimes literally. *The Babadook* uses the presence of a haunted pop-up book to begin a deeper conversation on how stories must be fully realized and articulated—perhaps even made tangible—before we can fight them. In the end, however, it warns us that fighting these stories may only be the first step out of our own prisons.

This essay will consider how *The Babadook* examines the ways we deal with trauma, analyzing how Kent's film sifts through different variations of narrative mediation and depicts the paradoxical entrapment and liberation found in stories. It first compares *The Babadook* with Robert Weine's 1920 *The Cabinet of Dr. Caligari*, in order to place Kent's film aesthetically and thematically within a larger cinematic context—particularly the cinema of narratives, internal stories and macabre books. It then considers how Kent breaks with cinematic tradition, presenting and problematizing the power of stories through a modern lens in a way that clarifies the inherent dangers of destructive stories and the way Amelia breaks through and free of them. The essay concludes by addressing a key distinction between *The Babadook* and *Caligari*: that Kent's film posits a path through and away from narrative—a positive way forward.

"Don't let it in!" The Story Is Already Inside

The Babadook begins with a traumatic memory. Amelia dreams of the night her son Samuel was born—the same night her husband was killed in a car accident. Since then, things haven't been going well. Amelia is becoming distant from her friends, and spends her nights becoming mentally submerged in the stories that come through her television.

And then the Babadook arrives.

Samuel loves bedtime stories. One night, he chooses a new one called "Mister Babadook." It has a deep red cover, and a splotch of black ink at its center—a bedtime Rorschach test. Maybe it's the shape of a man. Maybe it's the shape of a monster. The pop-up book starts innocently enough—a story about a mysterious man who hides behind cabinets, peeks around corners—but soon takes on a darker tone. The Babadook will come to your house. He'll knock three times. If you look at him directly, you'll wish you were dead.

The Babadook is concise, evocative, and effective. Its overall conceit, narrative structure, and filming technique give nods to previous Gothic horror films while pushing the genre forward. Beyond the jolts, shadows and eerie soundtrack, however, *The Babadook* also provides a fascinating look at how individuals mediate grief through stories. Sometimes these stories are our own—the ones we've invented. We like some of these stories, suppress others, and re-write the ones we need to. Sometimes, though, "our" stories are *not* our own. Our 21st century storyscape is packed with narratives that influence us through films, television programs, ads, YouTube videos, and tweets. These narratives can wash over us, infect us, overcome us. But what about *tangible* narratives: the hardcover novels, celluloid strips of film, and pop-up books that launch their stories at the reader?

Amelia (Essie Davis) and Samuel (Noah Wiseman) read "Mister Babadook" together—the experience changes them in dramatically different ways in *The Babadook* (2014).

Beyond the stories in our mind, and the stories on our screen, what about the ones we can hold in our hands? At the intersection of these different types of stories, the internal and the external, is *The Babadook*'s protagonist, Ameila. It is through narratives that she is attempting to fashion a new peace out of old traumas.

Amelia's grief and eventual peace is mediated through three major types of stories. First, her trauma is recycled, obfuscated, and submerged through dreams, subconscious stories that are ripe for subversion by the Babadook. Second, Amelia subsumes and re-contextualizes her lingering traumas, and the emerging effects of "Mister Babadook," through the television programs, movies, and advertisements she gazes at each night. Finally, and most tangibly, her trauma is made manifest—and finally, addressed—through the experience of reading the pop-up book "Mister Babadook," and then interacting with the Babadook himself. The menacing figure is not confined to the realm of the tangible book, or later, Amelia's physical home. The Babadook also invades Amelia's personal story structures, her dreams, and the media she watches. Paradoxically, however, it is only through dealing directly with the Babadook—the film's most frightening story creation, the most present and tangible—that Amelia is finally able to come to grips with her grief, her role as a mother, and the trauma of losing her husband.

In order to better understand the film's use of stories, it's helpful to turn back a page and consider one of its predecessors: Robert Weine's *The Cabinet of Dr. Caligari* (1920). Beyond the obvious German Expressionistic connections—what Kent describes as aesthetically and cinematically "bringing the inside out"[3] of characters—the film provides a more protean and elemental version of what we find in *The Babadook*. This is particularly true in the way that *Caligari* links traumatic experiences to the search for ameliorating narratives. Like *The Babadook*, *Caligari* explores the seductive power of stories that comfort, distract or consume us—and, in the end, distort and corrupt the mind. Weine's film is an early and important example of how stories can "be the prison" to use Solnit's phrase. *The Babadook*, we will see, offers an escape plan.

Caligari's Wanderkino

When Jennifer Kent made *The Babadook*, she drew inspiration from a wide range of German Expressionist films, such as *Vampyr*, *Nosferatu*, *Faust* and *The Fall of the House of Usher*. Contrary to popular belief, however, *Caligari* was not one of them. In an interview with Max Evry, Kent notes that the film wasn't a "specific reference for her," but might have been in her mind "subconsciously."[4]

Perhaps. But a critical examination of *Caligari*—its structures, motifs and themes—reveals an early 20th-century distillation of *The Babadook*'s meditations on the problematic nature of story. Robert Weine's 1920 film *The Cabinet of Dr. Caligari* focuses on a small town that is being terrorized by a murderer. The murderer is revealed to be a sleepwalker who is being mind-controlled by a carnival showman, Dr. Caligari. Francis, the film's protagonist, attempts to thwart Caligari's scheme when his friend Alan is killed, and his fiancé Jane is terrorized, by the sleepwalker. The final act of the film presents its most important and resonant elements: Caligari, it turns out, has been inspired by a ghoulish history book, which outlines how a similar doctor used a similar sleepwalking killer as his murder weapon centuries before. As Francis finally captures Caligari with the help of the police, however, Robert Weine provides the final twist of the screw: the entire plot has actually been a construction of Francis's mind, and Francis himself is an inmate of an insane asylum run by, yes, yet another version of Dr. Caligari. The real Alan's days are consumed with building an alternative reality for himself to escape the real or imagined traumas of his past life, or perhaps his presently addled mind. It is therefore in *Caligari*'s presentation of emotionally traumatic triggers, and its examination of the power of stories and narratives, that the film can act as a useful refracting lens through which Kent's deeper vision comes into clearer focus.

Consider, for example, the initial traumas in *Caligari* that trigger character disruptions, internal narrative building, and the search for resolution. In *Caligari*, the protagonist Francis has dual traumas that set him on a disturbing path: He experiences a seemingly supernatural event that predicts his friend's murder, and then Alan is, indeed, killed. The effects of Alan's death on Francis are inextricably linked to his experience of Cesare, Dr. Caligari's human murder weapon, and the man who predicts that Alan will be killed in a few hours' time. Cesare's uncanny ability to predict the future is shocking, and Caligari's mental dominance over his somnambulist is existentially terrifying.

Following these ghoulish events, Francis is confronted with a lack of social and familial outlets—Alan is dead, his lover Jane is rendered catatonic after her own encounter with Cesare, and the authorities are useless. Francis's experience of these traumas, and his lack of emotional outlets in their aftermath, mirror Amelia's trauma as well. She is traumatized not just by the death of her husband, but by her inability to fully discuss her emotions with others in the years that follow. Her husband is gone. Her son is traumatized. Her friends have rejected her. When the Babadook begins to fully manifest itself, this intertwining of trauma, isolation, and the supernatural are further heightened. At first, no one believes Francis' theory that Cesare and Caligari are behind Alan's murder. Likewise, Amelia has no one to rely on to help confront the demons within her house and within herself.

When no one will hear our story, can it still liberate us, or does it imprison us? And when these stories wilt over years, what new, potentially darker stories will fill the vacuum?

Weine's *Caligari* also provides a cinematic antecedent in its presentation of the seductive power of outside narratives. When Francis and Alan first arrive at Caligari's carnival tent, Caligari's pitch, delivered outside the tent, promises a combination of miracles, the macabre and the power of predictions. But it takes a willing participant to fully activate the power of Caligari's supernatural story. Caligari asks for a volunteer, and Alan heeds the call. He asks "how long will I live?" and Cesare merely says "till the break of dawn." This is not a threat, only a prediction, an idea—a story, yet it is enough to send Alan into hysterics. That night he is, indeed, killed.

The intersection of supernaturally empowered stories and the role of the narrative consumer is key in *The Babadook* as well. Early on in the film, Samuel chooses a new book, "Mister Babadook," for his bedtime story. It has a blood-red cover embossed with a Caligari-esque silhouetted figure. At first, the book maintains an uneasy balance in its tone as it depicts a creature that is half demure, half demonic. It warns that "if it's in a word or if it's a look, you can't get rid of the Babadook." This warning is mixed with description of the creature being a "friend of you and me," whose outfit is "funny, don't you think?" Samuel giggles. But soon the book takes on far more ominous tone. As Amelia turns the pages, "Mister Babadook" warns of nighttime visits, nocturnal invasions. The illustrations become darker, sharper, and protrude into Amelia and Sam's space with more nightmarish shapes and angles. Amelia can see her son is getting upset, but it's the book's final command that rattles her: "Take heed of what you've read … You're going to wish you were dead." Samuel is frightened to tears as he imagines the Babadook under his bed. Amelia has caught a glimpse of the invasive power of a dark story, one that has been seemingly been in their midst without her knowing, sitting on the book shelf in Samuel's room, or perhaps in the dark recesses of her own mind.

This is a frightening enough experience, but it's the page in the middle of "Mister Babadook" that is most prescient to the film's plot, and the most specific to *The Babadook*'s theme of a narrative's influential power. As the tension builds, Amelia reads a page that warns that "you'll know he's around" when you hear three sharp knocks. Samuel opens a bureau in the pop-up book, reminiscent of the cabinet that contains Cesare in Cagliari's show, revealing the creature's key words, an onomatopoeia signifying his arrival—"Baba Ba Dook Dook Dook"—and then he says them out loud.

Has Samuel simply read some words in a children's book? Has he spoken a demonic incantation from a haunted book?[5] And what does Amelia think? She watches Samuel participate directly in the book's narrative. Soon after this scene, he is gripped with seemingly imaginary visions of a monster, that a doctor describes as simply phantasms of his young mind. But then, the thumps come to life. Has the book's prediction come to fruition? Is this a projection of Samuel's own childlike narrative? Or are all of these elements—her son's disturbed mind, the disruption of her home life, the gnawing experience of dread—pre-established narratives that already haunt Amelia, her conception of her son, and her ability to protect him?

Both Dr. Caligari's performance and Amelia and Samuel's reading of "Mister Babadook" are, at first, seemingly innocuous. Both involve supernatural or unnatural elements with predictive powers. And yet while Alan is sent into hysterics—echoed by Samuel's uncontrollable sobbing after reading the book—Amelia does not, ultimately, succumb to the power of this narrative. "Mister Babadook" may be the most shocking and lurid narrative in the film. But, paradoxically, it is also the most liberating, as it most acutely reveals what lurks inside Amelia. Unlike many of the other narratives Amelia consumes in the film, as we will see, the book doesn't shut her down—it wakes her up.

"Mister Babadook" reaches out—and Amelia (Essie Davis) ponders the many meanings of "Let Me In!" in *The Babadook* (2014).

The issue of audience has a further dimension, however. Without the audience, Caligari would have no power, and no victims. Like The Babadook without a reader, Cesare without a viewer would remain a two-dimensional outline on a cover. Without Samuel's desperate need for magical narratives, and Amelia's constant consumption of media, the Babadook would remain trapped inside a children's book, its insidious power diminished.

However, the Babadook doesn't just slip into Amelia's home and mind through thumps on the door or screeches on the telephone—indeed, those terrify and repulse her. The Babadook, like Dr. Caligari's pitch, is at first, and at its most effective, seemingly innocent. The creature appears initially as an innocuously beckoning creature in the book. The simplicity and inviting nature of "Mister Babadook"—like the lure of her dreams, the allure of the television she watches, and Caligari's pitch—is key to these narratives' power. And the requirement of the viewer/sleeper's participation—key to the power of the pop-up book, and Cesare's performance—is elemental to the attention-grabbing media Amelia consumes, and the sleep she craves. Once the seduction is complete, however, both *Caligari* and *The Babadook* address the ways in which their narratives corrupt the viewer/reader/dreamer, and possibly destroying them, or worse, in the end.

Indeed, at the root of *Caligari* is a different text, one that mirrors the effects of the "Mister Babadook" pop-up book as well. Francis believes he has completed his quest for answers by breaking into Caligari's office and discovering a book that outlines a rash of murders committed, in the 18th century, by a different Dr. Caligari and his own somnambulist killer. As Stefan Andriopooulous notes in his analysis of Weine's adaptation of hypnosis in *Caligari*, this history book acts as a hypnotic force.[6] The book's narrative infects Caligari with a "compulsive idea" to manipulate Cesare into becoming a killing machine. Francis also finds Dr. Caligari's journal, illustrated in a flashback sequence in which Caligari is literally surrounded by the words of the compulsion-inducing history book. The narrative leaps off the page, lodging itself in Caligari's conscious and subconscious.

These words, emerging from the page and infecting Caligari's personality, echo the visual motifs of the "Mister Babadook" pop-up book and its effects upon Amelia. The children's book, like the 18th-century history, has words, shapes, ideas, and figures that leap out at the reader, literally and figuratively. But the power of the book is not simply that it draws in monsters, or subconsciously infects and inspires Amelia. It changes her conscious experience and personality. It seems to compel her to vicious deeds. Its compulsive control is only broken through physical conflict with Samuel, and through Amelia's own confrontation with the manifested monster, whose narrative seems inextricably bound to her.

In the end, however, *Caligari* and *Babadook* diverge in one key way. While each film's protagonist interacts with traumas, narratives, and disruptive and corrupting books, *Caligari*'s Francis is trapped and Amelia is liberated. The difference raises crucial questions: How does Amelia survive her ordeal? How does Amelia escape the corruption of book-borne supernatural visitor, while the idea of Caligari completely overtakes Francis? Deitrich Scheunemann notes, in her discussion of Romantic and Gothic literature, that texts like *Caligari* (and, I would argue, *The Babadook*) feature characters that "create artificial beings who eventually escape their control, and usually end in self-destruction."[7] Mental self-entrapment—if not outright self-destruction—is central to the denouement of *Caligari*. For all of the seductive carnival imagery, illusionist acts, and horrific historical lore, the most powerful "artificial narrative" in *Caligari* is Francis' own.

But what about the Babadook? Amelia's past and present are filled with pain, but isn't a monster, lurching out of a haunted children's book, a more pressing problem? Perhaps. But a closer reading of the film, and a focus on Jennifer Kent's concept of the "inside coming out" of Amelia points to a different answer. The Babadook may be real, or it may be a figment or Samuel's imagination. It may be a projection of Amelia's guilt. But either way, the Babadook isn't the worst problem in this house, as Cesare, or Caligari, were to Francis. Francis was the problem, the originator of his own nightmare. Amelia, like Francis, is the originator of her own entrapping narrative. She is also, appropriately, the creator of her own liberation story.

Nightmares, Méliès and Mister Babadook

The Babadook opens with a dream. In the dream Amelia is on her way to the hospital to give birth to Samuel. In the dream, she re-experiences the moment of impact in the car crash that killed her husband. She is jolted out of bed, wrenched from this personal history that has become her repeating narrative of trauma. As the film continues, it explores the paradoxical relationship between Amelia and her dreams. After reading "Mister Babadook," the dreams become more and more unsettling, filled with new visual wrinkles and invaded by monstrous voices. Nevertheless, throughout the film Amelia yearns for the recuperative and numbing power of sleep. She even attempts to drug her son Samuel to get *him* to sleep.

Samuel, however, knows the truth. Samuel has watched his mother descend into seductive and numbing narratives of her own, through her personal grief, and the external media narratives she consumes to a stupefying level. Whether or not there is a Babadook monster, to literally and figuratively sleep through life will endanger him, and possibly destroy his mother. Samuel has already lost his father to an external accident. He knows that his mother is in the process of enveloping the remaining family members in a haze of false internal narratives, partial memories, and fractured experiences, creating a mediated somnambulist reality for Samuel and herself. If Samuel had seen Weine's film, he would recognize his mother as both Caligari *and* Cesare. Throughout the film, Samuel acts as a canary in the coal mine, warning his mother against the three forms of mediation that have become destructive in her life: her dreams, her television shows, and the "Mister Babadook" book itself.

The most elusive mediated experience—the intersection of dreams and memories—is one of the most subtly dangerous in *The Babadook*. Joana Rita Romalho has noted that in Gothic films, "memory [is] an oppressive, suffocating force,"[8] and Neil McRobert has taken this description further, noting that "Gothic stories are concerned with the violation of reality by the unreal, and detail the protagonist's attempt to sift through layers of dream, psychosis and dubious history."[9] Kent leverages these key elements of the Gothic tradition to further problematize and weaponize the seductive power of dream and memory narratives. And while Amelia yearns for the hazy internal narratives, Samuel sees that these dreams and "dubious" or incomplete memories are indeed "suffocating" his mother.

Additionally, television narratives create a literal and emotional pseudo-state of wakefulness/sleep for Amelia as she consumes and digests media narratives every night. Amelia spends her nights staring at her television set, taking in a cornucopia of advertisements, violent films, and increasingly nightmarish imagery. Like her dream narratives, these visual narratives are presented as yet another blunting element: a distancing force that separates Amelia from her traumatic memories and experiences, and even her son. The specific shot composition of these sequences, consistent across the film, emphasizes this point. When Amelia and Samuel share physical narratives from children's books, she cradles him, physically and emotionally sharing space and stories with her son. When she consumes television narratives, however, Amelia is often shot in glowing profile, sunken into her chair, her eyes transfixed by the screen. On the few occasions Samuel is in the room with her, he is on a separate couch, unseen by his mother. This literal and emotional distancing at night is hard enough for Samuel. But after the initial reading of "Mister Babadook," Kent braids together these external media narratives with the influence of the Babadook character and Amelia's own personal anxieties, dreams/memories and visual texts. Indeed, an external/internal hybrid narrative begins to emerge. It clarifies the influence of the Babadook, but even more profoundly illuminates the depth of Amelia's own internal trauma narratives.

Three major sequences show Amelia watching television after she reads "Mister Babadook." Each montage is increasingly disturbing, illuminating Amelia's fraught and destructive emotional state. Some of these sequences are influenced by the Babadook, but each sequence also works independently in illuminating the evolution of Amelia, and the effects of this distinct type of media, and not just "Mister Babadook," on her.

The first montage begins with Amelia watching a program depicting an innocuous kangaroo and a young boy. She then sees a piece of a romance film, followed by a film noir. Then, however, Amelia experiences her first exposure to the direct influence of the Babadook. A series of Méliès films clips are played, and fantastic figures from his feverish early works parade across the screen, confronting Amelia with an array of demons, witches, and headless men. "The Haunted House," with its garish and monstrous ghost-demon, follows. Méliès' "The Magic Book" is played as well—but with *The Babadook* in the film itself, the monster appearing in the *livre magique*.

The first montage thus shows the Babadook literally invading Amelia's mediascape. The horror-genre logic is clear here: Amelia reads a haunted book and invites a spirit into her house, and that spirit in turn infects her other narratives, media and stories. *The Babadook* quickly diverges from this predictable path, however, and Kent provides the viewer with an early indication within this montage that the tangible haunting will not be directly linked to new, visual media.

Consider, for example, the specific visual narrative the Babadook infects. The monster is paradoxically contained within an "old" media text, the dated and archaic Méliès film. Méliès' special effects were tangible, tactile—created using analog editing and physical sets and props. In this section, and only in this section, the "animation" of the pop-up "Mister Babadook" is linked to the protean cinema of Méliès. One would expect the Babadook to continue to infect Amelia's media narratives, but it does so neither directly nor literally. The next two media sequences complicate this trajectory, downplaying the explicit influence of the Babadook monster while implicitly pointing towards its true horrific nature.

Instead of reinforcing the Babadook's literal influence on Amelia's experience of "escapist" media, the final two sequences show her mediated evenings inspiring real-world nightmares. The montages evoke not murderous monsters, but the real-life accident that took her husband's life, delineating the darkness of the Babadook monster from the darkness within Amelia herself. The second montage of media clips is peppered not with Méliès films, but with more modern, strange and bizarre imagery, such as slow-motion car crashes and extreme close-ups of predators and carnivores. In the middle of the sequence, Amelia looks to her left to see Samuel on the couch, covered in blood. She wakes from this brief dream, but the implication is clear. Like the television, the world outside of her head is becoming a space of nightmarish potentialities and fantasies. She wakes to find Samuel screaming at her, a knife unknowingly clutched in her hand. Her increasing frustrations, echoed and encouraged by narratives of hunting and meat, pulse within her. Any visual iconography of the Babadook is absent, however; there is no shadowy figure or ink-black outline. Amelia is haunted by her own urges, the violence of the television narratives of hunters and blood and meat.

The final moment of the second sequence is even more instructive, both for its specific content, and for the absence of the Babadook. Amelia watches what she believes, at first, to be a simple news report. Police have found a dead body. It is that of a young boy, killed by his mother with a knife. Amelia, perhaps remembering her waking nightmare from moments earlier, is jolted to attention. Perhaps it is just a coincidence. Perhaps it is a mediated suggestion from the Babadook. But at the end of the sequence, Amelia peers into the corner of the frame. Behind a curtain in a house, where the dead boy was found, Amelia sees a face: not the Babadook's, but her own, with a slightly distorted rictus of a grin on her face. Kent ends this sequence with a sharp, audio pop of static. The lights blow out in Amelia's living room. In this moment—a prescient fever dream, a narrative of violent catharsis placed within a normalized "news" context—the Babadook isn't the monster. Amelia is.

This moment is crucial to the underpinnings of what *The Babadook* is saying about the power of narratives, both those we create and those we receive. This moment specifically points towards what McRobert has described as the "increasingly apocalyptic" content of televised narratives, both fiction and nonfiction, which ensures that "rather than being the antithesis to supernatural or monstrous threat, the factual media is now potentially more horrifying than anything that traditional cinema can deliver."[10] Has the "Mister Babadook" book supernaturally infected Amelia's media to evoke small-scale apocalypses in Amelia's future? Or is the predisposition to consider this dark eventuality already within her?

German neurologist Robert Gaupp has noted that modern visual media holds a "deep and often sustained suggestive power" that can "put to sleep all critical faculties in the receptive soul. We know that all suggestions are imprinted more deeply when our critical faculties are asleep."[11] By this point in *The Babadook*, Amelia has segued from the fraught narratives of her nightmares to the nightmares on the screen; she has shifted from a literal sleep to Gaupp's mediated one. It's possible that the Babadook is the direct cause of all of this, but Kent's visual grammar seems to tell us otherwise. The creature could be popping up in these texts, as it does in the Melies films, or in Amelia's neighbor's apartment, or at the police station when Amelia attempts to report it. When Amelia is alone with her televised narratives, however, she is enveloped by something else, something more potent. She isn't facing a supernatural monster, but the violence within herself.

The final montage of televised images is the shortest, and the most disturbing. Again, there is no Babadook. There is only, it seems, a series of shots from a horror film. A woman rises out of a bed. The sleeping, the dreaming, is over. She comes towards the camera. Another character off screen is screaming. The face of the rising woman is sickly pale, lit by neon greens and reds. The score is unsettling. The face, which echoes the distorted Amelia from the "news report," is fixed with a frightening stare, the teeth in the same leering configuration of glee and malice. By this point, the Babadook has "entered" Amelia, perhaps possessed her, and has certainly become bound up within her. But the televised narratives are devoid of the monster. They only show versions of Amelia, unbound by the morality, ethics, and responsibilities of the living. Then, finally, Amelia gets out of her chair. And she attacks Samuel.

But what about the book itself? Unlike Amelia's dreams (which she creates) and the television she watches (which she chooses), the "Mister Babadook" book is the sole text that is placed in front of her without her choosing. Samuel wants her to read it. Taken literally within the supernatural context of the film, the book seems to act as a homing beacon for the demon or creature. Once inside the house, it penetrates further, finally entering and, it seems, possessing Amelia.

The book's role in the film is, however, more complicated than that. It also acts as a quantifier and articulator of Amelia's grief, a signifier—a namer—of the demons within Amelia already—demons that need to be exorcised. Like applying pressure to a snakebite, to better bring the venom to the surface so that one can suck and spit it out, "Mister Babadook" does what Amelia's dream narratives and her television stories could not. They were diversions, but the book is a mirror. It acts as a reckoning. Paradoxically, it is both the most monstrous and also most liberating narrative of the film.

Indeed, this is the key paradox of the book. While "Mister Babadook" is a seemingly haunted text that attracts monsters, it is also the most tangible, physical, and galvanizing narrative—it breaks Amelia free from her dream narratives, her purely visual narratives, her repeating and reinforcing traumas. It lurches her out of her memorial stupor and her mediated nights. It compels her to action, to break through her emotional malaise. It ensures she doesn't experience a "nightmare death," and helps her shatter her nightmare life.

The Babadook creature acts as a method of identifying the monstrousness within Amelia and Sam's life. It helps to isolate, challenge, and hopefully eliminate that malignant force. As Jessica Balanzategui notes in her analysis of *The Babadook* and Australian cinema, the act of naming elemental forces and monsters is powerful, and that in the case of The Babadook, "The monster's name is an intriguing blend of the 'Baba Yaga' of Slavic folklore; the European word 'bogeyman' [and] the Australian terms like 'bunyip' and 'Boobook' owl that suggest the dangers of the bush..."[12] Kent's amalgamated Babadook, composed of other folklore monsters, points towards Amelia's own process of hybridization she has to undergo to precisely understand how to move beyond her grief. Her dreams and televised narratives obfuscate and submerge the traumatic issues at hand. But the Babadook's inherent, named monstrousness creates the opposite reaction—it jars her out of her benumbing narratives, and forces her to face a far more quantifiable and terrifying threat.

The book, significantly, evolves throughout the film. When we tell a child about a bogeyman, we are simply using a fictional story to teach them that there are dark forces outside of their control, or even awareness. One day, we all outgrow thoughts of bogeymen and understand deeper, and sometimes more distressing truths about society. Amelia goes through the same trajectory thanks to the evolution of the "Mister Babadook" book itself.

She destroys the book, but it returns to her house, in a new form. In the new version, new illustrations have appeared. Some present the Babadook's monstrousness more clearly, but others feature Amelia herself committing the horror. As in the final moments of her television viewing experiences, Amelia begins to understand that the Caligariesque apparition of the Babadook is not the only, or even the primary issue. Unlike the televised narratives, which seem to hypnotize her into a violent stupor, the book—and later the monster—galvanize her to action. First she burns it. Then, when it returns in its new and more disturbing form, she rips this second version apart with her bare hands. Metaphorically, the book confronts Amelia with the most problematic issues within her suddenly made tangible. It forces her to actually and literally grasp them and wrestle with them, and previews her final active confrontations with demons both external and internal.

The "Mister Babadook" book does something that the other mediated experiences in Amelia's life do not: It manifests a tangible problem, and also triggers a specific, tangible reaction and solution. Amelia's disassociation from her son and her current life is both mediated through and abetted by dreams and televised narratives. Amelia's physical and emotional stupor is shattered only with the arrival of the Babadook, which acts as a tangible articulation of what her broken psyche may eventually bring: the destruction of Samuel, and herself.

Faced with a real threat—a physical narrative, a tangible book—that must be confronted, Amelia acts decisively, physically clutching Samuel while facing down the Babadook, and then expelling and restraining it after a makeshift exorcism by Samuel. Often, traumatic experiences must be mediated through narratives, sometimes illusionary or falsified to blunt the full force of the trauma. *The Babadook*, however, points towards a specific type of resolution for Amelia that other forms of mediation were not able to provide. While directly confronting a trauma may be the most painful and difficult form, it is also the most crucial. The ending of *The Babadook* reinforces this idea, while highlighting a key aspect of Kent's vision.

Fight? Flight? A Third (Female) Way

When an animal is challenged, it reacts in one of two ways: fight the challenge, or flee from it. Perhaps, however, there is a third way.

In *The Mother of All Questions*, Solnit notes that the "common sense" fight-or-flight duality was derived from studies of male mice, and male humans, only. A 2000 UCLA study, on the other hand, identified a "tend-and-befriend" urge among female test subjects. Solnit writes that "much of this is done through speech, through telling one's plight, through being heard, through hearing compassion and understanding in response to the people you tend to, whom you befriend."[13] This is precisely the approach that Amelia takes to dealing with the Babadook.

Prior to the monster's arrival, prior to reading the book, Amelia is fleeing from her trauma, her responsibilities, and her son. She is fleeing into dreams, attempting to send Samuel into dreams, and diving deeply into television narratives. When the Babadook fully manifests itself, however, Amelia doesn't flee—she fights, at least for a brief time. She screams at the Babadook, and *it* flees into the cellar.

At this point in *The Babadook*, it is easy to imagine an ending in which a final "fight" is staged in the cellar, or one in which Amelia flees the house, leaving it to be haunted forever. Instead, however, we get something else: Solnit's third way. "Mister Babadook" has made the demons within Amelia manifest. But instead of fleeing from them, or fighting them, she tends to them—in some ways, she befriends them. In the final coda of *The Babadook*, Kent alludes to a new cycle for Amelia—digging in a garden, calmly listening to Samuel, and bringing a dish of worms into basement. Amelia descends into the dark murk of the basement, where we last saw the Babadook flee. And as the camera rushes towards Amelia out of the shadows, for brief moment, it seems she is attacked by the Babadook again. It rushes out of the shadows at her. But she doesn't run, and she doesn't fight. She calms the creature. She gives it food. She knows this process may have to continue for as long as she lives (Samuel seems to know this too), but Amelia appears at peace with it.

Above ground, she is at peace with her new life as well. There is no more running from Child Services, no more mediated stories for them to disbelieve. There is just the truth, as hard as it may be. And in the garden, stories are back where they belong. Samuel dazzles her with a magic trick, a story of amazing ability and infinite possibility for the boy. Amelia may even, for a brief moment, believe Samuel's innocent story that he is "the world is not what it seems." But for her, finally, the stories have been shed—sloughed off like a brittle snakeskin. All that is left is the present, immediate truth: her caring, loving, and tending for her son.

There is, of course, a final paradox. By tending to the Babadook, she has both freed herself and also chained herself to this problem. But this unconventional story is what she has chosen for herself, a new narrative—unlike what has come before, and wholly her own. "A free person tells her own story," Solnit writes. "A valued person lives in a society in which her story has a place."[14] Jennifer Kent has, in *The Babadook,* created that place for Samuel, Amelia, and the monster.

Notes

1. Solnit. "Short History of Silence," 17.
2. *Ibid.*, 19.
3. Evry, "10 Movies."
4. *Ibid.* Kent also notes in this interview that Méliès' "The Witch House" is an influence, and clips of that film, and of course "The Magic Book," make it into *The Babadook.*
5. This moment in *The Babadook* also calls back to the mistakenly chanted incantation that unleashes demons in Sam Raimi's *Evil Dead.* In that film, campers stumble upon a similarly possessed book, speak a magical phrase, and unleash evil spirits that eventually kill almost all of them in a similarly haunted house.
6. Andriopoulous, "Spellbound in Darkness," 105.
7. Scheunemann, "The Double, the Décor, and the Framing Device," 618.
8. Ramalho, "Aesthetics of the Tangible," 106.
9. McRobert. "Mimesis of Media," 137.
10. *Ibid.*, 144.
11. Andriopoulous, "Spellbound in Darkness," 111 (which translates quotes from Gaupp's report on the intersection of hypnosis and contemporaneous burgeoning visual media texts).
12. Jessica Balanzategui, "*The Babadook* and the Haunted Space," 28.
13. Solnit, "Short History of Silence," 19.
14. *Ibid.*

Bibliography

Andriopoulous, Stefan. "Spellbound in Darkness: Hypnosis as an Allegory of Early Cinema." *The Germanic Review: Literature, Culture, Theory* 77, no. 2 (2002): 102–16.
Balanzategui, Jessica. "*The Babadook* and the haunted space between high and low genres in Australian horror tradition." *Studies in Australasian Cinema* 11, no. 1 (2017): 18–32.
Evry, Max. "10 Movies That Scared 'Babadook' Director Jennifer Kent Into Filmmaking." *Shutterstock,* October 31, 2014. https://www.shutterstock.com/blog/10-movies-that-scared-jennifer-kent-into-filmmaking.
Harari, Yuval Noah. *Sapiens: A Brief History of Humankind.* New York: Harper, 2015.
McRobert, Neil. "Mimesis of Media: Found Footage Cinema and the Horror of the Real." *Gothic Studies* 17, no. 2 (2015): 137–50.
Ramalho, Joana Rita. "The Aesthetics of the Tangible: Haptic Motifs and Sensory Contagion in Gothic Terror Films." *Irish Journal of Gothic and Horror Studies* 15 (2016): 96–112.
Scheunemann, Deitrich. "The Double, the Décor, and the Framing Device: Once More on Robert Weine's *The Cabinet of Dr. Caligari.*" In *Expressionist Film: New Perspectives,* edited by Dietrich Scheunemann, 125–56. New York: Camden House, 2006.
Solnit, Rebecca. *The Mother of All Questions.* Chicago: Haymarket Books, 2017.

Bad Books and Fairy Tales

Stigmatized Guardians in The Turn of the Screw *and* The Babadook

AUSTIN RIEDE

Jennifer Kent's 2014 film *The Babadook* was universally acclaimed by critics, who generally picked up on and praised the film's allegorical transformation of grief into haunting, unresolved monstrosity. Though the film is unique in many ways, and has a powerful and mysterious premise, it does fit into a specific tradition or subcategory of the domestic horror genre. Henry James's 1898 novel *The Turn of the Screw* is possibly the foundational narrative for the distinct domestic horror story that reverses the conventional top-down didacticism of the cautionary monster tale by putting children in peril at the hands of those charged with protecting them. These narratives, which reverse the moral logic of fairy tales, rely on a confusion between the parent or guardian of a child or children and a monster, ghost, or supernatural force that has specifically selected that child to terrorize. One aspect of several of these narratives is the reversal of the guardian relationship, as the child becomes more cognizant of the problems manifest in the adult's behavior—problems that the adult denies or does not recognize.[1] By contextualizing *The Babadook* within this tradition and reading it alongside *The Turn of the Screw*, I will argue that, while critics are correct in reading the film as a harrowing metaphor of grief, there is actually another and more illuminating metaphor presented by the titular monster. The Babadook is not only a manifestation of Amelia Vanek's grief for the husband who died on the night her son was born, but of the social stigma that she bears; it is, using sociologist Erving Goffman's terms, the spoiled aspect of her identity.[2] Reading the monstrous Babadook that terrorizes Amelia and her son, Sam, as a manifestation of permanent stigma rather than transitory grief reveals, I believe, the roots of the film's terrifying power: grief and stigma are both potential fates for anyone at any moment, but stigma *spoils* the identity that grief temporarily obscures, and the horror of Amelia's stigma lives on not in her grief for her dead husband, but in her horror at her own living son and her permanent exclusion from "normal" society.[3]

Metaphysical or Stigmatic Manifestations?

Unlike Amelia, James's unnamed protagonist is utterly naïve. She has been raised in a parsonage, and responds to an advertisement seeking a governess for two children at a country manor, Bly. She is interviewed by the uncle of the children and learns that their parents have died, and they have been left in his care. He is a charming bachelor who does not want his carefree life changed by this familial obligation, and so he stipulates that at no point, no matter what, should the governess ever contact him. The conditions of the job have been too off-putting for most would-be applicants, but the governess thinks she can do it. However, when she arrives at Bly, she begins to hear odd rumors about two former servants, Peter Quint, the valet, and Miss Jessel, the prior governess, both of whom are now dead. During her tenure at Bly, she begins to confront, or think she is confronting, both of these figures as ghosts, and her relationship with the children, Miles and Flora, which had begun as idyllic, begins to take a sinister turn.

The Turn of the Screw has famously been read in two ways—both of which work, though they are mutually exclusive—and the text has at this point become, as Marcus Klein points out, "a kind of continuously aggregating palimpsest of itself."[4] Either the ghosts are real, or they are manifestations of the governess's disturbed psychological state and possibly of her sexual repression. The latter is the more productive reading, although it could go against James's insistence on the simplicity and homogeneous quality of the novel.[5] The central tale is told entirely by the narrator, although there is a frame device of Christmas guests at a manor house exchanging ghost stories that allows the tale, a now 60-year-old manuscript kept under lock and key by the faithful Douglass, who had heard it originally straight from the governess herself, to read it aloud. He must send away for it, and thus the manuscript appears among the houseguests, a bad book invited willingly into the house. While it is clear from her narrative that the governess was innocent initially, unblemished and of sound, unspoiled identity, the stigma that attached to the deceased Peter Quint and Miss Jessel, once she hears of it, activates a new knowledge in the governess that causes her, in a sense, to reconstruct them and bring them back to Bly. Like the children's book in *The Babadook*, which re-appears and keeps seeming to write itself no matter how much Amelia tries to destroy it, Peter Quint and Miss Jessel are continually resurrected, reconstructed, and made more sinister by the governess's growing hysteria and her desire to exorcize them. The former servants, who were too "free" and, it is hinted, possessed of a queer or illegitimate sexuality, bear the original stigma in the tale.[6] They are talked about by Mrs. Grose, the housekeeper, and by the nearby villagers, as shameful and wicked. That stigma certainly attaches to the governess, however, by the time she loses Flora's affection and attends, or possibly causes, Miles's death at the novel's close.

Goffman begins his analysis by identifying three types of stigma: there is visible physical stigma, stigma of character attached to what is known about an individual, and the stigma of being of a minority race, nationality, or religion.[7] Amelia Vanek fits into Goffman's second category. She can and does move about in her society looking like what Goffman would call a "normal," an individual free from any marks of stigma. It is only for those who know her situation that Amelia is effectively "reduced … from a whole and usual person to a tainted, discounted one," and we see several instances of this reduction occurring when Amelia's domestic situation obtrudes on her social and professional life.[8] Since her husband's death, Amelia has a "known record," not of bad behavior or addiction or disease, but of misfortune. She is an object of pity, but the resoluteness with which her grief clings to her sets her aside as tainted and excluded. In several interactions at her job, with her elderly neighbor Mrs. Roach, with her son's teachers, and most prominently with her sister and her sister's friends—even with a stranger at the supermarket—Amelia experiences the "mixed contact" of the stigmatized with the normal. Unlike James's governess, Amelia is painfully aware of her exclusion from the realm of the normal, and it begins to influence her relationship with her son.

Elizabeth Bruenig is one of the few authors so far to address stigma in *The Babadook*, but she focuses in her brief article solely on the stigma of Amelia's class. Amelia works in a nursing home and, the movie implies, she is constantly under surveillance in her interactions with the elderly patients. Her job allows her no escape from ministration, as her patients are in a kind of "second childhood." Bruenig is correct that, when Amelia goes outside her workplace or her home "her attire functions as a permanent reminder of the fact of her work, a kind of stigmata of the service sector," and Bruenig's excellent argument shows that Amelia's working-class status is, if less obviously, as responsible as the more apparent factors for her isolation.[9] I would add to Bruenig's analysis that her working class status also seems to derive from the instigating tragedy of the car crash, as her husband was a musician whose preserved clothing and belongings (guarded carefully by Ameila in the basement) mark him as an artist. When he was alive, Amelia, too, worked outside the service sector as a writer and, she reveals at one point, had done some writing for children, which is a clear hint that the bad book obtruding on her domestic life is a bad influence over which she may have some unconscious control. Bruenig focuses on the resolution of Amelia's problems through the beneficial intervention of the state child welfare workers, but before they arrive on the scene we can see *Mister Babadook* (the book) as a possible unconscious manifestation of Amelia's desire to write herself out of her identity as a permanently bereft, working-class, single mother of a troubled child. Moreover, although Bruenig points to the social workers as a sign that social aid programs work well for those they serve, the ending of the film is not as unambiguously happy as it may at first appear.

Although also in the service sector, if more liminally, James's governess does not immediately appear to suffer from an obviously spoiled identity, and throughout her unreliable narration, she never questions her own status as a normal young woman put into an abnormal situation. Although she has come from a humble background, there is no indication of a major trauma in her young life that would obviously make others view her as a stigmatized person, or make her conceive of her identity in such a way. However mundane the appointment of a governess over two children by an uninterested uncle may seem, there is, within the frame narrative that begins the novel, an indication of where the governess's trauma originates. The frame narrator implies to Douglass, the man into whose hands the governess has entrusted her story, that the governess must have succumbed to the handsome and rich uncle. When Douglass replies that she saw him only twice, the narrator says that is what makes her passion for him so beautiful. Without implying—as, indeed, the story never does—that she has succumbed to him in a sexual way, Douglass affirms that the narrator is correct: her limited exposure to the uncle does constitute the beauty of her passion for him, which, he implies, is the only reason she is willing to take a job that others see as dull, strange, and even frightening, given the uncle's main condition that the governess of his niece and nephew never, under any condition, attempt to contact him. It is partly a function of her obviously subservient role as a young woman from a lower social class than her employer that she has no decent voice or outlet for the anxieties which seem to manifest themselves in the ghosts that haunt Bly. Further, as for Amelia, there is either no possibility of development or advancement from this position, or she is in denial about any such possibility. She is single-minded in her desire to serve a man for whom she nurses an unrealistic longing, a hope for a storybook happy ending gleaned from her own experience of reading such fairy tales.

The Influence of (Bad) Books

Both *The Turn of the Screw* and *The Babadook* present narratives in which the trauma, stigma, and horror seem to be suggested by books that have gained a hold over the minds of the protagonists. For the governess, books have disciplined her, in a Foucauldian sense, to have unrealistically pleasant expectations, and so to be happy with her position in the knowledge that if she does her job well, she may be lifted miraculously into a fairy-tale ending. She is much younger than Amelia, and possibly believes in the moral lessons instilled by the "charming stories" she has read and to which she refers. For Amelia, older and experienced, outside narratives seem constantly to invade both her home and her identity. The name of the monster, and of the film, Babadook, is an anagram for "A Bad Book," and this clearly refers to the terrifying children's book that Sam finds on his shelf: a book that immediately threatens Sam with violence, but also, as its initially blank later pages are filled in, intimates violence against the family dog, and finally suggests that Amelia's own life must end in suicide. This threat—which seems to come from outside the home, and which reasserts itself after Amelia tries to destroy it—is mirrored in the threats emanating from the television. As Amelia sits up on cumulatively crushing sleepless nights, the television offers her narratives in old horror films, in ads for phone sex lines, and in an eerie news report of violence done to a child, in which Amelia recognizes her own face peering from a window. Amelia's actions mirror those of the phone sex models, and it is clear that she is interpreting behavior on the television as models for her own spoiled identity. As 21st-century subject, it is clear that Amelia has more than just books to influence and discipline her. While the 19th-century governess would have nothing more than books and print material, Amelia is under the influence of a broader range of discourse, including the television and the Internet. When Amelia does go to the police to report that someone or something is stalking her and her child, she withdraws the report when she sees some police clothes hanging up in the back of the station, behind the officer who begins to take down her report, that resemble the form of the Babadook as presented in the book; whether she is suspicious of the police officer, or afraid that he is suspicious of her, remains ambiguous.

Amelia may be under the influence of a bad book, as the governess was under the influence of insalubrious and unrealistic fairy tales and romances. The film suggests, however, that it is a book that she is unconsciously writing, a suggestion made all the more clear in a key scene at her niece's birthday party, discussed below, when it is revealed that Amelia used to be a writer, and had written, in addition to some magazine articles, "stuff for kids," presumably children's books.[10]

The governess's having read, and too seriously taken to heart, children's books is most evident in the first view of Peter Quint, the gingery and hatless villain, who, she conceives, particularly wants to seduce her young ward Miles into some kind of indecency. She first sees him at the top of a corner tower, one that she has already visited, setting up the pattern that she will consistently see the ghosts in physical spaces that she herself has occupied or will also occupy. Her thoughts, immediately before perceiving him, demonstrate that she has been preconditioned by her education to expect something from the uncle, for whom she is barely conscious that she pines. She recalls first seeing Peter Quint at the hour of the day that she reserves for herself, and in which she can cultivate and form her own sense of identity, independent of the children or her professional obligations: "It was plump, one afternoon, in the middle of my very hour: the children were tucked away and I had come out for my stroll. One of the thoughts that, as I don't in the least shrink now from noting, used to be with me in these wanderings was that it would be as charming as a charming story suddenly to meet someone. Someone would appear there at the turn of a path and would stand before me and smile and approve."[11] Although she doesn't say that she is fantasizing about the uncle in Harley Street, her odd defensiveness makes that obvious. She is concentrating on exactly what it would be like to see his face when she suddenly sees Peter Quint. Her first thought, she writes, is a "sense that [her] imagination had, in a flash turned real."[12] This suggestion that Peter Quint is a manifestation of her imagination is strengthened by his location. He is "at the very top of the tower to which, on that first morning, little Flora had conducted [her]." Looking back at the tour Flora had given the governess earlier, we see that she had been conducted to the top of this tower, which had made her dizzy.

In that same tour, in contemplating Bly, she writes: "I had the view of a castle of romance inhabited by a rosy sprite, such a place as would somehow, for diversion of the young idea, take all the colour out of story-books and fairy-tales. Wasn't it just a storybook over which I had fallen a-doze and a-dream?"[13] Beyond the reading that the ghosts of Bly are manifestations of the governess's own psychology, Peter Quint's first appearance has two significant dimensions. First, he appears when her thoughts reveal that she has in some way been indoctrinated or interpellated by storybooks to see herself as the heroine of a charming romance, in the fairy-tale location of an old castle tower upon which she had already experienced disorientation. Second, the actual appearance of Quint is brought on by her allowing herself to fantasize about the man in Harley Street. The condition that makes her sense of self-identity precarious is her lower-class status in regard to both the uncle and his niece and nephew. Her fantasy—the very thing that Quint is faulted for by Mrs. Grose, who describes him as being too "free" with the children—is to transgress class boundaries in a desired but forbidden attachment to the uncle.

Son or Stigmata?

Although the conditions of the two women differ immensely, there are similarities between the Governess and Amelia Vanek. One major difference is that Amelia's identity has been spoiled by a single traumatic event, which blossoms into a network of traumatizing situations, whereas the governess has been unable to form an independent sense of identity as a grown woman, and so arrives at Bly with a fertile and mutable imagination. The death of Amelia's husband, on the other hand, is at the core of the film's allegory, but not merely as grief. His death precipitates the profound stigma under which we see her struggle, publicly, during the first half of the film.

Amelia's stigma is manifold. First, grief is a kind of stigma itself, albeit a socially sanctioned and generally temporary one. The old outward signifiers of mourning, the "trappings and the suits of woe," as Hamlet calls them, are meant as a warning to others. They set the bearer apart, and this is sanctioned for a time. Like Hamlet's, though, Amelia's grief seems to have surpassed the allotted time. Her sister, Claire, upbraids her for dwelling on her husband Oskar's death, and it becomes clear on a few occasions that she cannot stand to even hear her husband's name.

Being a single mother of a young child carries another stigma, and being the single mother of a child with what Sam's school principal describes as "significant behavioral problems" is a much greater stigma. Throughout the first half of the film Jennifer Kent relentlessly underscores Amelia's frustration and her lack of individual agency or identity in the face of her son's behavior. As she grows more publicly alienated from the other characters in the film, and from the social institutions such as the school and the police, which offer no help, the presence of the Babadook continues to grow within her house, as we see her son embarrass her in public, smash property, endanger other children, and push his cousin out of a tree-house, breaking her nose. Simultaneously with this event, Amelia accuses Claire of not taking an interest in her life, and Claire responds that it is because she cannot stand to be around Sam. This is a shocking admission of dislike for a child, and Claire has clearly broken a social taboo in speaking of her own nephew this way, but the film puts both her and the viewer, who probably feels the same way about Sam at this point, clearly in the category of "normal" individuals who don't want to be touched and defiled by the stigma of others.

The central problem that Amelia must face in the film is that this feeling resonates with her, as well. Her resentment of her son comes across in many ways. Though she is defensive of him, it is evident that he is an omnipresent mark of stigma. In an early scene at the grocery store, the friendly mother of a little girl says to her daughter, in Sam's proximity, that they have to get home to Daddy. Sam, unprovoked, says that his Daddy is in the cemetery, having died while driving his mother to the hospital to have him. This confrontation is a perfect illustration of the way stigma works in a mixed contact situation, according to Goffman's description. One "normal" subject engages in an interaction with another putatively normal subject, bringing a host of assumptions about how their normal social interaction should proceed. The woman with her daughter sees another mother with a child close to the same age as her own. There is nothing to mark Amelia in this moment as different, until Sam makes his declaration. The woman is subtly but visibly taken aback for a moment, coming to an understanding of Amelia's condition. She gallantly offers a comment to the effect that Amelia is very lucky to have Sam, then. This is probably as tactful a way to resolve the encounter as possible, but it could also be one of several suggestions to Amelia's psyche that she is more cursed with her son than blessed, as he insists on making public a stigma that could otherwise remain private.

Another scene that underscores both her son and her grief as stigmatic markers occurs at her niece's birthday party, before Sam's violent outburst. Her sister's friends appear wealthy, and beside them Amelia looks particularly haggard. When one of the friends makes a tactless comment about how she does charity work with some "disadvantaged women" who have also lost their husbands, Amelia hardly responds. When the woman then changes the subject talking about how she's become so busy lately that she can barely find time to go to the gym, Amelia's bitterness erupts. "That's a real tragedy," she declares, in a dark and cuttingly sarcastic voice. "Not being able to go to the gym. You must have so much to talk about with those disadvantaged women."[14]

Amelia Vanek (Essie Davis) has become haggard with grief in *The Babadook* (2014).

Though the sister's friend is aware of the stigma of grief, and now possibly failure, attached to Amelia, she is not in a position to be what Goffman would call "wise" to Amelia's condition. The wise, a term that Goffman explains originated in the gay community, are those who know, understand, and can sympathize with the stigmatized. This woman is certainly not in that position vis-à-vis Amelia, but it is not a breach of etiquette, I would argue, that draws out such ire from Amelia. Rather, it is the implicit suggestion, which Amelia recognizes to be true, that the "normal" lives of her sister and her friends are no longer attainable for her. Again, using Goffman's terms, these are not her "own" people. Rather, her "own" people are those pitied-but-condescended-to, "disadvantaged women who have lost their husbands." Further, as she will realize in a moment when Sam breaks his cousin's nose, her "own" people are those affected by something akin to madness.

The House as a Metaphor of the Mind

A common reaction of viewers of *The Babadook* is to point out how annoying they find Sam.[15] It is a testament to Kent's ability as a director that she can bring out such a performance in such a young actor as (then) six-year-old Noah Wiseman, and to his acting ability. He is monstrously hard to bear throughout the first half of the film, but we see a transformation as the Babadook begins to get under Amelia's skin, and the role of aggressor slips from son to mother. In the first half of the film, we are taught to feel what Amelia feels towards Sam: a deep and enduring annoyance. As the roles begin to shift, though, our sympathies lie more and more with Sam, and not only because we see the threat to his life, but we see that he is dealing with it in a child-like but remarkably mature way. He is keeping his promise to protect his mother, despite her becoming the threat from which he needs to protect both of them. As a boy with no memory of a "normal" life, who has always felt the stigma of his fatherlessness, he is uniquely equipped to understand what his mother is going through.

Their relationship has been read by many critics through the lens of the Oedipal complex, a clearly inviting and rich discourse openly suggested by the fraught maternal relationship. Such readings are in keeping with the Jamesian tradition, as James was writing contemporaneously with Freud and is the forerunner of an intensely psychological modern literary impressionism, in which novels are concerned as much with the psychology of their unreliable narrators as they are with the ostensible facts and events of the stories they tell. The governess, however troubled her relationship with her wards, certainly seems to care about them excessively, and they create a chiasmatic arc corresponding to Sam's development—as he becomes more actively protective of his mother, Miles and Flora, whom she first described in exaggeratedly angelic terms, become more alienated and hateful towards the governess. The governess's mania comes, possibly, from a repressed sexuality that finds an outlet in a dangerous affection for the children, especially Miles. Amelia's problem is the reverse. She is charged with protecting a son who is a daily burden and whose existence spoils her own identity. A scene in which Sam interrupts her as she tries to have a moment of solitary sexual pleasure makes clear that, in the absence of a partner to help her bear the burden, his existence profoundly disrupts her ability to forge a healthy sense of self.

To situate *The Babadook* in the larger historical context of the domestic horror genre read through psychoanalysis, I would like to point out a structural aspect of the film's different manifestations of the horrific Babadook, which can be seen as a primal figure of the id urging Amelia simply to dispense with this problem, her son, that interrupts every level of her identity formation as a healthy adult woman, and I'd like to do so through reference to a very well-known and foundational horror film. Slavoj Žižek has pointed out that in Alfred Hitchcock's *Psycho*, the Bates mansion reflects the three levels of Norman's subjectivity. The first floor is the ego, where Norman behaves more or less as a normal man.[16] The second floor, where the mother's body is preserved and where Norman takes his unbearable lessons, functions as the maternal superego, preventing Norman from engaging in sexual activity. The cellar, to which he transports the mother's body, is the id, the reservoir of illicit desires. Žižek points out that this transposition of the maternal superego to the space of the id reveals the fundamental connection between the two, which are both inhuman forces plaguing the subject who tries to find some kind of space in which to be a Goffmanian normal and no longer the prey of either an insidious guilt or an insidious desire. *The Babadook*, too, structures Amelia's subjectivity through the house. It is on the first floor where we see her interact with visitors, such as her would-be suitor and colleague, the sympathetic Robbie, and the pair who come representing Child Protective Services to inquire why Sam has not been in school. The basement, to which Sam brings his own mother, serves throughout the film as the place where Amelia has metaphorically buried Oskar and where, as the ending of the film implies, she will continue to keep alive her now-domesticated grief and stigma. The second floor becomes the battleground on which most of this narrative is fought.

The place of repose and sleep becomes the site Amelia must protect from her darker urges. It is here that she battles the Babadook, and claims a decisive victory. The angriest line she delivers in the film is directed not toward her son, but toward the Babadook, which can of course be read as the force encroaching on her identity, the stigma that threatens to extinguish her entirely from the race of normal, even if normally stigmatized, human beings. She yells at this force "You are trespassing in my house," and it is through this realization—that the house is a metaphor of the mind—that she is finally able, with the help of her son, not to defeat the monster, but to domesticate it, and shackle it in the basement, where she can nourish it just enough on the grubs and bugs that turn up in a well cultivated garden, but where it must obey her commands.

A Fairy Tale Ending?

In *The Babadook* the monster is tamed, rather than destroyed. Amelia learns how to live with it, and in the perpetual duality between eros and thanatos, eros has won, in an odd sort of way. While a wedding is the traditional happy ending that means the continuity of a community, a birthday party may mean much the same thing for a child turning seven, and Sam has, for the first time in his life, a birthday party of his own, not shared with the cousin whose nose he recently broke, and whose birthday parties he had always been glommed onto in the past, as a sort of messy afterthought. It may not be well attended, but the very fact that Amelia has put it together—fulfilling a parental duty she had been too horrified to face since the day of Sam's birth and Oskar's death—demonstrates that Amelia has fought and won the battle that has made her able to accept her son on the horrible terms under which fate presented him to her. While James's governess loses her fight—either with a malevolent spirit or her own desire to possess Miles—Sam ends the film unharmed and happy, and even apparently healed of his own violence, producing doves of peace from a hat as he performs a magic trick in imitation of the magic DVD that has served for him, in the most recent stage of his fatherless childhood, as a kind of outside discourse of guidance and influence.

The triumph, though, is conditional. Sam's magical ability to produce doves, and the hyper-peaceful atmosphere of the closing scene—echoing the opening of David Lynch's *Blue Velvet* in its suburban pastoral images cut with a foray into the subterranean brutality of grubby insect life—suggests that this happiness is only as real as the Babadook itself, and no more real than the book in which he appears. The stigma of spoiled identity can be managed, sometimes and to some extent, but it does not go away. You can't get rid of the Babadook.

NOTES

1. Some examples of this type of psychological horror narrative are Stephen King's novel *The Shining* (1977) and its film adaptation (1980), quite clearly Alejandro Amenábar's film *The Others* (2001), and to some extent Shirley Jackson's *The Haunting of Hill House* (1959).
2. Goffman, *Stigma*.
3. Stigma similarly drives the actions of the protagonists of the texts mentioned in the first note. John Torrance is an alcoholic and a failed writer, Eleanor Vance suffers powerful feelings of familial and social rejection, Grace Stewart in *The Others* suffers an even more primal stigma as one of the only remaining Britons on a German occupied island.
4. Klein, "Convention and Chaos," 595. Klein offers an overview of the evolution of the two interpretations of the novel.
5. James, "Preface to the New York Edition," 123.
6. James, *Turn of the Screw*, 25.
7. Goffman, *Stigma*, 4.
8. Ibid., 3.
9. Bruenig, "Keeping Up with the Babadooks," 11.
10. *The Babadook*.
11. James, *Turn of the Screw*, 15.
12. Ibid.
13. Ibid., 9.
14. *The Babadook*.

15. I have seen such commentary repeatedly in online discussions of the film. Further, when I have taught the film, students do not hesitate to say things like "I hated that kid."
    16. *The Pervert's Guide to Cinema.*

BIBLIOGRAPHY

The Babadook. Directed by Jennifer Kent. 2014. Surry Hills, NSW: Causeway Films, 2015. DVD.
Bruenig, Elizabeth. "Keeping Up with the Babadooks." *The Baffler* 27 (2015): 10–12.
Goffman, Erving J. *Stigma: Notes on the Management of Spoiled Identity*. Englewood Cliffs, NJ: Prentice-Hall, 1963.
James, Henry. *The Turn of the Screw*, Second Norton Critical ed. New York: Norton, 1999.
Marcus Klein, "Convention and Chaos in *The Turn of the Screw*." *The Hudson Review* 59, no. 4 (Winter 2007): 595–613.
The Pervert's Guide to Cinema. Directed by Sophie Fiennes. 2006. Charlottesville: Amoeba Films, 2009. DVD.

Diaries and Scrapbooks

Dreadful Girl Diaries and the Promise of Transparent Girlhood

Karen J. Renner

In the 2012 horror film *The Cabin in the Woods*, a group of characters discover that the eponymous cabin in which they are staying to enjoy some summer fun has a basement filled with a variety of strange objects—an old wedding dress, a reel of 8 mm film, a music box. One character finds an antique diary written by Anna Patience Buckner and begins reading it aloud to her friends. Entries reveal that Patience witnessed terrible things as a member of the Buckner family, whose male members appear to have concocted their own perverse form of religion to justify their sadistic tendencies. One of Patience's entries reads, for example: "Mama screamed most of the night. I prayed that she might find faith but she only stopped when papa cut her belly and stuffed the coals in." Another states: "I want to understand the glory of the pain like Matthew, but cutting the flesh makes him have a husband's bulge and I do not get like that." The young woman reading the diary then discovers a series of Latin phrases, which, with the encouragement of her friends, she recites. In a clear homage to Sam Raimi's 1981 cult classic, the words literally summon the evil dead: outside, the Buckners—including Patience herself—rise from the grave and begin shambling, zombie-fashion, toward their prey in the cabin.[1]

If this sounds a bit cliché, that's because it's supposed to be: *The Cabin in the Woods* is a self-reflexive film that playfully points out the tropes of the horror genre while simultaneously employing them for scares. Patience's diary is a nod toward the many horror texts that feature diaries and an acknowledgment of the various roles that they play. Diaries—and letters, their close counterpart—often provide important backstory that helps characters understand the gothic mysteries that they face. In addition, diaries commonly act as a summoning device for evil. The discoverer of the diary, once initiated into its gothic secrets, seems doomed to experience them for him- or herself.

However, Patience is no innocent bystander. She comes back from the dead as murderous as her male kin, and she survives long after, proving, in fact, to be the most enduring monster in the movie. And, after all, it is her diary that allowed the Buckners to return in the first place. The suggestion is, then, that Patience's diary is not simply the innocent transcript of a guileless victim but rather belies her complicity in the Buckners' violent family traditions. Patience thus also recalls those girls, both fictional and factual, who reveal their homicidal tendencies by confessing them to their diaries. On the one hand, these dark diaries subvert the image of innocent girlhood so prevalent in our culture. On the other, they still uphold the comforting assumption that the true nature of girls can always be accessed and known and therefore potentially controlled. Behind the obsession with dreadful girl diaries, I argue, is a fantasy of feminine transparency—a desire to believe that girls cannot help but reveal their hearts whenever they pick up a pen.

Diaries and the Gothic

Diaries and similar types of records, such as letters, have long been a gothic trope. Some texts, such as Bram Stoker's *Dracula* (1897), embed these types of documents throughout their narratives; other works take on the diary format entirely. An example of the latter, Charlotte Perkins Gilman's short story "The Yellow Wall-paper" (1892) details the narrator's descent into madness due to the restrictive gender roles of the late 19th century. The diary format of the story creates horror by allowing the reader to bear immediate witness to the psychic unraveling of a sympathetic woman. Gilman's "Yellow Wallpaper" is one of the most famous pieces of gothic fiction that calls upon the diary trope but it is hardly the only one.[2] And the trope continues to thrive today. *The Pink Backpack*, a short graphic story that was published on the web and later went viral, poses as the diary of a very young girl. Written on penmanship paper in an elementary script checkered with childish misspellings and accompanied by crude illustrations, *The Pink Backpack* describes the narrator's relationship with Lisa, her imaginary friend, whom the reader quickly infers is the ghost of a murdered girl. As we read, we realize that Lisa has killed everyone who interfered with their relationship, including a substitute teacher and the narrator's own father, but the narrator remains ignorant of the full implications of Lisa's actions and just describes everything that happens with an innocent earnestness.[3]

The diary has become a common trope in other types of horror texts as well, including film, television, and video games. In *An American Haunting* (2005), an old journal describes one young girl's suffering at the hands of the supposed Bell Witch, and its reader soon discovers that her daughter is suffering the same fate. A central event in the original television series *Twin Peaks* (1990–1991) is the discovery of the diary of a murdered girl. In fact, this diary proved so compelling that a book version, *The Secret Diary of Laura Palmer*, was published in 1990. Furthermore, if we expand the definition of "diary" to include formats other than pen and paper, we find even more instances. In fact, the diary trope is so common to horror video games that Ewan Kirkland has claimed, "In survival horror, everyone, it seems—research assistants, academics, mercenaries—keeps a journal,"[4] though these journals more often appear in audio form. Video logs—essentially a video version of a diary—are a common feature of sci-fi horror, appearing in films like *Event Horizon* (1997), *The Astronaut's Wife* (1999), *Serenity* (2005), and *Day of the Dead* (2008). Furthermore, many films that fall into the popular "found footage" horror subgenre could also be considered video diaries; the famous scene in *The Blair Witch Project* (1999) in which the female protagonist weepily apologizes to the camera for the danger in which she has placed her companions and herself sounds profoundly similar to a diary entry.[5]

Diaries and Girl Culture

As is clear from the examples above, the version of the trope that appears most frequently is the diary of a young girl. This is hardly a surprise, considering that, as Rebecca Hogan explains, in the last hundred years or so, diary-writing has undergone a "feminization," shifting so that it is now primarily seen as woman's work.[6] Jane Hunter argues even more specifically that today's diaries "are almost exclusively the domain of the preadolescent girl—often merchandised in pastel colors with lock and key already affixed."[7] Even though the digital possibilities for diaries in today's world are endless, diaries still seem to have far more appeal when they are physical items that one can hold and hide.[8] Studies have shown that not only are girls the primary keepers of digital versions of diaries,[9] such as blogs, but also that most prefer a material version: "83% of today's teenage girls keep a personal pen-and-paper diary—compared with 69% in [the] 1990s."[10] That diaries are an important part of girl culture is also evident in how frequently they feature in children's and young adult literature.[11]

The prominence of girls' diaries in adult culture requires another explanation, however. Megan E. Friddle argues that girls' diaries play a dual role in today's culture: "to serve as a site for identity-making and self-understanding [for girls], while simultaneously offering parents and other authority figures an authoritarian glimpse into adolescent girls' hearts and minds."[12] The appeal of girls' diaries for adults lies, in other words, in their supposed ability to provide unfettered access to a girl's most private fears, fantasies, and feelings. Laura Palmer's diary begins with just this sort of pledge. Addressing the diary itself, she writes, "You shall be the one I confide in the most. I promise to tell you everything that happens, everything I feel, everything I desire. And, every single thing I think. There are some things I can't tell anyone. I promise to tell these things to you."[13] An excellent metaphor for the ways that adults nefariously consume girls' diaries appears in *Harry Potter and the Chamber of Secrets* when Voldemort explains how he fed off of the secrets that one young girl wrote down in his diary: "I grew stronger and stronger on a diet of her deepest fears, her darkest secrets."[14] Not surprisingly, the diary's ability to provide its unauthorized reader special access to the most intimate moments in a girl's life often takes on sexual connotations.[15]

The first and foremost function of the girl's diary in horror film is to provide clues to the mystery the protagonists are facing without even meaning to. In *Nightmare on Elm Street 2: Freddy's Revenge* (1985), for instance, the central character finds the diary of Nancy, the teen protagonist of the first movie. The sequel thus imagines that Nancy took the time to record the horrors she suffered during the first film in a diary, which is then made available for the benefit of later characters. It is through Nancy's diary, after all, that one character learns that Freddy gains his power by evoking fear in others. A girl's diary functions similarly in the 2016 horror film, *Restoration*. In this movie, a couple discovers a teddy bear behind the walls of their new house while doing renovations. Inside the teddy bear is a diary that details the ominous experiences of a young girl who used to live in the house. Her revelations provide the protagonists the answers they need to understand the haunting they suffer.[16] Horror films thus often imagine the girl's diary as an innocent document that only unintentionally offers up valuable information—a comforting confirmation that girls are, like their diaries, open books ready for adult perusing.

Diaries and Girl Killers

However, a second trend surrounding the girl's diary has been on the rise in horror films. In recent decades, diaries of criminal girls have become an equally frequent plot device. While the omnipresence of this device has gone a long way toward subverting the image of innocent girlhood, the dreadful girl and her diary still uphold the idea of feminine transparency: even bad girls are unable to hide their badness. These diaries confirm a central ideology about girlhood: that they are incapable of deceit. If our culture is no longer so naïve as to believe in the unquestionable innocence of girls, the next best thing, perhaps, is to trust in their transparency.[17]

This desire to see girls as fundamentally incapable of effective deceit is especially evident in the real-world cases of juvenile homicide in which female culprits were caught because they confessed their crimes in their diaries. One of the earliest cases—and perhaps most famous—would be the murder of Honora Parker in 1954, committed by Honora's daughter, Pauline (16), and her best friend Juliet Hulme (15) and later dramatized in Peter Jackson's film *Heavenly Creatures* (1994). Parker wrote extensively in her diary about the girls' plan to kill her mother, and the entries were a central focus of both the legal proceedings and the media coverage. As Julie Glamuzina and Alison J. Laurie explain, Pauline's diaries "were read aloud during the trial and … sensationalised by the media"; images of the actual diary entries were also frequently included alongside news stories.[18] The passages from Parker's diary were played for shock value by media and magistrate alike, and certainly the emotionless way that she details her homicidal plans is fitting material for any horror film.[19] However, these entries were also presented as proof of Parker's true state of mind. Rarely do we find sustained attempts to analyze the entries psychologically. They are just taken at face value.

Diaries that appeared in other cases of female juvenile homicide have been similarly sensationalized. After Shirley Wolf (14) and Cindy Collier (15) murdered Anna Brackett, an 85-year-old woman, Wolf wrote in her diary, "Today, Cindy and I ran away and killed an old lady. It was lots of fun." The diary entry is directly referenced in the title of the movie about their crime, *Fun* (1993), and is prominently mentioned in the *Killer Kids* episode devoted to the story.[20] Similarly, when it was discovered that Sharon Carr (12) had murdered Katie Rackliff in 1992, Carr's diary entries were pointed to as signs of her complete lack of remorse, even though the extremity of her violent rage at such a young age suggests deep psychological issues: "I bet she's all bone and maggots by now. She shouldn't have tested," "If only I could kill you again, I promise I'd make you suffer more, you slay. Your terrified screams turn me on," and "Last night it occurred to me, that killing her did me good. I know what I'm capable of, and will do it again."[21] The diary of Pearl Moen, a 17-year-old who in 2015 stabbed another woman 21 times, has been paraded around in the media in similar fashion: "I stabbed an innocent woman to death earlier today.… It was absolutely fantastic. Murder gives me a high unlike any other."[22] These diaries are all presumed to be trustworthy indicators of the evil dispositions of these girls and are all capitalized on for their horrific potential.

Alyssa Bustamante's diary might be the most famous of all. After killing nine-year-old Elizabeth Olten in 2009, the 15-year-old wrote in her diary: "I just fucking killed someone. I strangled them and slit their throat and stabbed them now they're dead. I don't know how to feel atm [at the moment]. It was ahmazing. As soon as you get over the 'ohmygawd I can't do this' feeling, it's pretty enjoyable. I'm kinda nervous and shaky though right now. Kay, I gotta go to church now ... lol."[23] As in other cases, Bustamante's diary is often treated as straightforward evidence that her motive for murder was simply a sadistic desire to kill, even though such a claim dramatically downplays the years of abuse and neglect that Bustamante suffered. This is exactly the stance taken in dramatizations of Alyssa's crime. In the episode of *Deadly Women* devoted to Bustamante, "No Good Reason," Alyssa is shown eyeing her future victim while writing in her diary.[24] In their analysis of the episode, Isabel Scheuneman Scott and Jennifer M. Kilty point out that the abuse that Bustamante suffered in childhood is "mentioned in passing at the very beginning of the segment but [is] never examined further, shifting instead to emphasize her badness by focusing on her expression of homicidal thoughts in her diary."[25]

In short, coverage of these crimes typically ignores the possibility that these diary entries, rather than being expressions of these girls' truest selves, could in fact be performances of a desired identity or ways for their writers to cope with the terrible deeds they had committed. One reason people tend to consider the diary an authentic and accurate transcript of its writer's inner life is that it is supposedly a private document, with no other intended audience than the writer. Consequently, it would seem that the writer would have no reason to lie or pretend. However, many scholars have contested the idea that diaries are solely intended to be private documents.[26] Others argue that the diary is less a record of an already established identity and more a way for a writer to try out different versions of herself.[27] And although Judy Simons was referring to older women's diaries from a much earlier period, her claim that some "turned to private writings to reconstruct themselves in transgressive mode" could very well be the case for young girls today, too.[28] Moreover, girls in severely dysfunctional situations—as so many of the girl killers previously discussed were—may use their diaries for other purposes: as a cry for help, for example, as Barbara Crowther argues.[29] Glaumuzina and Laurie wonder if this was the case with Pauline Parker's diary: "The question may be raised as to whether she hoped to be discovered and prevented from carrying out the plan.... [I]t seems as though the diary process functioned either as a sounding board or as a way of letting others know about her ideas and feelings."[30] While dreadful girl diaries may very well reveal the sociopathic personalities of their authors, journalists rarely question their motive or meaning, finding it far more comforting to believe that as evil as these girls may be, they cannot hide their true nature.

True cases like these may very well be responsible for the proliferation of another trope surrounding girls' diaries in horror film: that dreadful girls are driven to confess their crimes. In *The Crush* (1993), for example, Darian, a mature and highly intelligent girl, manages to damage property, attempt murder, and falsely accuse a man of battery and rape without detection. However, Darian is unable to resist revealing all in her diary. Her best friend claims that Darian "writes everything" in her diary because "[s]he thinks no one knows about it." However, Darian frequently is seen throughout the movie scribbling in her diary in public, so there's no suggestion that she believes her diary is a secret. Although Darian is ultimately caught in the act, rendering the diary a Chekhovian gun that never needs to go off, the movie still hints that had it been found, it would have served as a consummate tell-all, definite proof of the girl's guilty actions and inexcusable motives.[31]

Orphan (2009) relies on similar assumptions. In the film, a homicidal woman in her 30s with hypopituitarism manages to pose as a young girl. Time and time again, she is adopted into a family, attempts to seduce her new "father," and then murders the whole family when he rejects her advances. Though literally wise beyond her years, Esther still cannot but help reveal her true nature. However, she is smart enough not to do this is diary form—having learned that lesson when she discovers the diary of her new "mother" and uses its contents against her. Instead, Esther's inescapable need to confess comes through in her paintings, which reveal terrible truths once exposed to the black light of her aquarium: a seemingly sweet portrait of her mother has stab wounds and a slashed neck, a drawing of a house suddenly appears on fire.[32] As cunning as Esther is throughout the entire film, she is incapable of complete deceit. The 2017 adaptation of Agatha Christie's *Crooked House* (1949) has clearly been influenced by recent criminal girl diary confessions as well. In the story, a 12-year-old girl, Josephine, murders her grandfather (and later her nanny) and confesses all in her diary, to which we are given access at the very end of the book. However, while the excerpts we receive in Christie's novel are brief and childish, the movie indulges us in far more detail. Although a conniving girl, Josephine can't help but reveal the minutiae of her crimes in her notebook, even though doing so is incredibly dangerous since everyone knows about its existence, and indeed it is the diary that is her downfall.

Although these texts may fit more firmly into the psychological thriller subgenre, more conventional horror films are beginning to appropriate the device as well. Perhaps the most striking example is Australian director Sean Byrne's *The Loved Ones* (2009). The movie focuses on a girl named Lola, a shy, mousy girl who repeatedly turns homicidal when she feels mistreated by boys. Assisted by her father, she kidnaps those she perceives as having rejected her and subjects them to a night of torture, all staged as an elaborate prom ritual. The evening begins with Lola pasting a picture of her most recent victim, Brent, into her scrapbook. The cover is decorated in pastel colors, the crayoned name Lola framed by hearts and stars. The first pages are equally childish—a picture of a knight colored with marker, a simplistic castle drawn in pink crayon. Then, the pages contain more mature material, images of men's torsos, advertisements for make-up. Around the picture of Brent, Lola draws a large heart that culminates in a red circle on his forehead. The red dot, we learn later, is no token of love; rather, it foreshadows the hole that Lola plans to drill into Brent's forehead, into which she will pour boiling water, Dahmer-fashion, effectively lobotomizing him. She performed this procedure on all of her previous victims, and they now live like feral animals in her cellar, feeding on the roadkill she periodically throws down to them. We see more of Lola's scrapbook later in the film, for she shares it with a badly injured Brent while her father smilingly looks on—a perverse parody of a boyfriend being subjected to his prom date's baby album before leaving for the dance. The first page we see is a simple drawing of a boy and girl holding hands in red marker. "That's me," Lola declares, pointing at the figure of the girl. Later pages feature the missing posters of various boys, all decorated with Lola's doodles and angry captions.[33] As devious as Lola may be, her scrapbook ultimately serves as a confession to all of her crimes.

In horror narratives, therefore, the girl's diary has transitioned from an innocent record of terrors suffered to a terrifying confession of horrors committed. These diaries have been integral to revealing that girls are made of other ingredients than sugar and spice. However, no matter how transgressive their behaviors may prove, their diaries are consistently used to provide the comforting assurance that no matter what, dreadful girls can't help but confess their crimes and submit themselves to the proper authorities.

Notes

1. To view this scene from *Cabin in the Woods*, go to https://youtu.be/IqRnnk37vx4.
2. Other examples of gothic texts that include fictitious diary-like documents of some kind or which borrow the diary form include Mary Shelley's *Frankenstein* (1818), Guy du Maupassant's "The Horla" (1887), H.P. Lovecraft's "The Call of Cthulhu" (1928), Richard Matheson's "Born of Man and Woman" (1950), Robert Bloch's "Notebook found in a Deserted House" (1951), Stephen King's "Survivor Type" (1982), and Mark Danielewski's *House of Leaves* (2000).
3. The entire book and some background can be found here: http://popcornhorror.com /story-lisa/.
4. Kirkland, "Storytelling in Survival Horror Video Games," 67. And not only survival horror but other more narrative, atmospheric games rely on the trope of the diary as well. For example, the entire point of *Gone Home* (2013) is to figure out why, after returning from a year abroad, no one is home to greet the first-person player character in her very gothic house. As a storm rages outside, you slowly discover secret passages and rooms, all the while piecing together your sister's journal, which details her struggles with lesbianism.
5. To view this scene, go to https://youtu.be/oVpU8_QMsfc.
6. Hogan, "Engendered Autobiographies," 95.
7. "Inscribing the Self," 75.
8. Deborah Anne Sosin argues that the reason for this is that diaries serve as "transitional objects" for female adolescents, a sort of safety blanket that "facilitates the passage into adulthood." Sosin, "The Diary as a Transitional Object," 93.
9. See, for example, Scheidt, "Adolescent Diary Weblogs."
10. "Dear Facebook."
11. Although the *Adrian Mole* (1982–2009) and *Diary of a Wimpy Kid* (2007–present) series each focus on a boy's diary, they are exceptions to the rule. Diary fiction for children and young adults far more frequently involves the journaling of girls. A short list of examples includes *Amelia's Notebooks* (1995–present), *Dear America* (1996–2004, 2010–), *Alice, I Think* (2000, 2004, 2005), *The Princess Diaries* (2000–2015), *From the Files of Madison Finn* (2001–2006), the *Jessica Darling* series (2001–present), *Dear Dumb Diary* (2004–2016), *My Story: Girls* (2008–2012), and *Dork Diaries* (2009–present). Darker versions of girls' diaries are common as well. Beginning with *Go Ask Alice* (1971), Beatrice Sparks published at least a dozen books that she falsely claimed were the real diaries of teens dealing with a variety of problems, from drugs to pregnancy; subsequent research has revealed that Sparks herself was the author. Other books taking a similar tack include John Marsden's *So Much to Tell You* (1987) and *Letters from the Inside* (1991)—the latter a series of letters not unlike diary entries. More recently, Laurie Halse Anderson's *Speak* (1999) deals with rape while *Love Letters to the Dead* (2014) the death of a sibling.
12. Friddle, "From *Betsy-Tacy* to the Blog," 167.
13. Lynch, *Secret Diary*, 22 July 1984.
14. Rowling, *Chamber of Secrets*, 310. In an interview on the *Chamber of Secrets* DVD, Rowling described diaries as dangerous: "[T]he diary to me is a very scary object, a really, really frightening object. This manipulative little book, the temptation particularly for a young girl to pour out her heart to a diary." In another interview with the *Sydney Herald*, Rowling further elaborated on the "My sister used to commit her innermost thoughts to her diary. Her great fear was that someone would read it. That's how the idea came to me of a diary that is itself against you. You would be confiding everything to pages that aren't inanimate." Renton, "The Story behind the Potter Legend."
15. Sara K. Day inadvertently reveals these sexual connotations in her claim that "popular culture frequently represents young women writing furiously in pink notebooks that are then stashed *under mattresses* or *in underwear drawers* in the hopes of being kept secret from the prying eyes of parents and siblings." Day, *Reading Like a Girl*, 145, my emphasis. In Jeffrey Eugenides's *The Virgin Suicides* (1993), the impenetrability of one girl's diary to the boys who adore her seems to cause them almost a sexual frustration, as though the diary is refusing to "give it up": "Almost daily we met to go over the evidence once again, reciting portions of Cecilia's journal.... Nevertheless, we always ended these sessions with the feeling that we were retracing a path that led nowhere, and we grew more and more sullen and frustrated." Eugenides, *Virgin Suicides*, 233.
16. Scenes from *Restoration* can be viewed here: https://www.youtube.com /watch?v=MVKhh1O88rY.
17. However, even this tendency may be increasingly portrayed as foolish, at least if Gillian Flynn's novel *Gone Girl* (2012) and its 2014 cinematic adaptation are any indication. The story bounces back and forth between an investigation into the disappearance of Amy Elliot Dunne and dramatized events from Amy's diary, which detail the Dunne's relationship. Amy's diary entries portray her as a sweet and innocent woman

increasingly mistreated by her husband. The story's twist comes when we realize that the diary is an elaborate fake, part of Amy's vengeful ploy to frame her husband for her own murder, and that we, like the police officers who read the diary, have been fooled by it. In the novel, Amy claims that "Diary Amy ... is designed to appeal to the cops, to appeal to the public should portions be released. They have to read this diary like it's some sort of Gothic tragedy" (238). To view relevant scenes from the film, go to https://youtu.be/hbrWfl79LnM.

18. Glamuzina and Laurie, *Parker and Hulme: A Lesbian View*, 76.

19. Two nights before they killed Pauline's mother, Pauline wrote about the plot, snidely referring to murder as "moider": "We discussed our plans for moidering [sic] mother.... Peculiarly enough I have no qualms of conscience (or is it peculiar we are so mad?)." The day before, Pauline wrote, "We discussed the moider [sic] fully. I feel very keyed up as if I was planning a surprise party. So the next time I write in the diary mother will be dead. How odd, yet how pleasing." And on the morning that the murder was planned, which Pauline blithely dubbed "The Day of The Happy Event," Pauline described herself as having been very excited and 'The night before Christmasish' last night."

20. The Collier and Wolf story appears in the first segment of season 2, episode 4, "Thrill Kill and Poisoned," which can be viewed here: https://www.youtube.com/watch?v =n2FN1eEsXxI.

21. "Murder Charge Girl's Chilling 'Diary of Death.'"

22. Andrews, "'I'm So Proud of Myself.'"

23. Associated Press, "Teen who butchered 9-year-old neighbor."

24. To see these scenes from *Killer Kids* and others from the *Deadly Women* episode in which Bustamante features, go to https://youtu.be/GIflqx1XekU.

25. Scott and Kilty, "'When She Cracks,'" 90.

26. See, for example, Martinson's *In the Presence of Audience*, Lynn Z. Bloom's "'I Write for Myself and Strangers,'" and Elizabeth Podniek's *Daily Modernism*.

27. Jane Greer and Miriam Forman-Brunell claim that "[d]iary keeping can be a highly performative act for young women as they represent themselves, constructing and censoring how they wish to be viewed" (211) while Margo Culley likens the diary to "a kind of mirror before which the diarist stands assuming this posture or that" (219). In her study of journaling self-help books, Anne Whitney discovered that the journaling was frequently portrayed "as a means of self-construction.... Whereas the notion of journaling as self-discovery implies an existing self found through writing, here writing is the genesis of identity; it creates a self" (n.p.).

28. Simons, "Invented Lives," 263.

29. Crowther claims, "Family therapists have sometimes found that in cases of severe problem behavior, where communication between the adolescent girl and her parents has completely broken down, the girl has used her diary to throw down a challenge to the parents." "Writing as Performance," 202.

30. *Parker and Hulme*, 81.

31. To view scenes from *The Crush*, go to https://youtu.be/8zeigNxxOWY.

32. To view these scenes, go to https://www.youtube.com/watch?v=20jKJmNTU4c.

33. To view these scenes from *The Loved Ones*, go to https://youtu.be/JogHUtGDpg4.

Bibliography

Andrews, Travis M. "'I'm so proud of myself. I stabbed her like 20 times': Teenage Girl's Diary Leads to 15-year sentence." *The Washington Post*, 24 January 2017. https://www.washingtonpost.com/news/morning-mix/wp/2017/01/24/im-so-proud-of-myself-i-stabbed-her-like-20-times-teenage-girls-diary-leads-to-15-year-sentence/?utm_term=.2a8e52212a36.

Associated Press. "Teen who butchered 9-year-old neighbor wrote that killing was amazing, enjoyable in her journal before she went to church." *New York Daily News*, 6 February 2012. http://www.nydailynews.com/news/national/teen-butchered-9-year-old-neighbor-wrote-killing-amazing-enjoyable-journal-church-article-1.1018171.

Bloom, Lynn Z. "'I Write for Myself and Strangers': Private Diaries as Public Documents." In *Inscribing the Daily: Critical Essays on Women's Diaries*, edited by Suzanne L. Bunkers and Cynthia A. Huff, 23–37. Amherst: University of Massachusetts Press, 1996.

The Cabin in the Woods. Directed by Joss Whedon. Santa Monica, CA: Lionsgate, 2012. DVD.

Cardell, Kylie. *Dear World: Contemporary Uses of the Diary*. Wisconsin Studies in Autobiography. Madison: University of Wisconsin Press, 2014.

Christie, Agatha. *Crooked House*. 1949. New York: William Morrow, 2011.

"Conversation with J. K. Rowling and Steve Kloves." *Harry Potter and the Chamber of Secrets*. 2001. Directed by Chris Columbus. Burbank, CA: Warner Home Video, 2002. DVD.

Crowther, Barbara. "Writing as Performance: Young Girls' Diaries." In *Making Meaning of Narratives*, The Narrative Study of Lives, vol. 6, edited by Ruthellen Josselson and Amia Lieblich, 197–220. Thousand Oaks, CA: Sage, 1999.

The Crush. Directed by Alan Shapiro. 1993. Burbank, CA: Warner Home Video, 2000. DVD.

Culley, Margo. "Introduction to *A Day at a Time: Diary Literature of American Women, from 1764 to 1985*." *Women, Autobiography, Theory: A Reader*, edited by Sidonie Smith and Julia Watson, 217–21. Madison: University of Wisconsin Press, 1998.

Day, Sara K. *Reading Like a Girl: Narrative Intimacy in Contemporary American Young Adult Literature.* Jackson: University Press of Mississippi, 2013.
"Dear Facebook, to Know the REAL Truth, Read My Diary." 14 January 2013. http://www.channel4.com/info/press/news/dear-facebook-to-know-the-real-truth-read-my-diary.
Eugenides, Jeffrey. *The Virgin Suicides.* New York: Farrar, 1993.
Flynn, Gillian. *Gone Girl: A Novel.* New York: Crown/Archetype, 2012. Kindle ed.
Friddle, Megan E. "From *Betsy-Tacy* to the Blog: Diary-Keeping, Self-Narrative and Adolescent Identity in American Girls' Books." In *Girls' Series Fiction and American Popular Culture*, edited by LuElla D'Amico, 165–86. Lanham, MD: Lexington, 2016.
Glaumuzina, Julie, and Alison J. Laurie. *Parker and Hulme: A Lesbian View.* Auckland: New Women's Press, 1991.
Gone Girl. Directed by David Fincher. 2014. Los Angeles: 20th-Century Fox Home Video, 2015.
Greer, Jane, and Miriam Forman-Brunell. "Diaries." In *Girlhood in America: An Encyclopedia*, vol. 1, edited by Miriam Forman-Brunell, 206–11. Santa Barbara, CA: ABC-CLIO, 2001.
Heathers. Directed by Daniel Waters. 1989. Troy, MI: Anchor Bay Entertainment, 2001. DVD.
Hogan, Rebecca. "Engendered Autobiographies: The Diary as a Feminine Form." *Prose Studies* 14, no. 2 (1991): 95–107. doi: 10.1080/01440359108586434.
Hunter, Jane H. "Inscribing the Self in the Heart of the Family: Diaries and Girlhood in Late-Victorian America." *American Quarterly* 44, no. 1 (March 1992): 51–81. doi: 10.2307/2713180.
Lynch, Jennifer. *The Secret Diary of Laura Palmer.* New York: Gallery, 1990.
Kirkland, Ewan. "Storytelling in Survival Horror Video Games." In *Horror Video Games: Essays on the Fusion of Fear and Play*, edited by Bernard Perron, 62–78. Jefferson, NC: McFarland, 2009.
The Loved Ones. Directed by Sean Byrne. 2009. Los Angeles: Paramount Home Entertainment, 2012.
Martinson, Deborah. *In the Presence of Audience: The Self in Diaries and Fiction.* Columbus: Ohio State University Press, 2003.
"Murder Charge Girl's Chilling 'Diary of Death.'" *Independent*, 27 February 1997. http://www.independent.co.uk/news/murder-charge-girls-chilling-diary-of-death-1280819.html.
"No Good Reason." *Deadly Women*, season 6, episode 8, October 2012.
Podnieks, Elizabeth. *Daily Modernism: The Literary Diaries of Virginia Woolf, Antonia White, Elizabeth Smart, and Anaïs Nin.* Montreal: McGill-Queen's University Press, 2000.
Renton, Jennie. "The Story behind the Potter Legend: J. K. Rowling Talks about How She Created the Harry Potter Books and the Magic Harry Potter's World." *Sydney Morning Herald*, 28 October 2001. http://www.accio-quote.org/articles/2001/1001-sydney-renton.htm.
Rowling, J. K. *Harry Potter and the Chamber of Secrets.* New York: Scholastic, 1998.
Scheidt, Lois Ann. "Adolescent Diary Weblogs and the Unseen Audience." *Digital Generations: Children, Yong People, and New Media*, edited by David Buckingham and Rebekah Willett, 193–210. Mahwah, NJ: Lawrence Erlbaum, 2006.
Scott, Isabel Scheuneman, and Jennifer M. Kilty. "'When She Cracks': The Visual (Re)Construction of '*Deadly Women*' in Infotainment Media." *The Annual Review of Interdisciplinary Justice Research* 5 (2016): 72–97.
Simons, Judy. "Invented Lives: Textuality and Power in Early Women's Diaries." In *Inscribing the Daily: Critical Essays on Women's Diaries*, edited by Suzanne L. Bunkers and Cynthia A. Huff, 252–63. Amherst: University of Massachusetts Press, 1996.
Sosin, Deborah Anne. "The Diary as a Transitional Object in Female Adolescent Development." *Adolescent Psychiatry* 11 (January 1983): 92–103.
"Thrill Kill and Poisoned." *Killer Kids*, season 2, episode 4, 17 December 2012, http://www.mylifetime.com/shows/killer-kids/season-2/episode-4.
Whitney, Anne. "Writing by the Book: The Emergence of the Journaling Self-Help Book." *Issues in Writing* 15, no. 2 (Spring/Summer 2005): 188–215. *EBSCOhost*, 18 July 2017.

"Do not read the Latin"

The Summoning Diary in Horror Film

Lisa Cunningham

Films featuring the summoning of demonic entities or vengeful spirits are plentiful—so much so that it is difficult to discuss them as a single, coherent genre. They are more profitably approached as a loose collection of subgenres, such as that comprised of films in which a diary, when read by the protagonist, summons violent entities, leading to concrete and messy consequences in the protagonist's world, which had (prior to the encounter with the diary) largely functioned by "normal" rules. This essay considers three such films—*Harry Potter and the Chamber of Secrets,* *The Cabin in the Woods,* and *Evilspeak*—all of which employ the trope of a summoning diary in order to explore and expand on existing dialogues regarding boundaries of the "public" and the "private" as dichotomous.

We construct private spaces that we see as having less value than the public spaces we construct, and so we don't expect them to interact with real-world public spaces in any meaningful way. Diaries that summon things, however, invert this relationship. They are purely private spaces that enact their own will upon the public world, thus reminding us that private spaces can still be spaces of danger, that public spaces are not made inherently safe by simply being public, and that the two are not as concretely divided as we think. When these diaries are read by an intruder—someone with no personal, private connection to the diary or its author, who finds the diary in some kind of a public space—the realm of the private (acting through the diary) responds to the intrusion by powerfully and violently affecting the public sphere.

Private Spaces on the Page

Any discussion of public and private spheres requires a definition of the boundaries of the concepts. As Jeff Weintraub suggests, this discussion can be rife with definitional vagueness, the distinction being "equivalent to establishing the boundary of the political" or even "used as a conceptual framework for demarcating other important boundaries: between the 'private' worlds of intimacy and the family and the 'public' worlds of sociability or the market economy ... and so on in rich (and overlapping) profusion."[1] His eventual conclusion that "the public/private distinction ... comprises, not a single paired opposition, but a complex family of them, neither mutually reducible nor wholly unrelated"[2] is borne out by these films, which establish different boundaries for the "private" and play with them in many different ways. Many cultural distinctions between public and private do, notably, seem to privilege the public sphere as the half of the dichotomy with the most power and the most ability to enact its will (or whim) on the other. This may, indeed, be the site of the horror that summoning-diary films are identifying and explaining: The diaries act upon public space in a way that calls into question whether public spheres ever even had the authority and power we ascribe to them when we describe them as impersonal and "objective."

The "private" sphere in these films is so private that it is individual: a person's diary is presumed to exist in order to keep their most private thoughts—their innermost attempts to process the world around them—away from literally everyone else. The "public" sphere is the world of the protagonist character who reads the diary: a world with structures and rules and authorities (religious, governmental, familial, otherwise bureaucratic, monetary, etc.) which they have been taught can protect them from any non-structural threats, such as unexpected violence or the summoning of demons. Joseph Campbell's monomyth identifies "crossing the threshold"[3] as a basic component of storytelling: The protagonist will, in the arc of the story, move into a wholly unfamiliar space, but there is always a presumption that they will return to a familiar space when their journey is complete. The spaces of the familiar and unfamiliar are demarcated by a solid and identifiable threshold, and they remain separate.

Slasher movies frequently employ this trope by having protagonists move from spaces of urbanity to spaces of extreme rurality, whose private "uncivilized"-ness is both their appeal and their eventual source of horror—such as Camp Crystal Lake in the *Friday the 13th* films, which claims by name and structure to be an inviting public space, but which the killer considers his private domain. The fact that diaries are considered, by their nature and social history, to be entirely ensconced in the private sphere (as *Harry Potter and the Chamber of Secrets* explores rather deftly) grants them a kind of invisibility while at the same time rendering them vulnerable. People presume that they can pick up, read, write in, or otherwise violate the diaries with impunity, and their very presumption of the harmlessness of the "private" diaries (which are in no way directly tied to the violators' own personal, familial, or private spheres) allows the diaries to enact significant violence on the public.

The Evil Dead (1981) and its reboot *Evil Dead* (2013) efficiently employ this trend by having their demons summoned via, respectively, playing an audio-recorded research journal aloud and following a series of hand-written notes—"leave this book alone" and "don't say it don't write it don't hear it," most relevantly—that led to an incantation. While the Sumerian *Book of the Dead* was, in both cases, the powerful artifact that summoned the titular creatures, the ritual could not have taken place without the personal notations or journaling which, for the students who engaged with the text, coexisted completely with the book. The private productions of someone reading (visually or audibly) the Sumerian *Book of the Dead* were what allowed for the entrance of the evil into the world at large, making—quickly but clearly—the point that the protagonists' damning choice was to intrude on a private space (the journals') which was not theirs. The space itself reacts against the intruders—the trigger, in *The Evil Dead*, requiring only that the protagonists not stop the tape in time—invading the entire rural space (the cabin) that the outsiders considered public and therefore safe—a part of the real, understandable, "normal" world.

A Repository of Secrets

Harry Potter and the Chamber of Secrets specifically engages with the cultural construction of the diary as a private space. The film, though rated PG, is structurally a fairly traditional horror film: the plot hinges on identifying and destroying a monster that sneaks through the walls; whispers violent thoughts that only our protagonist, Harry (Daniel Radcliffe), can hear (much to the chagrin of his concerned, yet disbelieving friends); and both ossifies and murders children. The villain—a part of the soul of the dark wizard Lord Voldemort (Christian Coulson) that had been housed in an antique diary—is summoned and strengthened by the misplaced trust of a girl he considered unassuming: Ginny Weasley (Bonnie Wright), the younger sister of Harry's best friend and, later in the series, his girlfriend. A cohort of the villain slips the diary into Ginny's shopping-bag-cum-cauldron one day while in public, immediately making the diary seem as though it had magically (and privately) manifested for her alone. Ginny begins using the diary to write about her daily life, slowly (and inadvertently) giving life to the evil it contains; the private sphere becomes manifest and violent when given the opportunity.

The diary is a site of horror here because it acts vampirically. By providing the book with intimate details of her daily emotional and social life, Ginny unwittingly strengthens it. She assumes that a diary is necessarily a mode of private expression, regardless of the fact that it speaks back to her. Inviting the diary into her private sphere actually invites it into a larger sphere than she anticipates. Her thoughts and feelings about her surroundings may be considered private in relation to the realm of her schoolmates/peers, but they are quite public when compared to the world of a diary possessing half a soul and bereft of social interaction. Ginny makes the structural mistake of thinking of herself as an individual rather than as a member of her societies—of the concentric public spheres that compose her social self.

One of the subtleties on which the film hinges is that diaries are so closely identified with the realms of the private and adolescent, the ineffectual and unthreatening, that the danger posed by this specific diary—a worldwide threat—is completely ignored by everyone around it. No one takes notice of a young girl scribbling constantly in an ancient leather diary, nor does anyone in her extremely impoverished family (whom the narrative describes as being able to take stock of everything they own) even notice her carrying it. Diaries are, by several cultural definitions, beneath notice; the plot requires that this be true in order to progress comfortably.

Even academics have tended to treat the realm of the woman as interconnected with that of the private (and thus with that of the diary), canonizing confessional poetry (Anne Bradstreet), diaries narrating captivity and slavery (Mary Rowlandson and Harriet Jacobs), "sensation" writing (from Jane Austen to more recent bodice-rippers like those of Charlaine Harris), and the *feminine ecriture,* along with personal writing and life narratives, privileging autobiographical modes of truth-telling in contemporary feminist thought. The identification of diary keeping and personal storytelling as modes of truth discourse is deeply and significantly tied, at least in our current modes of thinking, to womanhood. Femininity's well-established link to harmlessness in public discourse is a product of the same associations that led to the assumptions that diaries could present no real threat.

Harry Potter, however, demonstrates the capacity of the private sphere to threaten and destroy. The diary itself is the site of the horror to the point that, in order to kill the villain, the hero must destroy the book (by stabbing it, creating wounds which bleed black ink and destroy the summoned spirit with bright light). The last taunting line delivered by the villain highlights the diary's capacity for destruction: "Funny, the damage a silly little book can do, especially in the hands of a silly little girl." Clearly, "silly" is the last thing either of these powerful tools were, but "silly" and inconsequential is all anyone thought them until the climax of the film.

Reading Other People's Lives

We imbue firsthand or primary accounts of events with authenticity and importance, perceiving them as truthful narratives. The use of diaries as narrative devices in horror films trades on this. The diary is a quick and easy way to allow a character from the past (who, in the context of a diary, ostensibly has no reason to lie) to communicate with the contemporary characters in a way that is imbued with authority. When diaries appear in horror films, they are generally found by one of the protagonists early in the film, and are read—often aloud—to the others in their group as well as to the audience. The author is typically from the distant past of the space the protagonists occupy, or is a character with whom the protagonists have interacted but who has reason to be less than truthful about their current situation. Diaries in horror films thus primarily exist either to inform protagonists about events that happened long before their presence (or even their birth), in which all the characters who took part are dead (or lying), or to inform the characters about the space that they are presently in (and usually intruding upon).

The Cabin in the Woods makes use of this particular version of the trope. When a group of college students goes on vacation to a remote cabin, they find that its basement resembles that featured in *The Evil Dead*. Investigating, they discover a plethora of odd and intriguing objects in the basement. Their presence is not happenstance: As a "meanwhile" sequence reveals, the basement and the protagonists are under the control and observation of a group of unnamed scientists who stocked the basement with objects which, when read or worn or solved, are designed to summon some familiar type of horror movie monster meant to kill those who unleashed it.

Dana (Kristen Connolly) and three other characters simultaneously choose objects to pick up (such as a puzzle box similar to the one that summons Pinhead from Barker's *Hellraiser* series), but Dana picks up the diary of Anna Patience Buckner (Jodelle Ferland) and begins reading it aloud, distracting the others before they fully commit to their choices. The text reveals that the Buckners, of whom Anna was the youngest, were a rural family—practitioners of a religion that revered pain and the experience of pain as bringing one closer to God. Once Dana reads this information, Marty (Fran Kranz) implores: "Uh, guys, I'm not sure it's awesome to be down here…. Okay, I'm drawing a line in the fucking sand, here. Do not read the Latin."[4] Heedless of the warning, Dana moves from reading background information about the pain-worshipping family who swore to return from the grave into reciting what proves to be the summoning invocation.[5] Immediately, the "Redneck Zombie Torture Family" (as they are identified by the shadowy scientific organization that controls the cabin and its monsters) rise from their "graves" by way of an elevator in the ground. Reading the Latin—and thus completing the ritual of summoning the Buckners—is clearly identified as the specific action needed to release the monsters.

Structurally, *Cabin in the Woods* suggests that private/public barriers are being constantly transgressed and questioned. The horrors of slasher films are typically private horrors—that is, they only happen to a clearly identified group of people who have intruded upon an unfamiliar location and are thus "asking for" the horrors that befall them. The location could be someone else's private space, such as Camp Crystal Lake in *Friday the 13th* (1980) or the suburban house of *The Amityville Horror* (1979), or a prohibited mythological space, like that of *Candyman* (1992) or *Krampus* (2015). There is some imagined comfort in the idea that, if one simply does not go to places that are known to be isolated or dangerous, and if one does not toy with legends or mythological beings, no horrific events should take place.

Cabin, however, features a group of young people who have been preselected and led to the titular cabin, which has been arranged as a purportedly inescapable death trap. The cabin itself is outfitted with cameras, microphones, chemical dispersal systems, and at least one two-way mirror; underneath the cabin, however, lies the larger danger—a vast underground complex of caged monsters and bureaucratic employees orchestrating the attack on Dana's group and monitoring the entire proceedings. They, in turn, are only doing this as a way to fulfill a ritual that keeps at bay the danger underneath *them*: the vast underground Hell of the Ancient Ones. The scientists seem to be recreating the deaths of iconic slasher-film characters, deliberately ensuring that the group included the "fool," the "scholar," the "athlete," the "whore," and the "virgin" or "final girl," so that they might be stereotypically "punished" for their sins. Apparently, the punishment of the transgressions of these archetypes—a feature frequently noted in slasher film studies—is necessary to forestall the Ancient Ones. However, since the film stresses the cyclical nature of performance, survival is not victory. Being Carol Clover's "final girl"[6] will help Dana only inasmuch as she might survive that specific instance of the ritual. The Ancient Ones, however, are only barely kept at bay, and so she can never truly be safe from that overarching danger.

In a final rejection of the archetypal role into which she has been thrust (as the "virgin" or "final girl"), Dana elects to keep Marty (the "stoner" or "fool") alive through the night, deliberately causing the ritual to fail and allowing the Ancient Ones to arise and destroy the world. Marty begins the trip with a "rant" that encapsulates the stance of both protagonists at the end of the film: "Society is binding. It's filling in the cracks with concrete. No cracks to slip through. Everything is recorded, filed, blogged, chips in our kids so they don't get lost—society needs to crumble. We're all too chickenshit to let it."[7] Not only are his fears about surveillance and the filling-in of the earth and its (literal and figurative) cracks proven true, but his stance on society "needing" to fail is eventually adopted and enacted by Dana when the unleashes the Ancient Ones.

Anna Patience Buckner was, therefore, the diarist who composed the words that ultimately led to the end of the world; her need to create a private space in which to keep her secrets—secrets, it turns out, that were more impressive than one might expect a pre-adolescent girl to have—created a space that threatened the stability of the world at large. Ultimately, all humanity dies because of Anna's diary, and so the narrative brings this space that was kept so secret crashing violently through the ultimate and permanent public space: the world. *Cabin* wants us to consider that there is *always* a larger context, a *more*-public sphere of which a particular sphere (family, peer group, corporate/government organization, humankind) is only a single component. There is, as the multilayered spaces beneath the house suggest, always another, larger, and more-encompassing level.

A Tome of Insight and Power

The diary at the center of *Evilspeak* is a similarly powerful object, but the antiestablishment focus of the film—its protagonist is the target of social and structural derision by everyone around him—transforms the diary's destructive power into a positive force. *Evilspeak* exists in a world where all established structures of power and authority are cruel, abusive, and overreaching, and the position expressed by Marty and enacted by Dana in *Cabin* (that society deserves to crumble) becomes a narrative through-line rather than a climactic revelation.

Stanley Coopersmith (Clint Howard) is a poor orphan trapped in a community that values lineage and familial money. Enrolled as "the charity case" at West Andover Military Academy, where he is bullied by peers and administrators alike—even the chaplain and the headmaster—Coopersmith is a complete social and structural outcast. The public spheres in which he attempts to take part unanimously and violently reject him. Two specific moments of cruelty starkly stand out. In one, the school's soccer coach (Claude Earl Jones) suggests that another player, the leader of the group of predatory bullies, should injure Coopersmith in order to prevent his playing in the next game. In the other, the bullies find Coopersmith's secretly adopted dog, murder it, and leave it for him to find. No single adult in the film interacts with Coopersmith in a positive, kind, or compassionate way; in fact, they are humiliating and encourage his peers to similarly mistreat him, largely citing his situation as an orphan as cause for the abuse. Having a family is, itself, an expected element of the dominant structure—both through family-structured public sphere expectations, and through the public space necessarily created by the constitution of a family unit. This helps explore ways in which families, while often thought of as "private spheres" of their own, are microcosmic participants in the hegemonic structures, necessary parts of the public sphere in both their intrapersonal interactions and in their interactions with other family units. When confronted with a member of no-family, the reaction of the larger sphere is to reject it entirely as too small and insignificant. Coopersmith is, therefore, an icon of this lesser sphere, seen as completely less-than and non-threatening to the larger, presumed-to-be more powerful public spheres (his school, religion, etc.).

Coopersmith is made to clean out the cellar beneath the school's chapel as a punishment, highlighting both that his school and his religion—which use him for labor while simultaneously shunning him—consider him literally and figuratively "beneath" them. While cleaning, he stumbles upon a small secondary chapel, disused and forgotten, attached to the cellar: the home chapel of Father Esteban (Richard Moll), a priest from the Inquisition who ended his life worshipping Satan. Pledging one's soul to Satan in a black mass is not a terribly difficult feat to accomplish, as Coopersmith soon finds out. He finds Esteban's diary—a leather book with a jeweled pentagram on the cover, written in Latin—and takes it to a computer, where he enters the text into a translation program, allowing him to understand the diary. The first entry reads: "January 13, 1520: I, Esteban, have come to know that the entire world is a domain of evil, ruled over by an evil spirit. And since the power that dominates the world is evil, then it follows that Satan must be God." There is never a moment when the diary is unclear about its intention or content; it immediately identifies itself as a book of forbidden knowledge.

Coopersmith enters the entire text of the diary into his computer, which is fortunate, as the book is stolen, briefly, by a secretary. Once she tries to damage the diary, it summons a herd of pigs to murder her in her bathroom, then fades away from her entryway and reappears behind Coopersmith, on Esteban's coffin. Coopersmith's torture at the hands of his peers ramps up, until eventually, at the diary's direction, he sacrifices a teacher in order to complete the black mass. The film climaxes with Coopersmith's possession by Esteban and then by a green demon (presumably Satan), backed by a chanting chorus and heavily-percussive orchestra music. An explosion occurs, and Coopersmith levitates into the now-flaming chapel where, wielding a demonic sword and accompanied by the murderous hell-pigs, he slays those—peers and authority figures alike—who have tormented him.

It is significant that the diary is found by, and manifests its power through, a young man who is defined as non-threatening by everyone he encounters. Coopersmith is cast out of hegemonic masculine structures (the church, sports team, and military academy) and embraces feminine pastimes, adopting the smallest puppy of a litter to raise as his own and reading dusty old books he finds in the cellar of the chapel. His sphere is judged, by those around him, to be too private. He is consistently abjected (and abused when confronted) by the bureaucratic public spheres of the school—the church and the military—as well as organized education, sports, and social groupings. He has even, as an orphan, judged to have "failed" to participate in the microcosmic version of the public sphere that the family represents. The public sphere thus rejects him angrily as non-participatory (as though he had a choice). It is, as a whole and in any incarnation in which he confronts it, a Kafkaesque, unwinnable game for him. All of this changes, however, when he finds Esteban's diary and finally finds a blend of the public (demonic) and private which will accept him.

Diaries Writ Large

Stephen Barber identifies the experience of urban space on film in relation to our perception of real space: "Once the image has been fixed, its residue in urban space abruptly becomes vulnerable to erasure or alteration—the city is subject to the intrusive power of capricious elements beyond its own domain, in the form of the great upheavals that incessantly amend cities' faces."[8] Each space of summoning in the three films considered here has the exact opposite significance to us as viewers: The summoning spaces *are* the "intrusive" spaces that allow for massive upheaval in public spheres. The geographical spaces in which each summoning occurs are the exact opposite of public space and of urban space: a palatial bunker hidden under a bathroom, the cellar of a cabin that connects to a system of underground tunnels and control rooms, and the basement of a chapel that houses a forgotten and desecrated second sanctuary. The cellars in which our heroes encounter the summoning diaries are all unlit (except by shafts of light through which dust visibly falls) and full of cobwebs. Each is described as smelling dank or unpleasant, and they share a host of visual signifiers of forgotten places, ones which have been passed on by the "capricious elements" or "great upheavals" that constantly roll through urban spaces. These are specifically spaces that were once public—which once had life of some identifiable type—but have now been de-civilized. The diaries themselves are, likewise, both extremely private spaces and sites of knowledge that are inaccessible to the public. The public does not have complete access to anything through the diaries, but simply to a select set of information and a select type and amount of power. The concerns about change or impermanence that affect urban space are not an issue for these hidden spaces, which are not perceivable in the way that cities or other actively public locations are. The un-public spaces (which were once public, creating their uncanny atmosphere) thus stand in for the unperceivable spaces in which we can find ourselves and which we fear because we cannot know them in the way that we can know an urban space: the space of the past, or of unfamiliar rurality, or of insurmountable bureaucracy.

Ultimately, these films provide a line of inquiry into the way that we consider personal/emotional discursive spaces like diaries to be private spaces, which we then consider unthreatening. The films question both diaries' existence as private spaces—they contain text which is produced, to which people can gain access, and which can drastically affect the world at large—and the general assumption that private spaces are not threatening to the social structures that exist as larger, public spaces.

NOTES

1. Weintraub, "Theory and Politics," 2.
2. *Ibid.*
3. Campbell, *Hero with a Thousand Faces*, 64.
4. *Cabin in the Woods.*
5. Immediately before reading the invocation, Dana remarks, "It doesn't even mean anything." Interestingly, the invocation is read aloud as "*Dolor supervivo caro. Dolor sublimus caro. Dolor ignio animus,*" which is later translated to mean "Pain outlives the flesh. Pain raises the flesh. Pain ignites the spirit," but which does not *actually* mean anything. As pointed out in a personal interview by the author with Nanette Eisenhart (senior lecturer of Latin at Georgia Southern University)—the Latin in *Cabin in the Woods* is "primarily gibberish." The correctly conjugated Latin should be "*Dolor carnem supervivit. Dolor carnem sublimat. Dolor animum ignit.*" Clearly, it is not the words nor the incantation itself that raises the zombies, but the act of having read aloud the (nonsense) Latin phrase from the diary.
6. Clover, *Men, Women, and Chain Saws.*
7. *Cabin in the Woods.*
8. Barber, *Projected Cities*, 20.

BIBLIOGRAPHY

Barber, Stephen. *Projected Cities: Cinema and Urban Space.* London: Reaktion Books, 2002.
The Cabin in the Woods. Directed by Drew Goddard. 2012. Santa Monica, CA: Lionsgate Home Entertainment, 2012. DVD.
Campbell, Joseph. *The Hero with a Thousand Faces*, 3d ed. Novato, CA: New World Library, 2008.
Clover, Carol J. *Men, Women, and Chain Saws: Gender in the Modern Horror Film.* Princeton: Princeton University Press, 1992.
Evilspeak. Directed by Eric Weston. 1981. Troy, MI: Anchor Bay Entertainment, 2004. DVD.
Harry Potter and the Chamber of Secrets. Directed by Chris Columbus. 2002. Burbank, CA: Warner Home Video, 2003. DVD.
Weintraub, Jeff. "The Theory and Politics of the Public/Private Distinction." In *Public and Private in Thought and Practice: Perspectives on a Grand Dichotomy*, edited by Jeff Weintraub and Krishan Kumar, 1–40. Chicago: University of Chicago Press, 1997.

"That book lies!"
Lost Texts and Hidden Horrors in The Whisperer in Darkness

A. Bowdoin Van Riper

It is night in the hills of southern Vermont. In a remote cabin, two men—desperate, agitated, under extreme stress—carry on a rapidly escalating argument. "It's all there in the book—let me show you!" the first man insists, gesturing at a century-old leather-bound volume on a table beside him. He is Albert Wilmarth, a professor of English from Miskatonic University in Arkham, Massachusetts—a tweedy, bespectacled outsider deeply out of place among the taciturn farmers of rural Vermont. He is a folklorist, drawn by mysterious tales of hill-dwelling monsters that have been passed down among those farmers for generations, some of which are recorded in the book. He reaches for the volume, intending to consult its wisdom, but the second man—Will Masterson, caretaker and handyman to the cabin's owner—is having none of it. "That book lies!" he screams at Wilmarth, drawing a revolver and firing a shot, followed by four more in rapid succession, into the inert tome. He saves the last round for himself: sudden, violent deliverance from a battle that, he believes, neither he nor humanity can possibly survive.

The scene is among the most strikingly memorable in *The Whisperer in Darkness* (2011), Sean Branney's adaptation of a 1931 H.P. Lovecraft novella of the same title. It is also among the most disturbing—no small distinction in a film that features conversations with disembodied human heads floating in metal cylinders, attacks by malevolent insect-creatures from other dimensions, and Masterson's daughter Hannah—a girl of 11 or 12—plucked by the monsters from the open cockpit of a biplane carrying her to safety and dropped to her death in the forest below. A man emptying his revolver into an antique book, angrily denouncing it as if it were a conscious and malevolent entity, could easily be played as comedy. It plays as horror in *The Whisperer in Darkness* because of the book's previously central role in the film, the nature of its "lies," and their implications for Wilmarth. Masterson is, at the moment he denounces the book and pulls the trigger, deep into the gray borderland that divides sanity from madness. The five shots he fires at the book are not, however, an act of madness. They are—along with, arguably, the sixth shot that ends his life—his last flicker of sanity: a final, desperate attempt to shock Wilmarth into awareness of the danger into which he has stumbled.

The horrors in *The Whisperer in Darkness* come in two distinct, yet intertwined, streams. The first is physical: the alien Mi-Go and their human allies: the strange noises in dark forests, disembodied heads in jars, and alien insect-monsters swooping out of the darkness to attack Wilmarth and the girl as they attempt to fly to safety. The second—as in so many Lovecraft tales—is intellectual: the protagonist's discovery that what they think of as "reality" is, in fact, a tiny corner of a vast, unruly, and terrifying universe. Wilmarth is, in the print version of "The Whisperer in Darkness," a man who goes in search of the truth and, upon finding it, immediately wishes that he hadn't. Robert Price describes him as "the model Lovecraft protagonist ... [who] starts out blissfully ignorant and only too late learns the terrible truth, and that only after a long battle with his initial rationalistic skepticism."[1] The film adaptation elaborates on the original, deepening and intensifying the intellectual horrors that Wilmarth suffers. This essay is an exploration of this fresh hell into which the film plunges its hapless hero—confronting him not just with the short, sharp shock of a revelation that there are aliens among us, but with the systematic overturning of everything he held sacred—and the book's central role in the process.

Monsters in the Hills

The Whisperer in Darkness begins like many Lovecraft tales, with a mystery. Spring rains swell the rivers of southern Vermont, and as the waters recede there are reports that the remains of strange-looking creatures have been found along the riverbanks. The discoveries revive centuries-old stories of mysterious, secretive beings living in the Vermont hills, and draw the attention of Wilmarth (Matt Foyer), an expert in New England folklore. Newly in possession of a rare book by fellow folklorist Eli Davenport, who recorded similar stories a century before, Wilmarth argues that the hill-creatures are nothing but legends—folkloric vestiges of a more primitive age. Vermont farmer Henry Akeley (Barry Lynch) believes otherwise, and in a series of increasingly agitated letters tells Wilmarth that the creatures have besieged his house. Wilmarth initially dismisses Akeley as a crank, but when the farmer dispatches his son George (Joe Sofranko) to Miskatonic to present Wilmarth with photographs and a wax-cylinder recording of the creatures, the folklorist's skepticism begins to waver.

Wilmarth encounters George Akeley moments after a disastrous, nationally-broadcast public debate about the existence of the hill-creatures, in which he was routed by Charles Fort (Andrew Leman), the author of bestselling books on paranormal phenomena.[2] Smarting from this humiliation—which was as much a product of his own arrogance as of Fort's considerable debating skills—Wilmarth resolves to take a more hands-on role in the investigation. Against the advice of his closest friend on the faculty, anthropologist Nathaniel Ward (Matt Langan), he continues his correspondence with Henry Akeley and—in response to a request in Akeley's last letter—agrees to meet him at his remote farmhouse to discuss the hill-creatures. The last letter differs radically from those that preceded it: sanguine, rather than fearful, and filled with praise for the creatures, whose motives Akeley claims to have misunderstood. Wilmarth's journey is unexpectedly difficult—complicated by rain, washed-out bridges, and encounters with locals (like Masterson) who seem to be hiding something. When Wilmarth reaches the farmhouse, he finds that Akeley, too, is not as he expected: not the vigorous defender of home and hearth who (in one of the photographs delivered by his son) posed with his rifle beside the corpse of a hill-creature, but a frail old man with a rasping, wispy voice, wrapped in a heavy robe and seated in a darkened room.

Akeley beckons Wilmarth close and, in whispers, reveals what he claims to be the truth about the hill-creatures. They are a race of advanced alien beings called the Mi-Go, capable of travelling at will through space, and willing to share the experience with humans who are willing to cooperate with them. The human body, Akeley explains, is not capable of withstanding the Mi-Go's method of interstellar travel, but they are capable of surgically separating the brain (leaving the individual's consciousness fully intact) and preserving it in a specially designed cylinder that *can* make the trip. Akeley shows Wilmarth a rack of such cylinders, along with an electromechanical device that, when a cylinder is plugged into it, causes the individual inside to manifest as a holographic image capable of seeing and conversing with those in the room. One of the disembodied brains, identified only as B–67 (Sean Branney), echoes Akeley's glowing reports of the Mi-Go and, telling Wilmarth that he himself—or, rather, his consciousness—has visited 37 "celestial worlds," including alien planets and dark stars.

Wilmarth retires to Akeley's guest room deeply disturbed and unable to sleep. Hearing voices coming from downstairs, he rises to investigate, and is horrified to discover that the Mi-Go and their human collaborators—including all three of the locals he met on his journey to Akeley's farm—are about to begin a new phase of their plans, and plan to kill him in order to prevent him from disrupting or exposing it. Hannah Masterson (Autumn Wendell) helps him to escape the house and sends his pursuers in the wrong direction, buying time for him to flee the area, but instead he doubles back into the house, unwilling to leave Henry Akeley to the Mi-Go. He soon discovers, however, that the "man" who whispered to him in the darkness was actually a Mi-Go using an elaborate disguise to impersonate Akeley. The real Henry Akeley has been turned, without his knowledge and against his will, into a disembodied brain in a cylinder who, when Wilmarth connects him to the machine and explains the situation, begs for the release of death.

Eli Davenport's book after the climactic confrontation, its pages damaged by bullets and its credibility destroyed by Masterson's revelation that it was part of an elaborate deception perpetrated by the alien Mi-Go, in *The Whisperer in Darkness* (2011).

Wilmarth finds himself incapable of killing Akeley, and Will Masterson (Caspar Marsh)—who at that moment enters the room with his gun drawn—likewise rejects the Mi-Go's orders to kill Wilmarth. He shoots the Davenport book, then himself, but before dying reveals the full horror of the situation. The Mi-Go, he explains, are not benevolent explorers but ruthless invaders who, for centuries, have used their powers of mind control to manipulate and deceive unwary humans. The ritual they are about to perform atop Round Mountain will open an inter-dimensional gateway, allowing them to complete their long-planned conquest of Earth. "Mankind is finished!" a distraught Masterson tells Wilmarth before taking his own life. "They're what's next!"

Unwilling to accept this dismal assessment, Wilmarth—for the first time in the film—takes action against the Mi-Go. He climbs to the mountaintop and throws the cylinder holding Akeley's brain into the emerging vortex, disrupting the monsters' plans and granting the old man release from his nightmare. Returning to the farm, he finds Hannah and flees with her in a war-surplus biplane that Akeley (somewhat improbably) keeps in his barn. His triumph, however, is short-lived. The Mi-Go intercept the plane and attack it in midair, causing Hannah to fall to her death and forcing Wilmarth to crash land. The film's final scene reveals that Wilmarth, who has been narrating the action of the film in retrospect, has himself been reduced by the victorious aliens to a disembodied brain in a cylinder.

The Book as Scholarly Totem

As a scholar of the humanities, a member of a university English department, and a specialist in New England folklore, Henry Wilmarth lives in a world defined by books. Written texts produced by others are, for him and his colleagues, the object of study and the standard against which the quality of their own work is judged.[3] To look at a text that everyone else has looked at and see in it what no one else has seen instantly raises a scholar's reputation in Wilmarth's world. To be judged by one's colleagues to have "read more into the text than is there" lowers it just as swiftly. The books that Wilmarth and his colleagues publish themselves, making their work available to fellow scholars and to posterity, are the coin of their professional realm: the basis on which the concrete rewards of tenure and title, as well as the insubstantial (but no less treasured) prize of standing within the field. Asked by Ward, his friend and fellow Miskatonic faculty member, whether he plans to turn his latest discovery into another book, Wilmarth treats the question as vaguely absurd and the affirmative answer as self-evident.

Books are, to Wilmarth and his colleagues, primarily vessels for transmitting information—the texts they study, and the interpretations of them that they formulate—across space and time. Even Wilmarth, a folklorist studying tales whose "natural habitat" is the oral tradition, depends on written texts to gain access to those tales. Folktales are protean by nature, varying from place to place and constantly diverging and evolving, but when plucked from the wild by the act of transcription and pinned to the page as words on paper they are rendered permanent and transmissible. Collating the tales collected and published by other scholars with those he has collected himself, Wilmarth can stand, Newton-like, "on the shoulders of giants," and trace the evolution of folklore over multiple centuries and across all of New England. Wilmarth achieves mastery of his field not by venturing into the field (like Ward, an ethnologist) or laboratory (like the unnamed Miskatonic astronomy professor [Zack Gold] who examines Akeley's photographs) but by immersing himself in books.

Approaching books as vessels whose significance lies in their contents, rather than as objects significant in their own right, sets Wilmarth and fellow humanities scholars apart from rare-book dealers and collectors.[4] Occasionally, however, the lines blur; some books are vessels for contents so unusual, and so rare, that they *become* significant objects.

The copy of Eli Davenport's *Vermont: Tales of the Old Ones* that Wilmarth acquires in the opening scenes of *The Whisperer in Darkness* is such a book. In a scholarly community where books are literally everything, it is the scholarly equivalent of a pirate's buried hoard. The idea that the book is a treasure, not merely a tool, is reinforced by the silent scenes that show Wilmarth taking possession of it. He enters a darkened house and walks confidently down a hall as rats scatter before the probing beam of his flashlight. He is dressed in a suit and hat—the very image of an academic, even when moonlighting as a burglar—but carries a small pry bar that he uses to force open the door to a locked room. Once inside, illuminated by the light of boarded-up windows, he breaks the lock of a dust-covered trunk inscribed with the initials "E. D." and extracts the slender, oversized volume as if cradling a golden idol or priceless portrait.

The conversation that ensues when he first shows the book to Ward revolves around its uniqueness: "I thought all copies had been lost," Ward says upon seeing it, raising the question of just how few copies must have existed in the first place in order for them all to be lost or destroyed in the space of a century. "Didn't Armitage have the last one? And it was ruined in that business last year." Wilmarth acknowledges the point, and takes the opportunity to further underscore the book's rarity. "That was the last *printed* copy," he excitedly explains to his friend. "This is Davenport's handwritten original, and *all his notes*. There's knowledge in there that's recorded nowhere else." Wilmarth's exultant description of the book to Ward suggests that he values it for two overlapping reasons: Its rarity, which means possession of it raises his status among fellow academics, and the window into Davenport's mind and work that the associated notes provide. The fact that the book is a pre-publication draft makes it, for Wilmarth, even more valuable than an unexpectedly (re)discovered print copy: a complete record of Davenport's thoughts, before rough edges were smoothed off, unproven speculations pruned away, and loose thoughts set aside for publication.

The value that Wilmarth assigns to the book gives it, in his mind, qualities that verge on the magical. When Ward asks him what he intends to do with it, his first thought is to use it to arm himself for his upcoming on-air debate with Charles Fort. Ward warns him, presciently, that he will be out of his element against Fort's well-honed rhetorical skills, and urges him not to participate in the debate, but Wilmarth is undeterred. "I can convince people ..." he insists, but Ward cuts him off: "With the minutiae of New England folklore?" Ward, though an academic, is fully aware that the insular world of academia operates by different rules than the wider one inhabited by Charles Fort and the debate's radio audience. Wilmarth recognizes no such distinction. His personal life has—the film implies—collapsed into his professional life since the loss of his wife and child, his understanding of the world is defined by what transpires within his ivy-covered enclave at Miskatonic University. He assumes that the totemic significance ascribed to Davenport's book in the world of literature scholars will transfer, undiminished, to the world of the general public. Preparing for intellectual battle with Fort—who he views as a board-certified physician might regard a highly successful quack—he believes that the book will be his invincible secret weapon, and that its power will allow him to vanquish his enemy with ease.

The Book as Weapon Against Ignorance

The Whisperer in Darkness is a film about tales of monstrous creatures lurking in the shadowy corners of our world, and a man called upon to make sense of them. The first words spoken onscreen—voiceover narration by Wilmarth, played over a scene of a man finding *something* in a rain-swollen Vermont stream—make this framing explicit. In the aftermath of the 1927 floods, Wilmarth explains, reports of strange things found floating in the water became entwined with "a primitive, half-forgotten cycle of whispered legends, which the old people resurrected for the occasion." It was this resurgence of old legends, he continues, that drew him into the story as "many of my friends appealed to me to shed what light *I* could on the subject."

The unnamed "friends" are, given Wilmarth's ivory-tower isolation, almost certainly fellow academics, and he approaches the problem of "shedding light" on the subject in a manner perfectly aligned with his literature-scholar's worldview: He seeks out a book. The film cuts from his "shedding light" comment to Wilmarth shining a literal light into the darkened building—presumably Davenport's abandoned home—where he finds the long-dead author's manuscript copy of *Vermont: Tales of the Old Ones*. The purposefulness with which he moves through the house suggests that he already knows what he is looking for, and that he is involved not in a large-scale scholarly fishing expedition—trolling for obscure published sources that had hitherto escaped his notice—but in a targeted search for notes, manuscripts, or other unpublished records that Davenport might have left behind. Wilmarth's subsequent exchange with Ward underscores the idea. "Nobody in the entire world knows more about this particular area of folklore" than he himself does, Wilmarth declares, but possessing the book of (and imbibing the knowledge gathered by) his long-dead colleague Davenport makes him more knowledgeable, and thus more capable of carrying out his mission of "shedding light."

As Wilmarth's conversation with Ward unfolds, however, it becomes clear that he sees his mission not as a dispassionate investigation of a curious phenomenon, but as a crusade against ignorance, superstition, and credulousness. The legends are, for him, holdovers from a more superstitious age, with no legitimate place in the modern world. When he quotes a section of Davenport's text to Ward (all but verbatim, as a cutaway shot to the pages of the book makes clear), the words themselves are heavy with mystery and menace, but Wilmarth's tone, gestures, and facial expressions signal his amusement at the absurdity of it all. His voice quickly becomes mocking as quotes Davenport's description of folktales describing "a hidden race of beings which lurk somewhere among the remoter hills, in the deep woods of the highest peaks," and the claim that "evidence of their existence was seen by those who ventured far up the slopes of certain mountains" leaves him smirking and chuckling at the absurdity of it all. By the time he concludes with "or in the deep, steep-sided gorges that even the wolves shunned," he can no longer contain his laughter.

The mockery, it is important to note, is directed not at Davenport, but at his too-credulous informants who believed that monsters lurked in the hills. "The whole reason to study folklore," he tells Ward, "is to help us understand how and why we create myths. People can't go around believing that each bolt of lightning is a spear thrown by Zeus." Wilmarth makes the same point a few scenes later in his debate with Fort. Pointing out that citizens of the area around Arkham once believed, uniformly and with near-absolute certainty, in the existence of witches, he argues that the casting aside of such beliefs is essential to progress. "Cultural traditions and beliefs, even superstitions, shape our view of the world, but ... the world is what the world is, and if we're to progress beyond witch trials and superstitions, we must cultivate the discipline to separate objective fact from myth and fancy."

The link between monsters-in-the-hills folklore and the "superstitious" past beyond which humans must progress is, for Wilmarth, axiomatic: self-evidently true and beyond question. His first mention of the stories, in the opening narration, tags them as "primitive." In the debate he lumps them in with "myth and fancy," and—reaching for examples of patently "primitive" fantasies, compares them to Nepalese legends of "the dreaded Mi-Go" and "the Abominable Snowman of the Himalayas." They are, he insists, mere "beliefs" and "cultural traditions" which have acquired a spurious air of legitimacy through longevity and endless repetition. Having attained this status of quasi-truth in the minds of credulous rural Vermonters—the likes, Wilmarth implies but never explicitly says, of Henry Akeley—they gain the ability to warp popular perceptions of reality. Steeped in centuries of stories about strange creatures living in the hills, their imaginations see monsters where only floating tree branches actually exist.

Davenport's book becomes the linchpin of his argument because, he believes, it makes precisely this point: A century old in its own right, recording even older stories, it establishes the great antiquity of the "monsters in the hills" tales. The deeper into the past he can trace the tales, Wilmarth believes, the more obvious it will be that they are rooted in primitive superstition, and the fantasies that swirled through the minds of early settlers as they peered uneasily into the darkness beyond their homes and hearths. The book serves his purposes not by proving that the legends are wrong, but by proving that they are old. "A heritage of legend and a popular belief in something isn't enough to make it true," Wilmarth tells Fort in the debate, but for him it is more than enough to render something suspect.[5]

The Book as a Tool of Deception

The skepticism that Wilmarth exhibits in the first act of the film exists prior to, and independent of, his acquisition of the Davenport book. The book provides convenient reinforcement for his beliefs—a trump card he can play against newspaper reports, purported eyewitness accounts, and Fort's encyclopedic catalog of parallel legends—but is not the source of them. Davenport uses the approach that Fort claims to employ: collating and recording, but expressing neither belief nor disbelief. A reader who came to Davenport's book agnostic on the subject of monsters in Vermont (like Charles Fort) would find support for their existence, and a reader already convinced that they were real (like Henry Akeley) would read it as a ringing confirmation that humans had been encountering them for centuries.

Wilmarth gradually becomes such a person as his seemingly impregnable skepticism breaks down over the course of the second act, and the book is integral to the process. Viewing the photographs that George Akeley shows him after the debate, he dismisses the first several. They are indistinct, hovering just at the edge of comprehensibility and thus capable of supporting multiple interpretations. The "strange" footprints outside Henry Akeley's cabin could have been made by deer; the shape of "creature" he poses with like a hunter is indistinct.[6] Wilmarth is unimpressed and unconvinced, but an image of a strangely carved black stone collected by the elder Akeley brings him up short. "Look familiar, Albert?" Ward pointedly asks him, and of course it does: a sketch of a virtually identical stone appears in the unpublished notes associated with Davenport's book. Ward's point—that Akeley could not have seen the Davenport sketch—is not lost on Wilmarth,

Wilmarth (Matt Foyer) contemplates Henry Akeley's last letter, incurious about the multiple ways in which it differs from all those that preceded it and unaware that it, like the Davenport book, lies in *The Whisperer in Darkness* (2011).

who tacitly accepts the stone as the first corroboration of tales he had dismissed as myth. Photographs alone are not sufficient evidence of the strange beings that lurk in the hills, but photographs that align with Davenport's book—and, through its pages, touch the truth—are.

The Davenport book shifts, in that moment, from being a bulwark for his skepticism to being the touchstone against which he measures all subsequent evidence. Even as myth and reality trade places before his eyes, the book remains his lodestar, and the central pillar of his academic's worldview—that books in general are a portal to the Truth—remains comfortably intact.

Wilmarth begins the film convinced that Davenport's book contains fictitious tales about imaginary creatures. Midway through his long night at Akeley's cabin, he abandons that view and embraces its polar opposite: that the folktales Davenport recorded were essentially accurate reports about real creatures. Reeling from this wrenching paradigm shift, and the intellectual disorientation resulting from it, Wilmarth misses repeated signs that he is (still) seeing only glimpses of a larger truth. The implications of the creatures not appearing on ordinary film do not sink in. The abrupt difference in tone and form between Henry Akeley's last letter and all those that preceded it puzzles, but does not detain him. The fact that the writer misspells "his" own last name passes unnoticed, as does the uncanny similarity between the voices of the creatures recorded by Akeley on the wax cylinder and the voice of the man at the cabin who claims to *be* Akeley.

In the darkened living room of the cabin, Akeley—or, rather, the being he still believes to be Akeley—underscores the depth of Wilmarth's ignorance of the hill-creatures. "All your legends about what they offer men and what they wish in connection with the Earth," the Akeley-being declares, "are based on man's misconceptions of allegorical speech. Your most educated experts understand them no better than illiterate farmers and savage natives." Wilmarth's only response is a bland question, punctuated by a brief, skeptical smirk: "All right, Henry … what is it they want?" The erstwhile professor of English, whose job includes instructing Miskatonic students in the nuances of the language, takes no notice of the "Akeley's" use of the second- rather than the first-person to refer to humankind. The self-proclaimed expert in New England folklore offers no protests when he is casually lumped in with the "savages" and "illiterates" he described in such condescending terms only a few weeks earlier. The man who describes the answer to his question as "the foulest nightmares of secret myth revealed in concrete terms" seems only mildly surprised that Akeley seems to accept it. Wilmarth, who argued passionately and aggressively with Fort and presented himself as a defender of logic and reason, has become what he (implicitly) accused Fort of being: a passive, uncritical consumer of information offered by others.

Struggling to grasp the discovery that "mythical" creatures are alive in the Vermont hills, and struggling even harder to make sense of a world where disembodied brains float in cylinders while exotic machines summon the spectral faces of their owners, Wilmarth reflexively clutches at the Davenport book—still, in his mind, a source of certainty. The truth, for him, *must* lie in the text, just as the substance of the text *must* represent a form of truth; no other possibility is conceivable. When Akeley's disembodied brain struggles to articulate a vague memory involving the Mi-Go and a tunnel, Wilmarth visibly brightens as his own mind plucks an answer from Davenport's pages: a legend of the Penacook people suggesting that the "tunnel" is actually a gateway between worlds.

His newfound sense of certainty and control lasts only moments, however. When he offers his newfound insight to counter Will Masterson's claim that "it's too late for us … we can't stop them," Masterson brushes it aside. Wilmarth gestures at the book, invoking its authority one more time by using the same revelation that first pierced his own skepticism: "The Davenport book … it says the *same things*!" Masterson, growing more agitated by the moment, and visibly exasperated with Wilmarth's failure to grasp the obvious, delivers the awful truth: "Of course it does; those things *wrote* the book!" Unwilling, or perhaps unable, to imagine his erstwhile scholarly hero as a pawn of the Mi-Go, Wilmarth insists that Davenport merely collected the folklore of the settlers and Indians, only to have that illusion shattered as well. "Who do you think *told* the Indians the legend?" Masterson asks, his voice rising to a shout: "*They* did!" The two men rage at one another—Wilmarth insisting that the book holds the key to stopping the Mi-Go invasion of Earth, Masterson screaming that the book is a trap, "full of their lies"—until Wilmarth reaches for the book, and Masterson fires.

Conclusion

The Whisperer in Darkness is a rarity among horror stories in that the protagonist, Wilmarth, never faces a proximate threat of death. Hannah Masterson, George Akeley, and others die at the hands of the Mi-Go, and the disembodied consciousness of B–67 is subjected to excruciating agony by their agents. Henry Akeley has his brain separated from his body, and suffers the living death of confinement in a metal cylinder, at the mercy of his alien enemies. Will Masterson puts a bullet through his own brain as his daughter watches in horror, the shot spraying blood across her face. Wilmarth witnesses much of this, but is himself never in serious danger, at least onscreen. Even when the closing scenes that reveal that he has suffered Henry Akeley's fate—brain separated from body, and consciousness imprisoned in a Mi-Go cylinder—his voiceover echoes B–67's placid acquiescence, not Akeley's horror and despair.

The horror that Wilmarth endures in the film is, for all that, no less real. The opening scenes of *The Whisperer in Darkness* establish Wilmarth as a man whose life is devoted to seeking out, extracting, and disseminating the truths found in the pages of books. The remainder of the film follows him, the camera's gaze never wavering, as every foundational truth on which his world rests is torn to shreds before his eyes. Having achieved one of the greatest coups of his scholarly career by acquiring Davenport's handwritten book, he feels his triumph turn to ashes in his mouth. The book convinces no one—not Fort, not Akeley, not Ward, not the debate audience—of the "truth" that Wilmarth has devoted his life to meticulously establishing, and (when read in the light of the world beyond the Miskatonic campus) reveals that the polar opposite is true.

Wilmarth, having spent his life believing he was studying real stories about made-up monsters, discovers that he has actually been studying made-up stories about real monsters—stories made up by the monsters themselves, to serve their own deceptive ends. He enters the living death of the Mi-Go cylinder having experienced an academic's peculiar version of Hell: the realization that his life's work—decades devoted to the pursuit of truth on the printed page—produced nothing more than a tissue of lies.

Notes

1. Price, *The Dunwich Cycle*, xi.
2. Charles Hoy Fort (1874–1932) was a real historical figure, best known for *The Book of the Damned* (1919), *New Lands* (1923) and *Lo!* (1931). For an overview of his life and work, which helped to define "the paranormal" as an intellectual category, see Bennett, *Politics of the Imagination*.
3. On the evolution of the book as a tool for scholars, particularly in the humanities, see (among a vast literature): Grafton, *The Footnote*; and Grafton, *Worlds Made by Words*, and O'Donnell, *Avatars of the Word*.
4. And, for that matter, from the protagonists of many of the other films discussed in this volume, among them the scholar-sorcerer of *Night of the Demon* (1957), the resurrected title character in *Warlock* (1989), and the hapless college students of *The Cabin in the Woods* (2012).
5. Wilmarth is, in this respect, the antithesis of Lovecraft himself, who immersed himself in the folklore of his native region and sought in it a primordial (and thus, in his view, more "authentic") New England culture. See Evans, "A Last Defense Against the Dark."
6. The photographs vagueness is, as James Kneale notes, an artifact of Lovecraft grappling with what Richard Salomon calls "the problem of witnessing": how to reveal the horrors at the heart of a horror story without, in the process, describing them too concretely and robbing them of their uncanny power ("Monstrous and Haunted Media," 95, 100–01).

Bibliography

Bennett, Colin. *Politics of the Imagination: The Life, Work and Ideas of Charles Fort*. New York: Cosimo Books, 2010.
Evans, Tim. "A Last Defense Against the Dark: Folklore, Horror, and the Uses of Tradition in the Works of H.P. Lovecraft." *Journal of Folklore Research* 42, no. 1 (January–April 2005): 99–135.
Grafton, Anthony. *The Footnote: A Curious History*. Cambridge: Harvard University Press, 1999.
_____. *Worlds Made by Words: Scholarship and Community in the Modern West*. Cambridge: Harvard University Press, 2011.
Kneale, James. "Monstrous and Haunted Media: Lovecraft and Early Twentieth-Century Communications Technology." *Historical Geography* 38 (2010): 90–106.
O'Donnell, James J. *Avatars of the Word: From Papyrus to Cyberspace*. Cambridge: Harvard University Press, 2000.
Price, Richard M. *The Dunwich Cycle: Where the Old Gods Wait*. Ann Arbor: Chaosium, 1995.
The Whisperer in Darkness. Directed by Sean Branney. 2011. Glendale, CA: H.P. Lovecraft Historical Society, 2011. DVD.

Witches, Demons and Curses

Spellbound

The Significance of Spellbooks in the Depiction of Witchcraft on Screen

EMILY BRICK

Witches (and their male counterparts, warlocks) are unique among horror monsters in that they exist more commonly outside the genre than in it. Along with classic horror films such as *Suspiria* (1977), *Rosemary's Baby* (1968), and *Black Sunday* (1960), the witch also appears frequently in adaptations of secondary-world fantasy stories (*The Wizard of Oz* [1939]), romances (*Practical Magic* [1998]), comedies (*Bewitched* [2005]), fairy tales (*Snow White and the Seven Dwarfs* [1937]), coming-of-age stories (*Sabrina the Teenage Witch* [1996]), and historical dramas (*Witchfinder General* [1968]). This generic hybridity of witches reflects the complexity of the witch archetype as ambivalent figures who can occupy both heroic and monstrous spaces, and whose use of magic can be either beneficial or malevolent. Many texts that fall outside the horror genre while remaining in the realm of the fantastic—the Oz and Harry Potter stories for example—present both types of witches, even pitting them against one another.[1] A significant number of witch films—such as *Bell, Book, and Candle* (1958) and *The Witch* (2015)—operate, however, in the mode of magical realism, presenting witchcraft as a magical intervention in an apparently non-supernatural world.

The diversity of ways in which witchcraft is practiced, and magic is depicted, on screen reflects the diversity of witches and settings. Magical powers can be innate or learned, and the means of exercising them vary from the creation of physical objects such as potions and amulets, through the combination of words and gestures into spells, to the summoning of demons. Spellbooks and grimoires (an equally potent but less-familiar type of magical text) figure prominently in the onscreen activities of witches, but their narrative roles, like the identities of the witches they serve, are complex and varied. They may function as a critical aid-to-learning for neophyte witches, a repository of knowledge for experienced witches, a manual that establishes the rules by which the magical world operates, and a tool that grants access to lost, proscribed, or otherwise inaccessible magical knowledge.

A spellbook, for the purposes of this essay, is a magical recipe book: a collection of instructions on how to perform spells, including recipes for potions, formulas for incantations, and directions for conducting rituals. A grimoire, also featured in many of the texts discussed here, is more expansive than a spell book. It contains history, context, and discourses on the principles of magic as well as instructions on how to perform spells. Both, in varying ways, are "repositories of knowledge that arms people against evil spirits and witches, heal their illnesses, fulfill their sexual desires, divine and alter their destiny, and much else besides."[2] Despite the differences in their contents, however, there is a consistency in the aesthetic appearance of spell books and grimoires on screen. Both are presented as aged heirlooms creating a link with the past, and existing mythology, even in contemporary representations. The spellbook in *Hocus Pocus* (1993), for example, is an enchanted object, bound in leather, with a moving eye on the cover. It has agency, responds when it is summoned, and glows with energy when opened. The spellbook in *The Witches of Eastwick* (1987), titled *Maleficia*, is kept in a velvet lined glass case with a silver dagger, framed like a sacred object on an altar. As well as an instruction manual, the spell book can be a magical object in its own right. It may speak, glow, animate or burst into flames to demonstrate its magical qualities.

The four screen texts considered here as case studies illustrate the diversity of types of magic and spell books depicted on screen, and—because they feature both witches and warlocks—reveal the ways in which depictions of witchcraft are gendered onscreen In the television series *Charmed* (1998–2006), the spellbook is a plot device, and the means by which the witches' power is revealed; in *The Craft* (1996), spellbooks are a crucial part in the learning of magical practice; in *The Covenant* (2006), the grimoire is a

Spell books from *Hocus Pocus* **(1993),** *The Covenant* **(2006),** *The Craft* **(1996) and** *The Witches of Eastwick* **(1987).**

historical narrative and link with the past; and in *Warlock* (1989), a legendary grimoire is a key which unlocks a higher power. The onscreen practice of witchcraft is varied and fluid however, and unlike traditional forms of religion, there is no central text where the rules are written down and no hierarchical body to regulate and organize. This essay, then, is an exploration of the ways in which cinematic depictions of spellbooks and grimoires reflect that complexity and diversity.

Historical Context

Many films featuring witches create a clear link to the past and ground their narratives in the real-life history of witchcraft. *Hocus Pocus* and *Warlock*, for example, open with prologues set in at the time of the 17th-century witch trials, while the warlocks in *The Covenant* are descended from the original witches of Salem. History functions, however, as more than just scaffolding on which these films erect their plots. Modern depictions of witchcraft on screen also draw heavily on complex and contested historical beliefs about witches and their practices.

The Practice of Witchcraft

The most important aspect of the depiction of a spellbook on screen is the witch who uses it. It is often the act of using a spellbook and performing spells that separates the witch from other characters with supernatural powers, such as seers, psychics, and telekinetics. The term "witchcraft" traditionally covers a number of different practices that were traditionally split into two broad areas: maleficia and diabolism (Wicca, discussed later, is a 20th-century development, albeit one rooted in ancient pagan traditions). Maleficia, as it was understood in the medieval and early modern eras, could be practiced with either good or evil intent, and its spells generally had a clear purpose. It was "folk magic," designed to solve specific problems by manipulating the natural world (including the human body) in specific, predictable ways. It presupposed that a web of hidden forces, connections, and energies lay beneath the visible surface of the world, and that those with knowledge of it could use that knowledge to reshape the world around them. Practices associated with maleficia included the preparation of medicinal potions, incantations and the wearing of amulets and talismans.

Diabolism involves worshiping and making a pact with the Devil, and female witches believed to practice it were frequently accused of sexual liaisons with the Prince of Darkness. Fears about witches—predicated on a religious worldview shaped by fear of the Devil, demons and damnation—centered on this aspect of witchcraft, and were heightened by religious leaders' perception that the established Church was vulnerable to disruption. The Church's anxieties were also heightened by the obvious parallels between religion and witchcraft: a belief in higher powers and paranormal events, and an emphasis on ceremony and ritual. Incantations parallel prayers and blessings, blood rituals evoke the doctrine of transubstantiation, and the "black mass" of diabolism is a conscious inversion of the traditional Catholic mass. The era of the witch trials was, not coincidentally, a time of religious schisms and reformations in Europe and North America. The *Malleus Maleficarum* (1486), a guide to identifying witches, was designed to help users find evidence of diabolism and (in so doing) to create a plausible theological model of the Devil's activity on earth. As a religious document sanctioned by the Catholic Church, it is primarily concerned with the practice of diabolic witchcraft rather than folk magic.

References to spellbooks are rare in historical documents about witches. One obvious reason for this is that these documents were composed in an era before literacy was commonplace, particularly among women, and books were scarce and expensive. The details of magical practice would have been passed on, like other craft knowledge, by oral tradition rather than in writing. *The Malleus Maleficarum* refers to spells that witches perform and ways of remedying them but there is no direct reference to the books or grimoires that contain these spells. Wicca, a modern form of pagan witchcraft distinct from that which obsessed early modern religious leaders, is—in sharp contrast—organized around a particular text. It originated in the 1950s in England, spurred by Gerald Gardner's claims that, in 1939, he had discovered a secret pagan coven in the New Forest and that its members had given him *The Book of Shadows*, a grimoire detailing their practices and rituals, which had been handed down through generations. The *Book of Shadows* has become absorbed into modern Wiccan mythology, and Wicca in turn promoted what Owen Davies has described as "a new, positive image of the witch ... one that was empowering and defiant."[3]

Witches and Gender

Three-quarters of those executed for witchcraft in 17th-century Europe and North America were women, but what Hans Peter Broedel calls "the stereotype of the female witch" existed in Western culture well before the age of witch trials.[4] The majority of medieval and early modern texts depict witches as female, and references to them reach back to classical antiquity. Traditionally seen as a figure of horror and a threat to society, the witch has, in modern times, also been embraced as an icon of women's empowerment and defiance. Feminist scholars interpret the witch hunts of the early modern era as a religiously motivated attack on women—one grounded in misogyny, fear of women wielding power over men, and a lack of understanding of the female body. Modern Wicca—like traditional witchcraft, overwhelmingly practiced by women—represents a reaction against this traditional, misogynistic image of witches. It gained popularity throughout the 1960s and 1970s as a form of alternate spirituality—free of the patriarchal and hierarchical elements of traditional churches—and as part of a movement sometimes described as "magical feminism." Practitioners of Wicca embrace the title of "witch" as an empowering feminist archetype imbued with agency and wisdom, but—particularly when writing for the general public—take pains to distance themselves from its traditional association with diabolism and the use of folk-magic for malevolent purposes.

The witch's historical status as a shifting signifier—one whose mythology encompasses notions of monstrosity, abjection and fear as well as empowerment and liberation—is reflected in the evolution of the witch in horror and, especially, on screen. Barbara Creed reads the traditional witch of horror—grotesque, malevolent, and powerful—as an archetype of the monstrous-feminine. Linking representations of witches on screen to religious frameworks of abjection, she argues that the witch's monstrosity is rooted in her femaleness and male fears of women's "imaginary powers of castration."[5] Modern depictions of witches, influenced by Wicca and shaped by Western culture's growing acceptance of women's agency, are more complex. Women with the ability to reshape the world, and a willingness to wield it, are no longer seen as innately monstrous or inherently malevolent.

Witches on Screen

Until recently in British and American popular culture, the witch-as-heroine featured mainly in comedies, romances, and teen dramas, while the witch-as-monster inhabited the realm of horror, fantasy, and fairy tales. Witches of either type remained relatively rare on screen, however, until witches-as-monsters—absent from the classic Universal Studios monster movies of the 1930s and '40s—began to appear in British-made films of the 1960s and '70s. Whether outright horror stories (like *The Blood on Satan's Claw* [1971]) or historical dramas with horror overtones (like *Witchfinder General*) the British witch film—even those set in the present—referenced early-modern campaigns against witches.

Horror films that specifically use the witch trials as a reference point tend to represent witches as victims of zealous witchhunters rather than as monsters. A common narrative—used in *Black Sunday*, *Mark of the Witch* (1970), and *Necromancy* (1972), among other films—involves a witch returning from the past to seek vengeance for her torture and persecution. Presenting witches as victims of a sadistic patriarchy gave the films a veneer of social relevance during an era of emergent feminism and—combined with the loosening of censorship restrictions—gave filmmakers an opportunity to show female witches bound, tortured, and partially nude on screen. These dynamics created films where, as Creed notes, "emphasis ... tended to be more on the witch-hunt or the male leader of the coven than on the witch,"[6] and where witches were more sexualized than overtly monstrous. As Leon Hunt puts it "by the late 1960s, one thing was clear: the occult = sex."[7]

Rosemary's Baby, one of the first major American horror films to feature witches, positions them as unambiguously monstrous. The witches in the apartment next door to Roemary's use both maleficia and diabolism to arrange the birth of the Antichrist, and her husband makes a demonic pact in which he offer her to them in exchange for career success. Rosemary is raped by the Devil and, throughout her pregnancy, the coven uses folk magic to imprison her in her apartment building and control every aspect of her life. She is given an amulet to wear and potions to drink, the coven performs incantations and ceremonies around her. The coven consists of both men and women, but they use their magic for specifically anti-feminist ends: imprisoning Rosemary in her home, robbing her of all agency, and using her body to provide their (male) master with a (male) heir.

Spellbooks on Screen

Whether they depicted witches as fully formed monsters or hapless victims of a ruthless patriarchy, these films rarely featured spellbooks or grimoires. Innocents unjustly accused of witchcraft had no need of them, and tales of monstrous witches tended to focus on the effects of magic rather than the process of practicing it. The rising popularity of witches on both large and small screens in the 1990s changed this equation. *The Craft*, *Little Witches* (1996), and *Buffy the Vampire Slayer* (1997–2003) all depicted teenage girls in the early stages of experimenting with witchcraft, using spellbooks and grimoires to access and use (not always wisely) powers that would otherwise be beyond their grasp. Witchcraft in these texts is linked—perhaps due to the growing prominence of Wicca and the resulting redefinition of the witch archetype—with self-empowerment and teenage rebellion, and they depict a range of magical practices. In them, and in onscreen texts that followed, the spellbook comes into its own.

Charmed: The Book of Shadows

The Book of Shadows is central to the narrative of *Charmed*, a television series about three sisters—Prue, Piper, and Phoebe Halliwell—who discover a copy in their grandmother's house after she dies. It calls them to the attic and it reveals that, like their mother and grandmother before them, they come from a long line of witches and have innate magical powers. Over the first few episodes, a series of events convince them that what the book says is true. Each sister has a natural power—Prue is telekinetic, Piper can freeze time, and Phoebe can see the future—but to perform specific spells, they must come together and invoke the "power of three." Working in concert, they are the most powerful witches of their generation. The first episode intercuts between learning about the sisters and the police investigation into a serial killer who is targeting witches. The killer turns out to be a warlock who wants to steal his victims' powers and who, naturally, finds the sisters an irresistible target. This heroine/victim dynamic structures the show's narrative for its entire eight-season run. The sisters' magic makes them powerful, but also makes them targets (primarily of men and male demons).

Beyond revealing the sisters' true nature to them in the first episode, *The Book of Shadows* plays a central role in their practice of magic and their interactions with the supernatural world. It is a repository of spells, but also a compendium of information about the depth and breadth of the supernatural world, compiled by the generations of Halliwell witches who came before and so, also provides a tangible connection to their heritage. Having become aware of the existence of magic and their ability to practice it only in adulthood, the sisters are obliged to learn about magic on an ad hoc basis. With their mother and grandmother no longer available to guide them, the sisters are particularly reliant on the book. It gives them access to the collected wisdom of their ancestors, enabling them to use their magic with a degree of sophistication they would never be able to achieve on their own. When their natural power makes them targets for demons, monsters, and other dark forces, it also provides valuable foreknowledge of what their enemies are capable of and how they can be defeated.

The book is not simply a book, however, but a powerful magical object in its own right. When the sisters reach for it on any given occasion it may glow, snap closed, or move across the table or floor of its own volition. It appears, at times, to have both sentience and agency. Its evident powers make it a target for those who practice magic with malevolent intent, reinforcing the sisters' dual status as empowered heroines and perpetually endangered victims. *The Book of Shadows* makes it possible for centuries of magical knowledge to be reliably transmitted from person to person, across centuries

The multigenerational nature of the book also embodies familial bonds between women, a central theme in the series. *Book of Shadows* is a generic title in the *Charmed* universe: Every family of witches is encouraged to have one, and to add to it from generation to generation.[8] It links the past to the present, but also witches to one another.

The Craft: Invoking the Spirit

The Craft follows four neophyte teenage witches on their journey into magic. Sarah arrives a new school where fellow students Nancy, Rochelle, and Bonnie recognize her as a natural witch. Together they form a coven and they use magic as a way of bonding, escaping their problems and punishing those who have hurt them. Their magic initially empowers them, but they soon begin to abuse it: injuring or even killing those they believe have wronged them, and then turning on each other. Sarah tries to leave the coven, but the others attack her with dark magic. Sarah fights back, driving away Bonnie and Rochelle by making their worst fears come true, and then defeating Nancy, the leader of the coven and the most corrupted of the four, in a magical duel. The film ends with a disempowered Nancy confined in a psychiatric ward and Sarah safe and still in possession of her own powers, newly aware of how easily they can be abused.

The books the girls use are instructional spellbooks rather than grimoires. Spellbooks fill the *mis-en-scene* throughout the narrative, surrounding them as they hang out in their bedrooms, open on the table at school as they eat lunch, and crowding the shelves of the occult bookstore that they visit regularly to buy or steal books. The shop is a supernatural resource filled with books, candles, ingredients, and mystical objects. There is a temple at the back of the shop with a pentagram on the floor that animates, underscoring the message that the space is magical. The shop functions not as a site where hierarchy is reinforced, but as a place for witches to meet each other and learn from each other, mutually acting as guides, mentors, and arbiters of good and bad magic. The witch who runs it plays this role for the girls and acts as the audience's source of contextual information about witchcraft. She explains that magic is neither inherently good nor inherently bad, but that it is the intention in the heart of the witch that makes it so. On one visit to the store, Nancy buys a book titled *Invoking the Spirit* that enables her to venture into a new, more powerful form of magic involving the summoning of the all-powerful spirit of Manon. The book itself is marked as special because, unlike the other books, the shopkeeper warns them of the dangers: that they cannot undo spells and that whatever they send out will return to them threefold. She does not, however, prevent them from buying the book. Similarly, although the girls fail to heed the witch's warnings, it is to the bookstore that Sarah goes in search of sanctuary when she is under attack.

The Craft borrows the principles of Wicca, as well as its egalitarian ethos, loosely using them—rather than more traditional practices of witchcraft—as its magical reference point. Screenwriter Peter Filardi explains that the protagonists' approach to witchcraft is experimental: "They are sole practitioners. They're creating their own mythology as they go."[9] Each spell has a clear aim and direct effect. Their early magic is playful and its effects are aesthetically appealing, typified by "glamouring" and ceremonies surrounded by butterflies. At this stage, their books are always with them when they perform rituals. They choose spells that solve their problems: Sarah finds love, Bonnie's scars heal, Rochelle's bully is punished, and Nancy's abusive stepfather dies and leaves her money. When they perform the ritual of invoking the spirit—going to a beach at sunset and repeating the incantation from Sarah's book while seated in a circle—the tenor of the magic changes. An aesthetic shift accompanies the magical ones, and the powers they conjure are represented as a storm—crashing waves, lightning, and dark clouds. Their magic subsequently becomes more destructive.

The ceremonial summoning of Manon also evokes the summoning of the Devil in diabolic witchcraft. The film is rich with religious metaphor and Nancy discusses the process of "invoking the spirit" as a form of communion—"you take him into you, it's like he fills you, he takes everything that's gone wrong in your life and he makes it all better again." After the ritual, she walks on water in a Christ-like pose. From this point on, the girls' magic becomes more harmful and more powerful, and they begin to turn on each other. Nancy, Bonnie, and Rochelle use dark magic against Sarah. They appear in her dreams, convince her that her father is dead, and make her hallucinate snakes and insects. The abuse builds to a standoff between Sarah and Nancy, who fight using a combination of magically charged strength and spells.

The Craft exemplifies the depiction of a particular "feminine" mode of magic. There is an emphasis on the power of the collective—on women learning together and mentoring each other—and the four protagonists are depicted as strongest when they cooperate with one another. The girls' unwise experiments with the spell book, which allow them to summon Manon, endanger them as individuals, but also destroy their mutually supporting friendship, and thus the unity of the group.

The Covenant: The Book of Damnation

The Covenant is superficially similar in many ways to *The Craft* but there are key differences between the films' depictions of the way that magic is "possessed" and made visible. Male witches are rare on screen, particularly in horror, and neither "wizard" nor "warlock"—the terms used interchangeably in popular culture to refer to male witches—has the same monstrous connotations as "witch." The witch, Creed argues, is both persecuted and monstrous because she is female, but in *The Covenant* and *Warlock*, male monstrosity is constructed differently, and structured in relation to other men. The framing of magic in these films is as distinctly masculine as the framing in *The Craft* is feminine.

The Covenant is set at an elite private boarding school in the New England town of Ipswich, near the site of the original witch trials. Caleb, Pogue, Reid, and Tyler—the film's protagonists—are "the sons of Ipswich," seventeen-year-old descendants of the town's founding families. Unbeknownst to those around them, their ancestors actually *were* witches, and they themselves possess magical powers. They form a coven but, unlike the girls in *The Craft,* they experience no journey of discovery and spend no time exploring the limits of their magical abilities. Having been raised by their families with the knowledge that they are witches, they already known how to work magic and understand how to control their powers. The challenge—for them as for the witches in *The Craft*—is learning when *not* to use them.

As in *The Craft*, their use of magic begins as casual and fun, but gradually becomes dark and threatening. Early scenes show the members of the coven using magic for relatively innocent purposes: jumping off a cliff in order to join a beach party below, starting a stalled car, or defusing a fight by causing a rival to vomit. Caleb, the oldest and most responsible of the four, is the most aware of the price that magic exacts. "It's addictive, you moron!" he tells Reid, the most impetuous of the four, and reminds him that any use of magic ages the user prematurely. Chase, a new student who arrives at school and befriends the coven, quickly proves even more disruptive than Reid. A descendent of Ipswich's *fifth* founding family, he was raised by adoptive parents and so grew up without knowledge of his powers or guidance in using them. Addicted to magic, he tries to steal power from the other members of the coven, but Caleb confronts and—after a near-fatal struggle—defeats him.

The members of the coven possess pedigreed bloodlines and carry themselves with an air of privilege and entitlement that comes from "old money." Magical abilities are passed through families according to a system of primogeniture, as Caleb explains: "Every generation produces only one, the eldest male." The group dynamics of the coven follow a similar pattern: Caleb is the leader of the group because, as the oldest, he will be the first to ascend and therefore the most powerful. The power and privilege that magic brings is rigidly and specifically masculine. The young women in the film exist as little more than prizes for the male characters to compete for or fight over. The fights and near-fights, which begin in the first scenes of the film, are part of a steady string of confrontations in which the protagonists jockey with each other to establish their position in the masculine pecking order. Magic becomes a means by which this competition is carried out.

The magical Book of Damnation—an ancient grimoire controlled by Caleb's family—validates, explains, and reinforces the rules of this male-dominated system of magic. It first appears in the title sequence: an aged volume illustrated with images of witches being tortured. The camera zooms in on key passages: "age of thirteen," "powers develop," "age of eighteen," the first son ascends," "power to take life," and "visitation by a darkling." When Chase's arrival unsettles the coven's well-ordered universe, it is to the Book of Damnation that they turn for guidance and in the book that Caleb discovers the existence of the fifth Ipswich bloodline, to which Chase belongs. The book is kept in Caleb's family's barn and it is he, as the eldest of the group, who controls the coven's access to it. It is treated with reverence and ceremony and the barn where it is kept is a gothic space lit with candles. Caleb summons the book and it hovers over a circle of flames.

The book itself is a narrative grimoire—a history of the Ipswich families' magical powers and statement of the "rules" that govern them—rather than an instructional spellbook. Rather than offering the protagonists spells that they can use to change the world, it outlines the realities of the world as it is. The final scene of the film freezes and slowly dissolves into a hand-drawn image like those in the book, suggesting that the events of the film's narrative have become the next episode in the Book of Damnation, and a lesson for future generations.

Warlock: The Grand Grimoire

A similar masculine form of magic is also present in *Warlock*, where a male witch makes a diabolical pact in his quest for greater power. The film opens with the title character (whose name is never revealed) being sentenced to death in the 1690s. Before he dies, Satan appears and propels him, along with the witch hunter who condemned him, through time to 20th-century Los Angeles. The warlock goes first to a spiritualist book shop and asks the woman who runs it to channel a spirit for him. When she complies, Satan possesses her and tells the warlock to gather the three lost parts of his Bible—a book that, when assembled, will reveal the true name of God invoked during creation. If the name is spoken in reverse, all creation will be undone. When the book is finally brought together, the pages reconnect themselves and glowing orange writing appears on the cover as a storm breaks.

The stakes in *Warlock* are substantially higher than those of any other witch-centered tales considered here. The book that the title character seeks represents the power not just to change the universe but to unmake it. "The spellbook!" a character declares at one point. "All witches keep grimoires but one is indestructible, the Bible of black magic: the *Grand Grimoire*. Always, witches have lusted for it." Consistent with its expansive scope, *Warlock* depicts a wide range of magical practice. The warlock, in his pact with Satan, is promised power in exchange for the book. There is folk magic in the form of potions and pentagrams, and in strange happenings that take place in the warlock's presence (milk going sour, bread not rising, cows sweating). The warlock himself repeatedly exhibits superhuman powers—making objects move with his mind, hexing people by meeting their gaze, and healing his own wounds—but, like Nancy in *The Craft* and Chase in *The Covenant,* the power at his disposal does not satisfy him. The book, which promises literally unlimited power, becomes the focus of his desires and he pursues it ruthlessly, severing the finger of one victim to take their ring, and killing an unbaptized male child in order to prepare a potion. Both the warlock and the witch-hunter use magic, the line between them being drawn by the warlock's willingness to practice diabolism. The witch hunter, although motivated by his religious fervor, resorts to more straightforward forms of maleficia—using a "witch compass," for example, that allows him to track the warlock by using the magical "laws" of sympathy and contagion. Tellingly, it is basic folk magic that saves the day and the world, as the Warlock is killed with a saline injection and the *Grand Grimoire* is buried in a salt plain. Even the most powerful spell book in the world, the film suggests, has its limits.

Conclusion: Spellbooks, Grimoires and Fan Practice

Spell books and grimoires are an essential part of the *mise-en-scene* of witchcraft on screen. While the former allow an accessible bridge to the supernatural, even for those with no natural powers, the latter provide the "rules" of the magical universe the witches inhabit and give an ideological framework to the practices of magic. The two types of books underscore the significant differences between male and female witches, and the aesthetic differences between masculine and feminine forms of magical effect: Male magical power is displayed as literal physical power inherent in the body of the witch. Female magical power is rooted in external nature and accessed through knowledge that is shared between individuals and practices passed from one to another. For female witches, the spell book is more integral to their magical practice than it is for male witches. In the Harry Potter series, for example, it is Hermione who places her faith in spells learned through books, and Harry who relies on instinct and physical strength. Across all these texts, the spellbook has multiple functions: as a plot device, a learning tool, a sacred object, and as link between generations of witches.

The emphasis on empowerment, female bonding, and shared magical knowledge in "feminine" forms of magic have proven appealing to female audiences. Replica spell books and grimoires are popular pieces of show-related merchandise for fans of both *Charmed* and *Buffy the Vampire Slayer*. There are multiple editions of *The Book of Shadows*, from official mass-produced versions to hand-crafted versions on etsy.com. Buffy fans, meanwhile, can buy *The Official Grimoire: A Magical History of Sunnydale*, purportedly written by Willow Rosenberg, Buffy's best friend and the show's principal witch. The rise of the internet as a mainstream phenomenon in the 1990s allowed teen witches and fans to form online communities and participate in discussions replicating the sisterhood depicted on large and small screens. Hannah E. Johnson argues that one of the pleasures of witchcraft is the "sense of *communitas*, a shared experience of the world which celebrates the sacred through ritualized actions, language and behavior."[10] Julian Vayne's study of contemporary witchcraft practice, found, however, that despite the vast resources now available online, "printed books still seem to be the key resource.... For serious study, the contemporary British teen witch is perhaps more likely to consult a physical text."[11] Engaging in magical practice (whether they believe in it or not) through buying and using spell books, adds a further dimension to these viewing pleasures and fan communities beyond the usual pleasurable identifications of cinema and television.

Notes

1. The duel between Molly Weasley and Bellatrix Lestrange—the series' iconic Good Witch and Bad Witch—at the climax of *Harry Potter and the Deathly Hallows, Part 2* (2011) is regarded by fans as one of the Potter saga's high points. See Vary, "'Harry Potter': Julie Walters on 'Not my daughter, you bitch!'"
2. Davies, *Grimoires*, 1.
3. *Ibid.*, 279.
4. Broedel 'The *Malleus Maleficarum*," 43–47.
5. Creed, *Monstrous Feminine*, 73–86; quotation on 75.
6. *Ibid.*, 73.
7. Hunt, "Necromancy in the Uk," 83.
8. "We're Off to See the Wizard," *Charmed*, season 4, episode 19; aired April 25, 2002.
9. Kim, "How the Cult Horror Classic 'The Craft' Nailed These Four Iconic Scenes."
10. Johnson, "Vanquishing the Victim," 110, 99.
11. Vayne, "The Discovery of Witchcraft," 63.

Bibliography

Broedel, Hans Peter. "The *Malleus Maleficarum* and the Construction of Witchcraft." In *The Witchcraft Reader*, 2d ed., edited by Darren Oldridge, 43–47. London: Routledge, 2008.
Charmed. 1998–2006. Hollywood: Paramount Home Media, 2008. DVD.
The Covenant. Directed by Renny Harlin. 2006. Culver City, CA: Sony Pictures Home Entertainment, 2007. DVD.
The Craft. Directed by Andrew Fleming. 1996. Culver City, CA: Sony Pictures Home Entertainment, 2000. DVD.
Creed, Barbara. *The Monstrous Feminine: Film, Feminism, Psychoanalysis*. London: Routledge, 1993.
Davies, Owen. *Grimoires: A History of Magical Books*. Oxford: Oxford University Press, 2009.
Hunt, Leon. "Necromancy in the UK: Witchcraft and the occult in British Horror." In *British Horror Cinema*, edited by Steve Chibnall and Julian Petley, 84–98. London: Routledge, 2001.
Johnson, Hannah E. "Vanquishing the Victim: Discourses of dis/empowerment in 1990s teenage witchcraft." In *The New Generation Witches: Teenage Witchcraft in Contemporary Culture*, edited by Hannah E. Johnson and Peg Aloi, 97–112. Aldershot, UK: Ashgate, 2007.
Kim, Kristin Yoonsoo. "How the Cult Horror Classic 'The Craft' Nailed These Four Iconic Scenes." *Complex*, May 3, 2016. http://uk.complex.com/pop-culture/2016/05/the-craft-20-anniversary.
Vary, Adam B. "'Harry Potter': Julie Walters on 'Not my daughter, you bitch!'" *Entertainment Weekly*, October 28, 2011. http://ew.com/article/2011/10/28/harry-potter-molly-weasley-clip/.
Vayne, Julian "The Discovery of Witchcraft: A Exploration of the Changing Face of Witchcraft Through Contemporary Interview and Personal Reflection." In *The New Generation Witches: Teenage Witchcraft in Contemporary Culture*, edited by Hannah E. Johnson and Peg Aloi, 57–72. 2007. London: Routledge, 2016.
Warlock. Directed by Steve Miner. 1989. Santa Monica, CA: Lionsgate Home Entertainment, 2004. DVD.

Horror Comedy by the Book

Grimoire, *Carnival* and Heteroglossia in Kenny Ortega's Hocus Pocus (1993)

SUE MATHESON

"It's no use. I don't remember the ingredients. I've got to have my Book!"
— Winifred Sanderson in *Hocus Pocus*

In *The Order of Things*, Michel Foucault remarks that at the end of the 16th century or the beginning of the 17th century, encyclopedias not only reflected "what one knows in the neutral element of language, " they also reconstituted "the very order of the universe by the way in which words are linked together and arranged in space."[1] This privileging of the page was particularly evident in the magical encyclopedias—their purpose being the reconstruction of reality at their users' whims. Given the power ascribed to the written word to shape the world, it is not surprising that Christopher Marlowe's Dr. Faustus sold his soul to the Devil for "a complete magic encyclopedia ... a conjuring book that contains every spell that [its reader] would ever need to know and order the world."[2] In the 18th century, these books became known as grimoires, even though the word, originating from the Old French term *grammaire*, simply meant grammar. By the 20th century, the term, grimoire referred to "any kind of collection of magic, authentic grimoire were based off the magical traditions of Jewish, Muslim, and medieval Christian rituals and texts."[3] Recently, grimoires containing collections of spells, guides to summoning demons and angels, and instructions on how to create magical objects, have been featured in horror movies investigating the power of the written word like *The Ninth Gate* (1999), *The Book of Eli* (2010), and *The Spellbook* (2012); horror romances like *Practical Magic* (1998); and television series like *Buffy the Vampire Slayer* (1997–2003) and *Charmed* (1998–2006). The Hogwarts School library in the Harry Potter films, containing "tens of thousands of books on thousands of shelves,"[4] has intrigued millions of millennials interested in practical magic.

Capitalizing on the capacity of words to alter or even remake reality, Walt Disney's *Hocus Pocus* (1993) also features a book of practical magic that is an object of immense power. Now touted as "the best Hallowe'en movie of all time,"[5] repeatedly producing record viewing numbers as part of the ABC Family network's *13 Nights of Hallowe'en*, *Hocus Pocus* began as a box-office disappointment for Walt Disney Studios, grossing only $8.1 million in its first week and $5.2 million in its second before falling out of the top ten. It ended its run with $39.5 million and netting $11 million domestically.[6] Fourth in earnings behind Steven Spielberg's *Jurassic Park* (1993) and Simon Wincer's *Free Willy* (1993),[7] this high-concept horror comedy also disappointed critics, and received mostly negative reviews. Janet Maslin of *The New York Times* deemed the movie to be "aimed squarely at the Nowheresville between juvenile and adult audiences" and to have "flashes of visual stylishness but virtually no grip on its story."[8] Roger Ebert of the *Chicago Sun-Times* found the film to be "desperately in need of self-discipline," and likened the experience of watching it to "a party you weren't invited to, and where you don't know anybody, and they're all in on a joke but won't explain it to you."[9] Kenneth Turan of the *Los Angeles Times* judged *Hocus Pocus* to be "not quite bewitching" and wondered what Bette Midler, Sarah Jessica Parker, and Kathy Najimy, as a trio of 17th-century witches—"camping and vamping it up in a way few toddlers are of an age to appreciate"—were doing "in the same picture with a talking cat and bad guys who can think of nothing worse to do than steal candy on Hallowe'en."[10]

As a home video, however, *Hocus Pocus* became "a cult favorite among Millennials."[11] It "began hitting its stride in 2012, cracking the top 10 movies for DVD sales in October."[12] Since then, "there's been a sharp increase in *Hocus Pocus* DVD sales starting in the last week of September each year."[13] Jen Chaney believes that *Hocus Pocus* (1993) is now to Hallowe'en what Frank Capra's *It's a Wonderful Life* (1946) is to Christmas.[14] Millions of viewers watch this movie after trick or treating, and October has become "HOCUS POCUS MONTH!"[15] Chaney and Alex Abad-Santos attribute *Hocus Pocus*' puzzling popularity to 90's nostalgia, the increasing presence of Hallowe'en in American culture, and the Disney Channel's and Freeform's promotion of the film,[16] but the movie's IMDB users differ sharply with the critics—awarding it an overall score of 6.7/10,[17] and rating it highly for its comedy.[18] Sonya Saraiya also considers *Hocus Pocus* to be "a comedy veering from slapstick to tongue-in-cheek horror-movie references to groan-worthy puns and other wordplay."[19] As Aaron Wallace points out in *Hocus Pocus: In Focus*, *Hocus Pocus* has evolved into a film with real pop-culture currency.[20] Investigating how this film resonates with viewers who crave comic carnival after an entire year of obedience to the norms and forms of society and science, this essay examines Kenny Ortega's treatment of grimoire, the power of the written word, and *heteroglossia* in the upending of horror on Hallowe'en.

Three Hags—Back from the Dead

Hocus Pocus is the story of three witches who threaten the normality of Salem, first in the late 17th century, and then three centuries later, when they are brought back from the dead. The film begins on All Hallows' Eve, 1693, when three witches—sisters Winifred, Mary and Sarah Sanderson—are executed for sucking the life out of little Emily Binx. Before being hanged for their crime, the sisters curse the town of Salem, casting a spell that will eventually bring them back to life. Three centuries later, Max Dennison, a teenaged Californian who refuses to believe in witches, relocates with his family to Salem. When taking his little sister Dani trick-or-treating, Max encounters Allison, "the girl of [his] dreams," and dares her to make a believer of him at the old Sanderson house. Trying to impress Allison, he lights the Black Flame Candle at the Sanderson House Museum, and the Sanderson sisters return, plotting to suck the life out of all the children in Salem.

Max, Dani, and Allison steal Winifred's book of spells and thwart the witches' dream of living forever. American Horror by the book,[21] the witches' Otherness is a threat to human relations. Socially subjugated in 1693, the Sandersons frame themselves as being "three kindly old spinster ladies," Puritan outliers, women marginalized and feared by their community. In fact, however, they really are monsters: ugly, vicious, and vindictive predators like fairy tale witches who fly on broomsticks, sniff out their prey, stir cauldrons, and consume the lives of the young and innocent.

Oretga's depiction of the kidnapping, cold-blooded murder, and consumption of a young girl by three cannibalistic hags should be horrifying, as should young Thackery Binx's subjugation by his sister's psychopathic killers and subsequent transformation into a black cat. But this is not the case.[22] Throughout *Hocus Pocus*, the witches are entertaining. As Winifred brews her "Life Potion," she and her sisters cease to be Other. Mary squabbles with her older sister over who is working the hardest, while Sarah amuses herself by "dancing idiotically." Familiar and humorous, this bickering humanizes the witches, disclosing their birth order and making them recognizable and relatable. Bossy, confident, and aggressive Winifred, the oldest sister, takes charge of mixing the brew; easygoing and flexible Mary, the acquiescent middle child, spends her screen time compromising with her older sister; irresponsible and devil-may-care Sarah, the youngest, ignores the antics of the other two and does as she pleases in the background while singing cheerfully about running "amuck, amuck, amuck." When the witches return to brew another batch of "Life Potion" three hundred years later, the film continues to overturn horror conventions. After Max tries to prove the Sanderson legend is "just a bunch of hocus pocus," a series of unnatural events begin to occur, announcing Winifred, Mary, and Sarah's return from the dead. One by one, the museum's electric candles go out, a mysterious wind begins to blow inside sealed old house, and as its floorboards loosen and begin to shake, an eerie green light shines through from beneath them. The candles, which have inexplicably

The Sanderson sisters (left to right: Kathy Najimy, Bette Midler, Sarah Jessica Parker) decide what to do with Thackery Binx (Sean Murray) in *Hocus Pocus* (1993).

become wax, re-ignite one by one, before the wood in the fireplace also spontaneously bursts into flame. Maniacal laughter rings through the house and the front door bursts open to reveal the three sisters, dramatically silhouetted and ominously back-lit. Ortega's treatment of the familiar horror tropes in this sequence is not tongue-in-cheek, but as soon as the witches walk in the door it is apparent that they are not meant to be feared. Their experience in Hell has not changed them in the least. If anything, their family dynamics (which led to their hanging) are even more pronounced. Mary proclaims her older sister "perfect" as soon as she enters; Sarah discovers that her "lucky rat's tail" is just where she left it; and Winifred resumes her relationship with her Book.

Winnifred's Grimoire

A popular trope in horror stories since Faust sold his soul to the Devil, books containing mysterious and forbidden knowledge confer occult information on the uninitiated and have disconcerting effects on their readers. They also act as keys to understanding the action occurring on the page or on the screen. The books that appear in *Hocus Pocus* are no exception to this rule. The film begins with the image of a handsome, leather-bound volume that displays an impression of the Sandersons' house, crowned with cryptic, zodiacal symbols and the date 1693; as the camera tilts down and zooms in on the cover, the film's title is shown, positioned above a black cat inscribed sitting on a fencepost while a man ploughs a field. Generally spoken when some sort of change is brought about, the words "Hocus Pocus" announce that the film's narrative is about to begin and indicate that magic is about to take place. Correspondingly, the book's cover flips open of its own accord, revealing not vellum pages, but an aerial view of Sarah flying over the marshes near Salem, searching for children to bewitch and lure to the witches' house.

As J.R.R. Tolkien points out in "On Fairy Stories," the word "spell" means both a story told and a formula of power.[23] Itself a story told, *Hocus Pocus* is, by definition, spellbinding—a filmic book, written in light. As Stam remarks, film "does not only include utterances, it *is* utterance."[24] Identifying itself as meta-cinema, *Hocus Pocus* informs its viewers that they will be spellbound while watching, and invites them to consider the power of words, as the Sanderson sisters cast spells that enchant the living and the dead.

In *Hocus Pocus*, Winifred's spellbook is not just a knowledge repository (filled with words); it is also the source of the film's dramatic tension. Possessing it is a matter of life and death, as Winifred explains to her sisters: "Let me make one thing perfectly clear: The Magic that brought us back only works tonight on All Hallows' Eve…. Fortunately, the potion I brewed the night we were hanged will keep us alive and young forever. Unfortunately, the recipe for that potion is in my spell book and the little wretches have stolen it … we must find the Book, brew the potion, and suck the lives out of the children of Salem before sunrise or it is curtains! We evaporate! We cease to exist!" Given to her "by the Devil himself," Winifred's book is "bound in human skin and contains the recipes for her most powerful and evil spells." A sentient being, possessing one eye that opens when its mistress calls, it is has magical powers, including—like the *Grand Grimoire*[25]— imperviousness to fire. The source of Winifred's power, it gives those who read and use it the knowledge needed to unravel and repair the fabric of reality. Modeled after medieval household manuals (like *The Good Wife's Guide*, also known as *Le Ménagier de Paris*),[26] the grimoire blends herbalism, medicine, and cooking, and offers useful information and recipes to novice and expert in the black arts. Its spells enable users to create magical objects such as the Black Flame Candle, resurrect the dead, and attain everlasting life. There are also pages of incantations for making others sick or invoking spirits and demons.

In the film's textualized socio-ideological world, Winifred's book mediates its user's relationships with those around her. Caressing its spine and cooing, "My darling ... my little ... Book. We must continue with our spell now that our guest of honor has arrived," Winifred clearly loves her Book and treats it better than her sisters. "Wake up," she urges, "Wake up darling, yes ... come along." When the Book opens its uncanny eye and regards her, she whispers, "There you are. Hello ... hello." It is evident that the Book returns her affection. When Winifred rejects her sisters' ideas to barbeque Thackery, or hang him on a hook, because "his punishment must be more fulsome, more lingering," all she has to do is call, "Book, come to Mommy"—and the grimoire obediently floats across the room into her arms. When the Book opens itself for her perusal, she speaks for it as well as herself. "Let's see," she says, identifying the words on its pages, "[A]mnesia, bunions, chilblains, cholera. We can do better than that I think. Let's see what we have." Unlike her sister's suggestions, Winifred declares those offered by the Book to be "Perfect. As usual." Immediately adopting its recommendation, she tells Mary and Sarah that Thackery's "punishment shall not be to die, but to live forever with his guilt."

As Bakhtin notes in *Discourse in the Novel*, spoken words all "have the 'taste' of a profession, a genre, a tendency, a party, a particular work, a particular person, a generation, an age group, the day and hour. Each word tastes of the context and contexts in which it has lived its socially charged life; all words and forms are populated by intentions." In *Hocus Pocus*, socio-ideological dialects that identify the "high" and the "low" are "shot through with intentions and accents"; what is presented is not "an abstract sys-

"Soon the lives of the all the children will be mine, and I shall be young and beautiful forever!" Winifred Sanderson (Bette Midler) gleefully anticipates her eternal youth in *Hocus Pocus* (1993).

tem of normative forms but rather ... concrete *heteroglot* conception[s] of the world."[27] In *Hocus Pocus*, words contain powerful social connotations. At the Sanderson sisters' hanging, "the proliferation of competing and intersecting social 'languages' cohabiting within a 'single' language" and *polyglossia*, the simultaneous world-wide existence of mutually incomprehensible tongues"[28] quickly convey the dynamics of center/margin in 1693.

Representing the group hanging the witches, Thackery's father (Norbert Weisser) is a powerful New England patriarch. Conducting the execution, he delivers the townsfolk's ultimatum to the witches: "I will ask thee one final time. What hast thou done with my son Thackery?" Having the knowledge he needs, Winifred is ultimately more powerful than her executioner. She says, "Thackery. Hmm ..." When Thackery's father shouts, "Answer me," she becomes passive-aggressive. "Well, I don't know," she snickers, "Cat's got my tongue." Only Winifred's sisters and the audience can understand the cutting irony (and agency) of her statement, for Thackery, who Winifred has turned into a black cat, is watching the hanging. The *polyglossia* of this scene increases when the Sanderson sisters then use a magical language to curse the people who have gathered to watch them hang. Their curse is completely incomprehensible.[29] Thackery's father warns his followers not to listen to the witches, but he is unable to halt the *heteroglot* activity at hand, for Winifred's Book comes to her aid, opening itself to "The Magician's Pact." Reading its words, Winifred screams triumphantly: "Fools, all of you! My ungodly book speaks to you on All Hallows' Eve. When the moon is around / a virgin will summon us from under the ground./ We shall be back / and the lives of all the children shall be mine!" Her highly emotive, melodramatic speech contrasts sharply with the silence of Zachary's mother, an obedient New England wife, but in the end both witch and wife are silent. After Winifred has been hanged, normalization occurs. The patriarch's voice prevails, and no other voices are lifted to challenge it, but—ironically—the *monoglossia* that ensues, ensuring the restoration of order, also guarantees that father and son remain parted. Without Winifred, no counter-spell can be read to release Thackery from the Book's magic. Unable to recognize his enchanted son, the patriarch kicks at the black cat rubbing against his legs and shouts, "Away, beast!"

Hallowe'en Carnival and Mésalliance

On their return from Hell (the most marginal place of all), the Sanderson sisters discover Salem's markers of center/margin have shifted considerably in their absence. In Salem, All Hallows' Eve has become contemporary carnival—"a night of frolic where children wear costumes and run amok." As Bahktin would point out, "carnival is more than a mere festivity; it is the oppositional culture of the oppressed, the symbolic, anticipatory overthrow of oppressive social structures. Carnivalesque egalitarianism crowns and uncrowns, pulling grotesque monarchs off their thrones and installing comic lords of misrule in their place."[30] Accordingly, all that is oppositional takes over in Salem, breaking down social forms and natural norms. Complex and multi-layered *mésalliances* are created.[31] Allison (a rich girl) befriends Max (a middle-class boy), and then becomes his girlfriend. The living fraternize with the dead: Winifred's long-dead lover, Billy Butcherson, "a good zombie," befriends, confides in, and protects the children. Animals speak to human beings: Thackery Binx (as a black cat) guides the children to safety and lectures them on the history of the Sanderson sisters. And children take on adult responsibilities: Max, Allison, and Dani—not their parents—save Salem from the monsters.

Winifred and her Book also continue their unnatural *mésalliance*. Having returned from the dead, the first thing the witch does is to tap the glass of the display case in which the volume is stored and fuss over it. "Wake up," she says brightly. "Wake up, sleepyhead, I missed you. Did you miss me too? Come on now, we've got work to do." As before, the Book returns her affection. Because of this affection for Winifred, the Book proves to be doubly dangerous to the children. At the Old Burial Hill Cemetery, Thackery Binx wisely warns Max, Allison, and Dani to stay out of the Book. "No good of will come of it," he says, because "it holds Winifred's most dangerous spells." He could not have been more correct. When Allison and Max open it, the Book emits a beam of light from its pages that acts as an emergency beacon and reveals its whereabouts. Allison discovers that a circle of salt will protect them from magic, but Winifred, in short order, learns where her beloved Book is, recovers it from the Dennison house, and kidnaps Dani in the process.

Resting on causal relationships between the world and the word, Winifred's magical formulas are an important element of the carnival at work in Salem. They enable the marginalized to overturn the laws of God and nature. The magical power of words to upset and refashion reality is evident when Winifred casts spells without her Book. Her tail rhyming, for example, charms and hypnotizes her listeners. Hovering over the cemetery, she raises the body of Billy Butcherson using the imperative voice and regular, true rhyme (aa bb bb):

> Unfaithful lover, long since *dead*
> deep asleep in thy wormy *bed,*
> Wiggle thy toes, open thine *eyes*
> Twist thine fingers toward the *sky*
> Life is fleeting not to *shy*
> On thy feet, so say *I*!

Unable to resist Winifred's emotive assonance, Billy bursts from his grave. Her song, "I Put a Spell on You," an adaptation of Jay Hawkins' bewitching 1956 cult classic,[32] also uses the power of repetition in rhythm & blues created by chiming identical terminal vowel sounds to enchant its listeners.[33] After Salem's party-goers have been charmed by the song's matching vowels at its line ends, Winifred curses them with their related, yet opposite counterpart, consonance. Creating cohesion via internal rhyme, the repetition of hard "d's" in her final line, "Dance, dance, dance until you die!," introduce a pounding, inexorable rhythm that compels their imitation on the dance floor. Ensorcelled, Max and Dani's parents party until they are released from the spell when the witches themselves die at dawn.

The spells written in Winifred's Book, however, prove to be even more powerful than those she merely speaks (or sings). Written in blank verse, Winifred's "Life Potion" appears at first to be a simple recipe that uses the imperative voice, instructing the reader to bring the solution

> to a full rousing
> Bubble then add two drops
> Oil of boil and a dead man's toe.
> Next add a dab of newt saliva
> A dash of pox. Stir thrice.

> One final thing and all is done.
> Add a pinch of thine own tongue.
> Administer one drop to victim
> And stand back.

Once this potion has been taken, the book explains, "the life force of the victim may swallowed to reverse the passage of time." After sharing Emily Binx with her sisters, Sarah, no longer an elderly hag, exults, "I am beautiful! Boys will love me!" "We're young!" Mary cackles. "Well, young*er*," Winifred corrects her sister, "but it's a start!" Winifred leaves no doubt as to what her next act of magic will be. Bent on stopping time entirely and acquiring everlasting life, she tells Mary, "I will be a sprig forever, once I've sucked the lives out of all the children in Salem!"

As the All Hallows' Eve carnival in Salem continues on, words mediate its socio-ideological world, conveying the competing and intersecting contexts of its participants. A Lady of Misrule, Winifred Sanderson revels in the use of irony. Her use of formal syntax and sophisticated diction uncrown her, however, because the world has become topsy-turvy. To the trick-or-treaters, she is a "weirdo," an adult participating in a festival meant for children. Max occupies a similarly unstable position, vacillating between being an adult and a child. He refuses to participate in the masquerade while taking his little sister from house to house, but his middle-class use of language, typical of the late 20th-century teenager, is dotted with slang: "*[Y]ou guys here* in Salem are *into* these black cats and witches *and stuff*, but everybody knows that Hallowe'en was invented by the candy companies" (italics mine). Jay and Ice, the most disorderly and irresponsible characters on-screen, consistently use language inappropriately. Like Winnifred, they use words to hurt others. To them, Max is "Hollywood," Dani a "twerp," and women "babes." Unlike Winnifred's insults which are precise and clever, Jay and Ice's irregular and insulting use of the English language seals their unhappy fate when they call the witches "ugly chicks." The offended Sandersons hang the bullies in gibbets (that aptly resemble large bird cages). When the boys ineptly attempt to apologize to their captors by using equally casual terms—"We think you're really *cute*," Jay says—they do not right the situation. If anything, they make matters worse. The outraged witches do not accept their apology, and Winifred tells them to "hush."

Clearly, the most effective use of language in *Hocus Pocus* is contained in Winifred's grimoire. Written down, the meaning of words in her Book cannot be overturned or forgotten. In part, Winifred tells Mary, "I've got to have my Book" because she lacks an eidetic memory. More important, she knows that the formal langue found in her grimoire, correctly repeated, brings about lasting, meaningful change, and that the English vernacular lacks this power. Privileging the page, Winifred demonstrates the spoken word (as parole) is unstable and ineffective. When past and present paroles meet the primacy of the primacy of the written word becomes particularly evident—as they intersect, supplement, contradict, and compete, overturning one another's meanings.

The power of words to order and reorder the nature of reality in these scenes reminds the viewer that *Hocus Pocus*, itself a story told, "*is* utterance"[34] inscribed and presented in a book on screen. Collisions between past and present paroles sustain the film's hilarious *heteroglossia* and contribute to the film narrative's dramatic tension while its characters communicate in more than one *lingua franca*. Winifred's use of early modern English is highlighted outside the Old Burial Hill cemetery after she and her sisters fail to catch the children and retrieve her Book. The meaning of her Shakespearean turn of phrase, "I'll have your guts for garters, girl,"[35] is particularly clear. There is no doubt that she intends to disembowel her younger sister if Mary cannot find the children. Another prime example of the *heteroglot* nature of language in *Hocus Pocus* occurs when Mary suggests her sisters participate in a calming circle to dissolve Winifred's tension. "Sisters, I have an idea," she says, "Since this promises to be most dire and distressful evening, I suggest we form a calming circle." When Winifred snaps, "I am calm!" Mary replies, "Oh Sister, thou art not being honest with thyself, are we? Huh? Huh?" As the witches are thinking soothing thoughts about the Black Death and Mummy Scorpion Pie, a bus pulls up. At the bus stop, in their conversation with the Bus Driver (Dan Yesso), meaning and power are continually (and playfully) deferred. Flirting with the witches, the Bus Driver attempts to seduce them by bowdlerizing (or misquoting) the opening line of *Macbeth*. "Bubble, bubble, I'm in trouble," he says. The purpose of his bus, he tells them, is "to convey gorgeous creatures, such as yourselves, to your most forbidden desires." Ironically, the Driver's inflated idioms are Winifred's vernacular. Mistaking the Sanderson sisters' hunger for children as sexual innuendo, he adds another layer of irony to the *heteroglossia* that overturns the meaning of their conversation. Responding to Winifred's use of the word, "desire," the Bus Driver uses modern slang to reply. "Hey, it may take me a couple of tries," he leers, upending her meaning. "But I don't think there'll be a problem. Hop on up. I'm going to get some ice packs … you girls are giving me a fever."

Having picked up the Witches (in one sense, at least), the Bus Driver speeds on toward his destination. At first, it seems he is in control of the situation. Erasing barriers between the past and the present, modern slang becomes a *lingua franca* that mediates the witches and the Bus Driver's comic *mèsalliance*. Sitting on the Bus Driver's lap, Sarah learns to drive. When she flattens Thackery Binx, who cannot avoid the bus, both teacher and pupil exclaim, "Speed bump!" Sarah, however, declines the Bus Driver's attentions when the bus stops. "[T]hou wouldst hate me in the morning," she says, returning to her earlier idioms. When he responds, mashing modern contractions and 17th-century verb forms in "I wouldn'st," Winifred intercedes, correcting his *grammaire*, with the words, "Oh, believe me, thou wouldst." The proper response would have been "I wouldst not." Here the Bus Driver's relationship with the Sanderson sisters ends. *Polyglossia* is restored when he returns to modern slang with the term, "Party-pooper." Throughout this exchange, meaning, power, and control shifts from speaker to speaker.

The power of language to arbitrarily refashion reality explains why Winifred reacts so strongly when she is insulted. When Dani tells Winifred that she is "the ugliest thing that ever lived," Winifred becomes ugly indeed, baring her teeth and hissing to the child: "You die first." Throughout the film's narrative, the pluralism of language is an important element of the carnivalesque, for competing dialects, when juxtaposed, supplement and contradict one another,[36] centering the margins and marginalizing the center. At the Town Hall, for example, it seems that Max has taken control when he announces that Sanderson sisters are back in Salem. Winifred, however, immediately destabilizes his statement with one of her own. "Thank you, Max," she says, "For that wonderful introduction." Having shifted the audience's attention (and therefore the balance of power) to herself, she then proceeds to place a spell on everyone in the Hall who will listen to her. The ability of words to transform those who listen to them also affects those who speak them. Max, for instance, asks Allison if salt will protect her from "new boyfriends." On hearing these words, Allison finally realizes that Max has been just that to her all night long. If his use of the word "boyfriend" can elevate him to the status of boyfriend, it is not surprising that the words in Winifred's Book are to be feared and respected.

The Book Abides

Appropriately, Ortega leaves the viewer to consider Winifred's Book at the end of *Hocus Pocus*. Tilting upwards, overturning the movement of the film's opening shot, camera discloses the grimoire resting on its stand in the witches' house. As Winifred's voice sings "I Put a Spell on You," her Book opens its hideous eye, implying that another carnival is about to begin, and promising more "phenomena in the process of change and transition, finding in every victory a defeat and in every defeat a potential victory."[37] *Hocus Pocus* may not be, as Abel-Santos says, "scary enough to be a horror film, fast enough to be an adventure flick, or campy or whimsical enough to be a comedy or musical,"[38] but its record viewing numbers suggest that such concerns are beside the point. Filled with "festive laughter,"[39] the film resonates strongly at Hallowe'en with viewers who crave comic carnival after an entire year of obedience to the norms and forms of society and science.

On July 22, 1993, Lynn Smith of the *Los Angeles Times* interviewed children who had watched *Hocus Pocus* for the first time. Notably "not a single kid would admit to being too frightened by anything in this movie. Not the zombie in the graveyard. Not even the book of spells with the living eyeball. Nor the witches sucking the life force from little children."[40] Nine-year-old Julie told Smith, "I really liked it. I thought it was as good as 'Jurassic Park.'"[41] Ten-year-old Amanda told Smith, "You know you're good scared when you laugh."[42] As Amanda points out, the cognitive value of *Hocus Pocus'* "festive laughter" offers us the means we need, at any age, to confront without terror what is often the all-too-plastic nature of what we perceive to be reality.

In final analysis, Winifred's grimoire is the source of "festive laughter" as the Sanderson sisters overturn social forms and natural norms, and create complex and multilayered comic *mésalliances*. Inviting viewers to consider the power of language, especially the power of words, Winnifred's spell book, like the carnival it produces, is "an authorized transgression deeply dependent on a law that it only apparently violates."[43] As the written word, it participates in the authority that its users seek to overturn. Because *Hocus Pocus* is horror comedy by the book, we know that order will be restored—and in the end, the world is righted. The witches return to Hell (where they belong), the children's parents return home (where they belong), and Emily and Thackery Binx go to Heaven (where they belong). Also refracting a mediated version of the real, Ortega's filmic text does not represent the world in its changing forms—it exhibits the changing forms of our representations of the real. What keeps us all, as Smith would say, "from the edges of our seats, bouncing and squirming and chewing our nails"[44] is the realization that carnival, like comedy, is "parasitic on the rules it breaks."[45] The carnival that takes place in *Hocus Pocus* is spellbinding, but as Hamlet would point out, in *Hocus Pocus* one finds only "words, words, words."[46] When the wordplay is over and Winifred's Book is closed, the moving finger, having writ, moves on—to the next carnival on All Hallows' Eve.

Notes

1. Foucault, *The Order of Things*.
2. See Wall-Randell, "*Dr. Faustus* and the Printer's Devil," 266–67.
3. Hood, "Ten Most Significant Historical Grimoires."
4. For more information about the Library, see *The Harry Potter Lexicon* at https://www.hp-lexicon.org/place/hogwarts-school-of-witchcraft-and-wizardry/hogwarts-fourth-floor/library/.
5. Piester's "Freeform's 13 Nights of Hallowe'en Is Here!"
6. See "*Hocus Pocus*," at *Reality TV World*.
7. Abad-Santos, "*Hocus Pocus* is a garbage movie."

196   Witches, Demons and Curses

8. Maslin, "Bette Midler, Queen Witch in Heavy Makeup."
9. Ebert, "Hocus Pocus." http://www.rogerebert.com/reviews/hocus-pocus-1993.
10. Turan, "'Hocus Pocus' not quite bewitching."
11. Saraiya, "Revisiting *Hocus Pocus*."
12. According to Alex Abad-Santos, between October of 2008 and 2015, *Hocus Pocus* has generated $21 million in DVD and Blu-Ray revenues, the majority earned in the October months. In 2015, ABC's October 19 prime time debut of *Hocus Pocus* attracted 1.7 million viewers, according to data provided by ABC Family, and that year *Hocus Pocus* was No. 2 on Amazon's list of bestsellers in the movies and TV category, and second on iTunes' ranking of most popular movies for children and families. Also in 2015, for the first time, Orlando's Walt Disney World added a *Hocus Pocus* show—the "Hocus Pocus Villain Spectacular"—to its Halloween festivities, making the Sanderson sisters as integral to the Magic Kingdom as Space Mountain. For more information, see Abad-Santos' comments in "*Hocus Pocus* is a garbage movie."
13. *Ibid.*
14. Chaney, "Magical Tale."
15. *Ibid.*
16. Abad-Santos, "*Hocus Pocus* is a garbage movie."
17. See IMDb User Ratings for *Hocus Pocus* at http://www.imdb.com/title/tt0107120/ratings?ref_=tt_ov_rt.
18. See customer ratings and reviews of *Hocus Pocus* at IMDB, http://www.imdb.com/title/tt0107120/reviews?start=0.
19. Saraiya's "Revisiting *Hocus Pocus*."
20. Wallace, *Hocus Pocus: In Focus*, 26.
21. Robin Wood notes ("An Introduction to American Horror," 201) that the true subject of horror is the return of the repressed and the recognition of the Other or "the figure of the Monster" via "the re-emergence of all that our civilization *represses* or *oppresses*."
22. Saraiya and 137 IMDB reviewers have noted this.
23. Tolkien, ""On Fairy Stories," 36.
24. Stam, *Subversive Pleasures*, 44.
25. Also called the *Red Dragon* and the *Gospel of Satan*, The *Grand Grimoire* was discovered in the tomb of Solomon in 1750. Written in either Biblical Hebrew or Aramaic, this four-part book is owned by the Roman Catholic Church and is kept in the Vatican Secret Archives. For more information about this *grimoire* and other spell books, see Anderson, "*The 9 Most Eerie Books and Grimoires of All Time*."
26. An excellent example of the medieval household manual, *The Good Wife's Guide* was originally published in 1393. This manual provides practical advice for the medieval wife and her household, including treatises on gardening and shopping, tips on choosing servants, directions on the medical care of horses and the training of hawks, menus for elaborate feasts, and more than 380 recipes.
27. Bakhtin, *Discourse in the Novel*, 293.
28. Stam, *Subversive Pleasures*, 58–59.
29. The witches begin their curse with the words "Thrice I with Mercury purify and spit upon the twelve tables."
30. Stam, *Subversive Pleasures*, 173.
31. An important element of carnival, mésalliance is a social mismatch in which the high and the low mingle.
32. The power of Hawkins' song is evidenced by the staggering number of artists who have covered it. These include Creedence Clearwater Revival, Nina Simone, Alan Price, The Animals, Them with Van Morrison, Arthur Brown, Bryan Ferry, Buddy Guy with Carlos Santana, Tim Curry, Leon Russell, Joe Cocker, Marilyn Manson, Mica Paris with David Gilmore, Jeff Beck and Joss Stone, Diamanda Galas, and Annie Lennox.
33. The formula that Winifred uses to enchant the party-goers at the Town Hall is ababcdedab: "I put a spell on **you** / and now you're mine. / You can't stop the things I **do** / I ain't lyin' / It's been three hundred years / Right down to the ***day*** / Now the witch is back / And there's hell to ***pay*** / I put a spell on **you** / And now you're MINE!"
34. Stam, *Subversive Pleasures*, 44.
35. This phrase originated in the Middle Ages and first appeared in print in Robert Greene's *The Scottish Historie of James the Fourth* (c. 1592).
36. See Stam's discussion of *heteroglossia* in Bakhtin's "Discourse in the Novel" (*Subversive Pleasures*, 51).
37. Stam, *Subversive Pleasures*, 119–20.
38. Abad-Santos, "*Hocus Pocus* is a garbage movie."
39. Stam, *Subversive Pleasures*, 86.
40. Smith, "'Hocus Pocus': Fear Turns Into Fun."
41. *Ibid.*
42. *Ibid.*
43. Stam, *Subversive Pleasures*, 91. In his discussion of Umberto Eco equating carnival with the "comic," Stam also points out that Eco fails to discern carnival's present-day vitality and its progressive potential.

44. Lynn Smith asks, "What better way to send kids to the edge of their seats, bouncing and squirming and chewing their nails?" Smith, "'Hocus Pocus': Fear Turns Into Fun."
45. Stam, *Subversive Pleasures*, 91.
46. See Hamlet's comment to Polonius in *Hamlet*, II.2.

BIBLIOGRAPHY

Abad-Santos, Alex. "*Hocus Pocus* is a garbage movie that doesn't deserve your nostalgia." *Vox*, October 30, 2015. https://www.vox.com/2015/10/30/9646178/hocus-pocus-review.
Anderson, Jake. "The 9 Most Eerie Books and Grimoires of All Time." *ODDEE*, May 27, 2014. http://www.oddee.com/item_98972.aspx.
Bakhtin, Mikhail. "Discourse in The Novel." In *The Dialogic Imagination: Four Essays*, edited by Michael Holquist, translated by Caryl Emerson and Michael Holquist, 259–422. Austin: University of Texas Press, 1981.
Chaney, Jen. "The Magical Tale of How 'Hocus Pocus' Went from Box-Office Flop to Hallowe'en Favorite." *Yahoo! Movies*, October 30, 2015. https://www.yahoo.com/movies/the-magical-tale-of-how-hocus-pocus-went-from-144105863.html.
Ebert, Roger. "Hocus Pocus." July 16, 1993. RogerEbertwww. http://www.rogerebert.com/reviews/hocus-pocus-1993.
Foucault, Michel. *The Order of Things: An Archeology of the Human Sciences*. Oxfordshire: Taylor and Francis e-Library, 2005.
Greco, Gina L., and Christine M. Rose. *The Good Wife's Guide (Le Ménagier de Paris): A Medieval Housebook*. Translated by Gina L. Greco and Christine M. Rose. Ithaca: Cornell University Press, 2009.
Hocus Pocus. Directed by Kenny Ortega. 1993. Burbank, CA: Walt Disney Studios, 2015. DVD.
"Hocus Pocus." *Reality TV World*, http://www.realitytvworld.com/pophollywood/hocus-pocus-1993-film/information/.
Hood, Nathanael. "Top 10 Most Significant Historical Grimoire." *Toptenz*, October 5, 2001. http://www.toptenz.net/top-10-most-significant-historical-grimoire.php.
Maslin, Janet Maslin. "Bette Midler, Queen Witch in Heavy Makeup." *New York Times*, July 16, 1993. http://www.nytimes.com/movie /review?res=9F0CEEDE1031F935A25754C0A965958260.
Mitchell, John. "It'll put a spell on you." *IMDb Reviews & Ratings for Hocus Pocus*. http://www.imdb.com/title/tt0107120/reviews?start=0.
Piester, Lauren. "Freeform's 13 Nights of Halloween Is Here! Check out the 2016 Lineup." *Enews*, October 19, 2016. http://www.eonline.com/news/802667/freeform-s-13-nights-of-halloween-is-here-check-out-the-2016-lineup.
Smith, Lynn. "'Hocus Pocus': Fear Turns Into Fun." *Los Angeles Times*, June 22, 1993. http://articles.latimes.com/1993-07-22/news/ol-15429_1_hocus-pocus.
Stam, Robert. *Subversive Pleasures: Bakhtin, Cultural Criticism, and Film*. Baltimore: Johns Hopkins University Press, 1989.
Tolkien, J.R.R. "On Fairy Stories." In *Essays Presented to Charles Williams*, edited by C.S. Lewis, 38–89. Grand Rapids: William B. Eerdmans, 1966.
Turan, Kenneth. "'Hocus Pocus' not quite bewitching," *Los Angeles Times*, July 16, 1993. http://articles.latimes.com/1993-07-16/entertainment/ca-13536_1_hocus-pocus.
Wallace, Aaron. *Hocus Pocus: In Focus*. Orlando: Pensive Pen Publishing, 2016.
Wall-Randell, Sarah. "*Dr. Faustus* and the Printer's Devil." *SEL* [*Studies in English Literature, 1500–1900*] 48, no. 2 (2008): 259–81.
Wood, Robin. "An Introduction to the American Horror Film." In *Movies and Methods: Volume II*, edited by Bill Nichols, 195–220. Berkeley: University of California Press, 1985.

Unraveling Julian Karswell's Runic Curse in Jacques Tourneur's *Night of the Demon*

MICHAEL FURLONG

> Dr. Julian Karswell: "Funny thing, I always preferred sliding down the snakes to climbing up the ladders. You're a doctor of psychology, you ought to know the answer to that."
> Professor John Holden: "Maybe you're a good loser."
> Dr. Julian Karswell: "I'm not, you know. Not a bit of it."[1]

Jacques Tourneur's *Night of the Demon* (1957) is an atmospheric British horror film depicting books and runic symbols as tools for summoning malevolent demons. Artfully adapted from M.R. James' 1911 short story "Casting the Runes,"[2] *Night* tells the story of a psychologist who gradually discovers that the world of the occult is real, and that books and manuscripts are vessels of great power. The film provides a classic illustration of the ways in which grimoires and other such magical books embody otherworldly power and forbidden knowledge in mid–20th-century horror films.

S.T. Joshi refers to "Casting the Runes" as unique for James—the only one of his stories in which "a character even attempts (here successfully) to counteract the effects of the supernatural agency; in all other instances the Jamesian figure is singularly passive and resigned."[3] Joshi reminds us that "Casting the Runes" and *Night of the Demon* are more akin to an H.P. Lovecraft tale featuring cursed texts, mad scholars, and warlocks summoning creatures, than they are to a traditional Jamesian ghost narrative. *Night*'s devil-worshipping antagonist, Dr. Julian Karswell (Niall MacGinnis) attacks investigators who have been meddling in his affairs by surreptitiously passing them a cursed parchment covered with runic symbols, possession of which summons a demon to dispatch the bearer.[4] The film thus sets the stage for an intense confrontation between scientific materialism and belief in the supernatural and spiritual world.[5]

Tourneur's personal supernatural beliefs inform *Night of the Demon*, and he likely would not be pleased with its inclusion in the horror genre. In a revealing interview with Bertrand Tavernier, he stated: "I hate the expression 'horror film.' For me, I make films about the supernatural because I believe in it. I believe in the power of the dead, witches."[6] Despite Tourneur's assertion, *Night of the Demon* succeeds as a supernatural horror film that explores the divide between everyday reality and the occult. Dennis White notes that horror is "a continual loss of means of escape until there is no safety and no hope of safety."[7] We, as viewers, can escape into *Night of the Demon* because the film's characters cannot escape at all.

J. P. Telotte classifies *Night* as a vesperal film, referring to it as "the labyrinthine, indeterminate, and dark perspective on the modern world and its rule of reason which these works offered, as they repeatedly deconstructed our normal vision of things and our usual methods of formulating or narrating the complexities of human experience."[8] As we examine the narrative, this description seems particularly apt. Karswell's attempts to practice dark magic by using occult books and texts bring him into conflict with psychologist John Holden (Dana Andrews), who investigates Karswell's activities and becomes locked in a battle of wits with the warlock. Holden is a committed rationalist and unwavering skeptic; he boasts that even as a boy he deliberately walked under ladders and crossed paths with black cats. Over the course of the film, however, his understanding of reality is repeatedly deconstructed and his rationalist worldview constantly challenged. He experiences unexplainable events and attempts to maintain his belief system in the undeniable presence of the dark arts.

Holden first appears on a plane bound for London, where he will be attending a psychological conference on the supernatural. During the flight, he meets Joanna Harrington, who is traveling to visit her uncle, Professor Henry Harrington (Maurice Denham). She quickly bonds with Holden, becoming a potential romantic interest. Professor Harrington has been investigating a "devil cult," purportedly led by Karswell, that Holden is scheduled to discuss at the conference. Upon landing, however, the pair is shocked to discover that Harrington was found dead that morning—an apparent victim, viewers know from the film's opening scenes, of Karswell's dark magic. As the two examine the circumstances surrounding Harrington's death, Joanna helps Holden recognize that he will have to abandon his skepticism and accept the supernatural as real in order to keep from becoming Karswell's next victim.

Karswell curses first Harrington, and then Holden, by using an ancient book of forbidden occult knowledge from his vast library. He creates slips of parchment covered in runic symbols which, at a predetermined time, summon a malevolent fire demon to destroy the intended victim.[9] The curse attaches not to a specific individual, but to whoever holds the parchment at the moment time expires. The cursed individual can save themselves by passing the parchment to someone else, but once the parchment spontaneously bursts into flame and crumbles into ashes, the last person to possess it is doomed, and the fire demon arrives to seal their fate. Karswell uses the slips of cursed parchment to assert control over his victims, much as libraries of the era used call slips to maintain control over their books; even the "time allotted" to the victim (two weeks, in Harrington's case) suggests a due date. The fire demon the parchment summons is, these early scenes show, implacable: as it approaches Harrington, he attempts to flee. Before he can make his escape, he crashes his car and is electrocuted by the downed power lines that fall around it. One way or another, it appears, death will have its due.

The Rational Meets the Supernatural

Holden, upon his arrival in London, finds that his visit is front-page news, and reporters are waiting to interview him when he lands, eager for his views on parapsychology.

Without hesitation or equivocation, he proclaims it "bunk," deeming those who believe in it misguided at best and delusional at worst. His colleagues, Drs. O'Brien (Liam Redmond) and Kumar (Peter Elliott), are more open-minded concerning the unknown. When Holden asks his opinion on devils and demons, Kumar responds "Oh I believe in them—absolutely" (echoing filmmaker Tourneur's beliefs). Soon after Holden arrives in London, O'Brien describes his involvement with Harrington's investigation of "Karswell's devil cult," and identifies a farmer named Rand Hobart (Brian Wilde), as "the one cult member we persuaded to speak up." Hobart, O'Brien explains, is now an accused murderer, confined to a hospital for the criminally insane with his mind "in a state of total collapse." O'Brien explains that he achieved one breakthrough with the catatonic Hobart when, under hypnosis, the farmer drew a crude image of a monstrous winged creature. Characteristically open-minded, O'Brien notes that the image is strikingly similar to depictions of "fire demons" from numerous ancient cultures—depictions that Hobart, with his limited education, would never have seen.

Holden bluntly rejects O'Brien's suggestion that Hobart's vision of the fire demon may have come from firsthand observation, and that the demon—not Hobart himself—committed the murder with which he was charged. The American scientist quickly seizes, however, on O'Brien's use of hypnosis, which he sees as a legitimate tool of science. As the film unfolds, however, it is Holden who must adapt his rational belief system to the older, more superstitious European milieu, highlighting Holden's closed-mindedness and foreshadowing the shift in worldview that he must make if he is to survive.

Holden reads Professor Harrington's notes on his investigation of Karswell's activities and, while tracing a reference to an obscure text titled *The True Discoveries of Witches and Demons*, finds that the British Library's copy of the book has mysteriously gone missing. As he resigns himself to the volume's inaccessibility, he is approached by an oversolicitous figure in a Mephisophelean beard: Karswell, who is conveniently waiting to provide assistance. He gives Holden his calling card, and invites him to come to his country estate to view the copy of *True Discoveries* in his vast personal library of occult books. The offer of help is, however, merely a pretext. While talking to Holden, Karswell contrives to knock a sheaf of his papers to the floor, then returns them to Holden with a slip of the cursed parchment hidden inside—a morbid form of intertextuality. Unaware that this is meant to be his occult death warrant, Holden begins to hallucinate. His vision swims and he sees the departing Karswell walking away down the hall as if through a tunnel. His blurred and shifting vision overwhelms his other senses, leaving him unsteady. With this, the horrors of the curse begin.

Karswell's calling card is the first of two significant textual signifiers suggesting the warlock's supernatural powers. When Holden glances at it in the British Library, he sees its engraved printing overlaid by a mystical, glowing message, written in jagged letters, that announces, like a library date stamp: "In memoriam, Henry Harrington, allowed two weeks." The librarian to whom Holden shows the card, however, sees only the ordinary, engraved text, leaving him to doubt his senses. Later, Holden discovers a second signifier: The calendar pages after the 28th of October are all missing from his desk diary, suggesting that for him, time stops after that date.[10] He chooses to ignore these signs because, as he argues, they can be explained away: disappearing ink could explain the vanishing handwriting, the lab to which he sends the calling card for analysis (which also finds nothing) could have made a mistake, and someone could have torn out, unobserved, the remaining pages from the desk diary. When he learns that Professor Harrington found the pages after his death date missing from his own calendar, Holden clings to the argument that it is coincidence. He remains a skeptic, ascribing the strange events to human rather than supernatural actions.

Texts and Power

Night of the Demon begins with narrator Shay Gorman evoking the power of words, and written texts, in a voiceover that plays over location footage of Stonehenge. "It has been written since the beginning of time," he intones, "even unto these ancient stones, that evil supernatural creatures exist in a world of darkness. And it is also said man, using the magic power of the ancient runic symbols, can call forth these powers of darkness: the demons of hell." The narration's opening echo of the familiar phrase "it is written" underscores the traditional equation of text with power and authority, and Stonehenge serves as a powerful symbol of ancient mysteries and forgotten knowledge. The (fictitious) runes carved into its stones could not have been written by a man, but perhaps—the film suggests—were authored by some otherworldly, malevolent creature.

Hidden, mythic, or forgotten texts that provide access to enormous power are common tropes in film and literature. They provide the impetus for horror when old texts and sacred learning collide with the present. The horrors of the past return—fully revived or as a ghostly echo—and the denizens of the present, who have little knowledge of what the intruders are or how to defeat them, must fight for their lives against evils whose very existence they struggle to comprehend. In *Night of The Demon*, however, it is the ancient texts themselves that serve as material representations of the past. Holden—after discovering, with Joanna's help, the cursed parchment among his papers—visits Stonehenge and finds that the runes on his cursed parchment match the ancient written symbols carved into the stones.

Throughout the film, archival research and hidden texts set the stage for pursuits, captures, and escapes. *Night* also, however, mocks the ways scholars covet certain prized texts, and engage in guerrilla warfare with academic rivals over rare books. In M.R. James's source narrative, "Casting the Runes," Karswell attacks Holden for rejecting his grammatically dysfunctional "The Truth of Alchemy" paper for publication and Harrington for harshly reviewing his book, *History of Witchcraft*. The story illustrates the extreme repercussions of a seemingly minor dispute over Karswell's work, with no reference to larger stakes. The cinematic Karswell is not as petty: he merely wants the investigation into his affairs halted in order to continue his life and livelihood, undisturbed. *Night of the Demon* thus becomes a battle not just of individual academics, but of ideas, worldviews, and theories.

In the intellectual circles in which Karswell moves, texts are the means by which power is amassed and maintained. Original scholarship and the quality of written work confers power and status to authors, and those who have access to unique documents potentially gain additional status from them, such as when Karswell meets Holden at the British Library and offers access to the copy of *The True Discoveries of Witches and Demons* in his rarified personal library. In order to continue his investigation, the scientist must meet Karswell at his Lufford Hall estate and engage the warlock on his own terms.

Scholars also use written texts as vehicles for expressing and validating new ideas which, if widely adopted, become another marker of power and status for both individuals and the institutions they represent. *Night of the Demon* demonstrates this by using ancient texts to emblemize Karswell and Holden's duel over the validity of their respective worldviews, as each scholar attempts to assert that his beliefs are valid and his rival's are not.

The Transformation of a Rationalist

Supernatural narratives are often framed by the protagonist's need to find and take control of specific objects, and in *Night,* the ancient texts that Holden seeks out in Karswell's Lufford Hall fill this role. They are objects of literal—not just symbolic—power if they are to be useful to him. He must, in other words, change his worldview and allow for the possibility that the supernatural exists. Necessarily, Holden finds, he has no choice but to believe.

The film articulates the initial gulf between the two men's belief systems in a conversation between them as they take a walk at Karswell's estate. Karswell challenges Holden's logic with rhetorical aporia: "Do I believe in witchcraft? What kind of witchcraft? The legendary witch that rides on the imaginary broom? The hex that tortures the thoughts of the victim? The pin stuck in the image that wastes away the mind and the body?" Holden says, of the latter, "also imaginary." And Karswell responds: "But where does imagination end and reality begin? What is this twilight, this half world of the mind that you profess to know so much about? How can we differentiate between the powers of darkness and the powers of the mind?" What the mind perceives and what the mind imagines are interchangeable, Karswell asserts. If there is a difference, it is so minute that the two are all but indistinguishable. To discount imagination, Karswell insists, is to ignore something originating from the mind, where reason also dwells. The worldview that Karswell articulates in this scene could be as a reflection of the filmmaker's own: a commentary not just on the presence of the supernatural within the everyday, but on the nature of film itself. The audience, once immersed in the film, enters Karswell's twilight world, fascinated by its artifice and shadows, yet reassured by its ability to sustain a semblance of reality.

Dr. John Holden (Dana Andrews) learns to accept the unexplainable when he is menaced by the fire demon in *Night of the Demon* (1957).

Holden and Joanna's visit to Karswell's sprawling country mansion reveals a type of warlock rarely—if ever—depicted in a horror film. Karswell is a bachelor who lives with his mother, and his pastimes seem innocuous when taken at face value. While hosting a Halloween magic show for the local children, for example, he dons a clown costume and adopts the persona of Dr. Bobo the Magnificent, a legacy of his long-concluded career as a stage conjurer. "Dr. Bobo" is a tramp or hobo type of clown, characterized by a "hairy and florid face, seedy attire, [and] grotesque movements,"[11] but he is anything but threatening, giving away puppies and chocolate bars to the children.

Karswell demonstrates what seems to be a genuine fondness for the children when performing magic tricks for them, and they in turn like him.[12] His affection proves, however, to be not just a quirk of personality but a reflection of his larger belief system. He feels an affinity for children—and, we are invited to believe—they for him (especially in his "Dr. Bobo" persona) because they have not yet been corrupted by the blinkered rationality that afflicts adults. Seeing the world through innocent eyes, they believe implicitly in the existence, and power, of the supernatural. "If only we grownups could preserve their capacity for simple joys and beliefs," he laments to Holden, suggesting that if Holden and other adults could regain the open-mindedness they presumably possessed as children, they could once again accept the presence of the supernatural in the world. His comments echo an earlier admonition by Joanna: "You could learn a lot from children. They believe in things in the dark, although we tell them it's not so. Maybe we've been fooling them."[13]

Holden's willingness to believe in Karswell's supernatural abilities develops slowly over the course of the film. The missing calendar pages and the spectral message on the calling card do not persuade him, nor does a séance organized by Karswell's mother, at which a medium summons what Joanna confirms is the spirit of Professor Harrington. The warlock's display of his powers at the children's Halloween party—willing a cyclone into existence and conjuring lightning to strike a tree—is not sufficient to change Holden's mind, but it gives him pause. As the children run, screaming in fright, and Karswell laments that he misjudged the strength of the wind he conjured, Holden begins to look intensely concerned—his eyes narrowed and hooded by thick brown eyebrows, his forehead furrowed—as if, for the first time, he is taking seriously the possibility that Karswell's powers are something more than stage-magic tricks.

The overwhelming natural phenomena swirling around him chip away at his certainty, presenting an immediate, palpable danger that even the least observant onlooker cannot fail to recognize. The sudden windstorm at the estate highlights the contrast between the two men's worldviews: Karswell is casually certain that, as a man of science, Holden simply needs concrete evidence to convince him of the existence of occult powers. Holden, however, responds to Karswell's conjuring with visible confusion, unable to explain the storm's suddenness and intensity in naturalistic terms, but unwilling to accept the explanation that Karswell offers him: that occult texts can be used to call forth and direct dark powers. Unable to account for what is going on around him using his traditional logical-positivist outlook, he is at last obliged to consider other possibilities. Once kindled, his curiosity and desperation become so all-consuming that he even breaks into Karswell's residence at night, searching for the ancient manuscripts, but is caught in the act.

Holden's growing acceptance of the possibility of supernatural explanations does not, however, diminish his belief in the power of science. He continues to use scientific methods to evaluate patients, fully confident of science's ability both to explain and to control the natural world. When examining Hobart, for example, he uses hypnosis to awaken him from his catatonic trance and interrogate him. The film's depiction of the process gives it, however, some of the trappings of magic: Holden and O'Brien seem to hold Hobart in their thrall, passing control of him back and forth, using nothing more than their voices and the light reflected from a seemingly ordinary shiny object. Holden's use of science thus becomes, both in the scene and in the broader context of the film, a version of Karswell's use of magic: a specialized way of asserting status and wielding power—one that is simply more accepted and conventional.

The lines between science and magic blur further once Hobart is conscious. He reveals that he himself was initially cursed with the parchment, but saved his life by passing the parchment—and with it the curse—to his "brother," a fellow cult-member.[14] Holden then produces his own cursed parchment and shows it to Hobart, who recoils in shock, believing that Holden is trying to pass it to him. Hobart flees the room in terror, bolting down the hall and leaping through a window, from which he falls several stories to his death. Holden thus causes, by the use of scientific methods, precisely the same type of fatality that Karswell does when marking Professor Harrington for death with the parchment. Both victims die fleeing something in which they believe so intensely that its *actual* existence or non-existence is beside the point. Holden's blindness to explanation of the world *other* than the naturalistic one he prefers contributes, ironically, to Hobart's death. Holden's rationalist self cannot conceive of the parchment as anything *other* than an ordinary, if unusual looking, document. He cannot, until it is too late, comprehend that Hobart, who fully accepts the reality of both the supernatural and Karswell's power, believes equally strongly that the parchment holds the power of life and death. Holden's misapprehension, however, is clearly one of degree rather than of kind. He believes that Hobart will see the parchment as a threat, and uses it as a tool to test Hobart for a specific response. Here, too, Holden's behavior converges with Karswell's. The former's science, like the latter's magic, is merely a tool for achieving a desired result.

Hobart's reaction to the parchment succeeds, ironically, in opening Holden's mind to the possibility that Karswell has genuine supernatural powers, and uses the cursed

Holden (Dana Andrews) examines patient Rand Hobart (Brian Wilde), who is catatonic after witnessing the demon's attack.

parchment to direct those powers against his enemies. Holden's sudden change of worldview is, in keeping with his character, wholly rational. Pierre Simon Laplace, physicist of the French Enlightenment and intellectual model for generations of rationalists, famously declared: "The weight of evidence for a claim must be proportioned to its strangeness."[15] For Holden, it is Hobart's death—before his own eyes, in the midst of a scientific inquiry—that provides the extraordinary weight of evidence his mind requires.

Conversion and Confrontation

Much of *Night's* action is set around individuals' failed attempts to escape from impending danger: Rand Hobart, Professor Harrington, and even Karswell himself. The film's climax, in fact, takes place as Karswell attempts to make his escape from Holden. As the ten o'clock hour, when the demon will appear to claim Holden, draws near, Karswell flees the city by train with a hypnotized Joanna in tow, determined to be nowhere near his rival at the moment of the attack. Holden, alerted to Karswell's departure by Professor Kumar, boards the train himself, intending to return the cursed parchment to the demonologist before he can flee. When he enters Karswell's compartment, there is palpable tension between the two, and they engage in a game of cat-and-mouse—Karswell desperate to avoid the demon, Holden intent on forcing him to remain.

Karswell prepares to leave and Holden uses a series of pretexts to detain him, each time taking the opportunity to hand Karswell an object—a note of apology, a package of cigarettes, and a box of matches—all of which the suspicious warlock declines. Then, abruptly, Holden's tone shifts: "Sit down," he gruffly orders. "You're staying with me, Karswell. You've sold your bill of goods too well, because I believe you now." Karswell's fear is obvious as Holden outlines his plan: "I believe that in five minutes something monstrous and horrible is going to happen. And when it does, you're going to be here so that whatever happens to me will happen to you." Holden's declaration signals that he has converted to Karswell's worldview at last, and shifted from skeptic to believer. At that moment, the police arrive and, over Joanna's protests, order Holden to let Karswell leave. Holden proffers Karswell's coat, and the police urge him to take it, which—flustered and off-balance—he does, his desperate desire to leave overwhelming his previous caution.

Karswell hurries out of the train compartment, only to realize in horror that he has been hoisted by his own parchment, which Holden has slipped into the coat pocket. Ironically, it is the elemental wind, which Karswell proved so adept at conjuring earlier at Lufford Hall, that proves to be part of his undoing. Surging through the corridor of the train car, it tears the parchment out of his grasp and sweeps it out the open doorway and onto the tracks. Karswell rushes after the slip of paper, finding it between the rails just in time to watch as it bursts into flame. With a fire demon advancing on him from one side, and a hurtling train from the other, he dies beside the tracks, his body broken and torn.[16] It remains unclear to all (but not to the film's viewers) whether Karswell has met his gruesome fate at the hands of technology or the supernatural.

Karswell's death—whether by demon or locomotive—removes the immediate threat to Holden. Yet, it is far from clear that Holden has won his battle. While victorious over death, he has become more like Karswell in using supernatural forces against his enemy. He acts in self-defense but, rather than responding to devil-worship and demon-summoning with rationalism, he uses Karswell's own diabolism against him. Holden's single-minded devotion to his personal crusade also hardens over the course of the film, shifting from arrogance and dismissiveness toward those with contrary views into a willingness to sacrifice those who stand in his way. Over the course of *Night*, he commits trespass and attempted theft at Karswell's estate, holds Karswell against his will in the train compartment, and causes the mentally unstable accused murderer Hobart to be interrogated before an academic audience under circumstances that lead to Hobart's death.

The scene begins with Holden announcing to the packed conference attendees: "We are going to perform an experiment on the platform with a Mr. Rand Hobart who, through an experience related to devil worship, has lost contact with reality." Holden is a trained psychologist—he should be fully aware that a patient's delusions can be utterly "real" to them, and thus genuinely threatening—and Rand Hobart's death should not have come as a shock to him, given the circumstances.[17] Hobart was unrestrained prior to Holden's uncontrolled experiment, an oversight that suggests a dangerously cavalier attitude toward what a conscientious scientist would regard as routine safety measures. His attempted escape and resulting death, coming while he was under Holden's care, would have ruined most practicing psychologists' careers. All that, however, is seemingly as irrelevant to Holden as traditional standards of historical scholarship have become to Karswell by the time he uses the parchment to kill Harrington. Hobart's death becomes, in fact, the moment at which the two rivals' characters (and worldviews) converge. The knowledge gained from Hobart's death allows Holden to reverse Karswell's curse and save himself, but he arrives at his newfound acceptance of the power of cursed texts through the rationalist methods he applies during and after Hobart's interrogation.

Holden's encounter with Karswell changes his worldview from one of strict scientific materialism to one that acknowledges the power of mysticism and occult texts. After witnessing Hobart kill himself out of fear of the parchment's ferocious curse and observing the demon devouring Karswell, it seems likely that Holden will return to America without the rational worldview that he held prior to his London adventures. He will never again investigate occult phenomena from a wholly detached, rational standpoint, casually dismissive of any suggestion that supernatural forces might be at work. Having seen the world as it truly is, he can never go back to seeing it as he once believed it was. In the last scene of *Night*, Joanna—glancing across the railroad tracks at Karswell's body—declines to look closer, declaring: "Sometimes it's better *not* to know." Holden echoes those words a moment later, but with a different meaning: Having accepted the possibility that Karswell was right, he dwells on the loss of his old certainty, rather than the acquisition of new knowledge. Tourneur may have perceived Holden's change as being positive, given his own view of the supernatural, but when a researcher gives up his belief system his fundamental outlook and perception has been irrevocably changed.[18] Ancient books, runes, and rituals are no longer mere superstition to Holden; they have become sources of power and knowledge to be believed in, safeguarded and feared.

Notes

1. Jacques Tourneur, *Night of the Demon*, 1957.
2. *Night*'s official script credits went to former Alfred Hitchcock screenwriter Charles Bennett and *Night*'s executive producer, Hal E. Chester. However, according to Brian Neve, making a large uncredited contribution to the script was blacklisted writer Cy Endfield. Neve states "Endfield remembers writing his own shooting script for the film for and with Chester—drawing on his own interests in science and magic—and that he agreed not to take any credit because of his continued blacklisted status." Also, since Endfield was a magician I extrapolate that the portions of the script focusing on Karswell's magic owe a debt to Endfield. Indeed,

Orson Welles first discovered Endfield because of their shared interest in magic, and magic plays a large role in *Night*. At the same time, Bennett's own contribution is significant since *Night* has the pace and suspense of a Hitchcock script. Considering this information, M.R. James, Endfield, Bennett and Chester should share the screenwriting credit for *Night of the Demon*.

    3. Joshi, *Weird Tale*, 135.

    4. Karswell's character was reportedly based on occultist Aleister Crowley.

    5. Tourneur's research for *Night of the Demon* appears to have been scrupulous. According to Vincent Porter, Tourneur had "a long discussion with the oldest of London's nine authentic witches" for research purposes. Also, when forced to show the fire demon, Tourneur copied the monster from an old demonology text ("Strangers on the Shore," 121). Why did Tourneur want to avoid showing the demon? J.P. Telotte's thoughts on Tourneur's aesthetic give a good reasoning for this rationale. "Certainly, the limitations of time, money, and material necessitated that less concern be given to fashioning elaborate spectacles than to making audiences believe they had seen something unusual or nightmarish" (*Dreams of Darkness*, 22).

    6. Torneur, "Interview with Bertrand Tavernier," 54.

    7. White, "Poetics of Horror," 8.

    8. Telotte, *Dreams of Darkness*, 186.

    9. Executive producer Hal E. Chester forced the fire demon's appearance on Tourneur. Tourneur and Bennett preferred the demon largely unseen in the film so that audiences could make up their mind about what happened in the film. Bennett recalls that Chester "to some extent 'messed up' his screenplay" (Neve, "Crediting the Runes"). I take this statement to mean that Bennett is referring to being forced to show the demon. There is an argument over this cinematic choice with strongly held opinions either way. Furthermore, it would be difficult to omit the demon when advertising specifically stated, "You will actually see them on the screen!" with an accompanying illustration of the demon.

    10. The calendar marking Holden's remaining time also evokes, for modern viewers, Stonehenge's function as a prehistoric calendar; this interpretation, however, was not widely known until nearly a decade after the film's release.

    11. Towsen, *Clowns*, 289.

    12. Julian Karswell's Christian name means youthful in Latin, which matches his demeanor around children, living with his mother and Karswell's great fondness for children's open-minded thinking.

    13. Tourneur has significant creative influences imparted on him during childhood according to an interview with Bertrand Tavernier. Tourneur begins by saying, "My childhood was rather tough." Tourneur's parents would frighten him if he misbehaved, putting "the maid in the cupboard and she used to jiggle a bowler hat while my parents would tell me: 'That's the terrible Thunderman.' This is the root of one of my obsessions: to suddenly introduce something inexplicable into the shot, such as, for instance, the hand on the balustrade of the staircase in *Night of the Demon*." Tourneur explains that in "the reverse shot, the hand isn't there anymore. Incidentally I spent a great deal of time looking for the right hand and finally I chose that of an old man very close to death" ("Interview: Bertrand Tavernier," 48–49).

    14. Tourneur thus allows both O'Brien and the (presumably rationalist) police to both be right: Hobart, having passed on a parchment he knew to be lethal, is guilty of murder, but it was the fire demon—not Hobart himself—that killed his brother.

    15. In *Analytical Theory of Probabilities* (1812).

    16. From this perspective, it makes perfect sense Tourneur preferred not to show the demon onscreen. Without an onscreen demon, the audience gets to decide if this is the supernatural or superstition in a manner like Holden, rather than being bluntly shown it exists with an onscreen demon at the beginning and end.

    17. Holden also shows a disregard for human life by snapping on the lights prematurely at the end of the séance. He is warned that he could have killed the medium Mr. Meek (Reginald Beckwith) by suddenly turning on the lights. Holden appears nonplussed by this revelation and storms off, unconvinced.

    18. In the Tavernier interview, Tourneur is displeased by the negative stigma given to the supernatural: "But it is really exasperating that supernatural forces are always represented as malevolent. Why this racism? If they exist and if they are malevolent, we would have been swept away a long time ago" ("Interview: Bertrand Tavernier," 55).

Bibliography

Curse of the Demon and *Night of the Demon*. Directed by Jacques Tourneur. 1957. Culver City, CA: Sony Pictures, 2002. DVD.

James, M. R. "Casting the Runes." In *The Century's Best Horror Fiction*, vol. I, edited by John Pelan, 179–95. Baltimore: Cemetery Dance, 2012.

Joshi, S.T. *The Weird Tale: Arthur Machen, Lord Dunsany, Algernon Blackwood, M.R. James, Ambrose Bierce, H.P. Lovecraft*. Austin: University of Texas Press, 1990.

Neve, Brian. "Crediting the Runes." *Film Comment* 28, no. 4 (1992): 80. http://www.jstor.org/stable/43453656.

Porter, Vincent. "Strangers on the Shore: The Contributions of French Novelists and Directors to British Cinema, 1946–1960." *Framework: The Journal of Cinema and Media* 43, no. 1 (2002): 105–26. http://www.jstor.org/stable/41552318.

Telotte, J. P. *Dreams of Darkness: Fantasy and the Films of Val Lewton*. Urbana: University of Illinois Press, 1985.
Tourneur, Jacques. "Interview: Bertrand Tavernier." In *Jacques Tourneur*, edited by Claire Johnston and Paul Willemen, 48–56. Edinburgh: Edinburgh Film Festival, 1975.
Towsen, John. *Clowns*. New York: Hawthorn Books, 1976.
White, Dennis L. "The Poetics of Horror: More than Meets the Eye." *Cinema Journal* 10, no. 2 (1971): 1–18. doi:10.2307/1225234.

International Takes

Logical Horror

Axiomatic Magic and Strategic Murder in Death Note

Richard J. Leskosky

At the heart of an international multimedia sensation originating in Japan lies perhaps the most unusual magical book in contemporary fiction: the Death Note, a book that exists for the sole purpose of ending human lives. The property of a Shinigami, literally a god of death, the Death Note is, simply, a notebook that kills people.

Ryuk, a bored Shinigami, writes the following basic operating rules on the inside cover of his Death Note and drops it outside a Tokyo high school:

1. The human whose name is written in this note shall die.
2. This note will not take effect unless the writer has the person's face in their mind when writing his/her name.
3. If the cause of death is written within 40 seconds of writing the person's name, it will happen.
4. If the cause of death is not specified, the person will simply die of a heart attack.
5. After writing the cause of death, details of the death should be written in the next 6 minutes and 40 seconds.

Seventeen-year-old top-ranking student Light Yagami picks it up, and once he discovers its potential, he resolves to use it to change the world by terminating violent criminals. Soon, however, he is also eliminating other morally unfit persons and even any investigators who threaten to discover his identity.

Ryuzaki, a brilliant but eccentric young detective in the Sherlock Holmes mode, working under the code name "L," takes over Interpol's efforts to identify the unknown person (whom the internet and television have dubbed "Kira") behind the mounting death toll of criminals. Based on his deductions and a successful initial experiment to learn about Kira's powers, in which he publicly challenged Kira to kill him on television, L immediately centers the search in the Kanto region of Japan. While Ryuzaki endeavors to track down the supernatural assassin, Light tries to discover L's true identity so he can execute him with the Death Note—a reciprocal, deadly game of cat and mouse driven by logic and deception.[1]

Propagation of Death Note *Narrative Across Media*

The Death Note narrative originated in the Japanese graphic manga series *Death Note* (*Desu Nōto*) written by Tsugumi Ohba and illustrated by Takeshi Obata[2] which ran in the magazine *Weekly Shōnen Jump* from December 2003 to May 2006 for a total of 108 chapters. In a development typical for popular manga series, the individual chapters were subsequently collected into 12 *tankōbon* volumes published from May 2004 to October 2006. An additional *tankōbon* volume *Death Note 13: How to Read* (2006) comprised a compendium of character analyses, rules governing use of the Death Note, commentary by Ohba and Obata, explanations of the various gambits employed by Ryuzaki, Light, and other characters, and general background information.

Continuing a well-established Japanese pattern of migration from one medium to another, an animé series consisting of 37 episodes adapted from the manga series and directed by Tetsurō Araki appeared on Japanese television from October 2006 to June 2007. In August 2007, a two-hour animated TV movie *Death Note Relight: Visions of a God* (*Desu Nōto Riraito: Genshisuru kami*) recapped the first half of the animated series from Ryuk's point of view with some additional wrap-around scenes; and in August 2008 a second TV movie *Death Note: Relight 2: L's Successors* (*Desu Nōto Riraito 2: L o Tsugu Mono*) recapped the second half with a differently oriented set of contextualizing scenes introduced by Ryuzaki and some additional changes.[3]

In 2006, two live-action films, *Death Note* (*Desu Nōto*) and *Death Note: The Last Name* (*Desu Nōto: The Last Name*), both directed by Shûsuke Kaneko, again retold the manga story but with significant alterations and omissions. A third film, *L: Change the World* (2008), directed by Hideo Nakata, continued Ryuzaki's story as he works on another case, with only a few references to the Death Note narrative, including a brief appearance by Ryuk, apparently to permit the inclusion of his image in posters and other publicity materials in order to attract fans of the supernatural elements of the original story. An 11-episode live-action Japanese television series appeared in 2015, again adapting the manga story with significant changes and omissions.

In September 2016, a three part live-action mini-series, *Death Note: New Generation* appeared on Hulu Japan, continuing the alternate story line of the earlier live-action films. And in October 2016, the live-action *Death Note: Light Up the New World* (*Desu Nōto: Light Up the New World*) was released theatrically as a further sequel in this sequence. The animé series the *Relight* films, and the first two live-action films are available internationally on DVD and Blu-Ray.

An American live-action feature, *Death Note*, directed by Adam Wingard, appeared on Netflix beginning August 2017. In this version, which relocates the story to Seattle, Washington, the Death Note exerts far more control over objects and people's actions, and many of the deaths share the grotesquely macabre Rube Goldberg-esque circumstances that are hallmarks of the *Final Destination* films. The American film also supplies more conventional motivations for its characters—Light, for example, initially uses the Death Note in part to avenge his mother's death.[4]

In addition to the manga and the animated and live-action films and TV series in Japan, the Death Note multi-media franchise includes at least a couple "light novels" (what would be called young adult novels outside Japan), and several video games. On stage, *Death Note: The Musical*—music by Frank Wildhorn, lyrics by Jack Murphy, and book by Ivan Menchell—premiered in Tokyo in April 2015. Ancillary merchandise includes bobbleheads of the main human characters and Shinigami, as well as cosplay Death Note notebooks.

As the function and handling of the Death Note remain constant throughout its various venues, this essay will focus primarily on the animé series, the two animated television recaps, and the first two Japanese live-action films—the moving image narratives which most closely adhere to the manga paradigm.

Divergence in Animated and Live-Action Narratives

A significant difference exists, however, between the animated and live-action versions of the story. Both build to a climax in the Light/Ryuzaki conflict with the following developments. Because Light's father, Soichiro, heads the Japanese police force's Kira investigation, Light has access to information both about the investigation and about criminals to eliminate. Ryuzaki quickly settles on Light as the person most likely to be Kira. A second (would-be) Kira appears trying to help the original in his crusade and explicitly wanting to meet him: teen model Misa Amane, who identifies Light as the genuine Kira, falls for him immediately, and pledges to help him. Light uses Misa and later another surrogate to continue the killings to lead the investigation away from himself, but Ryuzaki still suspects him even though Light actively helps the task force in apprehending the third Kira.

At this point the animated and live-action versions diverge. With 37 episodes, the series had more time to follow the complicated plot of the manga which spans nearly seven years (November 28, 2003, to January 28, 2010, in the narrative).

In the animated series, the third Kira is Kyosuke Higuchi, a greedy business executive more motivated by furthering his own career than by bringing justice to evildoers. Shortly after Higuchi's capture, Light eliminates Ryuzaki by tricking Rem, the Shinigami haunting Misa, into killing him to protect Misa from imprisonment and heightened interrogation techniques. Light then assumes the L identity and continues his involvement in the primary Kira investigation, all the while killing criminals as Kira. After graduating from college, he formally joins the police and becomes the head of the task force.

At the same time, Near, a successor to Ryuzaki reared in the same orphanage training program for prodigies, comes to head a special task force in the United States to capture Kira and take control of the Death Note. The Light vs. Ryuzaki opposition now continues as Light vs. Near, with yet another would-be successor to Ryuzaki, Mello, working outside the law with the Mafia to capture Kira before Near. After years of his murderous campaign, Kira is close to becoming the ruler of the world: wars have ended and the crime rate has decreased 70 percent. Light, however, maintains his position as L to ensure that the task force does not discover his Kira plans. Once again, he uses surrogates in a complicated scheme to destroy his opponent, Near, but a rogue action by Mello leads to an oversight by Kira's prime surrogate, Teru Mikami, a prosecutor obsessed with punishing the wicked. This compromises Light's strategy and permits Near to end Kira's reign of terror.

The live-action version, conversely, ties everything up after the capture of television journalist Kiyomi Takada, who takes Higuchi's place as the surrogate Kira, and Light's manipulation of Rem to write Ryuzaki's true name in the Death Note. But here Ryuzaki uses a rule-based ploy of his own to capture Kira, and so no Light vs. Near conflict takes place in this version.

Unique Facets of the Death Note

In all its venues, the Death Note is unique among fiction's magical books. Though made from materials not found on this planet, it presents a nondescript, banal appearance and could pass for an ordinary school notebook. It contains no spells or recipes for potions; it summons no demons[5]; it grants no wishes; it provides no instructions for transmuting metals; it requires no contract signed in blood and no immediate sacrifices such as blood offerings in order to access its power. In fact, in its natural form it does not even contain any writing either on its pages or its cover until someone writes in it. Its sole function is to end human lives. It is, in effect, a weapon, and the narrative surrounding it does not represent it as anything else.

As a weapon, its powers can increase exponentially when the user specifies the conditions of a death. Disease and accident are two obvious possibilities, but so is suicide. When the Death Note's user specifies such circumstances, the Death Note is able to control its victims and, to a certain extent, the world around them as long as the specified conditions are possible. (If the conditions are not possible or if they would cause the death of other, unnamed persons, the default heart attack occurs.)

To utilize the Death Note one obviously must write in it, so it might be expected that its pages would become full at some point, but the Death Note never runs out of pages. A page or even a piece of a page removed from the notebook, moreover, has the same lethal properties as the notebook itself.

Unlike most magical books in films or literature, the Death Note itself is not a solitary item. Every Shinigami has at least one, and there are many Shinigami. Up to six Death Notes may operate in the human world at one time (exclusive of those actually carried by a Shinigami).[6] Three Death Notes from three different Shinigami fall into human hands in the animé series, and repeated changes in the ownership of those Death Notes underlie crucial plot developments.

Shinigami in Death Note

The Death Note functions in a way that is the polar opposite of the book carried by Shinigami in traditional Japanese lore. There the Shinigami's book simply lists humans' unalterable death dates, and the Shinigami constantly checks it to make sure the deaths occur at the proper times. When a human's time of death draws near, the Shinigami calls the human at the appointed moment.[7]

The Shinigami of *Death Note* are, themselves, also unlike those in other very popular manga/animé series. In the action series *Bleach*, the comic *Rin-ne*, and the gothic *Black Butler*, for example, Shinigami look like humans and pursue essentially benevolent careers guiding souls to the wheel of reincarnation and neutralizing evil spirits. Of course, exceptions do exist. Some Shinigami in *Bleach* are driven to dubious actions by rigid codes of honor or by the desire for more power. In *Rin-ne* the eponymous young Shinigami's father, an inveterate conman, has no scruples about sending souls to Hell for his own profit or swindling and stealing from his own family and anyone else who might develop an attachment to him. And the Shinigami in *Black Butler* generally act like uncaring bureaucrats, with at least one of them frequently engaging in psychotic behavior. But, by and large, the Shinigami in these different fictional universes work diligently and honorably at their spiritual duties.

Shinigami in *Death Note*, however, differ in virtually all respects. Physically, they are grotesque bipeds with retractable wings. Some are wholly or partly skeletonized; some appear stitched together like Frankenstein's monster; and others exhibit nightmarish features such as multiple eyes. Humans seeing them for the first time (after touching a Death Note) invariably react in shock, often compounded by fear and horror. Ryuk displays the most humanoid appearance among them but nonetheless looks monstrous, with a shock of black hair, a dead white face, shark-like teeth, large unblinking eyes, and a punk/goth black leather outfit draped with chains, inspired by the design of Tim Burton's Edward Scissorhands.[8] Rem most nearly resembles a partially unwrapped mummy with a head inspired by the Gorgon Medusa of Greek mythology.[9] The frightful appearance of these Shinigami (a mélange of features culled from 1930s Universal Studios horror films with an infusion of Lovecraftian details) links *Death Note* iconographically to more mainstream horror films. Ryuk's fondness for apples also suggests an affinity with the serpent in the Garden of Eden, though Ryuk is a desultory tempter at best.[10]

Death Note Shinigami inhabit an astral-plane wasteland, which they seldom leave because they do not need to come to Earth to end human lives—they can observe this world and select their victims through portals in their realm. They also possess the innate ability to see a person's true name and lifespan, which means they have no problem ending someone's life with the Death Note.

Only humans who have actually touched the Death Note associated with a particular Shinigami can see and hear that Shinigami. Humans who legitimately own a Death Note are haunted by the Shinigami who originally had it.[11] That simply means the Shinigami is obliged to hang around the human owner of the Death Note and cannot return to its home realm until that human relinquishes the Death Note or dies, though it is not required to be in constant attendance on the human. The Shinigami does not control the human, nor can the human command the Shinigami to do anything that violates the Death Note rules or that the Shinigami simply is not willing to do.

Death Note Shinigami are lazy slackers with no apparent duties in their home realm. They end people's lives by writing their names in their Death Notes, but not because those humans have reached the natural end of their lifespans—quite the opposite. Ryuk and his fellow Shinigami cut people's lives short so that they can appropriate the lost

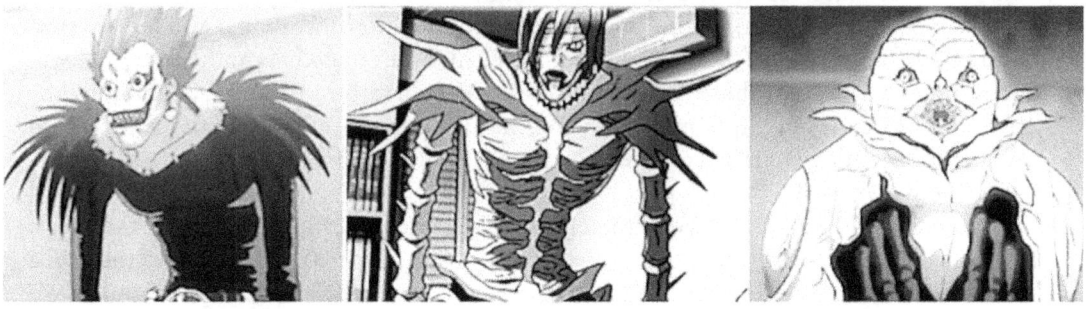

Death Gods as Monsters. From left to right: Ryuk, Rem, and Sidoh. Shinigami in *Death Note* (2003–2006) iconographically mix and match elements from familiar figures of horror—vampire, Frankenstein's creature, skeleton, mummy—as well as Edward Scissorhands, arthropods, and even stranger things.

years to increase their own lifespans. Ending a human life, therefore, is not their job but rather a means of self-preservation; they are simply predators here. So, unlike the Shinigami of the other fictional universes, they concern themselves not with the general human populace but rather with only a relatively small set of human victims.

With no apparent purpose other than extending their own lives, the Shinigami lead a bored existence. Ryuk's ennui drives him to visit this world and pass his Death Note to a human simply to see what will happen. So, he is fortunate that Light Yagami picks it up.

Light, too, is bored—like many teenagers—with school and with the world, which he sees as completely rotten. Once he discovers the power and potential of the Death Note, he makes plans to mold a better world by eliminating the worst people, simultaneously intimidating everyone else into being good, and ruling that better world as a god. His cleverness in pursuing this goal and avoiding capture provides Ryuk with plenty of amusement.[12] But Ryuk also finds himself and Rem being manipulated by Light as part of those plans.

Perhaps the oddest Shinigami trait, though, is their ignorance regarding their primary means of survival: they themselves do not know all the rules governing Death Notes. Incredibly, most of them seem to be unaware of the fatal rule that if a Shinigami uses its Death Note to save a human and thereby extend the human's lifespan, then that Shinigami will die.

Rule-Governed Death

Use of the Death Note is superficially simple—write someone's name in it while having that person's face in mind and that person will die. No special or magical implements or inks are required, nor are incantations or mystical gestures. The Death Note reduces murder to a mere ledger entry. That basic operation, however, is constrained by a surprising number of rules.

Although the five rules already noted are the only ones written in Ryuk's Death Note, over the course of its run the manga displays 97 rules on dedicated pages as bonus material for the reader, with some rules having multiple subsections. These pages are designed to look like Ryuk's printing on the inner cover of his Death Note, and these images also appear as bumpers bracketing the commercial breaks in the animé series. Some of these rules are descriptive rather than prescriptive—simple statements of fact about, say, Shinigami biology (they have no functioning internal organs) and the physical nature of the Death Note (there is no significance in different colors on the covers). Ryuk and Rem reveal many of these additional rules as the narrative progresses, although they are not obligated to tell humans anything about using the Death Note (and rules forbid them from revealing names and lifespans of possible victims or the identities of other Death Note owners).

The normal Death Note is completely blank to start with. Before dropping the Death Note into the human world, Ryuk printed "Death Note" on its front cover and inscribed the five basic rules noted earlier (in English, which he describes as the most popular language in the human world) on the inside front cover.[13]

But the rules do not apply as a result of Ryuk's writing them in the notebook; they apply *a priori*. Ryuk writing the rules in an ordinary notebook would not change it into a Death Note. He transcribed a small number of the basics merely to facilitate human use of the Death Note. Even orally he does not give Light all the rules governing use of the Death Note. Moreover, Light has Ryuk write two fake rules in his Death Note (that the user must employ the Death Note every 13 days or die, and that destruction of the Death Note will kill everyone who has touched it). He anticipates that Ryuzaki's task force will eventually acquire it and plants these false rules to mislead and manipulate them. But even though these fake rules are entered in the Death Note by its former Shinigami owner, they have no power to produce the effects they describe.

The genuine Death Note rules essentially provide instructions for creating well-formed sentences that kill people—literal death sentences. These sentences take the form <*NAME (will die of a certain cause) (at a given time) (under certain circumstances)*> where the elements in parentheses represent optional conditions; if none of these elements are specified, the rules mandate that the person named will die in 40 seconds of a heart attack. In other words, the Death Note rules constitute a grammar. Like the grammars of natural languages, this lethal grammar contains a component that depends on rule ordering to produce grammatical sentences.

So, for example, the first rule Ryuk transcribes, that anyone whose name is written in the Death Note will die, would seem to be the most rudimentary of all, yet it must apply only after the rule stating that anyone whose name is accidentally misspelled four times in a Death Note cannot then be killed by the Death Note. If it were to apply globally—meaning it would apply whenever its conditions were met and thus, in effect, operate prior to the four-mistake rule—then a correct fifth attempt at spelling the name would kill the victim and therefore violate the four-mistake rule creating a contradiction that would vitiate the whole system.[14] Other rules which must apply before Ryuk's first rule include those excluding victims less than 780 days old and older than 124 years.

Although the rules governing restrictions on possible victims and the circumstances of their deaths would seem to be the most crucial for the use of the Death Note, the rules defining ownership of the Death Note play a major role as well. Indeed, although the death-dealing nature of the Death Note and the urgency of finding it and stopping Kira motivate most of the action in these narratives, ownership and the rules governing it structure both the search for Kira and Kira's quest to discover Ryuzaki's true name—even though the forces opposing Kira may be unaware of that influence.

The Potency of Ownership

At first it would seem that ownership as such is not that significant a factor in the operation of the Death Note. After all, anyone can write a name in it, and the named person will die. And anyone touching the Death Note will thenceforth be able to see and hear the Shinigami who dropped it into the human world.

Who actually "owns" a Death Note, though, can be an opaque issue even for the original Shinigami owner. When a not very bright Shinigami named Sidoh lost his Death Note in the Shinigami realm, Ryuk found it and passed it off as his own. This is the Death Note Light picked up, but by the time Sidoh comes to Earth looking for it, Mello's gang has absconded with it. Ryuk is forced to admit to Sidoh that he does not know who owns the note at that time or where they might be. So Sidoh must return to the Shinigami realm to use their special viewing portals to search for it. When Light starts shifting around the ownership of his and Misa's Death Notes, Ryuk and Rem have to take some time to sort out what exactly is going on because their connections to specific notes change in the process as well.[15]

Two sets of rules concerning ownership have enormous consequences in the narrative.

First, if the human owner of a Death Note relinquishes ownership, he or she loses all memory of owning the Death Note and of everything (the Shinigami, the murders) relating to it. If that person subsequently touches a Death Note, those memories will return as long as the person remains in contact with the note unless the person once again obtains actual ownership, in which case the memories return permanently.

Second, owning a Death Note affects how the owner can be perceived by another human with "Shinigami eyes." When Shinigami look at a human, they can see that person's real name and remaining life span. The human user of a Death Note can acquire "Shinigami eyes" by trading half his or her remaining lifespan for them and so can then similarly read the name and lifespan of anyone whose face he or she can see either in real life or in a photo or video image. But someone with "Shinigami eyes" can see only the name of the owner of a Death Note, not his or her lifespan. That means that someone with the eyes power can tell whether or not someone is the owner of a Death Note even if the Shinigami haunting that person is not present.

Light exploits both rules to keep his identity as Kira concealed.

He insists that Ryuzaki confine him in a cell to see if the Kira killings stop while he is under surveillance; then he relinquishes ownership of the Death Note to Ryuk after weeks of incarceration so that he will have no memory of it. Misa, who had been taken into custody earlier, also relinquishes ownership of her Death Note at the same time and loses all memory of it. Meanwhile, Higuchi, the third Death Note user, continues the killings so it appears that the genuine Kira is still at large. This leads the task force members to demand Light's release. When Higuchi is subsequently captured and his Death Note (the one Ryuk had originally dropped) retrieved, the fake rule about the user having to write a name in the note at least every 13 days or die provides further spurious proof that Light and Misa could not have been involved in the Kira killings. The other fake rule, about the destruction of the Death Note triggering the death of everyone who touched it, ensures that the task force will not destroy it. Meanwhile, Light regains all his memories once he touches the note again, and ownership reverts to him when he kills Higuchi by writing his name on a scrap of a Death Note page he had concealed on his person before giving up his memories.

Years later, in the face of the combined assaults by Near and Mello, he again relinquishes ownership but keeps a Death Note strapped to his body so that he will not lose his memories again. His father, Soichiro, now deputy director of the Japanese task force, makes the trade for Shinigami eyes to assist in an assault on Mello's hideout. After that fails, on his deathbed Soichiro looks at Light and can see his lifespan, meaning that he does not own a Death Note, so he erroneously assumes that means that Light is not Kira and dies unburdened of that lingering worry.

Exploiting the Rules

The highly codified use of the Death Note meshes neatly with the logic of Kira/Light's and L/Ryuzaki's (and later Near's) mirrored attempts at discovering each other's identities.[16] Each operates on the assumption that his opponent is highly intelligent and will do anything to achieve his ends and so interprets all new evidence from that perspective. Thus, once Ryuzaki determines that Light is most likely Kira, he pretty much discounts anything that Light says or does to "prove" his innocence as something that Kira would logically say or do to mislead him. And in the anime version, Light sets a final trap for Near based on correct assumptions about how Near would interpret and act upon certain falsified circumstances; and that would have succeeded if Mikami had not acted on his own, disregarding Kira's orders to the contrary, thereby alerting Near that something was amiss.

In this extended duel, Light always operates with an inherent edge because he knows things about the Death Note that his opponents cannot know or else finds them out first. Ryuzaki and later Near and Mello can only deduce the rules of its operation from what they can see of its effects in the real world (much like linguists analyzing a new language, to return to the earlier linguistics analogy), although Mello does manage to learn quite a bit when he gains Sidoh as an informant. This is not to say that they cannot use the rules for their own ends, though.

In the anime version, Light has Mikami use a fake Death Note where Near's agents can observe him, so that Near will think it real and develop a plan to steal it and secretly substitute a copy. Light correctly predicted Near would figure that in a subsequent meeting between their investigative groups Kira would have Mikami spy on them with Shinigami eyes and kill everyone but Light, whom he would recognize as Kira because he would not be able to read his lifespan. Of course, the copy would not work, but it would list the names of everyone present except for Light's—sure evidence that he was Kira. But under Light's plan, Mikami would have the real Death Note, which had been safely hidden, instead of the copy and all his enemies and his own task force who would otherwise then know the truth about him would die. But the failed intervention by Mello a couple of days before the scheduled meeting led Near to realize the subterfuge and make copies of both the fake and the real Death Note, thereby in fact winding up with the anticipated proof of the list of names excluding Light's.

All that takes a considerable amount of time for characters to explain in the manga and the anime. The live-action *Death Note: The Last Name*, on the other hand, handles the final confrontation between Light and Ryuzaki succinctly and imaginatively. Ryuzaki resolves the case in probably the most unusual manner ever carried out by a detective: he commits suicide.

In this version, Light again maneuvers Rem into inscribing Ryuzaki's real name in her Death Note, and Ryuzaki collapses at his feet. Light explains to Misa what has happened and writes a controlling script in his Death Note that will make his father return Misa's confiscated Death Note to him and then die. But when his father arrives, he is not carrying a Death Note and knows now the truth about Light. Ryuzaki also shows up with the missing Death Note and explains to the astonished Light what has happened. Ryuzaki figured that Light would use the Death Note somehow to kill him, so he took advantage of a couple of rules himself. The Death Note has an operational window of 23 days (the 23-Day rule), so a couple days earlier Ryuzaki wrote his own name in the book with the notation that he would die peacefully of a heart attack in 23 days. After a period of six minutes and 40 seconds, the death sentence cannot be changed. So, although Ryuzaki has effectively killed himself by doing this, he has also guaranteed that for the next 23 days no one could kill him using a Death Note.

In both versions, Light's capture as a result of his opponents using Death Note rules against him leads to the application of further rules with a decidedly eschatological turn.

After the confirmation of Light's identity as Kira, he is wounded while trying to use a Death Note scrap to kill Near and faces at least life in prison if not a death penalty. In a panic, he begs Ryuk to kill everyone at the meeting. Ryuk, however, figures that, all things considered, Kira's career is over. He can also see Light's lifespan and knows that the rules require him to stay near Light as long as Light owns the Death Note to which he is attached. Thus, he would also have to spend all that time in prison, which would bore him. So Ryuk invokes another rule which says, "After a Shinigami brings a Death Note to the human world and gives its ownership to a human, the Shinigami has the right to kill the human using its own Death Note for any reason, such as disliking the owner." Ryuk writes Light's name in his Death Note and then reminds Light of another rule he told him about when they first met: "The human who uses this note can go neither to Heaven nor to Hell." Ryuk tells Light that for him it's Mu—"nothingness," in the Zen Buddhist tradition.

Existential Horror

Death Note functions as an existential, even nihilistic, horror tale. It begins with the existential position that humans live in an absurd, meaningless world and that anything can happen to anyone at any time (in contemporary horror film terms, "anyone can die at any time") and ratchets that up several notches.

Ryuk comes from a realm devoid of meaning. The Shinigami have only one task—prolonging their lives indefinitely at the expense of human lives. And they do not even actively pursue that any more than minimally necessary. Mostly they nap and gamble. His boredom with this meaningless existence sends him to Earth in search of diversion, and Light's parallel boredom with school and the world, which he sees as rotten, make him a prime candidate for taking up the Death Note and the power it confers.

Light sets out to impose meaning on his own meaningless world, and the rules governing the Death Note allow him to do that. But in the end, his only real accomplishment amounts to temporary amusement for Ryuk.

Dying Live on TV. Kira demonstrates his power in *Death Note* (2003–2006) by killing people on live TV. Lind L. Tailor is actually a decoy: a criminal facing execution made to act as detective L and challenge Kira on television. His murder tells the real L much about Kira. A second Kira kills an announcer at a specified time to show he has the same power as the original Kira.

Kira's campaign to change the world involves killing thousands and thousands of people to eliminate evildoers and to coerce everyone else into being good—or at least giving that appearance. For the general populace, the mechanism by which this happens remains a mystery albeit a very public mystery. Kira kills people while they are appearing live on television and kills them in groups (prisoners in their cells, gangs, government task forces investigating him). The Death Note even forces the President of the United States to kill himself. Literally, anyone can die at any time, and it is often in public.

For the task force members working with Light, existential anxiety reaches even greater heights. They know that because they are trying to find Kira, Kira regards them as enemies or at least hindrances to his plans. As a result, they are more likely to succumb to his power than ordinary citizens. In fact, early on, most of the police initially working with Soichiro opt out of the investigation to avoid facing the likelihood of sudden death, leaving only a handful of operatives to continue the search. As more becomes known about Kira's capabilities and as Ryuzaki makes his suspicions of Light known, the task force members realize how much more vulnerable they are becoming. And this is brought home to them even more when Kira manages to kill Ryuzaki. Ironically, their continued existence after Light subsequently takes over the investigation and the identity of L serves to bolster their doubts about Ryuzaki's belief that Light was Kira. The fact that Light has not killed them when he could so easily do so argues, for them at least, against his being Kira. But it is a false argument because Light plans to kill them all—have his surrogate kill them all—at his face-to-face meeting with Near.

Light's vision of an ordered world with him as its god vanishes when Ryuk writes his name in his Death Note and reminds Light that he is heading for Mu ("nothingness"), and the meaninglessness of existence reasserts itself.

Ryuk's aversion to boredom both begins and ends Light's career as Kira, by relying on Death Note rules. Those rules also provided the structure for his "fun" in observing Light exploiting them in his literal game of death with his intellectual opponents. That in turn produced a challenging story line for audiences of this multimedia narrative with its unique supernatural book and its equally unique consistent adherence to a set of defining rules.

Unfortunately, some of the *Death Note* fictional universe has slipped into the real world. Presumably identifying with Light due to his charisma, his disgust with the condition of the world, and his confidence that he knew how to fix it and rule it, teenagers in several countries have made their own Death Notes (non-functional, of course) inscribed with the names of hated classmates and teachers. In more disturbing developments, some have actually made preparations to accomplish what their handmade Death Notes could not. And a grisly 2007 murder in Brussels had sufficient references to *Death Note* features at the crime scene that Belgian media came to refer to it as the "Manga Murder."

Conclusion

The *Death Note* narrative's central conceit of a magic book that kills those whose names are simply written in it is unique among literary and cinematic horror books. Also unique is the rule-governed aspect of the Death Note's operation. This placed constraints on its use but also allowed for creative exploitation of those rules both by Kira, the wielder of the Death Note, and the detectives (first L and then Near) seeking to uncover his identity, leading to a complex reciprocal cat and mouse game with each trying to discover his opponent's true name.

The realization that anyone can be killed at any time if their name and face are known to Kira, and that there is no physical defense possible, creates a pervasive sense of existential horror that overshadows the supernatural horror component provided by the participation of Shinigami. Kira's willingness to kill people on live television—even his own supporters when they begin to display desires for money or power he deems unseemly in promoting his cause—spreads that anxiety well beyond the law enforcement organizations trying to find him.

The deductions, logical reasoning, and strategizing several moves ahead in both Kira's and L's/Near's campaigns hold appeal for older readers and fans of detective fiction. Adolescent readers/viewers, however, seem to be attracted more by—and even sympathize with—Kira/Light's disaffection with the state of the world and his idealistic belief that he can make it a better world—and perhaps even by his narcissistic belief that he is the ideal ruler of that world. And filmmakers continue to capitalize on the appeal of the central conceit of the Death Note and the supernatural and existential horror elements with further sequels and remakes.

Notes

1. Actually, "Ryuzaki" is also a pseudonym. The detective calling himself Ryuzaki has kept his face and real name and even his existence secret until this case. Even Interpol has known him only as L, a voice on a computer monitor.
2. I will employ the westernized order for proper names (given name, family name) throughout rather than the Japanese (family name, given name) because all translations of the texts under consideration here use that format.
3. Ryuzaki is an odd choice as a commentator here because in the portion of the narrative this film covers he is dead.
4. Light's departed mother is also described as something of a hippie, presumably to explain his unusual given name. The filmmakers also make Ryuk (voiced by Willem Dafoe) more actively sinister and leave both Light and L alive at the end of the film, obviously anticipating sequels.
5. Human ownership of a Death Note does come with the attendance of the Shinigami who had previously owned it, but this is not a summoning as such and the Shinigami is not obligated to obey the human owner's wishes.
6. A seventh Death Note would not become operational until one of the other six had been destroyed or returned to its Shinigami; names written in it up to that point would not cause anyone to die.
7. As described in Joya, *Mock Joya's Things Japanese*, 469.
8. Confirmed by manga artist Obata in an interview appearing in *Death Note 13*, 185.
9. Medusa inspiration confirmed by Obata in a comment on character design appearing in Ohba and Obata, *Death Note*, *13*, 137.
10. Old Testament resonances also occur in ancillary artwork in the manga.
11. The rule written in English in the manga states that the human who owns a Death Note is "possessed" by the Shinigami who originally had it, but that highly charged term mischaracterizes the human/Shinigami relationship.
12. "Yagami" translates as "night god." So Light Yagami's name symbolically encompasses his original righteous, albeit misguided, intention to make the world a better place, the dark means to that end, and his desire to be the god of that reshaped world.
13. The live-action Japanese films show at least a couple of pages of rules, and in the American version Light complains about the number of pages of rules.
14. In an early experiment to see if the Death Note actually does what it claims, Light writes in several possible spellings of the name of a motorcycle thug who is terrorizing a young woman in the street and whose name he hears without knowing the exact spelling. By chance, his first attempt at rendering the thug's name happens to be correct, so there is no violation of the four-mistake rule because the incorrect spellings do not occur before the correct spelling.
15. The switching of ownership of the three Death Notes in the manga and the animated series, both of which played out in weekly installments, is even more byzantine than described here, so much so that the amount of dedication and/or memory needed to keep abreast of these complications must have been tremendous.

16. The animé series often represents this parallelism graphically with a split screen presenting Light and Ryuzaki and then Light and Near facing each other in mirrored poses.

BIBLIOGRAPHY

Joya, Mock. *Mock Joya's Things Japanese*, 2d ed. Tokyo: Tokyo News Service, 1960.
Ohba, Tsugumi, and Takeshi Obata. *Death Note, 13: How to Read.* San Francisco: Viz Media, 2008.

Grotesque Adaptations
Bodies of Knowledge in Maléfique (2002)

Cynthia J. Miller

Éric Valette's film *Maléfique* weaves a tale of four imprisoned bodies—inmates, incarcerated for an array of crimes, sharing a spartan cell—each seeking freedom. When a loose stone in the wall reveals the hiding place of a journal, penned in 1920 by a prisoner who used blood magic to escape, the four formulate their own plan to free themselves. On their first test, they utter an incantation from its pages, and the cell floor bursts into flames, leaving a mysterious symbol etched in glowing embers. With each new experiment, however, it becomes clear that the book has its own plan. The four soon discover the horrific truth in one of the journal's lines, "Art creates and destroys a multitude of universes," as its powers grant their individual wishes for freedom at a gruesome price.

Situated firmly in the body of films known as the New French Extremity, *Maléfique* draws on traditions of body horror and exploitation to craft a claustrophobic tale about the imprisonment of bodies and minds, and the illusion of freedom. The characters' experience of captivity is shared, and yet individual and isolating. The journal appears to be a vehicle for granting their simple wishes for release from incarceration, but the words "freedom," "release," "escape" carry layers of meaning. This essay will explore the film's commentary on the nature of imprisonment and the agonies of freedom as those notions evolve for each character when the journal, once discovered, refuses to be banished until their longings have been fulfilled.

The Encounter

The confines of a prison cell offer the only view we have of the inmates. Just as our vision is limited by the cell's aging stone walls and murky light of its small, rectangular window, our understanding of who these characters are is restricted as well—partial and inadequate—as fragments of their past lives and inner worlds are revealed. They begin as caricatures: Carrère (Gérald Laroche), an over-privileged businessman jailed for committing fraud; Marcus (Clovis Cornillac), a bullying transsexual who has taken the infantile and mentally ill Pâquerette (Dimitri Rataud) as his lover, and Lassalle (Phillipe

Laudenbach), a taciturn intellectual. But as their crimes and interrelationships are exposed, they gain depth, complexity, and broader significance.

At the film's opening, Marcus lovingly cuts off the first joint of one of Pâquerette's fingers, so that the young man might have a few days of "vacation" from their dismal cell. After Pâquerette is carried to the infirmary, Marcus tosses the fingertop out the window, darkly musing that the young man is escaping one piece at a time. Meanwhile, Carrère has just been admitted to the prison, and is saying his goodbyes to his wife and young son. The tension between the two adults is as palpable as the affection between the man and his son. Carrère promises that they will be reunited soon—in time for the boy's birthday—and in an act of loving naiveté, his son gives him his action-figure doll to help him escape.

But escape is the farthest thing from Carrère's mind as he enters the cell. Convinced that his wife will bail him out quickly, he observes his cellmates with an air of detachment. He sizes up his new surroundings with an air of superiority, and settles into an uneasy coexistence with characters who seem transported straight from an absurdist tale. Marcus is a study in contrasts, with bulging muscles and pendulous breasts; Pâquerette, like a modern-day Renfield, compulsively snatches roaches as they scuttle across the cell and stuffs them in his mouth; and Lassalle's silence seems to guard desperate secrets, even greater, perhaps, than his periodic violation by Marcus.

When his release fails to happen, Carrère finds himself drawn more deeply into the collective life of his cell, and into thoughts of escape, as well. Day after day, he stares at "freedom" on the other side of the cell's small barred window. The group's thoughts of

Cellmates long for freedom in *Maléfique* (2002). Bottom left: Pâquerette (Dimitri Rataud); top left: Marcus (Clovis Cornillac); center: Carrère (Gérald Laroche); and top right: Lassalle (Philipe Laudenbach).

escape become more focused, however, when their fantasies take material form. One night, Pâquerette urinates in his sleep and drenches Marcus as he sleeps in the bunk below. When Marcus awakens in the morning and finds himself wet and stinking, he lashes out at Pâquerette and hurls him into the wall, then notices a protruding stone near where the young man struck. He removes the stone and, although a first attempt leaves him screaming in disgust when he withdraws an arm covered in roaches, he reaches in a second time and pulls out a dusty, leather-bound journal. Carrère surveys its pages, which are covered with Latin and Greek lettering, along with symbols from some unknown language. Dated October 7, 1920, it was written by another convict, Charles Danvers (played in flashback by Geoffrey Carey),[1] who mysteriously disappeared from within his locked cell and was never seen again.

"Another teacher's lost his marbles," Marcus mutters, alluding to what he imagines was Lassalle's former career, and articulating a link between arcane knowledge and madness—an intimate relationship noted throughout history which, as Foucault argues, creates both fascination and anxiety: "On all sides, madness fascinates man. The fantastic images it generates are not fleeting appearances that quickly disappear from the surface of things. By a strange paradox, what is born from the strangest delirium was already hidden, like a secret, like an inaccessible truth, in the bowels of the earth. When man deploys the arbitrary nature of his madness, he confronts the dark necessity of the world...."[2] Such interconnections of madness and knowledge belie our fear of the unknown—and those who attempt to gain access to and control its nature—and have long provided impetus for unspeakable horrors, in films such as *Night of the Demon* (1957), *The Dunwich Horror* (1970), and *Hellraiser* (1987), as well as in numerous Lovecraft-inspired tales.

As Carrère—not the brightest, but the most confident of the group—deciphers Danvers' notes, he discovers that Danvers was a serial killer. Obsessed with youth, he began stealing human placentas to make a rejuvenating lotion, then—growing first impatient, and then desperate—began killing pregnant women, rather than waiting for them to give

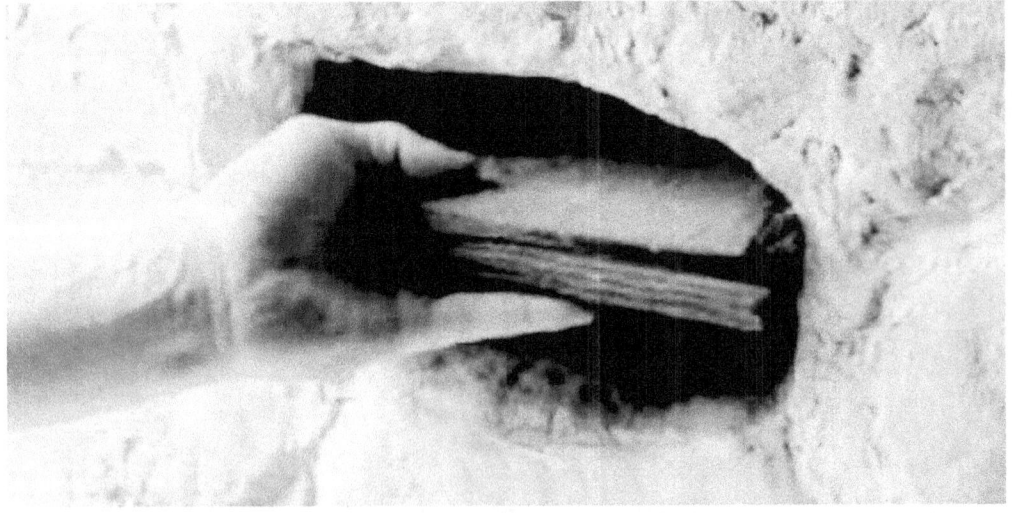

A loosened stone reveals the hiding place of Charles Danvers' (Geoffrey Carey) journal in *Maléfique* (2002).

birth. All the while, he related his obsessions in the journal: writing verses, sketching diagrams and symbols, attempting to conjure ancient magic that would keep him forever young. The cellmates are disbelieving and wary as Carrère relates what seem to be the chronicles of a madman, but the childlike Pâquerette is enthralled. He opens the book, unobserved, and copies symbols on the floor in Marcus's lipstick, then runs with the book to the small table where the others are eating, begging excitedly: "Read the magic! Read the magic!" Carrère indulges him, and chants a line from the book as the camera draws near to the page: "*imas qui sarat ez quier yuggoth.*"[3]

At this, the symbols on the floor burst into flames. Fearful, but fascinated, they resolve to test another verse. Carrère reads: "I placed the four points that mark the wind's direction and traced the lines that link them. Then I pronounced the spell and a wind came out from the stones." Carrère draws the symbols accompanying the text on the wall—a large P with an X through it—and reads "*Al Axif Veniversum Fhtagn.*" The symbol glows with fire and then explodes, hurling both men and furniture back across the room. Marcus demands that they stop, but Carrère counters, "Don't you want to know what we can do with it?… We didn't do it right—imagine if we could understand it." A compromise is reached: Carrère agrees not to open the book when Marcus and Pâquerette are present.

That night, however, Lassalle reads the volume by flashlight while the rest sleep: "Three times I have pronounced the spell I found tonight. the stones moved apart. *Thsathogga eimat.*" The book's true horrors begin to reveal themselves when Pâquerette twice repeats the words as he sleeps (making three times). As if in a trance, he then rises and walks to the outside wall of the cell, extending his hands. The first joints of each of his fingers disappear into the stone as blood streams down the wall and he quietly gasps in agony. He then returns to his bed and falls back to sleep. In the morning, the tops of all of his fingers are gone and the wounds are fully healed.

Confused panic ensues in the cell. Marcus beats Carrère, blaming him for Pâquerette's disfigurement, and then tenderly nurses the young man at his breast. They turn to the book anew, to undo the damage that has been done. When Lassalle suggests beginning at the end of the journal, Carrère finds new symbols and the line "My research has come to an end. Tonight, I will walk across the stones."

The three resolve to use Danvers' final incantation to make their escape, but fail, and a distraught Pâquerette begins to eat the book's pages in an act of mad retaliation. Almost immediately, he begins to levitate off the ground. As his cellmates watch in horror, limbs twist full circle, ribs splinter, and blood pours from his body, until his broken corpse falls to the floor. But when the grief-stricken Marcus attempts to toss the book out the window, Lassalle argues that the journal merely defended itself, and finally reveals his own interests: He is a devotee of Danvers, who was a revered practitioner of esotericism. He reveals that many have looked for the book that is now in their possession, some believing it was only rumored to exist. Lassalle confirms that Danvers escaped from the cell, using the book, but Marcus is unmoved. He rids the cell of its dark magic, pushing it through the bars of the window.

Before long, a new inmate arrives to claim the bunk above Marcus's—Picus (Didier Bénureau), a curious character wearing a bowtie and carrying a small home movie camera that he uses incessantly, documenting the inmates so that they, and what they cherish most, might be immortalized. His presence is not long in the cell, however. One night, while the others sleep, Picus vanishes. They awake to find only his camera, and the mysteriously-returned book in the middle of the cell floor. ("There's no use trying to get rid of it; it will always come back," Lassalle admonishes.) Watching the playback, they observe Picus reading from the book until a blinding light appeared in the wall. He walks to, and into, the light, never to be seen again…

Emboldened by this proof of the book's power, the three resolve to do the same. Lasalle recites Lovecraftian verses from the book, the light appears, and each walks through. The wall closes on an empty cell. The inmates do not, however, emerge to the freedom they were expecting. Like a cruel trick, they materialize, instead, in Danvers's original cell from 1920. The book has new pages now, with more drawings. "The book is guiding us," Lassalle proclaims, now enraptured by its mission, and slices his wrist with a shard of stone so that his blood fills in the book's diagrams. Admonishing that "the book doesn't want us to cheat," he slices Marcus's genitals and leaves him to die in a pool of blood. He turns to Carrère: "No one will escape. The book was never meant for that. All my life, books have asked me questions. This one possesses the answer. Answers to what? For you, I don't know; for me, to things I could never have learned in one lifetime." He explains further: "The book never helped anyone to escape. Danvers was a pervert, a killer. He used his knowledge of black magic to escape, but he made a mistake; his body was never found. Some believe the dark force didn't help him to escape, but they fulfilled his dearest dream, beyond his expectations…. It's my turn to fulfill my dearest dream." With this, Lassalle writhes in agony and becomes the book, ancient text and symbols carved into his flesh, their bloody knowledge covering his face and body.

Carrère is alone. He opens the book, hears his last conversation with his son, and begs the journal: "I just want to see my son. I just want to be able to look at him." The book emits a blinding light, he screams in agony as his body begins to transform, and the scene shifts.

The cellmates attempt to conjure with Danver's occult verses in *Maléfique* (2002).

The camera cuts back to the prison. Carrère's wife and son are collecting his few belongings, one of which is his son's doll. As they drive away, the child picks up the doll; the eyes looking back at him are not those of a plastic action figure, but of his father, looking out at his son.

The Extremes of Horror

Valette's film is among the first entries in the new wave of French horror of the 21st century. As Donato Totaro observes, *Maléfique*, along with films such as *Haute tension* (2003), *À L'intérieur* (2007), and *Frontière/s* (2007) marks "a viable, exciting rebirth in French horror film."[4] Interweaving elements of France's commercial film sector with its more esoteric, intellectual *art et essai*, or arthouse, cinema, the film draws on the popular supernatural and horror genres and merges them with arthouse themes and modes of representation. Valette's use of Dutch angles, single-point perspectives, and closed framing, combined with suffocating close-ups, and chiaroscuro lighting creates a claustrophobic atmosphere that balances on the edge of panic and disorientation throughout the film.

Yet it is *Maléfique*'s juxtaposition of intellectualism with the horrors of the body that shapes the film's identity and impact, as high culture collides with low, and cerebral pretensions are continually in tension with visceral nightmares. The camera watches with an unflinching eye, as imprisoned bodies endure agonies in their desperate quest for freedom: fingers and penises are severed, limbs are twisted and shattered; hands are thrust into gaping wounds and still-warm blood is smeared across stone walls, ghostly lips, and unyielding pages—all against a backdrop of reason and intellect stretched to the breaking point, as the cellmates struggle to unlock the journal's secrets. It watches defilement in the dark of night, as a sleeping Pâquerette slowly soaks his lover and protector in urine, and as Marcus, in turn, brutally sodomizes the cerebral Lassalle, who later claims that the act is never "rape," but choice—an exercise of liberty in the face of overwhelming force—the struggle of the mind to overcome the violation of the body.

Tim Palmer sees this "profaning of the sacred"[5] as characteristic of a larger trend in contemporary French cinema that blurs the boundaries of interpretation: "Mainstream pleasures permeate the rarified materials of the arthouse, as popular and intellectual paradigms interconnect, complete osmosis, on-screen."[6] In this case "mainstream pleasures" are those grotesque spectacles and voyeuristic thrills afforded by the horror genre, the terrors of the mind and the destruction of the body that have come to mark the genre's products. Scholars have long observed that horror allows its audiences to confront fears about their own mortality, and more recently, the study of "body horror" has drawn greater attention to individual's fears related to the integrity of their own highly vulnerable bodies—the "goop and innards which make up our physical being," as Matt Smith suggests.[7] Body horror films "promise to be sensational," and their displays of pain and pleasure are "on the edge of respectable."[8] These body-focused terrors are also cited as foundational elements of the New French Extremity, with its focus on the violation and disfigurement of the body. Its beginning credited to the late 1990s and its last gasps uttered between 2008 and 2012,[9] the New Extremity grew out of the instability of identity in rapidly changing times. James Quandt has decried the movement as "determined to break every taboo, to wade in rivers of viscera … to fill each frame with flesh … and subject it to all manner of penetration, mutilation, and defilement."[10] Grounded in the human condition, extremist films use cruel and sensational body imagery to craft commentary about reality versus ideals, perception versus fantasy. Following theatrical director and author Antonin Artaud's notion of the Theater of Cruelty, these films strip away the social veneer that masks humanity's true desires, and through "brutal humanity, experimental camera work … taboos and violence,"[11] force the subconscious into a confrontation with reality. Smith takes a somewhat more existential view, observing that "as the French seem intent to prove, it is not our corporeal existence that should be held sacred—[their] insistence on showing anything and everything is evidence of this. The body is meant to be examined, explicitly and externally, to deepen our understanding of our own humanity … and what we hope lies in wait for us at the other end of it all."[12]

This perspective offers an important lens for considering *Maléfique* as a visual essay on humanity. Using a language of violence, degradation, pain, and cruelty, Valette offers a glimpse of the human condition in its most desperate: four men who have been stripped of nearly everything, attempting to maintain their connection to the world outside the prison walls. Ultimately, the four have nothing to lose in their attempts to escape; they have hit rock bottom. We learn that Pâquerette's oral compulsions know no bounds; even driving him to eat his baby sister. When he dies, he leaves Marcus utterly alone and without purpose. Lassalle butchered his wife in a fit of insanity, and remains unrepentant. He tells Carrère of his brutal crime:

> I had to walk across my study to get to the kitchen—a circular vestibule covered with books. That morning, I stopped in the middle of the room. I had the impression that the books were looking at me…. Suddenly, the books began to throb; to pulsate, harder and harder. Words began to come out of the books. Hundreds, thousands of words, they were mocking me…. I didn't feel my hands tearing apart the covers. I didn't feel my arms dislocating the bookshelves, and I didn't feel my fingers ripping my wife's body. The shrink said it was two minutes of insanity. They were two minutes of lucidity.

And Carrère—not a violent criminal like the rest—becomes desperate enough to turn to the journal after receiving news that his wife has taken control of his business holdings (which he hid under her name) and is divorcing him. Once believing himself superior to the others, he is now one with them.

Valette forces viewers to observe these characters, to consider their lives, their motivations, and the lifeways and relationships they struggle to maintain; and then dares them to look away as each suffers the tortures of the damned—not because of their crimes, but because of their humanity.

Fathoming the Book

The nature of the human condition is the connective tissue that binds Valette's message—or more accurately, his question—to the film's graphic imagery. This is not a tale of crime and punishment, as it might seem, but a tale about the condition and limitations of human existence. Marcus, Pâquerette, Lassalle, and Carrère have all been incarcerated for crimes against society, and their punishment, at the hands of that society, now defines their existence. From the outset, these characters are shown as closely tethered to the harsh realities of their cell—grim, rough-hewn stone, dim lighting, poor food, and Spartan conditions. Upon discovering the journal, however, everything changes. Its presence signals a gradual shift in their collective understanding of their surroundings, and not only creates a thread between their historical moment and that of Danvers in the 1920s, but imports intangibles that had been stripped away by their circumstances: curiosity, hope, belief in forces larger than those found in the physical world, and introspection. Collectively, they all most desire freedom, yet the journal ultimately illustrates the gross limitations of their conceptions of that term.

Danvers, we learn, was an icon of esotericism, a collection of movements that has taken many forms over centuries, from Antiquity to the present day. Gnosticism, Christian theosophy, Kabbalah, Freemasonry, Thelema (founded by Aleister Crowley and followed, for a time, by L. Ron Hubbard, founder of Scientology), and contemporary occult groups, such as the Illuminates of Thanateros, are various manifestations of Western esotericism. The constellation of notions binding these esoteric movements together are both spiritual and intellectual, concerning themselves with the "universal spiritual dimension of reality"[13] Antoine Faivre, one of France's leading scholars on esotericism, articulated what he saw as fundamental characteristics of esoteric practice. Among these, we find webs of interrelationships: energy, or a "life force," that flows through and animates all things in the universe, joining them in interdependence; real and symbolic correspondences between those things—planets, animals, people—that affects behavior and wellbeing; the ability to evolve and transform to a higher level of being; and the power of imagination and mediations, "such as rituals, symbolic images, mandala, [and] intermediary spirits" to aid in that transformation and provide access to immaterial worlds.[14] As a result, esoteric beliefs are frequently framed as higher-order ancient spiritual knowledge—the domain of elite groups of individuals capable of fathoming esotericism's revealed wisdom. Danvers's journal provides a guide to just such mediations, with its occult rituals and supernatural symbols. Yet while the journal lays out the functional steps to achieve what appears to be the ends the cellmates desire, it does not provide the cellmates with the inner knowledge to comprehend the depth or complexity—the web of interrelationships—that inhere in the path they choose.

That path, we find, was opaque by design, intended to re-mystify the lives of those who travel it. Esotericism's followers often position themselves in opposition to positivist science, and the "dis-enchanting" of the world that the scientific revolution and its notions of causality have brought about.[15] Austrian philosopher Rudolf Steiner posits, "Now, it is possible for human beings to deceive themselves. We can succumb to the belief that there is no hidden element, that what appears to our senses and our intellect includes everything that can possibly exist. This deception, however, is only possible on the surface of consciousness, not its depths.... In one way or another [we] will always long for something hidden."[16] For Steiner, our understanding of the world around us is half-truth, rather than full truth, because it rests on what may be observed on the surface.[17] Human beings exist in three realms, or states of consciousness, in Steiner's view: body, soul, and spirit.[18] One must "awaken" from the physical realm (in much the same way that South Asian religions such as Hinduism consider earthly life to be *Māyā*, or illusion) in order to comprehend other realms of existence. Thus pain, disfigurement, violation, and even death are of little consequence, as the physical body and its instinctual realities are, in esotericism, the lowest manifestation of the human condition. The convict Lassalle comes to understand this by the time the group enacts the final ritual found in Danvers's journal. He has spent his life in the pursuit of knowledge, and in the journal he finds the universe open to him. His madness is that he follows the journal's mediations to his own ends, unable to turn away from his ultimate desire to possess all knowledge. "The book is a mirror of our vanity," he tells Carrère, and lets it overtake him.

Esotericism does not, then, represent a set of understandings and practices generally accessed by a group of brutal or scheming convicts, whose actions and desires have mired them in the lowest forms of the physical world. Yet, the discovery of Danvers's journal has literally laid his specialist knowledge at their feet. Its display of Greek, Latin, and other unknown texts and symbols signify that it, like so many other occult texts found written in books or on parchments, or carved into boxes or bodies, contains mysteries intended for an elite, erudite reader. Only the educated Lassalle has an inkling of what is in their possession, yet even his speculation is limited. The true horror of *Maléfique* begins, then, not with the deprivations of incarceration, but with the ill-informed striving for something more. In their attempts to translate and use the journal to escape, as they believe Danvers did, the cellmates venture into a world with which they have no experience, and which, in truth, they cannot fathom.

The Tortures of Freedom

"I call a thing *free* which exists and acts from the pure necessity of its nature...."[19]

Desire is a complicated thing. It is all too common to want what one cannot or should not have. It is also common to not fully understand the nature of what one wants, until, as with Valette's cellmates, it's too late. As different as they are, the one thing on which they all agree is that they desire freedom. Each day, they gaze, expressionless, out the cell's window, fixating on the liberty represented by the horizon on the other side. But their understanding of freedom, as the film's invocation of esotericism reveals, is confined to the physical world that they can see and experience. When they read Danvers's notes, they glean that he has used the occult knowledge written there to attain his own freedom, but they don't know the entire story.

The esoteric rituals he employed gave Danvers his freedom, but not from his prison cell. Freedom, for Charles Danvers, was freedom from succumbing to the ravages of aging. The fear of it drove him to madness, murder, and incarceration. His pursuit of freedom from aging drove him to experiment with occult mediations, which led to his disappearance and alleged escape. Danvers, however, did not escape in the conventional sense; rather, his "freedom" came as a form of devolution. As Lassalle finally reveals Danvers's true fate to Carrère, we watch, in flashback, as he grows younger—from adult, to young man, to child, to infant, to embryo—and finally disappears. His freedom was granted, in a way that he was too tethered to the physical world to ever anticipate.

As Steiner points out in his *Philosophy of Freedom*, esoteric freedom can never be freedom from an external physical state—a freedom granted or enacted from *outside* the individual—but rather, it is an inner (existential) conquest of external restraints.[20] Thus, we see for our inmates, freedom takes its own form, grotesque when considered in finite physical terms, perfectly logical in infinite, esoteric terms—and exquisitely rendered through the film's conventions of extremity. Pâquerette unknowingly began the cycle of freedom. Rather than finding liberty one finger joint at a time, the walls of his cell freed them all at once. His lover Marcus, longs to be freed of his gender status as a male, yet is still burdened by his penis. When Carrère asks what he will do once they escape, Marcus (who works out daily in their cell) replies, "I don't know. Maybe I'll get rid of the thing I don't want to work out." The journal's mediations grant Marcus his freedom, as well, when Lassalle severs his penis with a shard of stone. Marcus dies, no longer a man. In his turn, Lassalle is freed from his intellectual limitations and literally *becomes* the knowledge of the book, a vessel of bloody runes and symbols; and finally, Carrère is left alone.

When filmed by the mysterious Picus, who it is later revealed is merely a manifestation of Danvers's journal, Carrère confides that his son is thing he cherishes most. His one fervent desire is to be free to see him again. Picus comforts him with a promise: "No one will ever take him away from you." Now, in the film's final moments, Carrère echoes those sentiments. He opens the book, and hears his last conversation with is son; an illuminated image of the boy's eye covers the pages. He begs the forces residing within the book: "I just want to see my son. I just want to be able to look at him…." With this, the book emits a blinding light. Carrère screams in agony—his eyes are covered by skin, his body taut—and the cell goes dark.

When next we "see" Carrère, he is, indeed, free and able to see his son. But the eyes of the child's toy that he has become reveal not gratification, but confusion and panic. The journal has kept its promise, again in a way that could not have been foreseen by convention-bound thinking. The film thus ends with a touch of body horror that differs from the rest—not grotesque, but uncanny—reminiscent of Rodrigo Blass's short film *Alma* (2009), in which the character's "soul" is trapped inside the body of a doll, a material condition out of their control.

In each of these "escapes" from imprisonment, the inmates have achieved Faivre's element of transmutation, but through his use of graphic and disturbing body imagery, filmmaker Valette has posed questions about whether such physical and spiritual transformations are liberating or whether, when brought about through only partial understanding, they represent violation of body, soul, and spirit. At its most obvious, *Maléfique* serves as a cautionary tale about desire (as does the adage "Be careful what you wish for"), but by invoking esotericism as a driving force in the film's action, Valette asks us to consider this issue much more deeply, probing at the true existential meaning of freedom, and its inverse, imprisonment. Cell walls are a trivial form of confinement when compared to a life trapped in a body of the wrong gender, a mind straining against the limits of what it can comprehend, or eyes prevented from seeing the one thing that makes existence meaningful. We are all, perhaps, imprisoned by our own physicality—our earthbound existence—and by our failure to comprehend the vastness of the universe that operates around, through, before, and after us. As Martine Beugnet posits, "The ambiguity of horror is that it lodges itself between two planes, that of pure sensation and that of discourse, maintaining the link between the two through the variations in rhythm and visual regimes that it effects, 'thinking' its way through binary oppositions, disrupting them, reconnecting the disconnected."[21] By adapting the tenets that drive Western Esotericism, along with the techniques of the New French Extremity, Valette juxtaposes existential questions on the human condition with bloody destruction of the physical body, causing a collision of high culture and low. He confronts viewers with multiple layers of imprisonment—physical, social, intellectual, and emotional—and resolves them in torturous release, leaving viewers shuddering at the cost of freedom.

Notes

1. While all available materials cite the character as "Danvers," the character's name more closely resembles "D'enfer" as one listens to the dialogue. That name, of course, translates into English as "of Hell."
2. Foucault, *Madness and Civilization*, 23.

3. One of several Lovecraftian influences in the film. Conceptually, we may draw connections, as well, with the Lovecraftian theme of unfathomable, forbidden knowledge that leads to the seeker's destruction.
4. Totaro, "*A L'intérieur*."
5. Palmer, *Brutal Intimacy*, 97.
6. *Ibid.*
7. Smith, "Confronting Mortality."
8. Williams, "Film Bodies," 727.
9. As Alexandra West notes, these dates are moving targets. Elements of the movement were visible decades earlier, and while it ended in France in 2008, French filmmakers of the New Extremity continued to make films in the United States until 2012 (Khalfoun's *Maniac* being cited as the film that ended the movement in North America). The movement has continued in Europe to the present day.
10. Quandt, "Flesh and Blood," 18.
11. West, *Films of the New French Extremity*, 10.
12. *Ibid.*
13. Hannegraaff, *Western Esotericism*, 10–12.
14. Faivre, *Access to Western Esotericism*, 12.
15. *Ibid.*, 5.
16. Steiner, *An Outline of Esoteric Science*, 24–25.
17. *Ibid.*, 25–26.
18. Referring here to Steiner's work in both Theosophy and Esotericism.
19. Benedict de Spinoza, quoted in Steiner, *Philosophy of Freedom*, 12. Italics in original.
20. Steiner, *Philosophy of Freedom*, xvi.
21. Beugnet, *Cinema and Sensation*, 47.

BIBLIOGRAPHY

Beugnet, Martine. *Cinema and Sensation*. Edinburgh: Edinburgh University Press, 2011.
Faivre, Antoine. *Access to Western Esotericism*. New York: State University of New York Press, 1994.
Foucault, Michel. *Madness and Civilization: A History of Insanity in the Age of Reason*. New York: Vintage, 1988.
Hannegraaff, Wouter J. *Western Esoterism: A Guide for the Perplexed*. New York: Bloomsbury Academic, 2013.
Palmer, Tim. *Brutal Intimacy: Analyzing Contemporary French Cinema*. Middletown, CT: Wesleyan University Press, 2011.
Quandt, James. "Flesh and Blood: Sex and Violence in Recent French Cinema." *The New Extremism in Cinema from France to Europe*, edited by Tanya Horeck and Tina Kendall, 18–25. Edinburgh: Edinburgh University Press, 2013.
Smith, Matt. "Confronting Mortality: The New French Extremity, Part 2." *The SplitScreen*. https://thesplitscreen.wordpress.com/2011/06/28/confronting-mortality-the-new-french-extremity-the-hostel-series-and-outdated-terminology-part-2-of-3/.
Steiner, Rudolf. *An Outline of Esoteric Science*. 1910. New York: Anthroposophic Press, 1997.
_____. *The Philosophy of Freedom: The Basis for a Modern World Conception*. 1894. East Sussex, UK: Rudolf Steiner Press, 2011.
_____. *Theosophy: An Introduction to the Spiritual Processes in the Human Life and in the Cosmos*. 1904. New York: Anthroposophic Press, 1994.
Totaro, Donato. "*A L'intérieur*: A Rebirth of French Horror. http://www.offscreen.com/biblio/pages/esssays/french_horror/.
West, Alexandra. *Films of the New French Extremity: Visceral Horror and National Identity*. Jefferson, NC: McFarland, 2016.
Williams, Linda. "Film Bodies: Gender, Genre, and Excess." In *Film Theory and Criticism*, 7th ed., edited by Leo Braudy and Marshall Cohen, 727–41. Oxford: Oxford University Press, 2009.

The Appeared (2007) by Paco Cabezas
Redefining the Book of Hidden Memories and Cyclical Time

GRACIELA TISSERA

Films about historical events have always occupied a prominent place in the film industry, and continue to mesmerize audiences with their juxtaposition of two different visions of the same reality: naked facts and fictional interpretations of them. Sometimes the perception of horrific acts crosses the line into the fantastic, and such is the case in the film *The Appeared*, directed by Paco Cabezas.[1] The film tells the story of two siblings who, while traveling together in Argentina, discover a sinister notebook that details crimes committed by the author 20 years ago. Following the history of the book, the siblings slowly uncover the dark secrets of families who suffered the horror of a repressive military regime, and witness how one family in particular was persecuted, tortured, and killed. Their journey becomes a nightmare in which it is not clear if the events are real or manifestations of supernatural forces, as the past begins to fade into the present, and the present moves into the past. Argentinean history is plagued with revolutions and unresolved conflicts. Of these, the "Dirty War" (1976–1983) left the most significant trail of unanswered questions, and generated the fiercest determinations on the part of victims to find closure, and an end to their pain and suffering—a task still ongoing for many.[2] In his film, Paco Cabezas looks back at the history of Argentina through the eyes of both victims and oppressors, creating an intersection where historical memory[3] and fantastic elements collide.

The Appeared is not simply a horror film designed to remind both forgetful and new generations about the lingering consequences of the war. Cabezas goes beyond merging objective facts with ghostly apparitions, instead exploring the underlying roots of fear through the metaphysics of time and space, the possibility of parallel universes, and the secret power of books. Belief in the occult is deeply rooted in Latin American culture due to religious syncretism[4] (the blending of beliefs from conquerors and indigenous groups), which makes Cabezas' perspective both commercially attractive and artistically thought-provoking. The idea of a book as a portal to labyrinthine levels of consciousness and hidden memories underscores the idea that the supernatural is an inextricable part of the human condition.

The Book as a Passage to Knowledge

In *The Appeared*, Cabezas sets out to recover a conflicted past through the testimony of lost souls condemned to repeat their deaths in an endless loop of time. The trigger that unleashes the events is a book—the film calls it a "diary"—that has recorded in detail the actions of a character called "The Doctor." This diabolical figure (Pablo Cedrón), whose real name is Gabriel De Luca, participated in illegal activities ranging from kidnapping to the torture and murder of families considered subversives by the government during the Dirty War, a brutal campaign waged by Argentine government security forces against suspected dissidents and radicals. As the film begins, a frantic woman named Malena (Ruth Díaz) takes her wounded brother Pablo (Javier Pereira) to the hospital and is terrorized by an unknown threatening presence. The story then drops back in time, recounting the events that led to the first scene, returning at the end of the film to that conflict and its resolution. When the main story begins, De Luca is in a coma and Malena and Pablo, his children, travel to Argentina to visit him and take care of his affairs. De Luca is in a hospital in Buenos Aires and his condition is explained by doctor Lehrmann (Héctor Bidonde) who is also an old friend: "We did the medical internship together at the hospital in Tierra del Fuego. I remember the day when he came here. He had known about the tumor for a month and had not said a word to anybody. He drove 1,800 miles by car, a seventy-two-year-old man with a brain tumor."

The siblings spent the first years of their lives in Argentina, until their parents separated and their mother took them to live in Spain. Pablo is hesitant to make the decision to disconnect De Luca from life support because, after years apart, he yearns for the opportunity to get to know his father and share some moments with him. Pablo knows that if Malena could make the decisions, she would disconnect the life support machine herself to let their father die, but he refuses to give his consent until Malena helps him to find out more about their family history. Malena did not have a good relationship with her father and always regretted the lack of attention she experienced as a child; when she asked him what she did wrong, he replied: "What you did wrong was not being born a boy." Pablo takes the car that his father used to drive to the hospital in Buenos Aires—which "smells of dad"—and convinces Malena to visit the house in Tierra del Fuego, where they lived as children. Unaware of their father's violent past, the siblings embark on the 3,000-kilometer trip, which becomes a journey of self-discovery with an expected turn and unforeseen outcome.

Gabriel De Luca kept his diary hidden in his car, the same vehicle that Malena and Pablo use on their journey. During their trip, in a remote and isolated area of the countryside, they discover the diary through an encounter between Pablo and a mysterious little girl (Isabella Ritto)—a seemingly chance event that is, in fact, the beginning of a supernatural experience without end. The presence of the girl foreshadows their interconnection with the past. In fact, the girl indicates the location of the diary in the car and disappears, leaving Pablo to investigate the book and become intrigued by its content. The diary includes notes, maps, newspaper clippings and photographs. One of the photographs is of the scene of a now-forgotten twenty-year-old crime: Room 206 of the Hotel Altantida.[5] The hotel is on the route to the south and Pablo wants to spend the night in that room, but they stay in Room 207 instead. Following the information in the diary, Pablo sums up to Malena an account of what happened in the room next door on June 23, 1980: "At 3AM a man breaks in. He has an iron bar and a cattle prod. The first to wake up is the mother. The man hits her with the bar, the girl starts crying. The father gets up to fight but the man stuns him with the cattle prod."

It quickly becomes apparent that the diary contains De Luca's minute-by-minute account of his crime. Pablo now reads from the diary to make sure to understand the scientific explanations provided by De Luca: "3:27 AM. Shocks should always be applied to the nerve centers. In this case the victim receives a strong discharge to the neck which produces a double effect: the trachea contracts, impeding oxygen intake and the vertebral column is numbed. I hold his head under the water and feel the veins in his neck bursting. Incredible how stubborn the human body can be when it comes to survival." Pablo, as he reads from the diary, is unaware that the people in Room 206 were his biological parents. The woman (Leonora Balcarce) was pregnant at the time and De Luca took the baby to raise him as his own, since he always wanted a son, as he constantly reminded his daughter Malena. Paco Cabezas makes the audience aware, however, and turns this link into one of the focal points in the film, with Pablo representing the children who, under the military regime in Argentina, were taken from political prisoners and illegally adopted.

As Pablo reads passages from the book describing the events in Room 206, a portal is created, allowing him and Malena to witness the events first-hand. At 3:29 a.m., the noises and screams in Room 206 alert Pablo, who suspects that the crime committed against the members of the family are happening again to them. The same events are taking place in the same order in time and at the same place. The photographs in the diary also corroborate that the same family is being tortured. Malena and Pablo can see someone kidnap them as Pablo reads from the book: "The child and the woman got away. I haven't even had time to regret my clumsiness. They just appeared on the road. They come to me like Isaac came to Abraham to be sacrificed." While the man (Luciano

Pablo (Javier Pereira) tries to understand the sequence of events as described in the diary with notes and pictures in *The Appeared* (2007).

Cáceres) died at the hotel, the woman and the girl managed to escape only to be captured on the road and placed on a pickup truck. Following them, Malena and Pablo arrive at an abandoned factory where they find the body of the man and the woman asking for help. They are unable to help because someone else is at the site blinding them with a strong flashlight and dragging the woman outside. They realize that they are confronting a power that threatens their lives, and run away to contact the police. According to the diary, De Luca killed the man, buried his body at the factory, and continued his trip to the south with the abducted woman and girl.

Pablo's initial hesitation when he encounters the diary soon transforms into a crusade to change the fate of the victims. The psychological contrast of characters is clear: Pablo wants to investigate the fate of the family but Malena wants to get rid of the book. Malena is more hesitant to accept the fantastic as a part of her life, and convincing her to do so will involve a long debate tainted by fear. Her objective and practical nature prompts her to disregard any strange events as everyday evils in disguise. She is unable to see the presence of the supernatural in the book, but focuses instead on the influence of her father and the actions that follow the accounts in the diary. Her attitude will change during the next series of events when she and Pablo find the pickup truck in a nearby town and rescue the girl. This action will unleash the fury of "The Doctor" who will pursue them, eventually using his truck to force them off the highway.

De Luca, though on life-support in a hospital room in Buenos Aires, also functions as a virtual character in the story. At first, he is present in the film only at the hospital and then through the reports of his misdeeds in the diary, but the book stimulates his

Pablo (Javier Pereira) and Malena (Ruth Díaz) are the only witnesses of the supernatural representation of the murder of the girl in *The Appeared* (2007).

brain activity, allowing him to manipulate events even though he is in a comatose state. He is reenacting the past, causing an intersection of the two times, and thus modifying the present. As a figure out of the past, he appears now to Pablo and Malena as a young man who can be perceived only when his image is reflected in mirrors or polished surfaces. As Pablo continues reviewing the notes in the book, he notices photographs showing the girl already dead from several injuries. Cabezas creates tension to prepare the audience for the violent scenes to come. In a remote town, Malena, Pablo, and the girl seek out a restaurant to use the phone and call for help. Exactly at 12:25 p.m., as indicated in the diary, the presence of De Luca is visible in the mirrors. He stabs the girl and her body levitates, covered in blood. No one at the restaurant can see the crime except for Malena and Pablo. The presence of the supernatural is announced through flickering lights and reflections of De Luca holding a knife. The siblings struggle to separate reality from false manifestations of their senses as they attempt to comprehend what they are seeing. Malena's first thought is to escape the nightmare, while Pablo searches for a connection between the real events documented in a newspaper and the supernatural events they are witnessing, believing that his intervention can alter the past. While his car is repaired, Pablo reviews the printed information he found in a collection of old newspapers in a thrift store from Rawson, Chubut: "Possible remains of Manuel Leonardi found. His wife Amalia and his daughter Andrea have been missing since 1980." The identity of the victims is thus revealed and Pablo recognizes the family he encountered at the hotel through the photos included with the material about their case. Another old photograph in one of the newspapers is labeled: "Detail of the necklace found near the body." It was the same necklace—a cross—that Malena lost at the factory where the body of Manuel Leonardi was buried by De Luca. Pablo can conjecture that if an action in the present left a trace in the past corroborated by physical evidence, then it is possible to alter the chain of events as it seems that past and present are intertwined at a level at which the same events are taking place again with significant modifications.

When the photographs in the book begin to change, Pablo finds another reason to concentrate on the idea that the events he is witnessing are cyclical, and that the repetitions could produce other outcomes. Another photograph showing Malena being tortured at an undisclosed place also prompts Pablo to return to the hotel where the transgression started to save the lives of the Leonardi family and thus change the future. He returns alone, since Malena continues to Tierra del Fuego, to her father's house. His actions, however, prove futile. The details of the gruesome crime may have changed, but the consequences remain the same: Manuel Leonardi dies and his wife and daughter are listed as missing. As Pablo is devastated by his failure, he concludes that he does not want to see them die again.

The film includes, at this point, specific information about the victims to give a context to the story and make a connection to the Dirty War in Argentina. Pablo and Malena receive the information, after they separate, through different sources documented in local and national newspapers: Pablo calls a reporter in Buenos Aires and Malena, at her father's home, discovers a rented storage unit belonging to him. It becomes clear that the Leonardi family was running away and were considered "disappeared." The bodies of the woman and the girl were never found, she realizes, and their possible deaths were related to an unknown doctor who worked for the military regime. Malena also confronts her suspicions about her father and his cruelty when the administrator of the storage unit, Amanda (Graciela Tenembaum), tells her details about the Dirty War and her husband's ordeal during his arrest and subsequent torture: "The 'Triple A' kidnapped him (the Argentine Anticommunist Alliance).[6] They said he was a subversive. After torture, his body was mangled. There were military doctors who measured the amount of pain a human being could take without the heart stopping." Paco Cabezas thus provides a general explanation about the kidnappings and torture that took place in the civil war and highlights the participation of De Luca in the events and his complicity, as a doctor, in the disappearance and torture of citizens considered subversive by the regime. The information also functions, within the film, to prepare Malena for the disappearance of her brother. While reviewing her father's documents in the storage space, she is informed that the police found her brother's car abandoned in the woods near Tolhuin (a town in the province of Tierra del Fuego) and she needs to report his disappearance. Nobody but Malena can see blood in the car and when the officer gives her an old photograph—found at the scene—of her family at the house in the south (the same photograph that Pablo kept as a souvenir), she considers it as a clue she can use to find Pablo, assuming that her father kidnapped him. Her childhood house becomes her next destination, and she plans to drive there in the wrecked car.

The house is in an isolated part of Tierra del Fuego, and looks deserted. Soon after arriving, Malena perceives the spectral presence of his father. To avoid his fury, she explains to him that she is his daughter, but De Luca is living in a fragment of time back in the past. He says: "My daughter Malena is six years old and she is at home with my wife. You are just a subversive." Malena's confrontation with De Luca enables him to explain how he sees himself: as a patriot, fighting to protect his country's values against the threat of communism: "We are here to educate you people, so you won't stray again. What you have to understand is that the church and the state are the parents of the motherland. That requires a sense of responsibility and deserves respect. You people don't respect anything so we have to take a hard line." In this way, filmmaker Cabezas presents both sides of the conflict with a strong implicit message about the abuse of power and the extermination of citizens by their own government. By showing victims and repressors reenacting the conflictive past the film immerses the audience in the history of Argentina, and advocates for the right of new generations to fight for just causes as a tribute to the victims of the past. Malena embodies this fight through a change from her previous uncommitted attitude to a newfound determination. Positioned at the intersection of different moments in time, Malena witnesses two parallel scenarios: Pablo unconscious next to her and the moment of his birth. She watches as De Luca performs a cesarean section and kills Amalia Leonardi, who was held captive with her daughter in the basement. This vision reveals the resting place of these disappeared victims, as well as Pablo's legitimate genealogy. In her amazement, Malena is forced to acknowledge the paranormal potential of the book. She is eventually able to escape and rescue Pablo who is being treated at the hospital where De Luca is in a coma. Pablo's condition takes a turn for the worse and Malena identifies the same occurrences that signal the presence of her father: his reflections in the mirrors and the fluctuation of intensity in the lights. Realizing that the supernatural presence of her father depends on the connection between the book and his brain activity—which started and increased during her trip to the south with Pablo—Malena disconnects her comatose father from life support, ending his life and his attacks. The book remains active, however, and the final scene shows the spirits of other victims surrounding Malena and Pablo in the streets of Buenos Aires.

Labyrinths of Space and Time

The action of the film takes place in Argentina and, within this space, combines two different and interconnected periods of time, creating a double separation of space and time for the characters. They can recognize the places, yet simultaneously doubt this recognition. Malena and Pablo are exploring a territory unknown to them, trying to recover their roots, and this literal purpose transforms itself into a supernatural experience. They bring the past to the present, through the influence of the book, only to feel a sudden terror between the familiar and the extraordinary. The depiction of characters in the film intends to explore the process of deliberation and decision making in relation to the fantastic elements. Todorov has defined the fantastic as "that hesitation experienced by a person confronting a supernatural event" establishing certain parameters to judge the uncanny and marvelous.[7] Filmmaker Cabezas crosses the limits in the film when he plays with the idea of destiny, cyclic repetition, and parallel universes.

Pablo is overwhelmed by being forced to witness, again and again, the final demise of De Luca's victims, and he seeks to separate himself from the unbearable pain. His conception that the time could be cyclical parallels philosophical theories. Friedrich Nietzsche[8] postulated the idea of "eternal recurrence," indicating that events will recur again in time: "And in every one of these cycles of human life there will be one hour where, for the first time one man, and then many, will perceive the mighty thought of the eternal recurrence of all things." The eternal return could be a mental nightmare, since for Nietzsche time is infinite and the atoms that form the universe have the quality of being limited. Pablo is confronted with this nightmare and he does not have the tools to stop the repetitions since he is not fully aware of the power of the book. The film seems to favor the infinite series of events in different combinations with the same outcome. When Pablo finds Malena's photograph in the book, he understands that he needs to save her from a future event that already occurred in the past. He will soon note that everything is tied to the same fatal resolution. That brings to the equation the concept of human fate, impossible to alter unless the links to the source of violence in the film are broken in order to discontinue the intrusion of the past in the characters' lives. Cyclical time and *fatum* have a long-lasting presence in the film as a reminder of the concealed episodes of Argentina's history.

With the insertion of the concept of inexorable fate into the story, Pablo is not simply playing an intellectual game, but rather becoming subject to the power of the book. Pablo believes that he is following a logical plan that it is resolved through clues that could be considered illogical or absurd, thereby creating a rupture in his mind. The creation of this character is also a challenge for the audience, hence the portrayal of a distant person coming from Europe without knowledge of the Dirty War in Argentina, someone who lives outside his realm and has different habits so that imagination flows more freely. Pablo embodies the characteristics of a pure thinker with something of the adventurer in him, but he has problems reconsidering all the possible paths of the process because the book has set down the coordinates of the sequence of events in order to control everything and everybody. Thus, the destruction and rebirth of characters in the film is prompted by the book creating a conflict over personal identity. Pablo ignores his true identity. He believes that De Luca is his real father. The book creates the means for him to meet his biological parents—Manuel Leonardi, writer and journalist, and his wife Amalia. While searching for details about the Leonardi family he is in a sense uncovering his own past but he will remain ignorant of his origins, a truth that Malena intends to reveal to him but cannot. Since Pablo does not discover his relationship with the Leonardi family, his compassion for the victims becomes a metaphor for a set of spiritual values that sees all individuals as equally deserving of such compassion. The director thus proposes the convergence of identities, and frames Pablo's search as a national search in Argentina, where the members of the organization Mothers of Plaza de Mayo are still working to find the victims' children and unite them with their families.[9]

Paco Cabezas confronts the audience with a forced involvement in the film, creating anticipation and doubt. The game of logic and magic lies in this anticipation. Intelligence and imagination are intertwined, dissolving the boundaries between reality and unreality. Following Pablo's desperate communication with the victims, the film encourages constant participation from the audience to analyze Pablo's gradual development from a simple to a more complex personality, and transformation from a mere analyst of the situation into an actor participating in it. He is attracted to the book, and becomes the axis of the story (he has been all along, but does not initially recognize it). Once under the book's power, he remains there—closing the circle of logic and opening a door to the unknown. The mere presence of a book that tells past tragic stories evolves into an enactment of those same tragedies. At the beginning of the film, Pablo holds to the common assumption that the present is the only "real" concept connected with time, but as the film unfolds, he is immersed in the book and in a more profound consideration of time as a relative perception at conscious and unconscious levels. He can analyze his situation with a degree of controlled observation but below the level of conscious thought, he has a pronounced influence on behavior from the material contained in the book. When he sees the photographs changing and new ones replacing the old ones, he follows his impulses to overturn the past. But he cannot comprehend the ramifications originating from the book. Like a series of analogies, the book reproduces and creates patterns of interaction influencing his conduct and emotions.

The characters' encounters with the supernatural in the film can be seen as an example of parallel universes—an idea, emerging from one interpretation of quantum mechanics—that is sometimes explained using the paradox of Schrödinger's Cat[10]: "A cat, a flask of poison, and a radioactive source are placed in a sealed box. If an internal monitor detects radioactivity, the flask is shattered, releasing the poison, which kills the cat. The Copenhagen interpretation of quantum mechanics implies that after a while, the cat is simultaneously alive and dead." In the film, the Leonardi family is interacting with Pablo and Malena, discussing their situation and asking for help. At the same time, in another version of time, they are dead. The book reveals both instances through the reports and photographs. The projection in images is presented in repeated sequences that show the torture, the killings, and the disposal of the bodies, then start again with the family at the hotel confronting the aggressor. The director presents the sequence to emphasize the circle in which the characters are trapped, but also includes the photographs of the dead bodies and the victims still alive. This combination of techniques creates the impression that they are dead and alive at the same time. Pablo corroborates this idea when he tells Malena: "Do you know what really doesn't make sense? Trying to save a dead person's life." The most striking example of the paradox is the presence of the little girl throughout the film dying in a violent manner and also alive begging Pablo for his protection. The girl—Pablo's biological sister, Andrea—also appears at the end of the film, trying to communicate with Pablo amidst the representations of other victims in the city as tortured figures that only Pablo and Malena can see.

Paco Cabezas has imagined a fantastic power irradiating from the book. Diaries are a common source to document personal or historical experiences, but, more than that, Paco Cabezas has utilized this kind of document to rescue the historical memory of Argentina during a period of state terrorism in which military forces and death squads hunted down and killed political dissidents, and anyone believed to be associated with socialism. Cabezas thus humanizes his film and provides the victims a voice with which to recount a time of senseless crimes. Making the book the vortex of the story allows him to create characters as symbols of the past and of new generations leading interconnected lives. The open-ended nature of *The Appeared* matches the lack of resolution felt by those whose relatives disappeared during the war, who are still requesting a full investigation from the Argentinian government. The film presents memory, reason, and willpower as the highest faculties of the human spirit, and positions them as decisive in resolving the plot. Pablo is only a piece in the intricate chain of events. Guided by the power of the book, he traverses the corridors of the victims' memory, and becomes lost in the alternate avenues of his own identity, his love for the man he believes to be his father, and his experiences with physical and psychological torment. He lacks the ability to fully discover the secret meaning of the book, which leads him to consider the absence of such meaning. The incessant quest for knowledge is his only hope.

Conclusion: Worlds Collide

Paco Cabezas' horror film uses innovative techniques to show the collision between secret worlds. It reverses time in order to immerse characters in a past of violence and repression. Phantasmagorical figures reenact their demise, bringing the living characters into a confrontation with real terror that, far from ending in the past, continues to project itself into the present.[11] Since the families of many "disappeared" victims are still looking for answers, the film proposes to recover this particular historical moment of Argentina's Dirty War in different ways. The characters in the film are condemned to relive the distant past and to find the truth through the representation of extreme experiences in virtual and fantastic realities. The supernatural book is not only a connection to the events represented in the film but also a document carrying magical elements able to bring to life the traumatic past experiences of a family that, just like many during the civil war, was deprived of human rights. Beyond historical facts, the book is a symbol of the enduring nature of memory transcending time and space.

NOTES

1. Paco Cabezas (Spain, 1976) is a Spanish film director and screenwriter. In 2007, Cabezas wrote and directed Spanish language horror film *The Appeared*; following that, in 2008, he wrote the screenplay for the Spanish horror comedy film *Sexykiller*. He also directed action-crime film *Rage* (2014) starring Nicolas Cage and an action-comedy romance film *Mr. Right* (2015) starring Sam Rockwell and Anna Kendrick.

2. The National Reorganization Process was the name used by its leaders for the military dictatorship that ruled Argentina from 1976 to 1983. Many cases of forced disappearance were never reported and infants were generally illegally adopted by military or political families affiliated with the administration.

3. Pierre Nora (French historian) argues that memory becomes a subject of study especially when great changes take place in society and rupture the existent flow of events. The rupture with the past leads to a self-conscious quest of memory.

4. This happens quite commonly when a culture is conquered, and the conquerors bring their religious beliefs with them, but do not succeed in entirely eradicating the old beliefs or, especially, practices.

5. The hotel is located in Rawson, capital city of the province of Chubut in Argentina, 700 miles from Buenos Aires.

6. The Argentine Anticommunist Alliance was a far-right death squad founded in Argentina in 1973 and acted against a wide range of government opponents, not just communists.

7. Tzvetan Todorov (1939–2017) was a Bulgarian-French historian and philosopher. He defines the fantastic as being any event that happens in our world that seems to be supernatural. Upon the occurrence of the event, we must decide if the event was an illusion or whether it is real and has actually taken place.

8. Friedrich Nietzsche (1844–1900) was a German philosopher whose work has exerted a profound influence on Western philosophy and modern intellectual history. Nietzsche's writings have been described as the unique case of free revolutionary thought. The concept of "eternal recurrence" is central to his writings.

9. The Mothers of the Plaza de Mayo is an association of Argentine mothers whose children "disappeared" during the military dictatorship. They organized while trying to learn what had happened to their children, and began to march in 1977 at the Plaza de Mayo in Buenos Aires.

10. Erwin Schrödinger (Austria, 1887–1961) was a Nobel Prize-winning Austrian physicist who developed a number of fundamental results in the field of quantum theory. In 1957, Hugh Everett (USA, 1930–1982) formulated the many-worlds interpretation of quantum mechanics, which does not single out observation as a special process. In the many-worlds interpretation, both alive and dead states of the cat persist after the box is opened.

11. According to Nöel Carroll the imagery and figures in the horror genre are arranged to cause the emotion that he calls "art-horror." Paco Cabezas configures images that can produce terror but also a profound cathartic emotion in the audience due to their symbolic meaning.

Bibliography

The Appeared [Aparecidos]. Dir. Paco Cabezas. Performance by Javier Pereira, Ruth Díaz, Leonora Balcarce, Pablo Cedrón, Luciano Cáceres, Isabella Ritto, Graciela Tenembaum. Morena Films, 2007. DVD.
Byrne, Peter. *The Many Worlds of Hugh Everett III*. Oxford: Oxford University Press, 2010.
Carroll, Noël. *The Philosophy of Horror*. New York: Routledge, 1990.
Gribbins, John. *In Search of Schrödinger's Cat: Quantum Physics and Reality*. New York: Bantam Books, 1984.
Hodges, Donald. *Argentina's Dirty War. An Intellectual Biography*. Austin: University of Texas Press, 1991.
Nietzsche, Friedrich. *El Eterno Retorno* [Eternal Return]. Translated form the German by Eduardo Ovejero y Mauri. Buenos Aires: Aguilar, 1974.
Nora, Pierre. *Rethinking France. Les Lieux de Mémoire*. Translated from the French by Marie Trouille. Chicago: University of Chicago Press, 2001.
Ricoeur, Paul. *Memory, History, Forgetting*. Translated from the French by Kathleen Blamey and David Pellauer. Chicago: University of Chicago Press, 2004.
Todorov, Tzvetan. *The Fantastic: A Structural Approach to a Literary Genre*. Translated from the French by Richard Howard. Ithaca: Cornell University Press, 1975.

"No one who sees it lives to describe it"

The Book of Eibon *and the Power of the Unseeable in Lucio Fulci's* The Beyond

Philip L. Simpson

A critical plot development in Lucio Fulci's *The Beyond* (1981)—a film set largely in the spooky Seven Doors Hotel, in a mysterious Louisiana landscape practically oozing with portent—is the characters' discovery of an ancient book titled *Eibon*. The book, like many other (in)famous "evil" books found in literature and cinema, is a physical, written record of valuable occult knowledge that attempts to codify—accompanied by dire warnings that careless or ignorant deployment of that power will result in horrific consequences—what is otherwise usually represented as literally "unseeable." *The Beyond*, with its pervasive images of blindness and eye mutilation as the consequence of encountering evil, betokens that the price of venturing too far into such forbidden occult realms is the opening of doorways to Hell that will expose the world to an invasion of horrors it was meant to never see.

The film posits that there are seven of these doorways, with the hotel being built atop one of them. Just as H.P. Lovecraft found horror and monsters in the archaic and degenerated environment of New England and the incomprehensible and meaningless gulfs of infinite space, Fulci sets *The Beyond* in a forbidding American landscape with in-terdimensional gates that, when opened, not only allow intrusions of zombies and flesh-eating spiders into this world but also reveal the fathomless realm of Hell itself to eyes that are meant to glimpse it. The dark magic, and the dire warning against careless or ignorant use of it, is the power leading—through the "blind," ignorant actions of the film's central characters—to the opening of those gates that should never be opened. In horror, the physical power of the written word, as symbolized in the metaphor of the evil book, and the knowledge codified in that word is never to be treated lightly. To misuse or ignorantly deploy that power is a "grave" mistake, dooming the two central characters of *The Beyond* to go through the door of Hell to "face the Sea of Darkness and all therein that may be explored," to quote *Eibon*, presumably never to return to the world of the living.

Fulci and the Abyss

Fulci was arguably at the peak of his formidable powers as a horror filmmaker in *The Beyond*. The film is the second of an unofficial "Gates of Hell" trilogy, of which the other two entries are *City of the Living Dead* (1980) and *The House by the Cemetery* (1981). Made within two years, as if in a frenzied spasm of creativity, all three are connected by the trope of hapless mortals literally living on top of an entrance to Hell and then inadvertently falling into it.

Fulci, a veteran of the Italian *giallo* genre by this time in his career, was already known for graphic set pieces (e.g., a woman whipped to death with chains in *Don't Torture a Duckling* [1972]), before turning to zombies and the living dead in *Zombi 2* (1979), a follow-up to the success of George Romero's *Dawn of the Dead* (1978), which was marketed in Italy as *Zombi*. The extreme violence, surrealistic imagery, and narrative illogic that Fulci worked with as conventions within the giallo easily translated into *Zombi 2* and the "Gates of Hell" trilogy. Peter Hutchings characterizes Fulci's violent set pieces as "disturbingly beautiful" because of "inventive staging and editing," and in the "Gates of Hell" films these scenes contribute "to a much more developed lurid, visionary quality. The films' narratives ... did not make a great deal of sense. Despite (or perhaps because of) this, Fulci managed to produce not just a series of remarkable set pieces but also an extraordinarily oppressive atmosphere."[1] Typically, if reductively, celebrated among horror aficionados for gore effects, his signature violent set pieces in this film—a suspected warlock whipped with chains and crucified by a lynch mob, a number of people who suffer graphic ocular injuries, a blind woman whose throat is ripped out by her own dog, a man whose face is eaten by spiders—do not disappoint. These sequences, often focused on the spectacular destruction of the face and eyes by acid or violent penetration with fingers or some sharp object, are as disturbing as any found in his canon.

To think of these scenes as gratuitous, however, would be to misunderstand Fulci's thematic and philosophical approach. Wheeler Winston Dixon, for one, emphasizes that "gore is just one component of Fulci's work. Also running through all his films is a strangely dreamlike, hyper-violent abandonment of narrative which seeks to disrupt normative social preconceptions, perhaps as a result of Fulci's youthful excursions into Marxist political thought.... Fulci continually operates against audience expectations in terms of both characterization and plot."[2] Fulci himself states that his intent, which the evidence found in *The Beyond*'s text bears out, is "to make an absolute film, with all the horrors of our world. It's a plotless film; a house, people, and dead men coming from *The Beyond*. There's no logic to it, just a succession of images."[3] Noting this tendency toward deliberate incoherence or inconsistency in Fulci's "zombie" films, of which *The Beyond* is one, Steven Zani and Kevin Meaux write that "zombies present many possibilities.... any possibility for discovering some essential character of the zombie remains impossible. Fulci's films, with zombies that are physical and not physical, who have conflicting etiological explanations and subplots that go nowhere, deliberately raise questions that are beyond answering."[4] Fulci's deployment of zombies that exist in some interstitial zone between reality and nightmare, logic and irrationality, and nature and the supernatural in the film fits his larger thematic conception of "the beyond": the infinite abyssal void that lies just beyond the rim of this observed world, waiting to erase all mortal life. As the film's protagonists Liza and McCabe discover to their horror, "the beyond," in the end, is a great unknown in which they will be lost forever.

Forbidden Books and the Lovecraft Connection

Key to the film's surreal, foreboding atmosphere is *Eibon*, the book of forbidden knowledge upon which the entire plot hinges and a fictional example of a type of magical book often called a grimoire. As defined by Owen Davies, a grimoire is a written, physical repository of occult knowledge, including charms, conjurations, spells, instructions on how to create magical objects, secrets of divination, and the like. A grimoire is really a kind of "tangible magical archive," dating back to the ancient Babylonian civilization of the second millennium BCE.[5] The grimoire is a manifestation of the power of the written word to transcend the place-bound limitations and uncertainties of generational, oral transmission of occult knowledge. As a trope in fiction, the grimoire features prominently in Gothic literature of the 18th century. In fact, the founding novel of the Gothic literary genre, Horace Walpole's *The Castle of Otranto* (1764), presented itself as a found manuscript dating from the 16th century, with Walpole purporting to be little more than an editor of another, anonymous writer's work. Building on this tradition, forbidden manuscripts appear in the fantastic fiction of Victorian and Edwardian novelists such as Robert W. Chambers, Arthur Machen, and W.H. Hodgson.

Among these examples, however, H.P. Lovecraft's fictional *Necronomicon* stands as one of the most famous and influential grimoires. First cited by name in the short story "The Hound" in 1922, the *Necronomicon* is said to have been authored by the "mad Arab," Abdul Alhazred (a name also invented by Lovecraft and first mentioned in his story "The Nameless City" in 1921). As Lovecraft published more stories, the *Necronomicon* made frequent appearances. So convincing was Lovecraft in presenting a description of this fictional book as an actual non-fiction text that to this day many are convinced the book exists. The publication of several bogus tomes called *Necronomicon* have only added to this belief.

A direct genre line can be drawn from *The Beyond*'s occult text to Lovecraft and his influence. *The Book of Eibon*, or *Liber Ivonis* in Latin, is an occult text, supposedly written by a Hyperborean wizard named Eibon but actually invented by Clark Ashton Smith for his story "Ubbo-Sathla," published in July 1933 in the pulp magazine *Weird Tales*. Smith was one of Lovecraft's literary protégés: a member of the so-called "Lovecraft Circle" that included, among others, Robert E. Howard, Frank Belknap Long, August Derleth, and Robert Bloch. The members of this circle wrote, both during Lovecraft's life and after his death, stories that borrowed from and expanded upon (with Lovecraft's blessing) many elements of his literary mythos, including the use of fictitious occult books containing forbidden knowledge as a plot device. Indeed, in the words of Donald Tyson: "The creation of a fictional book filled with mind-destroying occult secrets seems to have been almost a requirement for membership in Lovecraft's inner circle of literary friends."[6] As one of these writers, Smith in "Ubbo-Sathla" references Lovecraft's own invented occult tome, *The Necronomicon*, as well as one of Lovecraft's most well-known alien godlike entities who menace the existence of humanity: Cthulhu. The *Book of Eibon* also appears in Lovecraft's stories "The Haunter of the Dark" (1936), "The Dreams in the Witch House" (1933), "The Horror in the Museum" (1933), and "The Shadow Out of Time" (1936).

It seems incontestable that *Eibon* in *The Beyond* owes its name to Smith's *The Book of Eibon*. Or is it? The screenwriter of *The Beyond*, Dardano Sacchetti, denies this connection rather adamantly when he says in an interview: "Actually, the real *Book of Eibon* is a positive book.... We needed to have a sort of authentic legend; I found this *Book of Eibon*, don't remember which part I read, and I put it in the script.... Years later I found out that, in reality, *The Book of Eibon* is one of the first books by one of the first prophets, so really, it's as if it were a sort of positive pre–Bible, with its share of negative things in it just like in the Bible, where you can find anything, you name it and it's in the Bible. So it wasn't the 'damned book,' it wasn't the '*Necronomicon*.'"[7] Clearly Sacchetti has heard somewhere along the way from some critics and/or fans that his invention of *Eibon* is in the Lovecraftian tradition of the *Necronomicon*, and it appears to rankle him, right down to his sarcastic use of air quotes with his fingers when he cites the latter. His description of "the real *Book of Eibon*" doesn't seem to fit Smith's work, in that Smith referenced the existence of the book and provided clues to its content but never actually wrote it. Nor does Eibon, a fictional mage in Smith's tale, exist independently as a historical figure or a prophet in Biblical tradition, let alone someone who wrote a book of prophecy. In any event, whatever book it was that Sacchetti read that guided his own invention of *Eibon*, it doesn't particularly matter in the sense that *Eibon* and Smith's *The Book of Eibon* co-exist as examples of a fictional occult book within a fictional narrative that provides the key to understanding all the supernatural events that transpire.

"We blind see things more clearly": Eibon's Unheeded Prophecy Fulfilled

Blindness, most often manifested in a series of horrific ocular injuries, is one of the most persistent tropes in the film. This trope is inextricably linked to the occult book that also appears at key moments. The film's prologue, set in 1927 (perhaps not coincidentally at the height of Lovecraft's writing career and the same year that he composed his "History of the *Necronomicon*"), immediately introduces *Eibon*, an antiquated tome with a leather-bound cover bearing a passing resemblance to human flesh. The book is prominent from the opening seconds of the first scene, and appears frequently throughout the rest of the film, magically porting itself from place to place as the narrative unfolds. The book's magical and occult properties associate it with the literary and cinematic trope of the arcane, cursed, or otherwise forbidden text that provides the key to comprehending and interpreting the otherwise inexplicable supernatural events about to unfold. However, virtually none of the characters in the film can see clearly enough, so to speak, to read the book, let alone apprehend its message. Only Schweick, an artist murdered by a mob in the opening scene of the film, and Emily, a seeress who transcends temporality to attempt to warn others about the gateway to Hell, possess the necessary sight.

The film opens in 1927 with Emily carrying an oil lamp as she sits down in a darkened room in her house to read *Eibon* amid flashes of lightning and apocalyptic clashes of thunder, an appropriately Gothic setting that will accompany other appearances of the book throughout the film. As the camera moves in close on her face and eyes, Emily intones, in voiceover, that "In this book are collected the prophecies of Eibon, handed down from generation to generation over more than 4,000 years." Through the oracular voice of one of the few characters in the film to see and thus comprehend the message, the book further warns its reader (and by extension the cinematic audience) that the "seven dreaded gateways are concealed in seven cursed places. Woe be unto him who ventures near without knowledge. Woe be unto him who opens one of the seven gateways to Hell, because through that gateway evil will invade the world." Emily's prophetic words not only set the moody atmosphere but summarize the plot of *The Beyond*, in which unaware characters accidentally open a portal to Hell through their careless, uninformed actions.

Jumping forward in time to 1981, the film introduces the audience to Liza Merrill, a young New Yorker who has inherited the Seven Doors Hotel—the primary site of the starkly grim opening sequence—in Louisiana. The book-as-artifact unites the two disparate timelines. Exploring the hotel's Room 36 in which the murdered artist Schweick resided in 1927, she discovers the book of *Eibon*, open on a desk; while she does not consciously know what the book is, at some level she recognizes its significance because she gasps upon seeing it. This discovery triggers the malign energy latent in the room. When she opens the bathroom door, she is terrified by sudden bursts of lightning and a vision of Schweik's hideously burned and rotting corpse nailed to the wall. As she flees downstairs, lightning flashes illuminate a painting of Hell produced by Schweick decades earlier, establishing a connection between *Eibon* and the painting as manmade signifiers of the underlying hellish reality of the gateway—a reality that Liza has finally begun to see.

Dr. John McCabe, Liza's reluctant ally in the film, also finds the cobweb-shrouded book of *Eibon*, albeit in a different location (the house established, in the opening scenes of the film, to have belonged to Emily). He reads the passage about the seven gateways to Hell concealed in seven cursed places. Intrigued, he returns with the book to the hospital morgue to examine a moldering corpse (which turns out to be Schweik) that had been brought in earlier. Examining the body, he discovers a runic symbol on Schweick's wrist matching the one visible on the basement wall in the film's opening scene depicting Schweick's murder and now on the page to which John has opened the book. The rune serves as the film's final confirmation (as if there were really any doubt in the audience's mind) of the validity of *Eibon*'s grim prophecies, including one now heard in John's voiceover: "And the day the gates of Hell are opened, on that day the dead will walk the earth."

In spite of all that he has seen by this point in the film, however, the firmly rationalistic John regards the book as manufactured evidence of some kind of ruse or con that Liza is running. Returning to the hotel, where Liza has escaped an attack by a zombie in the basement, John does not believe her latest story because there is no evidence of a violent attack upon her: no cuts or bruises. He accuses her of leaving the book at the old house at the crossroads for him to find, asks who she really is, and then unwisely recites to her what he has read: "According to the book of *Eibon*, this hotel is one of the seven gateways to Hell." Ironically, however, his skeptical words serve as the final catalyst for the gateway to open fully. The basement turns into a storm of wind, lightning, sprays of blood, and falling stonework, forcing them to flee upstairs past Schweick's painting, itself now beginning to ooze blood through the canvas. The painting and the Hell it represents are fast becoming one as the film winds toward its conclusion, a point made by Michael Grant when he argues the painting "does not simply *depict* hell—it *is* hell ... a disruption of temporal order takes place in *the film*, and it does so at the moment when image and what is imaged become one, a unity achieved as the film concentrates at the end on Schweick's painting. What occurs here ... reveals the film's fixity and subordination to a time impotent to go anywhere except interminably back to its beginning."[8] The conclusion tracks Liza and John's futile effort to escape the destiny their shared blindness to the book's prophetic warning has already determined for them.

The Price of Knowledge

The book is thus a source of knowledge about the dangers of the gate to Hell—knowledge that carries with it a ghastly price. Those most familiar with the effects of the opening of the gate, such as Emily or the little girl Jill, who sees her parents killed, lose their physical sight and, it is implied, their souls. Equally unfortunate for the characters in the film, however, is the price of remaining ignorant (either unwittingly or obstinately) of the proximity of the doorway to Hell. In Fulci's idiosyncratic cinematic signature, these varying prices are paid in spectacularly gory set-pieces that emphasize the excruciating vulnerability of the human face (and the eyes in particular) to violence.

The first victim we see pay the price of knowledge is the artist (and suspected warlock) Schweick in the film's opening scene when he is murdered by local vigilantes. Schweick, as a tortured visionary artist who has glimpsed Hell and now is driven to represent it compulsively through art, could have stepped directly from Lovecraft's pages. Locked in his cloister of a hotel room, he slavishly paints a hellish landscape that has seemingly driven him mad. The distorted, broken human figures he represents in the painting as sufferers in Hell reflect not only his psyche but portend the extreme violence that will be inflicted upon most of the film's characters. Fulci's nimble camera and lighting ensure that Schweick's face is never seen without some kind of rupture; for example, an expressionistic shadow line divides his gaunt face between light and dark, and his face appears in uncomfortable close-up and then blurs to focus upon the hotel room number ("36") on the wall behind him. The camera's bisecting and dissolving of the artist's face foreshadows the extreme violence of his death, his mutilated features dissolved by quicklime. Dragged into the basement, he desperately tells his tormentors that the hotel is built upon one of the seven doorways to Hell, and only he can save them. His prophetic words are completely ignored by the men who, just as the prophecies foretell, are "venturing near without knowledge." They pitilessly beat Schweick, nail his wrists to the rock wall of the basement in a mockery of the Crucifixion, and then hurl the caustic lime onto his head. The camera closes on Schweick's bubbling, dissolving face to capture it from several angles before pulling back to reveal a runic symbol carved into the wall next to his outstretched left hand: the marker for the gate of Hell that John will later see on a page in *Eibon*. Schweick's warnings, like those contained in *Eibon*, are ignored by the men who do not see Hell literally beneath their feet and, through their sacrificial murder of Schweick, open Hell's door.

Unbeknownst to Liza decades later, the renovation work she authorizes for the hotel has dire consequences for her and those around her—again, portrayed by Luci as a gory comeuppances for ignorance. The laborers working on the house (painting its exterior, fixing its plumbing) and the staff in the house awaken the latent evil inhabiting it. A painter, Larry, looks into a window from his perch on a scaffold and is startled by the face of a spectral woman (whom the audience recognizes as Emily from the prologue) with blind eyes whitened as if by cataracts; recoiling, he plunges off the scaffold and is terribly injured. A plumber named Joe—his "Jesus Christ Is the Answer" license plate, head bandana, flannel work shirt, and denim overalls establish him as Fulci's vision of a rural laborer "yokel"—descends into the basement to investigate the source of a persistent flooding problem and meets an even grislier fate. He unknowingly retraces the path to the location where Schweick was killed and then entombed by the mob. His single-minded focus on his task blinds him to the unsettling clues (the endlessly streaming water, the crumbling walls, the rune on the wall that signals the audience this was indeed the location where Schweick was killed) that this basement flood is no ordinary plumbing disaster. His metaphoric blindness to the evil surrounding him becomes gruesomely literalized when, as he digs into the sodden wall behind which Schweik was entombed, a corpse-like hand (zombie Schweik's) lunges from the hole to grab him by the face and gouge out his eyes. Later in the film, Joe reappears as a zombie rising (ironically for a plumber) from the filthy water of a clogged bathtub to kill Martha, the maid, by impaling her head on a nail projecting from a wall. The nail pushes out one of her eyes in an inversion of the way in which Joe lost his eyes to the demon attack. Martha's son, Arthur, is also killed in the flooded basement near the wall where Joe was killed. Though Arthur's death is off-screen, the logical conclusion is that Schweik killed him too.

The sacrifice of these rural tradesmen and domestic workers parallels the first act's murder of Schweick, symbolizing the dehumanizing consequences of Liza's desperation as a transplanted New Yorker to capitalize upon the labor of these locals to save her from pecuniary ruin. A subtext of economic anxiety and class consciousness persists throughout the film, beginning with the opening murder of the outsider Schweick by the locals. The hostility of place-bound rural locals toward an urban outsider is nothing new in American horror film, of course. Bernice M. Murphy, for example, identifies a trend that she calls the Rural Gothic, "characterised by negative encounters between individuals who have permanently settled in one place, and those who are defined by their mobility and lack of permanent relationship with the landscape."[9] Viewed through this lens, Schweick's transitory status in Louisiana (signified by his staying in Room 36 of the hotel) marks him as a target for violence driven by the superstitious beliefs of the ignorant locals. When, as a zombie, he returns as the ultimate outsider to take revenge on the living, most of his victims are drawn from the same strata of the local class hierarchy as the vigilantes who killed him.

With the film's temporary leap forward to Liza's story, this economic dynamic subtly shifts, but the focus on class difference remains. Liza, while an urbanite, has as little working capital as the locals, a condition she makes clear in her opening scene with her architect, Martin Avery. She tells Avery that she has to wait before beginning the extensive renovations he is recommending because she cannot afford more than painting and cleaning work—a course of action that Avery, as an upper-middle-class professional, tries to dissuade her from by telling her she has no idea how much impact double-digit inflation will have on housing and construction costs. Her status as an urban out-of-towner, however, carries its own kind of not-so-positive cultural capital among the tradesmen and union employees of the bayou. While the workers she employs are courteous enough to her in life, if for no other reason than that they are dependent upon her for payment, their employment with her ends in their deaths and eternal damnation. The curse extends even to Joe's hapless family. His wife, coming to the hospital morgue to dress his body, is killed by an unseen presence that dissolves her face with spilled sulfuric acid; his daughter, Jill, witnessing the traumatic event, is rendered blind and is, the audience later discovers, possessed by the evil of the open gateway. When the malign energies of the Hell portal reanimate all of these characters to stalk its borderlands as zombies, they try to kill Liza and those around her. Their victimization of her is a kind of karmic retribution for her ignorance, which put them in harm's way for the sake of her own economic gain.

Liza's architect Avery gets another kind of comeuppance for being her accessory in reopening the gateway. Unlike Liza herself, whose exploitation of those who work for her is more of a reflection of her self-absorption than anything else, his contempt for those from a lower socioeconomic level is quite explicit. In this regard, an exchange Avery has with a union employee just before Avery dies is telling. When he goes to the library section of the town hall to retrieve hotel records, he asks the town employee who is serving him for help. The employee, whose name is Lucio and thus may be credibly interpreted as a mouthpiece for Fulci's own take on such condescending well-to-do types, politely but firmly declines on the grounds that he needs to take his union-mandated lunch break now. Lucio is obviously proud of this small benefit his union has obtained for him; just as obviously, Avery is contemptuous of Lucio's status as a union employee. He sarcastically wishes Lucio a "happy lunch" and, while climbing the ladder to find the manual containing the information he seeks about the hotel, mutters to himself in reference to the lunch hour change: "First from 1 to 2, now from 12 to 1. A great labor victory." Following this sarcastic slap against unionism, Avery locates the book he is seeking and opens it to find a diagram of the hotel clearly showing the open gate to Hell. This discovery summons a great clap of thunder and blinding flash of lightning, which frightens him into falling from the ladder, just as Larry the painter fell from the scaffold and with similar injurious result. What happens next as Avery lays helpless and paralyzed from his fall is, in context, as much punishment for his contempt for Lucio as it is for discovering the diagram. In one of the film's most notorious scenes, tarantulas crawl from the baseboard and across the floor to him, their skitterings and chirrings increasingly magnified on the film's soundtrack. As they crawl over him, they tear away chunks of his lip, nose, tongue, and (of course) one of his eyes. When he dies, the diagram in the book, open on the floor beside him, disappears from the page.

Willful Blindness

As the horrible deaths of Liza's laborers, domestic help, and architect demonstrate, then, her single-minded focus on opening the hotel to save her financial life renders her blind to what is really happening around her until it is far too late. When the ghost-like Emily reappears in the film, now blind and accompanied by a guide dog named Dickie, her sole purpose is to dissuade Liza from reopening the hotel. After Liza encounters Emily while driving across a bridge, Emily takes Liza back to her house near a crossroads. Were Liza less blind to mythology and folklore, she would have realized at some point that this house's location is significant, in that crossroads are traditionally believed to be intersections between this world and the next, serving as conduits for spirits and other paranormal phenomenon. While playing the piano for Liza, Emily immediately warns her to give up her plans for the hotel and go back to New York. As it becomes clear that Liza will not heed her, Emily explicitly states the danger to her and, in so doing, gives voice to one of Fulci's primary themes in the movie: "We blind see things more clearly. I wanted to spare you but now I'll have to tell you everything." In keeping with the well-known dramatic trope of disabled characters acquiring mystical powers, those who are physically blinded in this film by their contact with the supernatural (such as Emily and Joe's young daughter Jill) gain compensatory clarity of understanding of the opening of the gates between worlds, while the sighted move forward blindly ignorant of their peril even when an oracle like Emily tries to alert them.

Emily tells Liza what happened to Schweik 60 years ago and says he "had found a key [to] the seven gateways to Hell. This house was constructed on one of the seven." Schweik's painting of Hell as seen in the film's prologue now occupies a prominent position in the hotel lobby and Emily can sense his ghostly presence as well as the aura emanating from the painting; when she touches the painting, the lobby bell for Room 36 rings in response. A few minutes later her palms begin to bleed as a kind of stigmatic connection to the dead painter (whom the audience later sees in his zombie form). When Emily tells Liza never to enter Room 36, Liza responds irately: "I've lived in New York all my life. And if there's one thing I've learned not to believe in, it's ghosts. I was lucky to inherit this hotel. It's the first good break I've had. It will take more than a faulty electrical contact or some crazy story to make me give it up." Liza's stubborn refusal to listen to Emily compels Emily to flee the hotel with Dickie. Though Emily has one last significant scene in the film, in which her own dog turns against her as a result of a zombie invasion of her home and kills her, Emily's exit from the hotel also marks the transition in the film when Liza begins to confront the supernatural energies of the hotel and become a believer.

The shift is signaled by Liza closing her eyes and seeing, as if in a loop, the recurring image of Emily and Dickie running from the house. This recursiveness foreshadows the film's climax, in which Liza and John's attempt to flee the hotel only brings them back to the hotel in a kind of spatio-temporal loop from which there will be no escape and an infinity of time in which to relive it as damned wanderers in the Sea of Darkness. Significantly, Emily's eyes are closed or "blinded" as she sees the looped images of Emily and Dickie fleeing, which paradoxically means that in this moment she gazes upon her eventual fate without realizing its import.

Liza's equally "blind" companion and reluctant ally through much of the movie is John, a rational man of science. Toward the film's climax he tells Liza that, as a doctor, he "won't accept irrational explanations." This doggedly rationalistic perspective prevents him from accepting the eerie and increasingly frightening events of the film's plot as supernatural in origin. When he finds Liza terrified after her sighting of Schweick's corpse in the bathroom of Room 36, he begins his own investigation. His failure to find anything in Room 36, not even the book of *Eibon* in the desk, leads Liza to begin to doubt herself. Clearly dubious of Liza's sanity himself, John then breaks into the abandoned house at the crossroads to make sure no mysterious blind woman is living there. Ever the man of science, until the last few seconds of the film, John thinks he can find the answers to the inexplicable events at the hospital, a bastion of rationality and science for the doctor where he hopes to consult with his colleague, Fisher. However, there he finds Fisher cowering in fear from the zombies who have infested the surgical theaters, morgue, and corridors of the hospital. In a clear and probably commercially necessary nod to George R. Romero's zombie mythos, John discovers the one tactic that seems to put down a zombie for the second and final time: a gunshot to the head that destroys the brain. John's logical response plague of zombies, however, is no match for the sheer number of zombies and the limited amount of ammunition at his disposal. Black magic defeats John's scientific approach, as is illustrated by an explosion of supernatural energy that kills Fisher with lethal shards of glass. John and Liza flee the morgue, only to find themselves back at the hotel where they started, and where the air itself is now filled by the moans of the damned. John stubbornly proclaims that what he has seen is impossible, but the despairing look on his face suggests that even he may finally be accepting the supernatural truth, as Liza did long before him.

The film ends with Liza and John running through the basement and toward a light, seemingly the only escape route, that radiates with an eerie blue luminescence from the hole in the wall where Schweik was entombed. Once on the other side of the wall, however, they discover that they have entered the desolate, otherworldly landscape captured in Schweik's painting. In a real way, they have been consumed by Schweik's painting itself, which proved to be as visually prophetic as the words of *Eibon*. Both the book and the painting are the portal, and the portal is both the book and the painting. All elements in play throughout the narrative have converged to a narrow access point but also broadened outward into an infinitely expanding Hell in which any forward motion as mortals understand it is lost in an infinite recursive loop. Liza and John are now figures within both Schweick's painting and the real Hell dimension it represents. Its verisimilitude that bleeds through the canvas, and their expressions of horror as they run hand-in-hand (in slow motion, adding to the surreal quality of the scene) indicate they have, at last, recognized what is happening. Most significantly, their eyes have turned white with the blindness that, in the cinematic grammar of *The Beyond*, signifies they now—too late—comprehend what it means to carelessly open the gateway to the Beyond and not heed the cautionary words of *Eibon*. Liza and John cannot, however, say they weren't warned.

NOTES

1. Hutchings, *A to Z of Horror Cinema*, 135–36.
2. Dixon, *Cinema at the Margins*, 11.
3. Schlockoff, "Lucio Fulci," 53.
4. Zani and Meaux, "Decaying Definition of Zombie Narratives," 112.
5. Davies, *Grimoires*, 2.
6. Tyson, *Dream World of H.P. Lovecraft*, 160.
7. Sacchetti. "Looking Back."
8. Grant, "The 'Real' and the Abominations of Hell."
9. Murphy, *Rural Gothic*, 10.

BIBLIOGRAPHY

Davies, Owen. *Grimoires: A History of Magic Books*. New York: Oxford University Pres, 2009.
Dixon, Wheeler Winston. *Cinema at the Margins*. London: Anthem Press, 2013.
Grant, Michael. "The 'Real' and the Abominations of Hell: Carl-Theodor Dreyer's *Vampyr* (1931) and Lucio Fulci's *E tu vivrai nel terrore—L'aldila* (*The Beyond*, 1981)." *Kinoeye* 3, no. 2 (February 3, 2003). http://www.kinoeye.org/03/02/grant02.php.
Hutchings, Peter. *The A to Z of Horror Cinema*. Lanham, MD: Scarecrow Press, 2009.
Murphy, Bernice M. *The Rural Gothic in American Popular Culture: Backwoods Horror and Terror in the Wilderness*. New York: Palgrave Macmillan, 2013.
Sacchetti, Dardano. "Looking Back: The Creation of *The Beyond*." Disc 2. *The Beyond*, special ed. Directed by Lucio Fulci. Grindhouse Releasing, 2014. Blu-Ray.
Schlockoff, Rob. "Lucio Fulci: Interviews Translated from the French by Federic Levy." *Starburst* 48 (1982), 51–55.
Tyson, Donald. *The Dream World of H.P. Lovecraft: His Life, His Demons, His Universe*. Woodbury, MN: Llewellyn Publications, 2010.
Zani, Steven, and Kevin Meaux. "Lucio Fulci and the Decaying Definition of Zombie Narratives." In *Better Off Dead: The Evolution of the Zombie as Post-Human*, edited by Deborah Christie and Sarah Juliet Lauro, 98–115. New York: Fordham University Press, 2011.

About the Contributors

Martin J. **Auernheimer** studied theatre, film and media science. His master's thesis discussed the depiction of the Trojan War in film and video games, and his doctoral thesis explored the incorporation and depiction of Greek mythology in television, film and video games.

Jessica **Balanzategui** is a lecturer in cinema and screen studies at Swinburne University of Technology in Australia. Her research is on the intersections of childhood, technological change and nostalgia—particularly in horror and gothic media—and the cultural, historical and industrial negotiations between cultural institutions and entertainment industries.

Emily **Brick** is a senior lecturer in film and media at Manchester Metropolitan University. Her research is concerned with representations of monstrous, transgressive and killer women in film and television. She is the co-editor *European Nightmares*.

Lisa **Cunningham** is an English instructor at West Georgia Technical College. Her work regarding cinema and film theory can most recently be found in *Lost Girls* and *The Laughing Dead*.

Learned **Foote** is a doctoral student in the Department of Religion at Rice University. He specializes in Tibetan Buddhism and participates in the Gnosticism, Esotericism and Mysticism (GEM) program on heterodox and marginal forms of religion.

Michael **Fuchs** is a fixed-term assistant professor in the Department of American Studies at the University of Graz in Austria. He has coedited three books and has written more than 40 published and forthcoming journal articles and essays on a variety of topics.

Michael **Furlong** is a regional campus librarian at the University of Central Florida. He has published on graphic novels, particularly the work of Will Eisner and Alan Moore, horror films and book reviews. He writes plays, screenplays and short fiction.

Mark **Henderson** teaches at Tuskegee University. His research has focused on 19th- and 20th-century American literature and psychoanalytic theory. His research interests include the American Gothic, American modernism and film—specifically horror, film noir, science fiction, dystopia and disaster.

Michael E. **Heyes** is an assistant professor in the Department of Religion at Lycoming College in Pennsylvania and is the author of *Holy Monsters, Sacred Grotesques* (2018). His research interests include magic, monstrosity and demons in the medieval and contemporary West; religion and film; pop culture and religion; and the history of Christianity.

Murray **Leeder** teaches at the University of Calgary. He is the author of *Horror Film*, *The Modern Supernatural and the Beginnings of Cinema* and *Halloween* as well as the editor of *Cinematic Ghosts* and *Refocus: The Films of William Castle*.

Richard J. **Leskosky** is retired from the University of Illinois at Urbana-Champaign. He formerly served as the director of the UIUC Unit for Cinema Studies and as the president of the Society for Animation Studies. He continues to write on animated film genres, Japanese animation and 19th-century proto-cinematic devices.

About the Contributors

Sue **Matheson** is an associate professor of English at the University College of the North in Manitoba. She specializes in American popular culture and film. Her articles have appeared in numerous periodicals; she is the author of *The Westerns and War Films of John Ford* and editor of *A Fistful of Icons*.

Cynthia J. **Miller** is a cultural anthropologist, specializing in popular culture and visual media. Her writing has appeared in a wide range of journals and edited collections across the disciplines. She is the coeditor (with A. Bowdoin Van Riper) of *Divine Horror* (McFarland, 2017).

Thomas **Prasch** is a professor and chair of the Department of History at Washburn University. His publications include essays on neo-noir/screwball fusion films of the mid–1980s, Michael Palin's travel documentaries, Robert Eggers's *The Witch,* and Alfred Russel Wallace's spiritualism and evolutionary thought.

Michael C. **Reiff** is a CollegeNow instructor of English at Ithaca High School through Tompkins Cortland Community College and teaches the Auburn Film Seminar through Cayuga Community College. He has contributed to the Popular Culture Association, *Science Fiction Film and Television* and *Film & History*.

Karen J. **Renner** is an assistant professor at Northern Arizona University, where she teaches classes in American literature and popular culture. Her work combines horror and childhood studies. She is the author of *Evil Children in the Popular Imagination* and editor of a collection of essays entitled *The "Evil Child" in Literature, Film and Popular Culture*.

Austin **Riede** is an associate professor specializing in British modernism and the literature of World War I at the University of North Georgia. He has published on Ford Madox Ford, W.B. Yeats, Vera Brittain, David Jones and Lewis Grassic Gibbon.

Philip L. **Simpson** is the provost of the Titusville campus and eLearning of Eastern Florida State College and. He is the president of the Popular Culture Association/American Culture Association and a member of the editorial board of *The Journal of Popular Culture*.

Graciela **Tissera** is an associate professor of Spanish at Clemson University. Her research and teaching interests include Hispanic and comparative literature and film, literary and critical theory, and Spanish for the professions. She is the director of the International Spanish Program and Internships in Seville, Spain.

Jeffrey M. **Tripp** is an instructor of religious studies at Saint Xavier University in Chicago, specializing in the New Testament and early Christianity. He has an ongoing interest in ancient apocalyptic texts and their influence on contemporary literature.

A. Bowdoin **Van Riper** is a historian who specializes in depictions of science and technology in popular culture. He is the author of *Learning from Mickey, Donald and Walt* (McFarland, 2011) and coeditor (with Cynthia J. Miller) of *Divine Horror* (McFarland, 2017).

Index

adaptation 5, 7, 19, 37–40, 42n29, 42n32, 45, 50–51, 62–63, 66–68, 125, 140n1, 150, 151n17, 162–163, 175, 192
agency 4, 11–20, 49, 114, 137, 176–180, 191, 198
Alan Wake (2010) 4, 11, 13, 15–21
alchemy 201
Alhazred, Abdul (fictional character) 23, 33, 44, 247
aliens 4, 162–172
ambiguity of horror 233
angels 5, 53n36, 74–92
Anti-Bible 5, 83–92
Antichrist 82, 74, 77, 79, 179
anxiety 27, 107–108, 116, 221–222, 226, 251
The Appeared (2007) 7, 235–244
Ariès, Philippe 109
Artaud, Antonin 230
At the Mountains of Madness (1936) 35, 41n8, 43
Auernheimer, Martin J. 4–5, 44–55, 255
author, role of 1, 12, 31–42, 45, 81, 154–161

The Babadook (2014) 3, 5–6, 107–141
Bakhtin, Mikhail 190
Balanzategui, Jessica 5, 107–119, 129, 131, 255
Beavis, Mary Ann 73–74, 79
Benjamin, Walter 35, 42, 68
Beugnet, Martine 233
Beville, Maria 13
The Beyond (1971) 7, 245–254
The Bible 4–5, 31, 37, 60, 64, 67, 73–86, 89, 183, 248
bogeyman 107–117, 129
"book objects" 17
Book of Damnation (fictional book) 182–183
Book of Eibon 7, 245–254
The Book of Shadows (fictional book) 178, 180
Book of the Dead 30, 32n20, 155
books 60, 129, 154–155, 174, 186, 190, 214; as artifacts 1, 73, 155, 249; artwork in 47–48, 189, 227–229, 232–233; children's 3, 5–6, 107–118, 120–139, 147–151; destruction of 46, 125, 129, 133, 135, 157, 162, 164, 166, 218; enchanted 176; as gateways 3, 7, 16, 51, 164, 170, 248–254; hidden 4–5, 13, 33, 79, 200–201, 219, 226, 236; as living entities 49–52, 162; lost 5, 73–81; pop-up 107, 111–121; rare/unique 33, 44, 78, 163, 165, 201; as repositories of knowledge 1–3, 7, 17, 78, 159–160, 166–167, 175–180, 184, 189, 191, 198–199, 201, 224–233, 236, 241, 245–250; as signifiers 2, 111, 129, 160, 249; as symbols 1, 45, 51–52, 94, 201, 245; and truth 1–2, 34, 38, 80, 150, 156–157, 163, 168–171, 201, 224, 231; use of blood for ink 30, 47–48; use of human skin 7, 47–49, 52, 189, 233; *see also* texts
bookstores/bookshops 34–35, 50, 181, 183
Brick, Emily 6, 175–185, 255
Broedel, Peter 178
Bruenig, Elizabeth 134
Bruhm, Steven 108, 119
Buckner, Anna Patience (fictional character) 145, 157–158

Cabezas, Paco 7, 235–243
The Cabin in the Woods (2012) 3, 6, 145, 154–160
"The Call of Cthulhu" (1928), 32n20, 44, 53n41
Cane, Sutter (character) 3, 13–16, 34–40
carnival/the carnivalesque 7, 186–195
Carroll, Noël 100–101, 244n11
"Casting the Runes" (1911 short story) 198, 201
The Castle of Otranto (1764 novel) 11, 247
Catholic Church 50, 66, 74, 80, 84, 177–178
Charmed (TV series, 1998–2006) 178, 180, 184, 186
childhood, nature of 85, 107–118

children's culture/"kinderculture" 5–6, 107–119, 147–148
Christianity 66, 80, 89
Clover, Carol 11, 38, 158
Cohen, Jeffrey Jerome 15
Constantine (2006) 74–80
Corman, Roger 24, 45
cosmology 36, 44–45
counter-narrative 85, 87
The Covenant (2006) 176–184
Cowan, Suzanne 59
The Craft (1986) 176, 179–184
Craven, Wes 11, 14–16, 20
Creed, Barbara 178–179, 182
Crooked House (2017) 150
Crowley, Aleister 4, 23–24, 27–28, 30, 231
Crowther, Barbara 149
The Crush (1993) 149
Cthulhu mythos 31, 3651, 247
Cuneiform 47, 49
Cunningham, Lisa 6, 154–161, 255
curses 7, 25, 95–99, 187, 191–192, 198–206, 248–251; *see also* spells

Darnton, Robert 1
Davies, Owen 178, 247
the Death Note (fictional book) 211–222
Death Note (transmedia franchise) 7, 211–222
Deliver Us from Evil (2014) 3
demons 50, 74–81, 100, 124, 127, 177, 179–180, 194–207; battles with 46–47, 123, 129–130, 251; possession by 26, 29, 51; summoning of 3, 6–7, 26, 30, 49–50, 67, 60, 129, 154–155, 174, 186, 190, 214; *see also* exorcism
desire 28–29, 133–136, 139–140, 149, 176, 184, 194, 205, 214, 222, 230–233; children's 113, 116; horror and 20; objects of 7, 147; for order 102
destiny 176, 241, 250
the Devil 5, 26, 29, 52, 74, 77, 81n18, 84–85, 88–91, pacts with 61–64, 69n2, 177–181, 186, 189; worship 66, 179–181, 198–206
diabolism 177–179, 184, 205

257

Index

diaries 6–7, 145–161, 200; *see also* journals
"Dirty War" 7, 235–236, 239, 241, 243
divine authorship 1, 74–75, 78
Dixon, Wheeler Winston 246
Dracula (1897 novel) 146
Drucker, Johanna 17
The Dunwich Horror (1929) 4, 27–29, 31, 36, 42, 44–45, 51–54, 226

e-reader 5, 94–103
Ebert, Roger 59, 187
Eisner, Lotte 59
Esotericism (movement) 28, 36, 231–233
evil 4, 6, 16, 44–52, 73–92, 145, 148–149, 155–159, 176–177, 189, 201, 214, 245, 249–251
The Evil Dead (1981) 3–4, 29–30, 33, 47, 155, 157
Evil Dead (2013) 47, 50–51, 155, 157
Evil Dead franchise 3, 5, 44–54
Evilspeak (1981) 6, 154, 159
exorcism 84, 90–91, 115, 130

fairy tales 15, 132–140, 175, 179, 188
faith 5–6, 143, 184; loss of 83–92
fantasy (concept, not genre) 1, 4, 6, 16, 18, 109, 136, 146, 230
Faust: Eine deutsche Volkssage (Faust: A German Folktale) (1926) 59–69
Faustbuch 60–67
Feather, John 1
Filardi, Peter 181
Flood, John 60
folklore 4, 45, 112, 129, 163, 165–168, 170, 252
Foote, Learned 5, 94–104, 255
Foucault, Michel 40–41, 186, 226
found-footage horror films 146
Freud, Sigmund 13, 112, 139
Friddle, Megan E. 147
Fuchs, Michael 4, 11–21, 255
Fulci, Lucio 7, 245–254
Fun (1993) 6, 148
Furlong, Michael 7, 198–207, 255

gateways 3, 7, 16, 51, 164, 170, 248–254; *see also* portal
gender 146, 176–178, 232, 233
ghosts 48, 127, 132–133, 135–136, 146, 198, 235, 252–253
giallo (horror film sub-genre) 246
Gilmont, Jean-François 60, 64
girlhood 6, 145–15; *see also* gender
Glamuzina, Julie 148
gods, ancient 24–25, 28, 45, 50, 158
Goethe 60, 63, 66–68
Goffman, Erving 132–133, 137–139
Gonce, John Wisdom, III 27
gore 45, 246
Gorey, Edward 113
Gothic 11, 13, 59, 107–109, 113, 122, 125–126, 145–146, 151*n*2, 183, 214, 247–248, 251

grief 3, 122, 126, 129, 132, 134, 136–139, 227
grimoires 3, 7, 33–35, 47, 175–184, 186, 189–190, 193, 195, 198, 247; *see also* spell books
guardians 6, 41, 85, 108, 118, 132–140

Haile, H.G. 62
Halberstam, Judith 12–13, 16
Haller, Daniel 27–28, 31
Halloween/All Hallows' Eve 187, 189, 191, 193, 202–203
Hanscomb, Stuart 101
Harms, Daniel 31
Harry Potter and the Chamber of Secrets (1998 novel /2002 film) 147, 154–156
The Haunted Palace (1963) 4, 24–26, 30, 45
heathen 88–89
Heavenly Creatures (1994) 6, 148
Heffernan, Kevin 39
Hell 7, 50, 52, 61–62, 75, 78–79, 84–85, 88, 90, 92, 158, 171, 189, 191, 195, 201, 214, 220, 245–254
Henderson, Mark 5, 83–93, 255
heteroglossia 7, 186–194
Heyes, Michael E. 4, 23–31, 255
Hocus Pocus (1993) 7, 176–177, 186–195
Hogan, Rebecca 147
home 3, 5, 24, 27, 87, 122, 124, 134–135, 163, 167–168, 179, 195, 253
horror (as genre) 2, 4, 11–12, 15, 38, 41, 45, 52, 100, 102, 108, 116–117, 127, 132, 139, 145–146, 150, 175, 198, 229, 246–247; domestic 6, 114, 132–140; postmodern 11–12
Howard, Robert E. 45, 247
Hulme, Juliet 148
Hunt, Leon 179
Hunter, Jane 147
hypertext 23

iconography 67–68, 159–160, 179, 215, 220, 231
identity: national 84, 88–92; personal 132–140, 147–149, 152*n*27, 211, 213, 218–221, 241–243
The Idiot (1874 novel) 94, 97–99, 103
images 14, 16, 27, 29, 40, 45, 63, 67–68, 71*n*88, 88, 100, 107–108, 110–113, 117–118, 150, 160, 164, 168, 183, 189, 213, 216, 218, 226, 231, 233, 239, 242, 244*n*11, 245–246, 249
imprisonment 7, 16, 98–99, 179, 213, 220–221, 224–225, 229–233, 237; by stories 16, 120, 122–123
In the Mouth of Madness (1994) 3, 4, 11, 13–16, 19, 20, 33–43
innocence 3, 6, 83, 107, 109, 121, 125, 131, 145–146, 148–150, 151*n*17, 182, 188, 203
inscription 3, 166, 189, 193, 216, 219, 221

irrationality 101–102, 108–112, 115–119
It Follows (2015) 5, 94–104

James, Henry 6, 37, 132–141
James, M.R. 198–201, 206*n*2
Jenks, Chris 108, 111, 112
Johns, Adrian 8*n*4
Joshi, S.T. 35, 41*n*2, 198
journals 6, 125, 151*n*4, 152*n*7, 155, 224–234

Kemp, Philip 59
Kent, Jennifer 5–6, 120–123, 125–130, 132, 137–138
Kilty, Jennifer M. 149
Kirkland, Ewan 146, 151*n*4
knowledge, dangerous 2–3, 7, 17, 44, 78, 108–109, 175–178, 189, 198–199, 201, 226–228, 231–233, 234*n*3, 245, 247–252
Kracauer, Siegfried 60, 69*n*9

language 2, 3, 16, 23, 36, 41*n*9, 70*n*49, 91, 186, 217, 219, 243*n*1; ancient 75, 78; *heteroglossia* 7, 191, 193–195
Laurie, Alison J. 148, 149
Leeder, Murray 4, 33–43, 255
legends 5, 28, 53*n*36, 62–63, 66, 158, 163, 166–169, 187–188, 248; *see also* myths
Lennard, Dominic 116
Leskosky, Richard J. 7, 211–223, 255
letters 2, 20, 45, 74, 145–146, 163, 169
libraries 27, 33–34, 44–45, 199; institutional 48, 186, 200–201, 252; personal 60, 199–201
literacy 2, 3, 65, 73, 170, 178
literature 16, 23, 28, 66, 68, 166–167, 201, 214, 245; apocalyptic 81*n*10; children's 107, 113, 118, 147; Gothic 125, 247; occult 4
Lost Souls (2000) 73, 74, 77
"The Love Song of J. Alfred Prufrock[qm] 99–100
Lovecraft, H.P. 4, 5, 12, 16, 23–24, 26–28, 30–31, 33–38, 44–45, 48–52, 102, 162–163, 198, 215, 226, 228, 245, 247–248, 250
The Loved Ones (2009) 6, 150
Lucifer *see* Devil
Luther, Martin 60–62, 65–66

magazines 135, 212, 247
Maggard, Dennis 33–34
magic 3, 5, 62, 64, 189, 192–193, 242; books used in 2–3, 5–7, 36, 38, 50, 60–61, 65, 67, 68, 175–176, 180, 186, 191, 211–223, 227; dark 181–182, 199–201, 224, 228, 245, 253; folk 177–179; gender and 174–184; historical practice of 23–24, 27–28, 31*n*9, 50, 66, 112, 229–231; imagination and 63, 111, 115, 127; science and 204–205, 206*n*2; stage conjuring

and 117, 127, 131, 202–203; transformation by 19, 231–233
Maléfique (2002) 7, 224–234
manuscripts 3, 4, 133, 198; ancient 75, 78, 203; book 11–12, 15–17, 19, 20n17, 41, 70n32, 167; occult 33
Matheson, Sue 7, 188–197, 256
Matthews, Gareth 112
McHale, Brian 11
McRobert, Neil 126, 128
Meaux, Kevin 248
Melanchthon, Phillip 60–61
Méliès, Georges 73, 126–128, 131
memory 1, 66, 121, 126, 138, 170, 193, 218, 222, 235, 243
Mephisto 59–60, 62–63, 67–68
Mesmerism 23–24, 26, 31
metafiction 12, 38
Miller, Cynthia J. 1–8, 224–234, 256
Miskatonic University (fictitious institution) 27, 35, 162–163, 165–166, 170–171
Mitchell, David Robert 96, 98, 101, 102
monsters 3, 50, 94, 158, 162–163, 175, 179, 180, 220, 245; control of humans by 34, 36–37, 168–171; fought by humans 74, 78, 130–131, 165, 192; origins in human psychology 108, 111, 114, 167–168; summoned by books 4, 11–22, 125, 129, 157; women seen as 179, 188
murder 79, 123, 125; of children 156, 188; by juveniles 112, 146, 148–150, 151n17, 152n19, 159–160; as revenge 24, 159–160, 248–251; state-sanctioned 235–244; under supernatural influence 3, 14, 99, 110, 200, 206, 207n17, 198–208, 211–221, 232
Murnau, F.W. 5, 59–72
myths 25–26, 33–34, 55, 57, 155, 158, 201, 252; American 83–84, 87, 89; association with the past 167–170, 176; Greek 215, 255; Middle Eastern 50; Wiccan 178, 181; *see also* legends

"The Nameless City" (1921) 32n20, 33, 44, 53–54, 237, 247
Naturom Demonto 46, 49, 51, 54n46
The Necronomicon (fictitious book) 3–5, 23–32, 33–43, 44–55, 73, 247–248
New England 4, 13, 36, 38, 88–89, 163–166, 170, 171n5, 182, 191, 245
New French Extremity (film movement) 7, 224, 229–230, 233, 234n9
newspapers 168, 236, 239
Night of the Demon (1957) 7, 171n4, 198–208, 226
Nightmare on Elm Street 2: Freddy's Revenge (1985) 147
notebook 7, 150, 211–216, 235; *see also* diary

nursery rhymes 107, 110, 115

Omen III (1981), 73, 74, 79–80
Orphan (2009) 150
Ortega, Kenny 7, 186, 187, 189, 195

Palmer, Laura (fictional character) 146–147
Palmer, Tim 229
parchment 7, 198–208, 232
Parker, Pauline 148–149
the past 17, 19, 51, 157, 161, 179–180, 193–194; American 84, 90–92; Argentinian 235–244; books as links to 168, 176
photographs 83, 165, 168, 236–237, 239–242
The Pink Backpack (short story) 146
portal *see* book, as portal
possession *see* demon, possession by
Prasch, Thomas 8, 59–72, 256
Price, Robert 163
print culture 5, 61, 64–65, 67–68, 70
printing, invention of 60, 62–65
prison *see* imprisonment
prophecy 248–250
The Prophecy (1995) 5, 73–74, 76, 78–79, 83–93
pseudapocrypha 78–81
Psycho (1960) 139

Raimi, Sam 29–30, 52, 131n5, 145
rationality 102, 109, 117, 253
readers 3–4, 16, 23, 33–36, 41, 45, 49, 81, 189, 222
reading 100, 102, 122, 124–127; as access to wisdom 75–80; as diegetic tool 14, 16; and seeing 39; as social activity 94, 98–99, 103, 160; as trigger for magic 3–4, 63, 145, 157–158, 161n5, 191, 228
reflexivity 11, 16, 38–39, 145, 170
The Reformation 5, 60–61, 63–66, 69–72, 177
Reiff, Michael C. 6, 120–131, 256
religion 28, 133, 145, 157, 159, 177, 231; *see also* Bible; Catholic Church; Reformation; Revelation
Renner, Karen 6, 145–153, 256
resurrection 25–26, 30, 52–53, 74
Revelation, Book of 52, 79–82, 86, 92
Riede, Austin 6, 132–141, 256
ritual 23–24, 26–29, 35, 77, 79, 95, 113–114, 150, 155, 157–158, 164, 177, 181, 231
Rohmer, Eric 59, 67–68
Romalho, Joana Rita 126
Roper, Lyndal 62, 66
runes 198, 201, 206–207, 233

sacrifice 28–29, 87, 160, 206, 214, 237, 251
Satan *see* Devil

Scheunemann, Deitrich 125
school 65, 74, 89–90, 109, 117, 137, 139, 159–160, 180–182, 186, 211, 214, 216,. 220
science *see* rationality
Scott, Isabel Scheuneman 149
screen 40; e-reader 94, 96–97, 99; television 122, 127–128; video game 14, 15, 17
scripture 5, 73–74, 78, 80–81
scroll 2, 82, 94
sexuality 24, 28–29, 80, 98, 133–134, 147, 151n15, 176–177, 179, 194, 224
Sheffler, Philip A. 34
Simonomicon 45, 50, 53
Simons, Judy 149
Simpson, Philip L. 7, 245–254, 256
The Slenderman 112
Solnit, Rebecca 120, 122, 130–131
sorcery 39, 62; *see also* magic; witchcraft
spells 3, 6–7, 45–46, 50–51, 53, 66–67, 80, 81–82n18, 175–185, 186–192, 195–197, 214, 222, 227, 247; *see also* curses
spiritualism 23, 26, 30
Steiner, Rudolf 231, 232
Sterritt, David 59
stigma 6, 132–141, 207n18
stories 37–38, 44–45, 50–51, 61–62, 135, 139, 175, 179, 189, 247; function 16, 120–122; nature 2, 4, 12–13, 33–34, 36, 68, 126, 163, 170–171; power 6, 107–108, 110, 113, 120–124, 127, 242
storyscape 122
storytelling 39, 155, 156
Strauss, Gerald 60, 65–66
subcreation studies 38–39
summoning 3, 6, 47, 53n25, 175, 176, 183, 191; books as tools for 154–161, 222n5; of demons 7, 26, 49–50, 186, 198–199, 205; of gods 25, 181–182, 214; of monsters 107, 111, 113
Supernatural (2005, TV series) 74, 77–79, 81n18
"supernatural irrationality" 109–111, 115, 117
superstition 167–168, 206, 207n16; *see also* legend; myth; rationality
synthetic folklore 45

teenagers/youth 33, 46, 50–52, 94, 95, 97, 147, 151n11, 181–185, 187, 193, 213, 216, 221
television 33, 96, 102, 116, 122–129, 135, 146, 148–150, 161, 166, 170, 185, 211–213, 215, 221–222
Telotte, J. P. 199, 207
temptation 66,150, 191
texts 11–13, 37–38, 40, 60–62, 64–66, 107; ancient 47; lost/forgotten/hidden/arcane 30–31, 74–75, 78–82, 83, 157, 159, 175, 177–178, 185, 227–228, 246–248; as objects of prestige 200; as

sources of truth 167, 170, 175; subversive 110, 125, 127, 129, 133; *see also* reading; writing
"Theater of Cruelty" 230
Thelema 23, 28, 31, 231
Tissera, Graciella 7, 235–244, 256
Todd, John 31
Tolkein, J.R.R. 36, 49, 189
Tourneur, Jacques 198, 200, 206, 207
transgression 4, 12, 14, 101, 136, 149, 158, 195, 239
trauma, psychological 3, 107–118, 120–131, 134–136, 243, 251
Tripp, Jeffrey M. 5, 73–83, 256
Tudor, Andrew 11, 16
The Turn of the Screw (1898 novel) 6, 132–141
Twin Peaks (1990–1991 television series) 146

Unaussprechlichen Kulten 45
the uncanny 3, 13, 17, 87, 96, 112, 161, 169, 171, 233, 241
undead 3, 46, 50, 53
universities 61–62, 161; Brown 34, 48; Heidelberg 64; Miskatonic (fictitious) 27, 35, 162, 165–166

Van Riper, A. Bowdoin 5, 161–171, 256
video games 11–22, 52, 146, 151*n*4, 212
Vogler, Thomas 17

Wall-Randell, Sarah 63
Walpole, Horace 11, 247
Warlock (1989) 3, 171*n*4, 177, 182, 183=184
warlocks 6, 25, 52, 175, 176, 177, 180
Warner, Marina 107, 109, 115
Weine, Robert 121–123, 125–126
Weintraub, Jeff 154
Wentersdorf, Karl 60
The Whisperer in Darkness (2011) 4, 6, 135, 162–171
Widen, Gregory 5, 83, 87

witches 6–7, 31, 66, 47*n*70, 202; belief in 146, 167; as comic figures 187–189; and dark magic 25–26; patriarchy and 178–179, 191; persecution 52, 88, 182, 183–184, 191; practices 175–185, 193–194; sexualization 29, 179, 191–192
wizards *see* warlocks; witches
writing (the act 38, 78, 134, 149, 151*n*15, 156, 218, 227, 248; automatic 30; as self-discovery 152*n*27; as world-creation 15–18, 34
writing (symbols on paper) 47, 68, 183, 200, 211, 214–216

"The Yellow Wall-paper" (1892 short story) 146

Zani, Steve 246
Žižek, Slavoj 18, 139

www.ingramcontent.com/pod-product-compliance
Lightning Source LLC
Chambersburg PA
CBHW081547300426
44116CB00015B/2786